LABOUR LAW, THE COLD WAR, AND THE RIGHT TO STRIKE

This book examines the origins, deployment, and legacy of Order 1305, a measure introduced in 1940 to make it a criminal offence to take part in a strike.

Surprisingly, the prohibition on the right to strike was retained by the Attlee administration after the Second World War, and was transformed to become a weapon of government during the Cold War to deal with what were wrongly claimed by ministers to be Communist-inspired strikes engineered for subversive purposes.

In a deep analysis of Order 1305, the authors provide a reassessment of the role of the State in industrial relations. Challenging much contemporary learning in labour law, the book is informed by a very detailed engagement with Cabinet and ministerial papers, which highlight the contradictions on the part of government in simultaneously promoting and containing trade union power. These sources also highlight the extent to which trade unions both relied on and were co-opted by the State.

The main focus of the book, however, is the use of Order 1305 for the control of trade union activists, with the continuing presence of the criminal law and allegations of communist inspired strikes ensuring an important role for MI5 and Special Branch in post-war industrial relations. Material unearthed at the National Archives demonstrates unequivocally not only that trade unions were deeply penetrated, but also that trade union activists were the subject of extensive surveillance, as the authors fully reveal.

Labour Law, the Cold War, and the Right to Strike

A Legal and Political History of Order 1305

KD Ewing
and
Andrew Moretta

•HART•
OXFORD • LONDON • NEW YORK • NEW DELHI • SYDNEY

HART PUBLISHING
Bloomsbury Publishing Plc
Kemp House, Chawley Park, Cumnor Hill, Oxford, OX2 9PH, UK
1385 Broadway, New York, NY 10018, USA
Bloomsbury Publishing Ireland Limited, 29 Earlsfort Terrace, Dublin 2, D02 AY28, Ireland

HART PUBLISHING, the Hart/Stag logo, BLOOMSBURY and the Diana logo are trademarks of Bloomsbury Publishing Plc
First published in Great Britain 2026

A catalogue record for this book is available from the British Library.

Library of Congress Cataloging-in-Publication Data

Names: Ewing, KD (Keith D) author | Moretta, Andrew author

Title: Labour law, the cold war, and the right to strike : a legal and political history of order 1305 / KD Ewing and Andrew Moretta.

Other titles: Labor law, the Cold War, and the right to strike

Description: Oxford ; New York : Hart Publishing, 2026. | Includes bibliographical references and index. | Summary: "This book examines the origins, deployment, and legacy of Order 1305, a measure introduced in 1940 to make it a criminal offence to take part in a strike, which became a weapon of government during the Cold War. Challenging much contemporary learning in labour law, the book is informed by a detailed engagement with Cabinet and ministerial papers, which highlight the contradictions on the part of government in simultaneously promoting and containing trade union power. The book demonstrates unequivocally not only that trade unions were deeply penetrated, but also that trade union activists were the subject of extensive surveillance"— Provided by publisher.

Identifiers: LCCN 2026009157 (print) | LCCN 2026009158 (ebook) | ISBN 9781509983162 hardback | ISBN 9781509983124 paperback | ISBN 9781509983155 Epub | ISBN 9781509983148 pdf

Subjects: LCSH: Strikes and lockouts—Law and legislation—Great Britain | Right to strike—Great Britain | Collective bargaining—Law and legislation—Great Britain | Labor unions—Law and legislation—Great Britain | Labor laws and legislation—Great Britain | World War, 1939-1945—Law and legislation—Great Britain

Classification: LCC KD3076 .E93 2026 (print) | LCC KD3076 (ebook)

LC record available at https://lccn.loc.gov/2026009157

LC ebook record available at https://lccn.loc.gov/2026009158

ISBN: HB: 978-1-50998-316-2
ePDF: 978-1-50998-314-8
ePub: 978-1-50998-315-5

Typeset by Compuscript Ltd, Shannon

For product safety related questions contact productsafety@bloomsbury.com

To find out more about our authors and books visit www.hartpublishing.co.uk. Here you will find extracts, author information, details of forthcoming events and the option to sign up for our newsletters.

For Cath

PREFACE

This book is about Order 1305, a remarkable wartime measure which helped to expand the coverage of collective agreements while also effectively taking away the right to strike. The order was all the more remarkable for having been conceived by Ernest Bevin, the General Secretary of the Transport and General Workers' Union who had been drafted by Churchill to become his wartime Minister of Labour, and more remarkable still for having been introduced with the full agreement of the trade union movement.

The main focus of the study, however, is with the continued operation of the wartime restrictions – again with the agreement with the trade union movement – for the whole period of the post-war government elected in 1945. Attlee's administration is remembered for having repealed the Trade Disputes and Trade Unions Act 1927 and for restoring the right to strike. But it did so while also retaining Order 1305's measures prohibiting strikes, failure to comply with which brought the risk of imprisonment.

As the Second World War ended, a new enemy emerged. Order 1305 was now to be used as a weapon in Cold War politics, as workers with grievances neglected by their trade union leaders organised unofficial groups within these unions and took unofficial industrial action in breach of the law. Ministers and trade union officials blamed the Communist Party, which having been tolerated during the Second World War was now suspected of encouraging disruptive industrial action in the interests of a foreign power.

Faced with huge challenges in 1945, many of which it addressed with such conspicuous success, much of the time of leading figures in the Attlee administration was nevertheless spent searching for evidence. Evidence with which to mount a prosecution to imprison the leadership of unofficial movements within the Transport and General Workers' Union in particular. Order 1305 was to emerge as the government's weapon of choice, to engage in a battle for which it was not designed and for which it was ill-equipped.

The story that follows is told through the lens of Cabinet papers and government documents now made available in the National Archives. We make no apology for telling the story in fine detail, in order to shed light on the positions taken by different Cabinet ministers, and to reveal the important role of the Attorney General in insisting on prosecutions. Also addressed is the political pressure placed on a sceptical MI5, as well as a compliant and less inhibited Metropolitan Police Special Branch.

Indeed, the material discussed in the pages that follow lays bare the extent to which trade union activity was subject routinely to MI5 and Special Branch surveillance. It also exposes the techniques that the agencies used for this purpose. Trade union activists at the time widely understood that police spies were hidden in plain sight, and that they were constantly being watched. Surveillance was used as an instrument of intimidation, as well as for the collection of information often gathered for no obvious purpose.

This penetration of the trade union movement raises disturbing questions about the role of the State. It raises even more disturbing questions about the extent to which trade union leaders were complicit in the surveillance of their members. The industrial and political wings of the labour movement at the time were closely intertwined, with trade unions having a much closer relationship with government than is imaginable today, as well as a much greater influence in the conduct of public affairs.

So although we were inspired initially by concerns about the surveillance of trade unionists, the study evolved into a wider examination of the role of trade unions in the post-war era and the role of the State in post-war industrial relations. It soon becomes clear when reading the official record that unofficial industrial action was regarded as subversive not only because of its alleged motivation, but also because it was seen to be 'unconstitutional' as undermining the social and economic constitution as well as the political constitution.

To write about a social and economic constitution may seem hyperbolic. But the fact is that the Second World War expedited a process of trade union participation in all forms of social and economic decision-making, which was retained after the war. The role of the Ministry of Labour was crucial. A government department headed during and after the war by a trade union general secretary (Bevin being replaced by George Isaacs), it was the voice of trade unions in government.

Moreover, the TUC was a recognised partner with government. As we will see, it was consulted and negotiated with, and as we will also see it had a de facto veto on major decisions. Otherwise, trade unions took part in an extensive framework of sectoral collective bargaining and wages' regulation, covering more than 80 per cent of workers. These arrangements were the construct of government, and in legal terms reached their apotheosis in the benign elements of Order 1305, which gave binding effect to joint industrial council agreements.

Within this carefully constructed system of economic democracy, it was anticipated that workers would participate through the formal processes of their trade unions, which were the vehicles for the representation of their interests. The vision was one in which trade union members would attend branch meetings, engage with the policy-making bodies of their union, seek election to various committees, and channel their grievances through their official trade union structures. Unofficial action was heresy and was to be contained.

The State thus empowered trade unions but sought to contain trade unionists. The benign elements of Order 1305 (on the regulatory effects of collective agreements) served the former purpose, while restrictions on industrial action (on the right to strike) served the latter. In the attempt to police industrial action, however, Order 1305 was to prove largely ineffective against the determined and loosely organised resistance of workers. This book is in part the story of how unofficial groups mobilised to resist and then break a bad law.

The revocation and replacement of Order 1305 did not, however, address the problem to which it had been deployed in the post-war era. One of the difficulties of labour law design never overcome was how to develop a system of sectoral collective bargaining, while simultaneously enabling workers to protest against their unions as well as their employers. It is a problem that raises wider questions about the purpose of the right to strike, revealed to be not only a tool in struggles with the employer, but also a safety valve against the union.

That apart, however, the book is a challenge to orthodox labour law scholarship which celebrates and to some extent worships at the altar of collective laissez-faire. Our examination of the primary sources reinforces our view that such labelling is not justified by the evidence. There was a British model of what we would today call labour law. The architecture was designed by the State, it was developed largely with State support, and it was given its fullest legal expression in Order 1305.

Finally, in the preparation of this book we have encountered many debts to many people, which we fully acknowledge. We would like to draw attention to the authors of several superb papers published in *Historical Studies in Industrial Relations* on whose shoulders we presume to stand. Thanks also to Timothy Evans Photography for assistance with the cover image. Above all, however, we owe a tremendous debt to Hart Publishing for reminding us of the joys of working with a kind, thoughtful, patient, conscientious, and professional team.

We are responsible for the errors that follow.

KDE/AM
7 March 2026

CONTENTS

PART III
RETENTION OF ORDER 1305:
THE LABOUR GOVERNMENT AFTER THE WAR

PART IV
REVIVAL OF ORDER 1305: UNOFFICIAL ACTION
AS ECONOMIC AND POLITICAL SUBVERSION

LIST OF ABBREVIATIONS

ACAS	Advisory Conciliation and Arbitration Service
AEU	Amalgamated Engineering Union
AESD	Association of Engineering and Shipbuilding Draughtsmen
BEF	British Employers' Federation
BOAC	British Overseas Airways Corporation
CCS	Chief Crown Solicitor
CEC	Cabinet Emergencies Committee
CIC	Chief Industrial Commissioner
CID	Criminal Investigation Department
CPPA	Conspiracy and Protection of Property Act 1875
CSEU	Confederation of Shipbuilding and Engineering Unions
CSU	Canadian Seamen's Union
CP and CPGB	Communist Party of Great Britain
DCIC	Deputy Chief Industrial Commissioner
DI	Detective Inspector
DPP	Director of Public Prosecutions
DR	Defence Regulation
ETU	Electrical Trades Union
GEC	General Executive Council
GMWU	National Union of General and Municipal Workers
HO	Home Office
IDT	Industrial Disputes Tribunal
ILO	International Labour Organisation
ILP	Independent Labour Party
IRO	Industrial Relations Officer

JCC	Joint Consultative Council
JIC	Joint Industrial Council
JTUDC	Joint Trade Union Defence Committee
KC	King's Council
M/L	Ministry of Labour
MP	Member of Parliament
NALGO	National Association of Local Government Officers
NASD	National Amalgamated Stevedores and Dockers
NAT	National Arbitration Tribunal
NATSOPA	National Society of Operative Printers and Assistants
NCB	National Coal Board
NEC	National Executive Committee
NI	Northern Ireland
NIC	National Industrial Conference
NJAC	National Joint Advisory Council
NJIC	National Joint Industrial Council
NSFU	National Sailors' and Firemen's Union
NUM	National Union of Mineworkers
NUSMW	National Union of Scottish Mineworkers
NUVB	National Union of Vehicle Builders
NUWM	National Unemployed Workers' Movement
PAYE	Pay As You Earn
PWC	Port Workers' Committee
RCP	Revolutionary Communist Party
RUC	Royal Ulster Constabulary
SIU	Seafarers' International Union
SR&O	Statutory Rules and Orders
TGWU	Transport and General Workers' Union
TNA	The National Archives
TUC	Trades Union Congress

TABLE OF CASES

PART I

Introduction

1

Introduction

I. The Setting

In normal circumstances, the introduction of an instrument containing measures such as those to be found in 'Order 1305' would be a matter of acute political controversy. On 25 July 1940, however, the country was preoccupied by more serious concerns. The Battle of Britain was barely two weeks old, and on that particular day German air attacks led to the loss of 11 merchant coal ships as well as two Royal Navy destroyers in the Straits of Dover. More importantly, a number of RAF personnel were fatally wounded or presumed dead as a result. It is thus perhaps unsurprising in the circumstances that a new war-time measure from the Ministry of Labour, introduced to keep wages within reasonable limits for the duration of the war, should receive little attention. This is despite the fact that the new Order would require the resolution of industrial disputes by conciliation and arbitration, make it an offence to take part in strikes and lock outs, and ensure the 'legalisation' of collective agreements.

It is nevertheless notable that Order 1305 had not been approved by Parliament before its introduction on 25 July. Legally there was no need for this to be done, with the Minister of Labour exercising sub-delegated powers under the Defence Regulations,[1] which did not require Orders of this kind even to be laid before Parliament. Defence Regulation 58AA made clear that the Minister of Labour 'may by order' make provision 'with a view to preventing work being interrupted by trade disputes'. Order 1305 was, however, well known by those to whom it applied, the contents having been considered not by the mother of Parliaments, but by a different Parliament summoned to meet at Central Hall, Westminster by the new Minister of Labour. This was an assembly of trade unionists to which 'every executive of every trade union in this country' was invited to consider whether 'they would forgo strikes, and if, in substitution for the strike, they would accept arbitration for the duration of the war'.[2] They agreed.

The Minister of Labour was of course Ernest Bevin, who had been appointed on 13 May 1940. At the time of his appointment, Bevin was General Secretary of the Transport and General Workers' Union (TGWU), a position which he continued to hold throughout the war, an arrangement that would be no longer constitutionally acceptable. Then as now, however, it was unacceptable for a minister not to be a Member of Parliament, with the result that a by-election was hastily arranged. The

[1] By an Order in Council under the powers conferred on the Minister by the addition of Defence (General) Regulation 58AA.

[2] HC Debs, 28 April 1944, col 1124 (Ernest Bevin).

General Secretary of the TGWU thus became the member for Wandsworth Central on 22 June 1940, succeeding Harry Cohen, who was elevated to the House of Lords. In addressing his responsibility to keep wages under control, Bevin concluded that 'the trade unions and the employers through their industrial relations machinery, might make a better job of it than if we introduced totalitarian methods', a decision he later felt had been vindicated by subsequent events, though the mines – to which we return – were in his words 'a black spot'.[3]

In this introduction, we give an account of the main provisions of Order 1305, having avoided doing so in earlier drafts of the book because of the rather dense nature of its text, mindful of the risks of beginning a work of this length with such material. But try as we might, it made no sense to launch into an analysis of a measure the main provisions and implications of which had not been fully explained. So what follows is an explanation in two parts, reflecting the two different but complementary aims of the Order. We begin with Parts I and II (dealing with the resolution of industrial disputes and the restrictions on the right to strike), followed by an account of Part III (providing for the *erga omnes* effect of collective agreements, the high water mark of British public policy in relation to the legalisation of such agreements). Although our concern in this study is principally with the right to strike, we are concerned also to ensure that Order 1305 is fully represented and that the strike restrictions are seen in the wider context of the Order as a whole.

Emergency Powers (Defence) Act 1939

The Emergency Powers (Defence) Act 1939 authorised the government by Order in Council to make regulations (known as Defence Regulations). These could be made where they appeared to be 'necessary or expedient for securing the public safety, the defence of the realm, the maintenance of public order and the efficient prosecution of any war in which His Majesty may be engaged, and for maintaining supplies and services essential to the life of the community' (section 1). The power to make Defence Regulations – which were subject to annulment by Parliament – were extended and clarified in 1940, and were used to make several instruments relating to industrial relations.[4] The latter included Regulation 58A, which enabled the Minister of Labour to direct individuals to work in essential services, subject to safeguards as to terms and conditions of employment, with regard to be had to any terms set by a relevant Joint Industrial Council.[5] They also included Regulation 58AA,

[3] ibid.

[4] See Emergency Powers (Defence) Act 1940 and Emergency Powers (Defence) (No 2) Act 1940 respectively. The extended powers enabled Defence Regulations to be made 'for requiring persons to place themselves, their services, and their property at the disposal of the His Majesty', where this appeared to be 'necessary or expedient' for securing public safety, the defence of the realm, the maintenance of public order and so on.

[5] Notable cases include *Horton v Owen* (1943) 87 Sol Jo 31; *William Dixon Ltd v Patterson*, 1943 JC 78; *Jackson v Fisher's Foils Ltd* (1944) 88 Sol Jo 103; *Barr & Stroud Ltd v Adair*, 1945 JC 34; and *Adrema Ltd v Jenkinson* (1945) 89 Sol Jo 358. These cases raise interesting questions of contemporary significance relating to the meaning of reinstatement and the effect of a contractual variation.

which provided that the Minister of Labour 'may by order' make provision 'with a view to preventing work being interrupted by trade disputes'. Unlike the provision for limited parliamentary scrutiny of the Defence Regulations, as explained in the text, there was no such scrutiny for the making of 'Orders' under Regulation 58AA.[6]

Regulation 58AA's marginal note made clear that its purpose was the 'avoidance of strikes and lock outs'. To this end, it was expressly provided that the Minister could by order make provision for: (a) the establishment of a tribunal for the settlement of trade disputes; (b) the prohibition, 'subject to the provisions of the Order', of 'a strike or lock-out in connection with any trade dispute'; (c) the requirement that employers should observe terms and conditions of employment as prescribed by the Order to be 'recognised terms and conditions' (that is to say, in effect the terms of any Joint Industrial Council agreement); (d) the recording of any departure by an employer with the obligation to comply with any 'rule, practice or custom' in respect of the employment of any person; and (e) the making of any incidental or supplementary provision the Minister 'thinks expedient'. It is thus clear that the Minister of Labour had delegated authority to make an Order prohibiting strikes relating to a trade dispute, the latter to have the same meaning as in the Industrial Courts Act 1919 rather than the Trade Disputes Act 1906,[7] though the definitions in both statutes are very similar.[8] While Bevin claimed that Order 1305 was 'virtually a collective agreement',[9] formally it was an 'Order' made under authority delegated to the Minister by the Defence Regulations.

II. Order 1305 and Compulsory Arbitration

Part I of Order 1305 made provision for unresolved trade disputes to be reported to the Ministry of Labour, with a view to these disputes then being resolved in accordance with the subsequent provisions of the Order. Thus, by virtue of Article 2(1):

> If any trade dispute exists or is apprehended, that dispute, if not otherwise determined, may be reported to the Minister by or on behalf of either party and the decision of the Minister as to whether a dispute has been so reported to him or not and as to the time at which a dispute has been reported shall be conclusive for all purposes.

A notable aspect of this power to report disputes to the Minister is that – unlike the corresponding provisions of Article 5 discussed in Part III below – there is no qualification to the effect that the report could be made on the workers' side only by a representative trade union.

[6] But the operation of Order 1305 could of course be the subject of parliamentary scrutiny. See HC Debs, 28 April 1944, col 1125.

[7] Defence Regulation 58AA(4).

[8] See Trade Disputes Act 1906, s 5(3); and Industrial Courts Act 1919, s 8.

[9] HC Debs, 28 April 1944, col 1125.

Once a report was made, the Minister was required by Article 2(2) to consider whether there existed procedures for its settlement – 'the recognised means of the industry' – and if so to refer the dispute to these procedures.[10] If this was done and the procedures failed to resolve the dispute, the Minister could thereafter refer the matter to the newly created National Arbitration Tribunal (NAT). In the absence of any such procedures, Article 2(3) empowered the Minister to make other arrangements – to take 'any steps which seem to him expedient to promote a settlement'.[11] This led the Ministry to refer disputes to its own conciliation officers, individual arbitrators, or ad hoc arbitration boards. Cases might also be referred for conciliation under the Conciliation Act 1896; to arbitration under the Industrial Courts Act 1919;[12] or to the NAT, the last being the only option available where one of the parties was un-co-operative.

Where steps taken by the Minister to resolve a dispute under Article 2(2) or (3) failed to provide a 'prompt settlement', Article 2(4) provided that the Minister 'shall' refer the matter to the NAT (if this had not already been done) for resolution. The reference had to be made within 21 days from the date on which the dispute was first referred to him unless, in the Minister's opinion, 'the special circumstances of the case make it necessary or desirable to postpone such a reference' (Article 2(4)).[13] That is to say, he was required to refer the matter for compulsory arbitration regardless of the wishes of the parties. It was compulsory in the sense that there was a legal obligation to have the dispute resolved in this way, and compulsory in the sense that the NAT award was legally binding. Thus, in accordance with Article 2(5), any agreement, decision or award made by virtue of the earlier provisions of Article 2 was to be binding on the parties to whom it applied. It was then to be an implied term of any contract of employment that the rates of wages to be paid and the other conditions of employment to be observed were to be in accordance with any such agreement, decision or award.

In addition to the foregoing were the parallel provisions dealing with the right to strike. Article 4 contained the prohibition on strikes and lock outs, permitting a strike or lock out in relation to a trade dispute only if a reported dispute had not been referred for settlement under the various procedures in Article 2(2)–(4) within 21 days:

> An employer shall not declare or take part in a lock-out and a worker shall not take part in a strike in connection with any trade dispute unless the dispute has been reported to the Minister in accordance with the provisions of Article 2 of this Order and 21 days have elapsed since the date of the report and the dispute has during that time not been referred.

[10] The phrase was used by the Ministry in a briefing note appended to the record of the 10th meeting of the JCC on 24 September 1940: see TNA, LAB 10/653 ('National Joint Industrial Council, Joint Consultative Committee, record set of minutes and agendas of meetings from 1st to 67th meeting May 1940–October 1947'). At the meeting, it was noted that after initial concerns about 'trivial' cases being referred to the NAT, the TUC had urged unions to 'supplement their machinery by arbitration provision', thus ensuring that more minor disputes could be tackled without recourse to the NAT (see also Bevin's response to the Wolverhampton batteries case featured on p 19, below).

[11] On art 2(3), see pp 215–216 below.

[12] Defence Regulation 58AA(3) stated expressly that it did not affect the power to refer disputes for settlement under the Industrial Courts Act 1919.

[13] This became a matter of concern for ministers and the Attorney General in 1950–51 when a dispute at Kemsley Newspapers Ltd prompted them to consider whether the Minister was obliged to refer all reported cases which had not been settled by other means to the NAT. See pp 212–217 below. During the war, the Ministry had been in no doubt that the Minister was so obliged.

The overall effect was straightforward. A strike lock out could take place in one of only two circumstances: (i) where the Minister had in breach of his duty failed to refer an otherwise unresolved dispute to the NAT within 21 days of it being reported; or (ii) where the strike lock out related to a dispute which did not fall within the definition of a trade dispute within the meaning of the Order.

Following the requirements of the Defence Regulation 58AA(4), for these purposes a 'trade dispute' was defined to mean 'any dispute or difference between employers and workmen, or between workmen and workmen connected with the employment or non-employment or the terms of employment or with the conditions of labour of any person' (Article 7). However, there was no definition of a 'strike' or a 'lock out' in the Defence Regulations, a matter thus left to the officials who drafted Order 1305. As a result:

- A 'strike' was defined to mean (i) a cessation of work by employed persons acting in combination, or (ii) a concerted refusal of a number of employed persons to continue to work for an employer, where (iii) this was done as a consequence of a trade dispute, (iv) in order to compel an employer, any other person, or any trade union to accept or not to accept terms or conditions of employment or affecting employment.[14] The definition also (v) applied to solidarity or sympathy action designed to 'aid' other workers in their trade dispute.
- A 'lock out' in turn was defined to mean action of various kinds by the employer (such as closing the workplace, suspending employees or dismissing employees) with a view to (a) compelling persons employed by the employer to accept or not to accept terms or conditions of or affecting employment), or (b) aid another employer seeking to compel their employees to accept or not to accept terms or conditions of or affecting employment.[15] The latter provision ensures that lock outs in support of another employer in a dispute were covered.

Liability for breach of Order 1305 was governed by Defence Regulations 90–93. What is notable is that the offence was committed by and the sanctions were applicable to workers individually rather than the union or union officials who called the strike. That said, Regulation 90 was significant for making clear that conspiracy to commit an offence was also covered,[16] while Regulation 91 (which would be relevant in the case of lock outs) provided that where the offender was a body corporate, company directors and officers would be personally responsible.[17] Regulation 92 applied to penalties for failing

[14] As Davies and Freedland point out, it did not include industrial action short of a strike: P Davies and M Freedland, *Labour Legislation and Public Policy: A Contemporary History* (Clarendon Press, Oxford, 1993), p 89. Chapter Two of the foregoing provides valuable political, legal and industrial relations context for the study of Order 1305, for which we are grateful. On the definition of a strike, compare Contracts of Employment Act 1963, sch 1, para 11(1), and now Employment Rights Act 1996, s 235(5).

[15] The symmetry of treatment of strikes and lock outs as a general principle has been retained in some areas: see Trade Union and Labour Relations (Consolidation) Act 1992, s 238, as well as in the area of jobseeker's allowance. There is not much litigation around lock outs, although see *Cummings v Charles Connell & Co (Shipbuilders) Ltd*, 1969 SLT 25.

[16] It also applied to acts preparatory to committing an offence.

[17] See *Sarna v Adair*, 1945 SLT 307 (penalties could be imposed on both the company and its directors, even in the case of a 'one man' company). It should be noted that just two companies were prosecuted in Great Britain during the war for breach of the lock-out prohibition (see TNA, LAB 10/173 ('Prosecutions of Strikers under Order 1305 (1) Undertaken (2) Contemplated')).

to comply with the Regulations or any 'Order' made thereunder (such as Order 1305). A person found guilty in summary proceedings was liable to imprisonment for up to three months or a fine not exceeding £100, or both. In the case of a conviction on indictment, it was two years or £500, or both. Regulation 93(1) (which did not apply to Scotland) was important in prescribing by whom proceedings could be launched: the police, the Director of Public Prosecutions, an employer with the consent of the DPP, or the Ministry of Labour.

The Right to Strike and Order 1305

To clarify, strikes could take place without the risk of criminal liability under Order 1305 in one of only two circumstances.

The first is that the strike was not 'in connection with any trade dispute'. However, in that case, those participating in or organising the action potentially faced criminal and civil liabilities at common law if their action was unprotected by the Conspiracy and Protection of Property Act 1875.[18] There was also the possibility of criminal liability under the Trade Disputes and Trade Unions Act 1927.

The second is that a strike 'in connection with any trade dispute' had been: (a) reported to the Ministry; (b) a period of 21 days had elapsed while the dispute was with the Ministry; (c) although unresolved, the dispute was not referred to the NAT for settlement by compulsory arbitration; and (d) there were no special circumstances that would permit the Minister to postpone any such reference.[19]

For the avoidance of doubt, it was illegal to strike 'in connection with any trade dispute' if the dispute had not been reported in the first instance to the Ministry of Labour.

III. Order 1305 and the Legalisation of Collective Agreements

Although Order 1305 is best known for requiring compulsory arbitration and restricting the right to strike (and lock out), that was only half of it. In agreeing to the suppression of their liberties for the duration of the Second World War, the Trades Union Congress got a much-coveted reward in return, albeit a reward consistent with the government's desire to ensure wage stability and to reduce the risk of industrial conflict. The reward in question was to be found in Defence Regulation 58AA(1)(c), which authorised the

[18] On the 1875 Act, see chs 4 and 9 below.

[19] If the reference was postponed for the reasons prescribed in art 2(4), it was assumed initially by the Ministry that the action could not go ahead: TNA, CAB 129/44/8 ('The Future of the Conditions of Employment and National Arbitration Order', Memorandum by the Minister of Labour and National Service, 10 January 1951), para 6. p 225 below.

Minister by Order to insist that employers comply with 'recognized terms and conditions of employment'. This was code for an obligation for all employers to comply with the terms of a relevant collective agreement, which at the time were concluded to a large extent on a sectoral basis. There was a concern not confined to trade unions that joint industrial council agreements were being undermined by employers who refused to comply with them, perhaps because they were not members of the employers' federation that negotiated the agreements in question, and seeking as a result to compete unfairly with their rivals by paying lower wages.

The 'legalisation' of collective agreements had been raised inconclusively by the Whitley Committee in 1917 when it recommended the expansion of collective bargaining through Joint Industrial Councils (JICs).[20] In the 1920s, however, the issue was promoted simultaneously by the Association of Joint Industrial Councils and by trade unions, a measure of the latter's support revealed by a TUC Annual Congress resolution in 1925. This urged the government to give JIC agreements the same validity as awards made under the Trade Boards Act 1918, 'with the objective of ensuring the observance of fair conditions of labour by all engaged in industry'.[21] It is thus disappointing that the idea was subsequently rejected by the Balfour Committee, appointed by the Labour government in 1924 to inquire into British industry and commerce with special reference to the export trade. Reporting in 1929, the Committee expressed concern that the 'legalisation' of collective agreements could lead to workers and their trade unions being exposed to civil action, and even criminal prosecution.[22]

Despite this setback, the TUC nevertheless commissioned the drafting of a Rates of Wages Bill in 1931, proposing that the Minister of Labour could, by Special Order, '[sanction] for the employees in that trade' the application of any collective agreement specified in the application and in the subsequent Order.[23] Despite falling some way short of giving JIC agreements the same legal status as trade board awards, the Bill was never adopted. But similar proposals were nevertheless accepted by the government for application to cotton manufacturing in 1934, it having been reported earlier that the abandoning by firms of collective agreements was a 'cause of constant friction'.[24] Questions were accordingly raised about the compulsory enforcement of agreements, the Cotton Manufacturing (Temporary Provisions) Act 1934 making provision for the collective agreements in the industry to be given statutory effect, the Ministry claiming that the 'increasing number of breaches of agreed conditions' was threatening a 'collapse of the voluntary system'.[25]

[20] Ministry of Reconstruction, Committee on Relations between Employers and Employed, Interim Report, Cmd 8606, 1917, para 6. It was suggested that 'it may be desirable at some later stage for the State to give the sanction of law to agreements made by the Councils', though the initiative for this should come from the Councils themselves (para 21).

[21] Once approved by the Minister, trade board recommendations were binding throughout the industry, sector or activity to which the trade board applied.

[22] Committee on Industry and Trade, Final Report, Cmd 3282, 1929, p 113.

[23] See KD Ewing, 'The State and Industrial Relations: "Collective Laissez Faire" Revisited' (1998) 5 *Historical Studies in Industrial Relations* 1 for fuller details.

[24] Ministry of Labour, Annual Report 1933, p 84.

[25] ibid.

Under the terms of the Act, employers controlling a majority of the looms and unions representing a majority of workers could make a joint application to the Minister for an order to be made for the application of collectively agreed wage rates to all workers employed in the industry. The Minister would appoint a board to investigate and could then make an order, but only if the board was unanimous in recommending the application of the collective agreement. The rates fixed by the Order were then to be a term of employment of every employed person in the sector, and it would also have been an offence for an employer to pay less than the applicable rate. In announcing that an Order had been made under the Act with effect from 15 July 1935, Ernest Brown, the Minister of Labour, said that joint representations by workers and employers in other industries had been made with a view to enabling statutory force to be given to their voluntary agreements,[26] and these representations would be considered in the light of the experience of the cotton industry.[27]

While it might be expected that the Second World War and the introduction of emergency powers focused on the war effort would scupper any plans for the extension of procedures of the kind found in the Cotton Manufacturing (Temporary Provisions) Act 1934, it had precisely the opposite effect. Order 1305, Part III addressed the substantive terms of collective agreements by responding more generally than the 1934 Act to the TUC demand for the 'legalisation' of collective agreements. Thus, by virtue of Article 5(1):

> Where in any trade or industry or in any district there are in force terms and conditions of employment which have been settled by machinery of negotiation or arbitration to which the parties are organisations of employers and trade unions representative respectively of substantial proportions of the employers and workers engaged in that trade or industry in that district (hereinafter referred to as 'recognised terms and conditions') *all employers in that trade or industry in that district shall observe the recognised terms and conditions or such terms and conditions of employment as are not less favourable than the recognised terms and conditions.* (Emphasis added)

In other words, JIC and other collective agreements would as a matter of law have an extended regulatory effect, applying to all employers throughout the sector in the district in which they operated, including those who were not members of the employers' association that concluded the agreement in question. In the event of a failure of an employer to observe recognised terms and conditions, a report could be made by a representative trade union or an employers' association to the Minister of Labour, who would then proceed to deal with the matter as if it were a report made under Article 2 (Order 1305, Article 5(3)). If it was necessary to refer the matter to the NAT, the latter could make an award so that here too, it would be an implied term of the contracts of employment of the workers to whom the award related that the employer in question should apply the terms and conditions set out in a specified collective agreement

[26] The industries in question were quarrying, asbestos, hosiery, cooperage, lock and latch, electrical contracting, gloves, heating and domestic engineering, pottery, furniture warehousing and removing: HC Debs, 5 March 1936, col 1539.

[27] ibid. The 1934 Act was judged to have been a 'successful experiment': Ministry of Labour, Annual Report 1937, p 63.

(Article 5(4)).[28] That said, a worker could not sue a recalcitrant employer until an award had been made by the NAT.[29]

IV. Conclusion

About six months after Order 1305 was introduced, Bevin was to inform the House of Commons that 'standard rates of wages' under collective agreements 'are paid over a more widespread area of British industry' than 'ever has been the case in the history of the country'.[30] In response to James Maxton, the Labour MP for Glasgow Bridgeton who asked whether this was done on a 'voluntary' basis, the Minister was unequivocal: 'No, that is compulsion.'[31] These results were achieved by the use of delegated powers, Bevin informing parliamentary colleagues some four years later that it was better to legislate by regulation and order rather than by primary legislation, given that the former would be easier to remove once the hostilities ended and the emergency passed:

> I did not want this war to be used to introduce any new Trade Union Bill. You can put a Bill on the Statute Book, but repealing it is another story. Therefore, I felt that anything I did, or advised my colleagues in the Cabinet to do, on this issue, should be limited solely to war purposes, and that, when the Defence Regulations went, this went, too, and the trade union law stood exactly where it was. I thought that was a wise decision, which commended itself to all my trade union friends.[32]

It is true that as late as 1945, it appears to have been assumed by the Ministry of Labour that Order 1305 would be revoked immediately after the war. As a result, and as explained more fully in Chapter 4, steps were taken in the Wages Councils Act 1945 to retain Order 1305, Part III, albeit only until 31 December 1950 (unless Parliament should extend the statutory expiry date). But in the end, these provisions were never invoked, for despite being 'limited solely to war purposes',[33] Order 1305 was to remain in force for the entire period of the first Parliament after the war, and was not revoked

[28] Although not without its limitations, this was an ingenious answer to the Balfour Committee (see above). Moreover, it is a model that was subsequently to be adopted on multiple occasions, and is visible today in the procedures for the enforcement of some Central Arbitration Committee awards: Trade Union and Labour Relations (Consolidation) Act 1992 (TULRCA), ss 181–85 (disclosure of information). See M Jones, 'CAC and Schedule 11: The Experience of Two Years' (1980) 9 *Industrial Law Journal* 28. See also B Doyle, 'A Substitute for Collective Bargaining? The Central Arbitration Committee's Approach to Section 16 of the Employment Protection Act 1975' (1980) 9 *Industrial Law Journal* 154, which deals with powers since repealed similar to those in TULRCA 1992, ss 181–85.

[29] See *Hulland v Sanders and Son* [1945] KB 78. See also the Ministry file on the case: TNA LAB 3/252 ('Court of Appeal decision on power of a workman to recover wages on the basis of recognised terms and conditions in the absence of an award by the National Arbitration Tribunal by which a term would have been embodied in the workman's contract'). Cases of non-observance of NAT awards had to be pursued in the civil courts (see TNA LAB 3/251 ('Enforcement of the conditions of Employment & Arbitration Order and of NAT awards')). It would clearly have been better if the obligation of the employer to comply with the agreement could be directly enforced without the need to go to the NAT for an award. The main point, however, was the unequivocal duty in art 5(1) that every employer must comply with recognised terms and conditions.

[30] HC Debs, 10 December 1941, col 1617.

[31] ibid.

[32] HC Debs, 28 April 1944, col 1127.

[33] ibid.

until 1951. As we discuss below, in the desire to retain Order 1305's 'benign' elements, no attempt was made to sever and remove the restrictions on the right to strike, an omission which contradicted the restoration of trade union freedom by the Trade Disputes and Trade Unions Act 1946.[34] Although it appears to have been clearly understood that the government would not use its powers to prosecute under Article 4, the temptation to do so was to prove irresistible in the face of what was perceived to be politically motivated unofficial industrial action at a sensitive time in international relations.

Yet while Order 1305 is thus about much more than the right to strike, it is with the latter that we are principally concerned in this study. Following this introduction, we proceed in Part II to consider the use of Order 1305 against strikers during the war – the period for which it was intended. Chapter Two deals with the position in England and Wales (though there were only three sets of prosecutions arising from Welsh disputes), while Chapter Three deals with the positon in Scotland and Northern Ireland where different legal systems led to more legalistic forms of enforcement. The lessons from all three jurisdictions were nevertheless similar and probably informed the initial strategy of the post-war government's engagement with Order 1305. From there we consider in Part III the decision to retain Order 1305 (Chapter Four), the role it played in helping the government to maintain tight control over wages (Chapter Five), and the machinery in place for monitoring and investigating those organising and participating in unofficial industrial action (Chapter Six). The last theme was to be a defining feature of post-war industrial relations, with ministers, officials and trade union leaders convinced that such action was inspired politically by communist instigators for subversive reasons.

In Part IV we move to consider the role of Order 1305 in dealing with unofficial strikes in the post-war era, beginning in Chapters Seven and Eight with the emergence of the Port Workers' Committee, an unofficial group of activists in the docks, and the attempts to use Order 1305 and other legal powers to control its activities. This is followed in Chapters Nine and Ten by an examination of the use of Order 1305 against striking gas workers, and the willingness of the magistrates to jail a number of the strike-leaders. Moving to Part V, in Chapter Eleven we show how the gas workers' case was a prelude to an attempt by the Attorney General to make greater use of Order 1305, only to be frustrated by his Cabinet colleagues who refused to consent until evidence of doubtful quality became available to move against the PWC in 1951. After considering in Chapter Twelve a Cabinet Review of Order 1305 in 1950, we move in Chapter Thirteen to give an account of the PWC trial at the Old Bailey early in the following year. The trial collapsed, the dockers walked free and, as we discuss in Chapter Fourteen, Order 1305 was revoked and replaced with the much more benign Order 1376, from which restrictions on the right to strike were removed. We consider the longer-term implications of Order 1305 in the Conclusion.

In what is ultimately a history of the abuse of state power by a Labour government, the malign elements of Order 1305 were rendered ineffective by a combination of inadequate drafting; ministerial incompetence and misjudgement; and courageous resistance by trade union activists to a bad law.

[34] The 1946 Act repealed the Trade Disputes and Trade Unions Act 1927, which had imposed a wide range of restraints on trade unions following the General Strike in 1926, including restraints on the freedom to take industrial action. See ch 4 below.

PART II

Order 1305 in War-Time

2

Order 1305 and the Right to Strike

England and Wales

I. Introduction

Order 1305 dealt with a number of important questions of collective labour law. Predictably, however, the most controversial provisions were the restrictions on the right to strike. In some senses, it may seem surprising that laws of this kind should be needed in war-time, when the country is united against an external enemy. But the reality is that employers and governments continue to take advantage, workers and trade unions continue to have grievances, and disputes continue to need to be resolved. As a result, strikes continued to take place, though to the extent that there was a real strike problem, it was mainly a 'problem' of unofficial action, ministers otherwise appreciative of the support and co-operation of trade unions and their full-time officials throughout the war.[1] This unofficial action would invariably be in breach of Order 1305 if only because the dispute to which it related was unlikely to have been referred to the Ministry. Given the sharp increase in levels of industrial action during the war, it was clear that Order 1305 was not having the restraining effect intended, while it was equally clear that it would not be possible to prosecute everyone who participated in an unlawful strike. So in what circumstances should the law be used and against whom?

In section II below, we begin with the role assumed by Bevin and the Ministry of Labour in the prosecution of workers who engaged in industrial action in England and Wales, and the policy adopted by the Ministry in relation to such prosecutions. Thereafter we consider in section III the type of cases in which Order 1305 was used, highlighting by way of example the prosecution at a company called Swift Scale, an engineering company where the Communist Party had a presence in the workforce. A major concern during the war, however, was the incidence of industrial action in coal mining, and

[1] N Stammers, *Civil Liberties in Britain during the Second World War* (Croom Helm, London, 1983), p 207, citing a junior minister claiming that 'almost without exception trade unions have not given official support to stoppages of work' (p 207). That said, in her classic article, Nina Fishman cited Ministry observations on the difficulty of distinguishing between unofficial and union backed action: N Fishman, 'A Vital Element in British Industrial Relations: A Reassessment of Order 1305, 1940–51' (1999) 8 *Historical Studies in Industrial Relations* 43, pp 52–53. Although strikes would almost invariably be presented as unofficial, trade union officials might offer informal *sub rosa* support, aware of the possibility of a prosecution.

in section IV we consider the reckless prosecutions following a strike at Betteshanger Colliery in 1941, the outcome of which made it clear that the law could not easily be used against large numbers of strikers.[2] By 1944, it was evident that Order 1305 was ineffective, as emphasised in that year by 'an outbreak of unofficial strikes in various coalfields on such a scale as had not been known since the beginning of the war'.[3] In section V we consider how Bevin was compelled as a result paradoxically to fall back on the Trade Disputes and Trade Unions Act 1927, and controversially to introduce even tighter restrictions with fresh Defence Regulations. Both of these latter initiatives were also to end in failure.

Order 1305, the Right to Strike, and the Common Law

Decided on 13 December 1941, the House of Lords decision in *Crofter Hand Woven Harris Tweed Co Ltd v Veitch*[4] served to highlight the significance of the restrictions imposed by Order 1305 in the previous year, and the use of the criminal law to enforce them. In redrawing the boundaries of civil liability for trade union activities, the judges in the *Crofter* case openly acknowledged the legitimacy of industrial action, with Lord Wright observing that 'where the rights of labour are concerned, the rights of the employer are conditioned by the rights of the men to give or withhold their services', adding famously that 'the right of workmen to strike is an essential element in the principle of collective bargaining'.[5]

It is presumably the *Crofter* decision and its reasoning that led DN Pritt KC to make the somewhat exaggerated claim in the House of Commons during a debate in 1944 when resisting additional criminal restrictions that 'strikes, of course, are legal at common law'.[6] Quite apart from being inconsistent with this common law principle, by its assault on an 'essential element in the principle of collective bargaining', Order 1305 was to confer enormous power on employers by depriving workers of their most potent weapon, thus making it 'easier to impose upon them (in the name of patriotism) much harder conditions than they would otherwise have accepted, or ought ever to have been asked to accept'.[7]

[2] These concerns were fully vindicated when Order 1305 was invoked against 1,000 or so striking miners at Betteshanger Colliery in 1942. See below pp 25–28. See also A Tyndall, 'Patriotism and Principles: Order 1305 and the Betteshanger Strike of 1942' (2001) 12 *Historical Studies in Industrial Relations* 109; and A Mak, 'Spheres of Justice in the 1942 Betteshanger Miners' Strike: An Essay in Historical Ethnography' (2015) 36 *Historical Studies in Industrial Relations* 29.

[3] R Page Arnot, *The Miners in Crisis and War: A History of the Miners' Federation of Great Britain from 1930 Onwards* (George Allen & Unwin, London, 1961), p 396.

[4] *Crofter Hand Woven Harris Tweed Co Ltd v Veitch*, 1942 SC(HL) 1.

[5] ibid p 24. For a notable account of *Crofter*, see D Brodie, 'The Scottish Case – *Crofter Hand Woven Harris Tweed v Veitch*' in KD Ewing (ed), *The Right to Strike: From the Trade Disputes Act 1906 to a Trade Union Freedom Bill 2006* (Institute of Employment Rights, Liverpool, 2006), ch 6.

[6] HC Debs, 28 April 1944, col 1103.

[7] DN Pritt, *Law, Class and Society: Book One, Employers, Workers and Trade Unions* (Lawrence & Wishart, London, 1970), p 88.

II. Role of the Ministry of Labour: Prosecution Policy and Procedure

In his British labour law debut article, Kahn Freund argued that 'even in the dire peril of the summer of 1940 Mr Bevin did not feel compelled or inclined to do what Mussolini had done openly and what Hitler had done surreptitiously in the days of peace: to suppress all strikes and lockouts'.[8] The prohibition in Article 4 was said to be 'conditional not absolute', in the sense that 'participation in hostile action becomes a criminal offence only if the Minister of Labour decides that the trade dispute is sufficiently important for him to intervene'.[9] This, however, may have under-estimated the implications of the way in which Order 1305 operated. At least on paper, the right to strike was for all practical purposes effectively removed. Workers could strike without reporting a dispute, in which case they risked prosecution; after a dispute was reported, they could strike during the three weeks that the minister was dealing with it or thinking about how to deal with it, in which case they risked prosecution; they could strike while the dispute was being considered by one of the disputes' procedures to which it was referred, in which case they risked prosecution; and they could strike if they were unhappy with the outcome of the procedure, in which case they risked prosecution.

Workers could strike only where the dispute had been reported but had not been referred for arbitration. But critically, it was by no means clear that there was a discretion not to refer, a matter to which we return in Chapter Twelve. So given that *all* strikes were likely to be unlawful, the real issue was not the wide powers of the minister to refer a dispute to arbitration, but the exercise of discretion whether or not to prosecute. Here we find that there was no great enthusiasm in government to use the powers, prosecution decisions constrained by the Ministry of Labour's policy set out in several memos by FW Leggett, then the Chief Industrial Commissioner (CIC).[10] Leggett began by pointing out that the main purpose of Order 1305 was 'to secure the maximum production of goods essential to the prosecution of the war and the continued operation of essential services'.[11] As he also noted, however, the Order was far-reaching in the sense that it applied to all industries and services, and thus included 'activities the interruption of which

[8] O Kahn Freund, 'Collective Agreements under War Legislation' (1943) 6 *MLR* 112, at p 126. For the broader significance of this article, see R Dukes, *The Labour Constitution: The Enduring Idea of Labour Law* (Oxford University Press, Oxford, 2014), pp 74–75.

[9] Kahn Freund (n 8) p 127.

[10] Note that the CIC was of equivalent rank to a Deputy Permanent Secretary. On the role of the CIC, see Sir Godfrey Ince, *The Ministry of Labour and National Service* (George Allen & Unwin, London, 1958), pp 23, 121 and 177. Ince succeeded Sir Thomas Phillips as Permanent Under Secretary in November 1944.

[11] TNA, LAB 10/116 ('Confidential Note from CIC to all CCOs and IROs on the Question of Policy, Raised by the Lord Advocate, to be Adopted under Part 4 of the Order as Regards Prohibition of Lock outs and Strikes') ('Prohibition of Strikes, Note by Chief Industrial Commissioner', 10 September 1940). Other sometimes tattered iterations of the Note, sent to – among others – the Lord Advocate in September 1940 and the DPP in November 1940, are to be found in TNA, LAB 10/199 ('The Crown Steel Trades Assn, Victoria House, Vernon Place, WC1: Position of Embargoes on Overtime to Enforce Wages Claims in Relation to the Conditions of Employment and National Arbitration Order and the Essential Work Order'), and TNA, LAB 10/895 ('Coal Mining Industry: Agreed arrangements between the Ministry of Power and Fuel and the Ministry for the handling of any troubles or stoppages that may arise – and that the new Labour Directorate be primarily responsible for industrial relations work').

would not cause any actual harm'.[12] This wide scope was said to have been adopted at the request of trade unions and employers' organisations for reasons not explained, though in Leggett's view, the failure to discriminate between 'disputes of vital importance' and 'those of a different character' weakened the force of the Order,[13] again for reasons not explained.

The law was to be administered in a way that would be consistent with the overriding objective of maintaining the maximum production of essential goods and services. This meant that the priority would be to ensure that disputes were resolved by industrial relations rather than legal procedures. The idea was to encourage employers and trade unions to remain responsible for the settlement of their disputes, and to eschew dispute settlement by coercive criminal sanctions. So although employers were seeking to persuade the Minister to prosecute strikers under Order 1305 in order to avoid discussing matters in dispute with trade unions, civil servants realised that such a course would pit state institutions against the rank and file. Moreover, to invoke the criminal law would be disproportionate (with most of the stoppages recorded in the early days of the war lasting only for a day or two as workers let off steam); impractical (many of the strikes were the consequence of deep-rooted problems for the resolution of which prosecution was not a solution); and counter-productive (in the sense that it would likely lead to the escalation rather than the resolution of disputes).[14] Leggett was thus concerned not to use legal powers for fear of provoking a political crisis, which he believed would arise if Order 1305 was to be invoked in all but the most 'defensible circumstances'.[15]

Consequently, it was important to maintain Order 1305's maximum utility, as a little-used 'substantial deterrent' in the background,[16] as emphasised in a Ministry of Labour note in 1940. While regretting that 'there has been a considerable number of stoppages despite the provisions of Article 4 of the Order', it was nevertheless 'the considered view of the Department that this Article has been (a) a deterrent and (b) a strengthening influence so far as the executives of the union are concerned'.[17] So as a secondary tool to deal with strikes and lock outs, Order 1305 would be best used only where the object of the strike (or lock out) was 'mischievous', Ministry of Labour policy crystallising in the following statement by Leggett as the government's approach continued to develop:

> The Department's policy has been to consider the question of prosecution for a breach of Part Two of the Order only where there is evidence that the stoppage is associated with subversive activities by the men concerned, or that certain people concerned are wilfully and maliciously inciting a stoppage for their own purposes, or that those concerned, although fully aware of

[12] ibid.
[13] ibid.
[14] ibid.
[15] ibid.
[16] ibid.
[17] TNA, LAB 10/653 ('National Joint Industrial Council, Joint Consultative Committee, record set of minutes and agendas of meetings from 1st to 67th meeting May 1940–October 1947') ('Note by the Ministry of Labour and National Service'). The Note was included in the record of the 10th meeting of the JCC held on 24 September 1940. The National Joint Advisory Council (NJAC) and the JCC were tripartite bodies comprising representatives from the Ministry, the TUC and the British Employers' Federation. Bevin almost always chaired meetings of both.

> the means available to remedy their grievance, wilfully and obstinately refuse to adopt constitutional methods.[18]

However, as we discuss below, these were not the only criteria, Leggett also suggesting, for example, that Order 1305 should not be invoked 'if any considerable body of workpeople should choose to defy it'.[19]

This policy of restraint was reinforced by Ministry guidance about prosecution procedure. It will be recalled that under the Defence Regulations, prosecutions could be brought by the police, by the DPP, by the Minister, and perhaps even by an employer with the consent of the DPP.[20] The files suggest that initial attempts by employers to prosecute were thwarted by the Ministry of Labour officials, as in the case of a Wolverhampton-based manufacturer of dry batteries. Said to be undertaking work of 'national importance', in October 1940 the company in question sought to prosecute six women for refusing to work with old reconditioned machines. The women were on piece work and their income would fall as a result of having to work with the less efficient equipment. When the employer rejected the women's objections, the women walked out and the company requested the DPP's consent to initiate proceedings under Order 1305.[21] On the basis that 'questions of policy may arise in connection with these prosecutions', the DPP sought the advice of the Ministry of Labour before responding.[22] Bevin's advice was unequivocal: there should be no prosecution. What was a trivial issue should be dealt with as a disciplinary matter in accordance with the industry's constitutional machinery.[23] In other words, Order 1305 was not to be seen as an instrument of labour discipline or an opportunity for employers to bully and coerce.

It was thus not until April 1941 that the first Order 1305 prosecution took place, in a case involving six apprentices employed by aircraft manufacturers in Manchester. Shortly thereafter, it was clear that the Ministry of Labour was not only consulted about when to invoke Order 1305 in individual cases, but that it was now in total control of prosecution decisions. A paper prepared for a Regional Industrial Relations Officers' Conference on 16 January 1942 revealed that there had been no change in the general policy determining whether proceedings should be taken under the Order, and that there should be no prosecutions without the Ministry's consent.[24] Cases would be

[18] TNA, LAB 10/895 ('Coal Mining Industry: Agreed arrangements between the Ministry of Power and Fuel and the Ministry for the handling of any troubles or stoppages that may arise – and that the new Labour Directorate be primarily responsible for industrial relations work') ('Ministry of Labour Note from 1940 included with a letter sent by the Ministry's Chief Industrial Commissioner to the Minister for Fuel and Power', 25 April 1944).

[19] TNA LAB 10/116 ('Confidential Note from CIC to all CCOs and IROs on the question of policy, raised by the Lord Advocate, to be adopted under Part 4 of the Order as regards prohibition of lock outs and strikes') ('Prohibition of Strikes, Note by Chief Industrial Commissioner', 10 September 1940).

[20] Defence Regulation 93.

[21] TNA, LAB 10/118 ('Statutory Rules and Orders 1940 – No 1305 Guidance sought by T H Cooper KC MP Crown Office Edinburgh on the administration of the above Order and the difficulties arising therefrom and the Minister's considered views on the points raised') ('Fowler, Langley & Wright to DPP', 31 October 1940).

[22] ibid ('DPP to Leggett', 2 November 1940).

[23] ibid ('Leggett to DPP', 6 November 1940).

[24] TNA, LAB 10/199 ('The Crown Steel Trades Assn, Victoria House, Vernon Place, WC1: Position of Embargoes on Overtime to Enforce Wages Claims in Relation to the Conditions of Employment and National Arbitration Order and the Essential Work Order') ('Regional Industrial Relations Officers' Conference,

brought to the attention of the Ministry of Labour from a wide range of sources, including an employer, an employers' association, and the police. However, it was observed in the Conference paper that the police were making inquiries and interviewing witnesses on behalf of employers. This led to concerns that police intervention could prejudice the settlement of a dispute or duplicate the inquiries already being made by local Ministry officials,[25] and attention was drawn to a December 1941 Home Office circular issued at the behest of the Minister of Labour instructing Chief Constables to report directly to the Ministry of Labour when they received a complaint from an employer and to take no further action.[26]

So although the Defence Regulations provided for prosecutions to be brought by multiple potential complainants, prosecutions in England and Wales were in practice a matter for the Ministry of Labour's Prosecutions Department and the Ministry's Chief Industrial Commissioner, in collaboration with the DPP (overseen in politically sensitive cases – such as they were – by the Attorney General). Ministry files indicate further that a report would be made by the Chief Industrial Commissioner (or the Chief Conciliation Commissioner) to Ministry officials, with either the Permanent Under Secretary or Deputy Permanent Under Secretaries sometimes being required to give a prosecution their blessing. The DPP had the junior role. In some delicate cases, as discussed below, the Minister himself was consulted, Bevin occasionally choosing to 'advise' against prosecution. The effect of Ministry control of most of the prosecutions is reflected in the prosecution figures, with remarkably few prosecutions in England and Wales relative to the number of stoppages and workers involved in the action in question. This is a point to which Bevin himself alluded in his own defence during a bad-tempered parliamentary debate about new Defence Regulation 1AA.[27]

Bevin's claims were clearly borne out by the evidence of the number of prosecutions relative to the number of stoppages and the number of workers involved in industrial action, both of which increased year on year from 1939 to 1945. As shown in Table 2.1, there were 113 sets of prosecutions in Great Britain for breach of Order 1305, Article 4, of which only 39 related to England and Wales (involving 3,861 workers over a period of five years, meaning that on average, there were five sets of prosecutions annually in England and Wales and an average of 772 workers convicted (if the 1,000-plus miners prosecuted following the Betteshanger Colliery dispute – discussed below – are excluded)). Given the population imbalance between England and Wales on the one hand, and Scotland on the other hand, the figures for England and Wales seem remarkably low. They are all the more remarkable in light of the rising levels of industrial action year on year, as shown in Table 2.2. Although the latter deals with the United Kingdom rather than Great Britain, or England and Wales only, it does nevertheless help to

16 January 1942, Note on Item 1, Trade Disputes-Proceedings in the Case of Illegal Stoppages, Procedure in England and Wales').

[25] ibid.

[26] ibid. See also ch 3 below.

[27] A point made forcefully by Bevin: HC Debs, 28 April 1944, col 1129: 'I have been careful about prosecuting men, and I could have prosecuted, in this war, thousands of men, and taken to the courts, as my hon. Friend knows, thousands of people.'

indicate the low levels of prosecution (particularly in England and Wales) relative to the number of stoppages and the workers involved.

Table 2.1 Prosecutions in Great Britain under Order 1305, Article 4, 1940–45

	Number of prosecutions	
Year	**England and Wales**	**Scotland**
1940	0	0
1941	4	9
1942	11	26
1943	21	38
1944	2	0
1945	1	1
TOTAL	39	74

Source: TNA LAB 10/998 'Legal Proceedings against Strikers in Wartime under Article 4 of Order 1305 (Conditions of Employment and Arbitration Order)'.[28]

Table 2.2 Industrial disputes involving stoppages of work in the UK

Year	**Number of stoppages**	**Workers involved (including directly)**
1940	922	255,200
1941	1,251	359,700
1942	1,303	456,400
1943	1,755	557,000
1944	2,194	821,100
1945	2,293	531,500
TOTAL	9,718	2,980,900

Source: Ministry of Labour, Annual Report 1939–1946 (TNA LAB 10/173 ('Prosecutions of Strikers under Order 1305 (1) Undertaken (2) Contemplated').

III. Limited Use of Order 1305 in England and Wales: Subversive, Mischievous and Unconstitutional

Prosecution for strike activity was thus exceptional rather than typical, the policy of the Ministry of Labour being to prosecute only the mischievous, the subversive, and the 'wilfully and obstinately' unconstitutional. The possibility of using Order 1305 against the mischievous and the subversive seemed slightly incongruous in light of the structure of the offence and the existing jurisprudence in related legislation. As we saw

[28] Two Scottish prosecutions of employers for instituting lock outs are included in these figures.

in Chapter One, Article 4 was directed principally at strike participants, not the instigators of strikes. And as we also saw, it was directed only at strikes connected with a trade dispute, a term defined in turn to mean 'any dispute or difference between employers and workmen, or between workmen and workmen connected with the employment or non-employment or the terms of employment or with the conditions of labour of any person'. A strike being undertaken for mischievous or subversive ends could arguably be said not to be connected with a trade dispute, given the definition of the latter.

The question of mischievous and subversive strike action had arisen years earlier in the context of the Trade Disputes Act 1906, section 3, which provided immunity from liability for inducing breach of the contract of employment for acts done in contemplation or furtherance of a trade dispute, the latter defined in terms similar to Order 1305, Article 4. In *Conway v Wade*,[29] Lord Loreburn gratuitously excluded the protection of the Trade Disputes Act 1906 (of which he was a principal author) from industrial action caused by 'some meddler' who 'sought to use the trade dispute as a cloak beneath which to interfere with impunity in other people's work or business'.[30] The conduct of the individual would be not in contemplation or furtherance of a trade dispute, but of 'his own designs, sectarian, political, or purely mischievous, as the case might be'.[31] What FW Leggett thus appeared implausibly to be suggesting in relation to Order 1305 was that conduct which could not be said to constitute action 'in contemplation or furtherance of a trade dispute' for the purposes of immunity from tort liability under the 1906 Act, could nevertheless be said to be 'connected with a trade dispute' (similarly defined) for the purposes of criminal liability (leading possibly to imprisonment).

One high-profile case which appeared nevertheless to meet the foregoing criteria of the Ministry is the prosecution of the strike leaders following a dispute at Swift Scale, an engineering company in North London. Perhaps because of its obvious importance for the war effort, Swift Scale was of interest to the Communist Party. Nina Fishman writes that Wal Hannington had worked there, getting a job courtesy of Claude Berridge, but had been dismissed 'due to Ministry of Supply pressure' in 1940.[32] Both Hannington (familiar to civil liberties lawyers),[33] and Berridge (an Amalgamated Engineering Union (AEU) full-time official who we encounter later in this book), were well known to MI5 and Special Branch.[34] There had been industrial relations problems at the company since at least December 1940, the workforce alleging 'gross inefficiency' and poor management practices, with union activists particularly concerned about what they saw as the anti-union behaviour of the employer. These had led to attempts to dismiss a shop steward (steps 'effectively prevented by strike action') and a subsequent Ministry of Labour inquiry chaired by Sir Charles Doughty KC.[35]

[29] *Conway v Wade* [1909] AC 506.
[30] ibid p 512.
[31] ibid.
[32] N Fishman, *The British Communist Party and the Trade Unions 1933–45* (Scolar Press, Aldershot, 1995), pp 290–92.
[33] See *Elias v Pasmore* [1934] KB 164. See also KD Ewing and CA Gearty, *The Struggle for Civil Liberties, Political Freedom and the Rule of Law in Britain, 1914–1945* (Oxford, Oxford University Press, 2000), ch 5.
[34] Hannington features in ch 10, and Berridge in chs 9 and 10 below.
[35] W Podmore, *Reg Birch: Engineer, Communist, Trade Unionist*, (Bellman Books, London, 2004), Appendix 1, pp 223–26, reproducing 'Report of the Trial of the Seven Shop Stewards', *Labour Research*,

Doughty's report was not published, though it was subsequently revealed that the inquiry had formed an unfavourable view of the shop steward who had evaded dismissal, claiming that Mr BE Leslie was '"out to look for grievances" and that it was unlikely that happy relations could exist between the workers and management so long as he continued to be employed'.[36] The inquiry failed to resolve the underlying tensions, and the steward was dismissed on 17 April 1941,[37] ostensibly for persistent lateness, but evidently because, according to a report on the dispute in *Labour Research* published four months later, he had been 'in the forefront of organising the men into the AEU, [and] had given much able assistance to the female workers in organising them into the TGWU'. There 'were other workers whose time-keeping was far worse', but Leslie was said to have 'always been a valiant protagonist for the workers generally'[38] and, in the circumstances, 'it was difficult to avoid the conclusion that Leslie's dismissal was a clear case of victimisation'.[39] The provocative, overtly confrontational nature of the dismissal of the popular convener was underlined by the report that a 'large posse of police was present at the work's entrance on the day of Leslie's dismissal'.[40] It was presumably merely coincidental that Leslie was said to be 'Jamaican'.[41]

According to the contemporary record, the workforce demanded that the company meet Leslie and his fellow shop stewards to negotiate a settlement, with 88 of their number taking strike action until it agreed to do so. Appointed to replace Leslie, one of the stewards was Reg Birch, at the time a Communist Party member and a well-known activist who 'virtually dared the state to proceed against the strikers',[42] though no mention is made of this in the Ministry of Labour record of the case. Birch and his colleagues sent a statement to Bevin claiming that the strike was an act of 'resistance' against attacks on 'trade union organisation and democratic rights'.[43] Their act of 'resistance' was met by a prosecution, though notably the Ministry chose not to bring charges against all the strikers, but only against the ringleaders, reflecting Leggatt's well-rehearsed view that the law could not be used against large numbers of workers, particularly where there was a risk that 'any considerable body of workpeople should choose to defy it'.[44] In what was only the second time that Order 1305 had been invoked, the three-day trial before a jury took place at the Old Bailey.

Represented by John Platts-Mills (later to be a Labour MP),[45] the defence expressed surprise that it should have been deployed in relation to a dispute in a 'small factory'

August 1941. The Labour Research Department had been the subject of MI5 surveillance since 1925 because of its links with the Communist Party: KD Ewing, J Mahoney and A Moretta, *MI5, the Cold War and the Rule of Law* (Oxford, Oxford University Press, 2020), pp 90–91.

[36] 'Report of the Trial of the Seven Shop Stewards' (n 35) p 226.

[37] ibid.

[38] ibid p 225.

[39] ibid.

[40] ibid p 224.

[41] Podmore (n 35) p 12.

[42] Fishman (n 32) pp 290–92.

[43] Podmore (n 35) pp 12–13.

[44] TNA, LAB 10/116 ('Confidential Note from CIC to all CCOs and IROs on the question of policy, raised by the Lord Advocate, to be adopted under Part 4 of the Order as regards prohibition of lock outs and strikes') ('Prohibition of Strikes, Note by Chief Industrial Commissioner', 10 September 1940).

[45] Platts-Mills had been instructed by William Sedley & Co, leading lawyers of the Left. Sedley was or was to become a member of the ultra-secret Communist Party Lawyers' Group. Some would have taken this as corroboration that there was subversive involvement in the dispute, as would the presence of Platts-Mills.

despite 'several hundred illegal strikes, many of them in large factories', having taken place since July 1940'.[46] Surprise too because the latest strike was simply a continuation of an existing dispute, the dismissal merely a skirmish in a much broader struggle which could not be regarded as a separate dispute. Because it was an element of a trade dispute already underway and unresolved, the defendants argued that it was unnecessary to report the dispute under Order 1305. Moreover, as the matter had been examined by the Doughty inquiry appointed by the Ministry of Labour, the Minister 'could not now certify that the dispute had not been reported to him' under Order 1305.[47] The defence was rejected by the court, and the ministerial statement that the dispute had not been reported was accepted, Article 2 of the Order providing that the Minister's decision as to whether a dispute had been reported was to be treated as conclusive for all purposes, a provision of the legislation that attracted strong criticism from contemporary commentators.

It took the jury about half an hour to find the defendants guilty. According to Birch's biographer, 'the government at first wanted a long prison sentence', until Bevin 'realised how much damage this would have done to the war effort'.[48] As a result, the Ministry of Labour Permanent Secretary (Sir Thomas Phillips) instructed counsel on 9 June 1941 that 'there is good cause for leniency' and that he would be glad if counsel could say that:

> [W]hile he had felt bound to enforce a law which was made in the general interests of the country and to make clear the seriousness of the offence in the circumstances in which the country was placed, he recognises that these workers were probably led astray by others and that they had no desire to impede the prosecution of the war.[49]

After uttering a eulogy about the defendants being 'good workmen', the Recorder co-operated and bound them over 'in sum of £5' to keep the peace for two years.[50] It seems that the Ministry was careful to control not only the prosecutions, but also their outcomes. Whether such a sympathetic outcome would have instilled fear into others minded to follow suit had the Communist Party continued to oppose the war seems at best contestable, the defendants regarding the outcome a 'great success for the working class'.[51]

But by 'a fluke', 'the workers were due to be sentenced on the eve of the Nazi invasion of the Soviet Union' in July 1941'.[52] Thereafter, it was thus not the fear of prosecution that brought Communist Party activists into line, but the Party itself. Operation Barbarossa and the Nazi invasion of Russia was a seminal moment in the conduct of the war, which led the Communist Party generally to support the Allies to such an extent that Communist trade union leaders were prepared to submerge the interests of trade union members to the demands of victory.[53] As we will discuss in Chapter Three, this

[46] 'Report of the Trial of the Seven Shop Stewards' (n 35) p 224.
[47] ibid.
[48] Podmore (n 35) p 13.
[49] ibid.
[50] 'Report of the Trial of the Seven Shop Stewards' (n 35) p 226.
[51] Podmore (n 35) p 13.
[52] 'Report of the Trial of the Seven Shop Stewards' (n 35) p 226.
[53] See especially J McIlroy and A Campbell, 'Beyond Betteshanger: Order 1305 in the Scottish Coalfields during the Second World War, Part 2: The Cardowan Story' (2003) 16 *Historical Studies in Industrial Relations* 39. See also Stammers (n 1) p 207.

was particularly true in Scotland and in relation to the Fife miners specifically. Although suspicion of the Communist Party (particularly in the engineering industry) persisted in government,[54] being most clearly expressed in a Home Office Memorandum authored by Home Secretary Herbert Morrison in 1943,[55] as MI5 pointed out in advice to ministers and officials looking for scapegoats, industrial action was not caused by Communist or Trotskyist agitators as the government sometimes wished to believe, but by genuine industrial grievances, which were inevitable in war-time. Paradoxically, industrial action increased as Communist Party support for the war intensified.

IV. Betteshanger and the Efficacy of the Criminal Law

Although the foregoing accounts for the general prosecution policy and practice throughout England and Wales, there was one important group of workers where the position was slightly different. This was in relation to the mines, with prosecutions initially the responsibility of David Grenfell, Secretary for the Mines. Said to be 'one of the best known of the miners' MPs from South Wales',[56] Grenfell held office from 1940 until 1942, when the department was transferred from the Board of Trade to the Ministry of Fuel and Power, where the new minister was Gwilym Lloyd-George, son of the former Prime Minister. A highly regarded minister who in 1943 was publicly to clash with Bevin,[57] Grenfell continued as Labour MP for Gower until his retirement in 1959, though there is no record of him having held any prominent part in the Attlee government after the war. The evidence suggests that under his stewardship, at least initially, the Mines Department took an even more relaxed approach to prosecutions under Order 1305 than did the Ministry of Labour, despite the high levels of industrial action in the mines, despite the importance of the supply of coal for the war effort, and despite what were probably unwelcome parliamentary questions about the number of strikes in the industry.

The files reveal that although the Ministry of Labour was keen to relieve the Mines Department of its responsibility for prosecution,[58] the Mines Department was just as keen to ensure that the law should not be used. Reporting on correspondence in 1941, a Ministry of Labour official wrote of the attitude of the Mines Department being that 'responsibility for taking action under Order 1305 is a matter for the Minister of Labour'. What this appeared to mean is that if Bevin wanted a prosecution to be brought, the initiative should come from him personally, because 'the Minister of Mines himself was not at all disposed to suggest prosecutions in the

[54] For government concerns of Communist Party influence which were downplayed by MI5, see TNA, LAB 10/281 ('Minute by CIC Harold Emmerson', 29 September 1943) and ('Note by Emmerson', 23 November 1943).

[55] TNA, CAB 66/35/9 ('Communist Party of Great Britain', Memorandum by the Home Secretary, 13 March 1943).

[56] Page Arnot (n 3) p 309.

[57] ibid pp 389–90.

[58] See TNA, LAB 10/895 ('Coal Mining Industry: Agreed arrangements between the Ministry of Power and Fuel and the Ministry for the handling of any troubles or stoppages that may arise – and that the new Labour Directorate be primarily responsible for industrial relations work').

mining industry'. Indeed, the Mines Department official noted that none of the 300 mining strikes in the first eight months of 1941 was said to be suitable for prosecution, though they were unusually thinking about sending over details of one case 'in which the local miners' lodge has supported the stoppage in defiance of the directions of the union executive'. The Ministry of Labour official concluded that: 'Save, however, in exceptional cases such as this, I do not think the Mines Department will take the initiative or welcome the initiative being taken by us in instituting proceedings.'[59]

Which makes it all the more surprising that a prosecution should have been brought following a strike at Betteshanger Colliery in December 1941, leading to one of the great *causes célèbre* of British labour law. The story of what is the best-known and most closely studied Order 1305 prosecution is told most famously by Sir Harold Emmerson, Leggett's successor as Chief Industrial Commissioner, in evidence to the Royal Commission on Trade Unions and Employers' Associations in 1966, the evidence being published as an Appendix to the Royal Commission's report.[60] An unusual – and perhaps the defining – feature of the strike is that it took place after the dispute had been the subject of arbitration, and after the men refused to accept the arbitrator's award. Another unusual feature of the strike is that, as Emmerson pointed out, it was not only 'illegal' as a breach of Order 1305, but 'to make matters worse', it had the support of local union officials. Keen after the event to pass the buck for the debacle to Grenfell, Emmerson advised the Royal Commissioners that in coal mining disputes, it was the Mines Department and not the Ministry of Labour that decided on action under Order 1305, with the Ministry of Labour acting as 'only their agents when it came to legal action'.

If Emmerson is to be believed, the role of the Ministry of Labour was reluctantly to 'set the machinery of the law in motion'.[61] But although it has been claimed that 'the decision to prosecute was taken 'against Bevin's advice',[62] Emmerson nevertheless also made it clear that Grenfell 'had Cabinet backing',[63] while Ministry of Labour records suggest that both Bevin and the President of the Board of Trade, Sir Andrew Duncan MP, favoured prosecution.[64] The problem, however, was that there were around 4,000 men on strike. Consequently, to make the prosecution more manageable, it was decided to concentrate on the underground workers, of whom there were approximately 1,000. Even so, preparing and serving summonses on 1,000 people was a formidable challenge, and extra police had to be drafted in for the purpose. Once charged, the proceedings might have lasted for months if the men had pleaded not guilty, so the union was asked if its members would plead guilty. The union agreed. Matters appear to have been conducted with remarkable goodwill, Emmerson describing a

[59] TNA LAB 16/53 ('The Conditions of Employment and National Arbitration Order 1940: PROSECUTIONS') ('Minute sheet note to Mr Emmerson and the Solicitor by HR Hodges', 4 November 1941).

[60] Royal Commission on Trade Unions and Employers' Associations, 1965–68, Report, Cmnd 3263, Appendix 6, para 1.

[61] ibid, Appendix 6, para 2.

[62] GG Field, *Blood, Sweat and Toil: Remaking the British Working Class, 1939–1945* (Oxford University Press, Oxford, 2011), p 116.

[63] Royal Commission on Trade Unions and Employers' Associations (n 60) Appendix 6, para 2.

[64] TNA, LAB 10/173 ('Prosecutions of Strikers under Order 1305 (1) Undertaken (2) Contemplated'). It is recorded there that '[t]he Minister agreed with the President of the Board of Trade and the Secretary for Mines that all the men should be prosecuted'.

party atmosphere on the day of the trial before the magistrates in Canterbury: 'local colliery workers made it an outing for their families and chartered coaches to take wives and children' to the hearing.[65]

Any concern that Order 1305 was about to be reduced to a circus act was quickly shattered when the three union officials were sentenced to terms of imprisonment with hard labour, 35 strikers were fined £3 (with the unattractive option of one month's imprisonment), and nearly 1,000 strikers were fined £1, with the option of serving 14 days.[66] As might be anticipated, this caused uproar: the men had pleaded guilty as requested, only to be met with sentences much more severe than expected. It was an industrial relations disaster, and the problem faced by the employer and the government was how to get production moving again, the men refusing to work until their leaders were released. It took 11 days for the three officials to be released, but only after significant political capital had been spent by those members of the Cabinet who had approved the prosecutions: in the first place it was necessary for the Secretary of Mines and the President of the Miners' Federation of Great Britain (which became the National Union of Mineworkers in 1945) to meet the men in prison, before an agreement could be signed between the local management and the local union, the agreement giving 'the men what they wanted'.[67]

Grenfell had then to organise a deputation to the Home Secretary, at the time Sir John Anderson, to persuade him to release the miners. But once that was done and they were back at work, there remained the question of enforcement of the unpaid fines as the criminal justice process unravelled in a way perhaps not even anticipated by Leggett. Unlike the prison sentences, the fines were not set aside. Yet only nine men paid their fines. Should the Clerk to the Justices prepare 'nearly a thousand commitment warrants', given that the county jail could accommodate only a few at a time, and that it would take years to work through the list? And should he do so in the knowledge that 'the men had been at work for some weeks, they had made good the lost output and he believed the country needed coal'?[68] The Clerk wisely sought advice, concerned that there would be an outcry if the men were sent to prison for non-payment of the fines, when the original prison sentences imposed on the leaders had been quashed. He was advised not to enforce the fines, but they were not remitted.[69] A request by the National Union of Mineworkers (NUM) in 1950 that the fines should be returned to the men who did pay was dismissed.[70]

The Betteshanger case clearly demonstrated the limited utility of Order 1305 and more generally the limited effectiveness of the criminal law in dealing with strikers, even if prosecutions were confined to dealing with the mischievous, the subversive and the wilfully and obstinately unconstitutional. It fully vindicated Leggett's concern that the law should not be used against large numbers of workers, as well as his concern

[65] Royal Commission on Trade Unions and Employers' Associations (n 60) Appendix 6, para 4. Not only that: 'the Mines Department authorised the Regional Petroleum Officer to allow petrol for the journeys'.

[66] ibid para 5.

[67] ibid para 6.

[68] ibid.

[69] ibid para 8.

[70] ibid para 9.

that the criminal law would cause more harm than good (it was completely counter-productive at Betteshanger), even in the limited circumstances of the three latter categories of case in which it was to be deployed. Emmerson's vivid and very influential evidence led the Royal Commission to go further and to claim that Betteshanger showed the 'fruitlessness of the use of penal sanctions for the purpose of enforcing industrial peace',[71] which of course raises the question about the purpose of Order 1305 in the first place. According to Sir Harold, the Ministry of Labour's view of the importance of Order 1305 lay in its 'moral effect', suggesting that it was intended mainly to restrain or prevent rather than to prosecute and penalise. If that was the purpose, the measure seemed to have little impact as the number of disputes continued to increase each year, while the number of workers participating in strikes continued to grow, as shown in Table 2.2 above.

Although the need for prosecutorial restraint was thus vindicated by practical experience, prosecutions nevertheless continued to take place despite the Betteshanger debacle, with a notable number launched in 1943, as shown in Table 2.1 above. The use of Order 1305 began to peter out only in the summer of 1944, paradoxically at a time when the number of working days lost to strikes – particularly by coal miners – was to rise exponentially, mainly as a result of unofficial/unconstitutional action. According to Henry Pelling, the coal industry was responsible for 'one half of the total loss of working days in 1943 and for two thirds in 1944'.[72] Yet only four of the prosecutions in 1943 and 1944 related to strikes by miners, which meant that there were only five sets of prosecutions of miners in England and none in Wales throughout the whole period of the war. In the four cases after Betteshanger, prosecutions were brought against 108, 297, 100 and 157 miners respectively in four different disputes at various locations. One of the cases was discontinued, and although the defendants were convicted in the other three cases, probationary sentences were imposed in two of the cases, with fines of ten shillings being imposed in the other. No doubt with Betteshanger in mind, the court ordered that the men's employer should collect the money.

V. 'Trotskyist Agitators' and Reliance on Other Powers

As the use of Order 1305 was beginning to decline, the government was faced with another concern which revealed other limitations of its war-time powers. This was a concern about the heightened activity of Trotskyist activists who did not share the Communist Party's support for the hostilities or its loyalty to the Soviet Union. Two small Trotskyist groups had fused in early 1944 to form the Revolutionary Communist Party (RCP), Herbert Morrison informing the War Cabinet that it had between 1,500 and 2,000 members.[73] Despite being a tiny organisation, the RCP was nevertheless

[71] Royal Commission on Trade Unions and Employers' Associations (n 60) para 486.

[72] H Pelling, *A History of British Trade Unionism*, 3rd edn (Penguin, Harmondsworth, 1976), p 217.

[73] TNA, CAB 65/42/3 (Cabinet Conclusions, 5 April 1944). For additional background, see Socialist Equality Party, *The Historical and International Foundations of the Socialist Equality Party, Part 3*, 12 March 2011, www.wsws.org; and M Upham, *The History of British Trotskyism to 1949, Part Two (1938–1944)*, 6 April 2004, www.marxists.org.

thought by ministers to be promoting unrest in the coalfields, Bevin citing 'definite evidence that members of a political organisation were fomenting trouble'.[74] There was particular anxiety about their involvement in the Tyneside Apprentices' Guild, which in January 1944 had 'issued a manifesto entitled 'Fight the Pit Compulsion Plot', attacking the government's plans to introduce a ballot for the conscription of young men to work in the mines, including those who were apprenticed elsewhere.[75] This had led MI5 to take a close interest in the Guild, with both the Ministry of Labour and the Home Office kept fully informed.

Opposition to the government's plans for industrial conscription was effectively run by the RCP and was seen by the Home Office as 'an interesting example of how Trotskyism is now providing the focus for discontented elements in industry which was formerly supplied by the CP'.[76] In a notable MI5 report – 'Tyneside Apprentices Guild: Trotskyist activities in connection with' – information was provided to the effect that early in January 1944, a notice of transfer to the mines was sent in error to an apprentice based in Wallsend, adding that 'by another error it was not until 9th February that the notice was cancelled'. In the meantime, the Apprentices Guild gave notice:

> [T]hat all apprentices would come out on February 14th unless the matter was put right. As it was put right the strike did not develop, but it is believed that the apprentices are thoroughly disturbed and awaiting another chance to come out.

However, in a covering letter, MI5 revealed that it otherwise had little information on the RCP, adding that some of its information came from Communist Party sources. It was nevertheless pointed out that 'the Party's intelligence service is not always completely reliable and generally speaking their definition of a Trotskyist is rather wider than ours'.

It soon became clear that four RCP activists – Jock Haston, Heaton Lee, Roy Tearse and Ann Keen – were playing a leading part in demanding that the Minister of Labour 'guarantee the unconditional exemption of all apprentices (irrespective of industrial group) from liability to direction under the Mining Ballot Scheme',[77] and were helping to organise a strike to begin on 28 March 1944. At the meeting of the War Cabinet on 3 April, the Minister of Labour informed his colleagues that 'the Director of Public Prosecutions was considering whether the ring leaders could be prosecuted under the Trade Disputes and Trade Unions Act 1927', adding that 'the existing emergency powers did not enable him to take effective action'.[78] This was likely to be a reference to Order 1305, Bevin having also said that it 'was clear that the apprentices' strike on Tyneside, the Clyde and in Yorkshire was a political one and had been instigated by a

[74] TNA, CAB 65/42/3 (Cabinet Conclusions, 5 April 1944).

[75] TNA, HO 45/25485/2 ('Disturbances: Revolutionary Communist Party: Reports on Activities') (Home Office G2 File 695517/70, 'MI5, Tyneside Apprentices Guild: Trotskyist activities in connection with. Fwd. copy of letter sent to M/L, and report'). The MI5 report 'Tyneside Apprentices Guild' was sent to Emmerson at the Ministry of Labour and Miss Nunn (then private secretary to Sir Alexander Maxwell, then permanent under-secretary at the Home Office) and to G2 Division, seemingly an earlier incarnation of what became F3 Division, the small group of Home Office civil servants with responsibility for supervising industrial policing. F3 features prominently in some of the chapters that follow.

[76] TNA, HO 45/25485/2 ('Disturbances: Revolutionary Communist Party: Reports on activities') ('Minute sheet note by Ministry official "JMP"', 29 February 1944').

[77] *R v Tearse* [1945] KB 1, at p 4.

[78] TNA, CAB 65/42/1 (Cabinet Conclusions, 3 April 1944).

group which had broken away from the Communist Party when Russia became our ally'.[79] It is because the strike was a political one, and would not have fallen within the definition of a trade dispute in Article 7, that Order 1305 could not be used. It was a dispute with the government about the conscription of apprentices to work in the mines; it was not a dispute with an employer about terms and conditions of employment.

Bevin was now weighing his options, advising ministers two days later that the TUC supported the idea for a new Defence Regulation (1AA) to enable action to be taken against the instigators of strikes.[80] In the meantime, however, he also told the War Cabinet on 5 April that he was considering the use of either the Defence Regulation 18B or the Trade Disputes and Trade Union Act 1927 against his Trotskyist tormentors.[81] The former was the provision under which Oswald Mosley and fellow fascists were interned,[82] Regulation 18B(1) providing that:

> If the Secretary of State has reasonable cause to believe any person to be of hostile origin or associations or to have been recently concerned in acts prejudicial to the public safety or the defence of the realm or in the preparation or instigation of such acts and that by reason thereof it is necessary to exercise control over him, he may make an order against that person directing that he be detained.

The use of such a power against political agitators would have been a big step, with an extensive Home Office note – 'The Possibility of Detaining the Leaders of the Revolutionary Communist Party under Regulation 18B' – dated 1 April 1944, having expressed caution, referring to likely trade union sensitivity, as well as MI5 advice that 'it is the centre of disturbance which attracts the Trotskyists, not the Trotskyists who create the centre of disturbance'.[83]

The latter advice was reinforced by an internal Home Office report to Morrison on 5 April advising him that it was not possible to say that 'the danger from these organisations is so great that it is essential to act at once under the special powers of Regulation 18B, without waiting to let the law take its normal course'.[84] That course had by now begun, following a police raid of a number of premises, including the homes of the RCP leaders as well as the RCP HQ in London, raids which had taken place in turn following the interception of letters about the apprentices' strike.[85] Although they were

[79] ibid. Bevin subsequently informed Parliament that this was 'not a trade dispute within the meaning of the law', the issue in dispute being that 'the Government should withdraw their decision to order boys to the mines': HC Debs, 28 April 1944, col 1128.

[80] TNA, CAB 65/42/3 (Cabinet Conclusions, 5 April 1944).

[81] ibid.

[82] The classic study is AWB Simpson, *In the Highest Degree Odious: Detention without Trial in War-Time Britain* (Oxford University Press, Oxford, 1992).

[83] TNA, HO 45/25485/2 ('Disturbances: Revolutionary Communist Party: Reports on Activities') (Home Office G2 File 695517/76 ('The fomenting of strikes by Trotskyist agitation: would it be right to use Regulation 18B against the agitators?').

[84] ibid. The final paragraph of the note mentions a meeting attended that afternoon by both the author and Morrison when it was expressly agreed that Regulation 18B detention would have no effect on the miners' strikes, 'and that the most that could be said was that while the use of Regulation 18B in connection with strike movements is extremely dangerous, the locking up of Trotskyites under that Regulation would create far less danger than the locking up of anyone else'.

[85] TNA, HO 45/25485/2 ('Disturbances: Revolutionary Communist Party: Reports on Activities') (Home Office G2 File 695517/76, 'The fomenting of strikes by Trotskyist agitation: would it be right to

still looking at 'certain documents' obtained by the police raids, the initial view of the police was that 'there will be no difficulty in launching prosecutions against Tearse, Lee and Davey, the Secretary of the Apprentices Strike Committee, for offences against the Trades Disputes Act (sic)'.[86] By now, the potential use of Defence Regulation 18B had all but been discounted, despite pressure from the Minister of Fuel and Power (Lloyd George), who had been pressing hard for its deployment.[87] The files reveal that Morrison was not happy about internment as a weapon against strikers, not least because it was 'likely to arouse grave apprehension amongst industrial workers', while questions would be asked 'why similar action was not taken against some more influential strike leaders'.[88]

Ten days later, Tearse and Lee were arrested, along with Ann Keen. Haston was arrested another 10 days thereafter, and the RCP premises were entered and searched again. With Order 1305 apparently discounted and the Cabinet in any event willing to use stronger powers, the Attorney General chose to invoke for the first time the Trade Disputes and Trade Unions Act 1927 in what was in effect a politically motivated attempt to decapitate the RCP. Introduced by way of reparations after the ill-fated General Strike in 1926, the 1927 Act provided that industrial action was 'illegal' if two conditions were met – that it:

(i) had any object other than or in addition to the furtherance of a trade dispute within the trade or industry within which the strikers (or employers locking out) were engaged; *and*
(ii) was 'designed or calculated to coerce the Government either directly or by inflicting hardship on the community' (section 1(1)).

Anyone who declared, instigated or incited others to take part in a strike or lock out declared by the Act to be illegal faced a fine or imprisonment, the Act allowing for a maximum fine of £10 or a maximum term of imprisonment of three months – two years if convicted on indictment. The four accused were charged with: (a) conspiring together to act in furtherance of a strike of shipyard apprentices declared by the Trade Disputes and Trade Unions Act 1927, section 1 to be illegal; (b) acting in furtherance of such a strike; (c) aiding and abetting the commission of such an illegal strike by aiding

use Regulation 18B against the agitators?') ('Trotskyist Organisations' addressed to the Home Secretary, 5 April 1944).

[86] ibid.

[87] See TNA, HO 45/25485/2 ('Disturbances: Revolutionary Communist Party: Reports on Activities') (Home Office G2 File 695517/73, 'Trotskyist activities among miners', Minute sheet entry, 30 March 1944). See also TNA, HO 45/25485/2 ('Disturbances: Revolutionary Communist Party: Reports on activities') (Home Office G2 File 695517/76, 'The fomenting of strikes by Trotskyist agitation: would it be right to use Regulation 18B against the agitators?', Minute sheet entry, 6 April 1944).

[88] TNA, HO 45/25485/2 ('Disturbances: Revolutionary Communist Party: Reports on Activities') (War Cabinet, Lord President's Committee: 'Use of Regulation 18B Against Fomentation of Strikes', Memorandum by the Home Secretary). This is a heavily hand revised typed draft dated 7 April, evidently signed off by Morrison on 12 April. It has not been possible to find the official final text at the National Archives, perhaps because the relevant file has been 'removed and destroyed', though the draft quoted here has been left in Home Office G2 File 695517/73, a faint note in pencil at the top of the paper appearing to state that it was the final version of Morrison's memorandum (LP (44)67).

others to act in furtherance of it; and (d) conspiring to incite the apprentices and others to declare such an illegal strike.[89]

It was some three weeks before the pre-trial preliminary hearings took place.[90] In the meantime, Bevin was the subject of excoriating criticism in the House of Commons in a lengthy debate on what was inevitably an unsuccessful prayer to annul the new Defence Regulation 1AA.[91] Shortly after the Cabinet meeting on 5 April, a draft copy of the Regulation had been prepared and shared with a TUC sub-committee, following which 'one or two amendments were made on their suggestion'.[92] Using the pretext of 'Trotskyist agitators', the new Defence Regulation 1AA provided that 'no person shall declare, instigate or incite any other person to take part or otherwise act in furtherance of any strike among persons engaged in the performance of essential services or in a lock-out of persons so engaged'. Note that although limited to 'essential services', the new Regulation was not confined to strikes in connection with a trade dispute. Breach of this latter provision carried the possibility of a five-year prison sentence and a £500 fine, in contrast to a maximum of two years and £500 on indictment under Order 1305. Bevin was strongly criticised from his own side for 'going behind the back of Parliament, and reaching understandings with outside bodies, and then presenting Parliament with a *fait accompli*'.[93] The new Regulation had been brought into operation on 17 April, 'the day before Parliament resumed after the Easter Recess'.[94]

Bevin was to be further embarrassed by the legal proceedings under the 1927 Act. The proceedings at the Newcastle Assizes, to which Bevin had been called by the defence, were held *in camera*, ostensibly because the police had not completed their investigations against other alleged offenders.[95] All four defendants were convicted on 19 June 1944. Tearse and Lee were sentenced to 12 months, Haston to six months and Keen to 13 days. The conduct alleged against them related to their 'helping the apprentices to prepare for a strike by organizing committees, preparing documents and propaganda and making speeches'.[96] Further reinforcing the dangers of using the criminal law to deal with strikes, however, the convictions of the three men were overturned on 25 September 1944.[97] According to the Court of Appeal, acts 'preparatory' to a strike could not be said to be in 'furtherance' of it. To make matters worse, such a construction would have implications not only for the 1927 Act (which was never used again), but possibly also for

[89] *R v Tearse* [1945] KB 1, at p 2.

[90] The committal hearings took place on 18–20 and 22 May 1944, and the trial on 13–17 and 19 June: TNA, HO 45/25485/1 ('Disturbances: Revolutionary Communist Party: Reports on Activities') (Home Office G2 File 695517/89, 'Prosecution of Haston, Tearse, Lee and Keen. Forward report of Police Court Proceedings').

[91] The government won the vote by 314 votes to 23. However, only 56 out of 165 Labour MPs voted in favour of the Regulation, in what was said to be the 'largest backbench rebellion over a civil liberties issue during the course of the war': Stammers (n 1) p 211.

[92] HC Debs, 28 April 1944, col 1062 (Aneurin Bevan MP).

[93] ibid col 1061.

[94] ibid.

[95] ibid col 1068. This did not prevent Special Branch recording the proceedings both at the Police Court and Newcastle Assizes: TNA, HO 45/25485/1 ('Disturbances: Revolutionary Communist Party: Reports on Activities') (Home Office G2 File 695517/89, 'Prosecution of Haston, Tearse, Lee and Keen. Forward report of Police Court Proceedings').

[96] ibid.

[97] The conviction of Ann Keen (Angel Rosalie Keen) was not quashed until 30 October. Her name had accidently been left off the original notice of appeal: *Daily Herald*, 31 October 1944.

the similarly worded Defence Regulation 1AA (which was never used at all).[98] Thus, it will be recalled that under the latter, it was an offence to 'declare, instigate or incite any other person to take part or otherwise act in furtherance of any strike' to which the new regulation applied.

Defence Regulation 1AA and Defence Regulation 1A

As indicated in the text, Bevin was to feel the wrath of a number of MPs following the introduction of Regulation 1AA. The criticism was of three kinds. First, as we have seen, there were constitutional objections from Bevan, who added to the passages already referred to in the text with other words of condemnation. The making of Regulation 1AA was 'an abuse of the Government's position' and 'an affront to Parliament'.[99] Second, there were concerns about the mischief to which the new regulation was addressed, Bevan scoffing at the suggestion that loyal miners were likely to be waylaid by Trotskyist agitators, adding that the reason why there was so much trouble in the coalfields was that the miners were represented by union officials who paid no attention to their interests.[100] But even if there was a problem of Trotskyist agitation as some on the left were prepared to accept, a third concern – raised by DN Pritt KC MP[101] – was that the new restrictions were wholly disproportionate and unnecessary.

Unsympathetic to his sectarian foes,[102] Pritt had warned for some time that 'the Trotskyists are sufficiently dangerous to be taken seriously'.[103] As he pointed out, however, Regulation 1AA was accompanied by an amendment to Defence Regulation 1A by which it was an offence to interfere with essential services (defined by Defence Regulation 100 to mean 'essential for the defence of the realm or the prosecution of the war or essential to the life of the community'). While seemingly close to including the instigators of strikes, Regulation 1A(a) was initially qualified by the proviso that 'a person shall not be guilty of an offence against this Regulation by reason only of his taking part in or peacefully persuading any other person to take part in a strike'. However, the amendment to Regulation 1A replaced the proviso so that 'no person shall be deemed to have committed an offence against this Regulation by reason only of his having in the course of a strike ceased to work or refused to accept employment'.

The result was that the continued exclusion of strike participants ceased to apply to strike instigators. According to Pritt, this rendered the new Regulation 1AA

[98] For a discussion of Regulation 1AA and the reaction to it, see Stammers (n 1) pp 210–12.
[99] HC Debs, 28 April 1944, col 1062.
[100] ibid cols 1065–66.
[101] On Pritt, see Ewing, Mahoney and Moretta (n 35) pp 143–50.
[102] About which he was teased by Sir Richard Ackland (also opposed to the new measure), who was 'amused to see the hon and learned Member for North Hammersmith (Mr Pritt) join the Minister in playing up the importance of this Trotskyist organisation': ibid col 1144. DN Pritt was closely associated with the Communist Party.
[103] ibid col 1108.

redundant: if 'your Trotskyite persuades people to strike', 'you can hit him at once for instigation' under Regulation 1A and 'you can hit him under 1305 for taking part in an illegal strike, because it is bound to be a trade dispute'.[104] Pritt challenged Bevin to suggest 'any circumstances which have any reasonable likelihood of ever happening in which 1A, as amended, would not cover'.[105] There was no convincing response, Pritt and the other critics being subsequently vindicated by events in the sense that Regulation 1AA expired at the end of the war unused, despite high levels of industrial action in 1944. It is unknown whether the failure of deployment was because it had been fatally wounded by the intervention of Bevan and others, or whether an appropriate occasion for its use never arose.

VI. Conclusion

Order 1305 was obviously not the first time that the criminal law had been fashioned for use against strikers. The Tyneside apprentices' strike notwithstanding, it was nevertheless an extraordinarily wide offence, the scope of operation of which was constrained only by departmental policy. Ministry officials were cautious about using the new legislation, their caution shown to be justified by experience, which revealed criminalisation to be unpredictable, inappropriate, and ineffective. It was unpredictable because outcomes could not always be guaranteed, with judges on occasion unhelpfully severe. It was inappropriate because – as in Betteshanger – it could not be used against large numbers of strikers, while any selective prosecution or victimisation of individuals was likely to be met with hostility from the workforce. And it was ineffective if the aim was to discourage strikes in order to support war-time production, assuming we are to judge effectiveness as being the impact of Order 1305 on restraining strikes. According to Robin Page Arnot, the prolific historian of mining trade unionism, 568,000 coalminers were involved in disputes in 1944, with 'the duration in working days of all disputes that year' reaching 2,480,000, 'a figure that had only once been exceeded in the previous seventeen years'.[106]

Yet rather than accept the limits of the criminal law, the response of Bevin and the Coalition government paradoxically was to take additional powers and to introduce even more criminal restrictions in what was to become Defence Regulation 1AA. The latter was more narrowly targeted than Order 1305, addressed only to those working in essential services, and applicable only to instigators rather than to participants, while the penalties on conviction were potentially heavier. But Defence Regulation 1AA

[104] HC Debs, 28 April 1944, col 1110. That may have been incorrect. As amended, Regulation 1A probably had a wider application than art 4 of Order 1305, in the sense that on its face, it appeared not to be confined to strikes in connexion with a trade dispute as defined in art 7 of Order 1305. That would make sense if the intention was to deal with problems such as those which had arisen on Tyneside in the *Tearse* case.

[105] ibid cols 1110–11.

[106] Page Arnot (n 3) p 396. A 'still more significant figure' was the 1,253 disputes 'big and small' in 1944, said to be 'half as many again as in the previous year', which 'had the highest total of disputes since the beginning of the century (ibid).

was no more effective than Order 1305. The reasons were made clear by Sir Frederick Leggett, by now Deputy Secretary at the Ministry of Labour, who was to comment with great foresight when Regulation 1AA was being contemplated. He argued that while it 'may be a deterrent in some cases', the 'general effect' will not 'be very great or wholly good'. Far more important was to 'take into account that there are grievances' and that 'it is only by dealing with them that we can hope to weaken the growing unofficial movement'.[107] This was a lesson that had to be re-learned after the war when the problem of unofficial action continued, albeit in the docks rather than in the mines, with the Communist Party rather than the RCP now being blamed for instigating disputes following the renewal of more familiar political hostilities.

[107] TNA LAB 10/281 ('Prosecution Policy in Relation to Unofficial Strikes: Draft Memo for Lord President's Committee and Powers of Prosecution Defence Regn 1AA') (Memorandum by Sir Frederick Leggett, 18 November 1943).

3

Order 1305 and the Right to Strike

Scotland and Northern Ireland

I. Introduction

In this chapter we are concerned with the operation of war-time restraints on the right to strike in Scotland and Northern Ireland. Order 1305 applied in Scotland as it did in the rest of Great Britain, but it did not apply in Northern Ireland for which an identical measure – Order 1508 – was made by the UK government.[1] A particularly important feature of both Scotland and Northern Ireland was the existence of different legal systems, operating independently of Westminster and Whitehall. There may have been a common body of rules operating throughout the United Kingdom, but there remained different personnel and different procedures in the three different jurisdictions for their enforcement. In Scotland the authority was vested in the Crown Office based in Edinburgh, which was led by the Lord Advocate. The latter was appointed on the recommendation of the Prime Minister to be the government's chief law officer in Scotland. At the time, the Lord Advocate was also a Member of the Westminster Parliament. In Northern Ireland, in contrast, law enforcement was the responsibility of the Attorney General for Northern Ireland. The latter was appointed by the Prime Minister of Northern Ireland to give legal advice to the Stormont government.

Both Scotland and Northern Ireland reveal very similar approaches to the use of the criminal sanctions in Orders 1305 and 1508. In doing so, they also reveal a sharp difference from the approach to prosecution in England and Wales, where as we have seen two different government departments were responsible for determining prosecution policy, namely the Ministry of Labour and the Department of Mines. Both of these departments appear to have been able to wrest control from the Attorney General, Sir Donald Somervell KC, who had served in that role since 1936, and both adopted a generally cautious approach to prosecution with the notable exception of the Betteshanger case. Led by Bevin and by Chief Industrial Commissioner Sir Frederick Leggett and his successor Sir Harold Emmerson,[2] the Ministry of Labour adopted what might be referred to as an administrative approach to law enforcement in relation to which the Donovan Royal Commission purred approvingly as being sensitive to the need to

[1] SR&O 1940 No 1508.

[2] Emmerson replaced Leggett as Chief Industrial Commissioner in June 1942 and was replaced by Robert Gould in 1944.

respect state-sponsored industrial relations procedures.[3] One of the oversights of the Donovan Report, however, was its failure to engage with the experience of Order 1305 in Scotland, and Order 1508 in Northern Ireland. Was the more legalistic approach to law enforcement any more successful in different legal systems? Or did the experience of these jurisdictions reinforce the lessons of Betteshanger?

II. Practice in Scotland

It is striking that there were many more prosecutions in Scotland than in England and Wales. Indeed, 74 of the 113 sets of war-time prosecutions under Order 1305 were from Scotland, with about 2,300 of the workers prosecuted being engaged there. This compared with 39 of the 113 sets from England and Wales, involving 3,861 workers, of whom over 1,000 are accounted for by the ill-fated Betteshanger convictions alone. The Scottish figures represented an average of more than six sets of prosecutions a month, compared to the position in England of only just over three a month. It seems extraordinary that about two-thirds of the cases should have been from a country representing less than 10 per cent of the national population, and that if Betteshanger is excluded, about half of all those convicted were from Scotland. It is true that Scotland was heavily engaged in the war-time economy, and that the Scottish prosecutions tended to be dominated by coal mining and shipbuilding, with 'Red Clydeside' being said to have had a higher incidence of strikes during the war than any other location. But other parts of the country also had shipbuilders and coal miners, and were just as important to the national economy, while as Table 2.1 in Chapter Two suggests, rising levels of industrial action were not unique to Scotland.

As suggested in the introduction, an important difference between Scotland on the one hand and England and Wales on the other, is the responsibility for prosecution and law enforcement. As we saw in Chapter One, Defence Regulation 93(1) authorised prosecutions by the police, the employer with consent of the DPP, or the Ministry of Labour. In practice, the authority to prosecute was seized by the Ministry of Labour, except in coalmining, which was the responsibility of the Mines Department in the Board of Trade until the creation of the Ministry of Fuel and Power on 3 June 1942. But Regulation 93(1) did not apply to Scotland, which meant that the Lord Advocate was in charge, the Lord Advocate performing a role equivalent to the Attorney General in England and Wales. At the beginning of the war, the office was held by Thomas Cooper KC, then a Unionist MP for Edinburgh West, but also a distinguished advocate at the Scottish Bar. He is most famous following his elevation to the Bench for being willing to question the extent to which parliamentary sovereignty as expressed by AV Dicey survived as a principle of the British constitution following the Treaty of Union,[4] and for his defence of the independence of the Scottish legal system as essential to 'what is left of Scotland's independent life and culture'.[5]

[3] Royal Commission on Trade Unions and Employers' Associations, 1965–68, Report, Cmnd 3623, 1968.

[4] *McCormick v Lord Advocate*, 1953 SC 396. In the end, his challenge did not amount to much: the Treaty of Union may be unalterable, but it is not enforceable in a domestic court to restrain the operation of a statute.

[5] Lord Cooper, *The Scottish Legal Tradition* (3rd edn by MC Meston) (Saltire Society, Edinburgh 1969), p 31.

Cooper was sceptical about using Order 1305, and no prosecutions were authorised while he was in post, though it is true that he vacated office only two months after Order 1305 was used for the first time in England following an apprentices' strike at an aircraft manufacturer in Manchester.[6] It appears that Cooper had been influential in determining Ministry of Labour prosecution policy as set out by Sir Frederick Leggett and explained in Chapter Two, with notable work on Cooper's concerns about the role of the criminal law in industrial disputes having been unearthed by Adrian Tyndall.[7] According to Tyndall, Cooper was concerned about the viability of the restriction on strikes, arguing that it was 'virtually impossible to prevent strikes where any considerable body of men was involved, and that the most dangerous industrial and political repercussions might easily ensue from an attempt to do so'.[8] Cooper is said to have been concerned that the law would be invoked by employers against workers in place of conciliation, and continued by emphasising that the Order would simply reveal 'the impotence of the Government to enforce the prohibition of strikes'. In his view, it should be used only in such 'rare cases as where strike is embarked upon by a small and subversive minority for mischievous ends'.[9]

Cooper's suggested criteria for prosecution were similar to Leggett's and would have greatly limited the impact of Order 1305. Following his appointment to the Court of Session as Lord Justice Clerk in 1941 (in which capacity he had to consider cases on Defence Regulation 58A dealing with the breach of essential work orders),[10] the cautious Cooper was succeeded by James Reid, then Conservative MP for Glasgow Hillhead. Reid is notable for having been subsequently appointed by Clement Attlee to the highest judicial office as a Lord of Appeal in Ordinary in 1948 (without having previously held a judicial post). Although also initially sceptical about the value of Order 1305,[11] it appears that Reid eventually felt himself less constrained than Cooper about the use of the criminal law. He appears also to have been less constrained than his counterparts in England and Wales, and more ready to invoke the penal provisions of Order 1305. Reid's starting point for prosecution was that he had 'no alternative to prosecution when offences were reported to him, unless he was advised by a Department that prosecution was contrary to the public interest',[12] and to this end it appears that Reid did routinely ask for the Ministry of Labour's views 'before prosecution action was considered'.[13]

Thus, on 5 November 1941, shortly after Reid's appointment, 680 men walked out of Hamilton Palace Colliery, Rothwell over a 'change in work arrangements without notice'.

[6] See HA Clegg, *A History of British Trade Unions since 1889, Vol III, 1934–1951* (Clarendon Press, Oxford, 1994), p 253.

[7] A Tyndall, 'Patriotism and Principles: Order 1305 and the Betteshanger Strike of 1942' (2001) 12 *Historical Studies in Industrial Relations* 109, pp 111–12, on which this account draws.

[8] ibid p 112 (Correspondence between Cooper and Bevin).

[9] ibid.

[10] On Defence Regulation 58A, see *William Dixon Ltd v Patterson*, 1943 JC 78.

[11] J McIlroy and A Campbell, 'Beyond Betteshanger: Order 1305 in the Scottish Coalfields during the Second World War, Part 1: Politics, Prosecutions and Protest' (2003) 15 *Historical Studies in Industrial Relations* 27, p 61.

[12] J McIlroy and A Campbell, 'Beyond Betteshanger: Order 1305 in the Scottish Coalfields during the Second World War, Part 2: The Cardowan Story' (2003) 16 *Historical Studies in Industrial Relations* 39, p 40.

[13] McIlroy and Campbell (n 11) p 61.

According to Ministry of Labour files, 'The Lord Advocate asked for the Minister's views before prosecution action was considered':

> The Minister replied that the men had resumed work on the status quo and assumed that no further consideration of prosecution would be necessary. He mentioned however, that the question of prosecution in cases arising in the coalmining industry is one of consideration by the Mines Department in the first instance, and that the Ministry of Labour had been in consultation with them about this case.[14]

This was by no means an isolated example. In another case in February 1942, around 1,500 workers walked out of the engineering department of the shipbuilding firm of John Brown's on Clydeside.[15] They could be said either to have been protesting at the lack of heating or to have gone home because it was too cold to work. Following advice that it was extremely doubtful whether cessation of work on a bitterly cold day because the heating apparatus was not working could properly be regarded as a trade dispute, 'the Minister advised the Lord Advocate against prosecution'.[16]

Consultations of this kind ought to have ensured a measure of consistency in prosecution practice between the two jurisdictions.[17] It is striking, however, that in 1942 the Deputy Chief Industrial Commissioner (DCIC) (equivalent to the Ministry's CIC in England and Wales, who in most cases had the authority in practice to decide to prosecute), 'reminded' the Ministry that in Scotland the decision to prosecute was 'a matter entirely for the Lord Advocate'.[18] So although the Scottish cases dealt with unofficial and unconstitutional action of a kind similar to the action for which Leggett had thought appropriate for prosecution under Order 1305, it did not follow that similar guidelines were applied with the same rigour in Scotland as they were in England and Wales. The position was particularly distinctive in relation to coal mining, where with the exception of Betteshanger there were very few prosecutions in England and Wales either before or after, notwithstanding high levels of industrial action in the mines. Scottish practice was for the Lord Advocate to consult the Scottish Coal Commissioner, a position held by Viscount Traprain (grandson of Arthur Balfour, the Conservative Prime Minister from 1902 to 1905) rather than the Mines Department in Whitehall.

We are by now several steps removed from Bevin and his advisers, with McIlroy and Campbell referring subsequently to an official source which reveals that Reid was having to deal with the 'inordinate rapacity' of the Scottish coal-owners, leading to demands for prosecutions from early 1942, in circumstances where the Lord Advocate seemed more inclined to act against the management than the strikers.[19] But it was not only in coal mining that employers took control. In one notable case in 1942, an unknown

[14] TNA, LAB 10/998 ('Legal proceedings against Strikers in Wartime under Article 4 of Conditions of Employment and National Arbitration Order, 1940'). As was pointed out in ch 2, in theory if not in practice, it was the Mines Department that was primarily responsible for prosecutions in coalmining.

[15] ibid.

[16] TNA, LAB 10/173 ('Prosecutions of Strikers under Order 1305 (1) Undertaken (2) Contemplated').

[17] But see McIlroy and Campbell (n 11) and McIlroy and Campbell (n 12) above.

[18] TNA, LAB 10/173 ('Prosecutions of Strikers under Order 1305 (1) Undertaken (2) Contemplated') ('DCIC Scotland to Industrial Relations Department, London SW1', 23 June 1942).

[19] McIlroy and Campbell (n 11) pp 58–61.

number of workers took strike action at Beardmore's engineering works in Glasgow,[20] the 24-hour action being taken in support of a '[d]emand for the dismissal of an assistant foreman on account of his behaviour to one of the female workers'.[21] A revealing entry in Ministry records indicates that the DCIC was 'not disposed to recommend prosecution', but that 'the firm pressed the matter'.[22] Nevertheless, the 'six ringleaders' were charged for instigating what appears to have been a stand against workplace sexual harassment by a charge hand, though charges against one of the six were dropped because of ill-health. This would be consistent with a document unearthed by McIlroy and Campbell, in which the DCIC reported in June 1943 that there was a:

> [V]ery marked tendency recently for firms, particularly where large numbers of strikers are involved, to press for prosecution irrespective any merits or extenuating circumstances but apparently simply in respect of any technical breach.[23]

Although they may have had the same starting points in terms of national guidelines for the circumstances in which the law should be invoked,[24] given the differences between the jurisdictions, it was thus implausible to assume that the law would be applied in the same way on both sides of the border. Enforcement in Scotland was the responsibility of the law officers, who had a duty to enforce the law. Enforcement in England and Wales was based in a labour department, which had an overriding interest in promoting good industrial relations. In addition, the Lord Advocate's position was unlikely to have been inhibited by political constraints of the kind that might have been expected to hold back Bevin and his officials. Reid was a Conservative politically and a lawyer by profession. His participation after the war in the parliamentary debates on the Trade Disputes and Trade Unions Bill reveal a man who was hostile to the repeal of the Trade Disputes and Trade Union Act 1927, suspicious of the extension of trade union power, distrustful of senior trade union officials, and not in favour of the emerging economic constitution and the role of trade unions within it.[25] More than a match for Hartley Shawcross (the Attorney General),[26] Reid was revealed in these debates as being strong minded, highly principled and forceful in expression.

III. Cardowan and the Efficacy of the Criminal Law

Thomas Cooper's remarks about the willingness of employers to resort to coercion rather than conciliation proved to be very prescient. So were his concerns that it would lead as a result to workers being investigated by the police, and would create the 'real

[20] See TNA, LAB 10/998 ('Legal Proceedings against Strikers in Wartime under Article 4 of Conditions of Employment and National Arbitration Order, 1940'). Beardmore's had the status of a Royal Ordinance Factory.

[21] ibid.

[22] ibid.

[23] McIlroy and Campbell (n 12) p 42.

[24] See pp 17-20 above.

[25] HC Debs, 26 February 1946, col 1765, particularly notable for the discussion of a speech by Walter Citrine, then TUC General Secretary.

[26] See in particular the exchanges at the Committee and Third Reading stages of the Trade Disputes and Trade Unions Bill, which had been introduced in 1945.

risk' of provoking industrial action. What could not have been anticipated, however, was the attitude of the unions to such risks, some union leaders apparently indifferent to the prosecution of their members. An important dimension relating to the Scottish mining unions in particular was their 'highly conscious outlook on the strategy of the war and the political implications behind that strategy'.[27] Even before the Soviet Union entered the hostilities, the Scottish miners' union was sending fraternal greetings to the Russian miners' trade unions, with support for the 'building of the Socialist state'.[28] After Russian entry into the war, the same union sent financial aid to Russia and campaigned actively for a Second Front to relieve pressure on the Red Army. 'Together with this keen attention to all the war issues', the historian of Scottish mining trade unionism wrote that 'the miners became increasingly conscious of their own part in the war effort', which 'took the form of a fight for increased productivity both in each pit and in the coal mining industry as a whole'.[29]

What is being said here by implication of course is that the mining union leadership was closely aligned with the Communist Party, which in turn strongly supported the war effort and the drive for productivity. Indeed, the legendary Scottish miners' leader Abe Moffat resigned his position as a Fife County Councillor (representing the Communist Party) 'to give his whole time to the job of President of the Scottish Mineworkers', whom he represented with great distinction.[30] The nature of the close alignment is highlighted by some far from flattering material revealed by McIlroy and Campbell. The material in question includes a government document which made reference to the 'fiery enthusiasm' for productivity which the 'Communist leaders' demanded of workers.[31] Among these leaders were trade union officials, one of whom was reported as saying that he looked forward to the day when 'the union would be able to return to its normal work of attending to the best interests of its members'.[32] This attitude documented elsewhere exposed the trade union leadership to strong if exaggerated condemnation as 'traitors', and of having 'borrowed' the usual phrases from the bosses' vocabulary 'to use at every industrial dispute since Holy Russia entered the war' to direct strikers back to work.[33]

These issues were highlighted by McIlroy and Campbell in relation to a dispute at Blairhall Colliery in the Fife coalfield in March 1942,[34] where 'the officials of the Union suggested prosecution' after 27 miners had 'very wantonly defied their Trade Union instruction'.[35] Although the strike ended after two days, 24 of those involved were prosecuted, found guilty, and fined £5 or 30 days for breaching Order 1305, the union refusing to represent them unless they pleaded guilty. Only four paid their fines, and when the police arrested a number of the others, their action was met by stoppages in solidarity which spread to other pits in the locality. The men returned to work three days

[27] R Page Arnot, *A History of the Scottish Miners* (George Allen & Unwin, London, 1955), p 259.
[28] ibid p 257.
[29] ibid pp 260–61.
[30] ibid p 257.
[31] McIlroy and Campbell (n 12) p 42.
[32] ibid p 42 (William Pearson, President of the Lanarkshire Mineworkers' Union).
[33] Anarchist Federation, *War Commentary*, Vol 4, No 23, October 1943, p 2.
[34] McIlroy and Campbell (n 11) pp 61–65.
[35] ibid p 61. See also 'Prosecutions' in TNA, LAB 10/173 ('Prosecutions of Strikers under Order 1305 (1) Undertaken (2) Contemplated').

later after a meeting addressed by Abe Moffat at which they were told that 'they were betraying the Dieppe raiders and the Red Army and also dishonouring the Anglo-Soviet Trade Agreement which demanded greater productivity'.[36] It is notable that the only concern raised by the local MP was not the conviction of the strikers or the imposition of fines, but the circumstances of their arrest for non-payment of the fines. The MP in question was William Gallacher, Communist MP for West Fife, who raised the matter in the Commons in questions to the Secretary of State for Scotland in September 1942.[37]

The Secretary of State was challenged about 'three miners, each of whom was fined £5, with a month to pay, during April, [who] were taken from bed and arrested, about 5 am on Friday, 28th August'.[38] There was no chance that the Secretary of State would yield to Gallacher's demand for the dismissal of the 'official who was responsible for ordering the arrest of these miners at such an hour in the morning'.[39] On the contrary, it was explained that the three men in question had been fined (with the alternative of 30 days) for contravening Order 1305, and that 'they had been given repeated opportunities over a period of more than four months to pay their fines, in instalments if they wished, and as they had failed to do so the alternative sentence of imprisonment had to be enforced'.[40] According to the Minister, the arrests took place at the time the men 'would normally have risen to go to work'.[41] They were 'given as much time as they wished to dress and breakfast'.[42] The fines were 'paid the same day, and the men were at once released'.[43] It is not clear how common were such practices, though the arrest of miners for the non-payment of fines was not the only opportunity Order 1305 provided for a police presence in Fife mining villages. It is claimed that those arrested in a later dispute were visited at home by the police 'with a view to determining their political records'.[44]

But just as the unions were prepared to encourage the use of Order 1305, so they were also prepared to act as instruments of law enforcement and assume the role of industrial peacemaker when unlawful strikes did take place.[45] In May 1943, a strike took place at Cardowan Colliery near Glasgow following the dismissal of a young miner for serious misconduct. The strike was reported by the procurator fiscal to the Lord Advocate, who consulted Lord Traprain, who in turn gave the go ahead to prosecute in view of the strike record of the colliery and the duration of this particular strike. On 27 July 1943, 34 miners were found guilty of violating Order 1305: one was fined £3 or 20 days as an alternative; the others were fined £5 or 30 days. The majority

[36] McIlroy and Campbell (n 11) p 64.

[37] HC Debs, 11 September 1942, col 518. The Secretary of State was Tom Johnston MP (West Stirlingshire), a revered figure of the Labour Left in Scotland, former editor of the Independent Labour Party's *Forward*, and author of *The History of the Working Classes in Scotland* (Forward Publishing Co Ltd, Glasgow, 1922).

[38] HC Debs, 11 September 1942, col 518.

[39] ibid.

[40] ibid col 519.

[41] ibid.

[42] ibid. Gallacher does not come out of this affair with much credit.

[43] McIlroy and Campbell (n 12).

[44] Anarchist Federation (n 33) p 4.

[45] These features of the NUSMW are not addressed by Page Arnot (n 27). Indeed, Page Arnot does not refer to either the Blairhall or the Cardowan prosecutions. The latter is addressed in the pages immediately following.

refused to pay the fine and were arrested as a result. On the day after their arrest, a notice was 'chalked' on the streets of the village near where the pit was located, the use of chalk being an inexpensive method of instant communication.[46] On this occasion, the notice read that a number of local men had been arrested, adding: 'Every pit out! Stand solid behind the men!' On the following day, a mass meeting at Cardowan Colliery did just that, with the men deciding to take strike action in solidarity with those who had been arrested.

Thereupon, the strike action spread throughout Lanarkshire and neighbouring counties so that by the following week, some 8,000–9,000 men were on strike in 32 pits nearby, the latter stopping work 'in sympathy with the imprisoned Cardowan miners'.[47] Thereafter, McIlroy and Campbell record that 'the miners' leaders did everything possible to break the strikes, invoking the sanctity of the law and the authority of the union as well as the agitator theory of industrial relations'. According to the union:

> The refusal to pay the fines was 'a challenge against the law of the country'. The stoppage had been achieved by 'intimidation' and 'deliberately engineered from the outset by subversive agents who were not even members of the union; these elements were said to be Fascist in nature under whatever disguise they may parade'.[48]

In a similar vein, Moffat was to claim in a statement on 29 September 1943 that the 'lads in prison' were merely 'the victims of a deliberate and planned attempt not only to destroy the trade union but to bring about a political situation for a group of people identified with the Anarchist Movement, the ILP, and the so-called Militant Miners'.[49] The last was said to be 'definitely opposed to the war against Fascism and have no interest whatsoever in the affairs of the miners'.[50]

It is notable that this assessment was disputed by the Cardowan branch officials who had endorsed the industrial action. Three branch officials were summoned to appear before the Lanark Executive Committee of National Union of Scottish Mineworkers (NUSMW) at a meeting in Hamilton, and asked to repudiate a leaflet that had been prepared by the Cardowan branch 'stating the position of the imprisoned men and calling on the miners in other pits to support the struggle'.[51] When they refused to do so, the three branch officials (the president, secretary, and treasurer respectively) were suspended from union office. Following the meeting, the deposed branch president (Andrew Stirling) made a statement which said that the three men had been asked if they would 'repudiate the dispute', but declined. According to Stirling, while 'the union executive blame Fascism, the Anarchists and the ILP for the Cardowan trouble', that was 'merely evading the issue'. As he made clear, 'the stoppage was a spontaneous expression of the unrest rampant in the

[46] On the practice of 'chalking', see *Thomas v Sawkins* [1935] 2 KB 249, at p 250.
[47] McIlroy and Campbell (n 12) p 52.
[48] ibid p 53.
[49] Anarchist Federation (n 33) p 2.
[50] ibid.
[51] ibid p 3.

Lanarkshire coalfield'.[52] The purpose of the strike was not only to secure the release of the prisoners, but also to bring about the improvement of working conditions at a nearby pit (Western Auchengeich), which raised wider questions about the 'evil system' of recruitment of miners by contractors as intermediaries between owners and miners.[53]

The matter was only resolved when on 1 October following the example of Betteshanger Colliery, four union officials (including Abe Moffat and William Pearson, Presidents of the NUSMW and the Lanark Miners' Union respectively) visited the men in prison to negotiate with them for their release. It appears that the NUSMW had persuaded the strikers to return to work 'on the understanding that they would get the men out of jail',[54] and that they were given permission to meet the jailed miners for this purpose by the Secretary of State for Scotland. The men voted by 14-2 to leave prison, their fines paid by money borrowed from the Lord Provost of Glasgow who was reimbursed by William Pearson,[55] the released miners making it clear that the 'struggle would be renewed' if 'any attempts were made to force the men to repay the fines'.[56] Having been shown to be ineffective and to have brought the law into contempt, as indicated by Table 2.1 in Chapter Two above, Order 1305 was thereafter taken out of active service in the Scottish coalfields, though as McIlroy and Campbell point out, not before ministers and officials considered startling proposals designed to improve the effectiveness of the enforcement machinery. These included putting pressure on Sheriffs to pass more lenient sentences, and for fines to be imposed 'without reference to the courts'.[57] Neither was adopted.

IV. Practice in Northern Ireland

As has already been pointed out, Order 1305 did not apply in Northern Ireland. There was, however, an equivalent measure – Order 1508, dated 9 August 1940 – which made identical provision. Like Order 1305, the latter was made under delegated powers conferred by the Emergency Powers (Defence) Act 1939, and was thus made under the authority of Westminster legislation rather than authority devolved to the Stormont administration. A strict division of labour quickly emerged in relation to the operation

[52] ibid. Coal mining in some parts of the country was a tinderbox for multiple reasons, including low pay, long hours, difficult working conditions, and poor management.

[53] ibid p 2. The system of contracting is described in Page Arnot (n 27) as follows: 'It is the system where one man has a contract with the company and has a few or several men working under him. He draws all the wages from the company and pays the men who are working with him individually. The workmen never know what the contractor has earned or the rates paid by the company. The system itself creates suspicion as some of these contractors have made huge sums of money at the expense of their fellow workers, and in most cases have done very little work for it'. It was said that 'many contractors are detested even more than some coal owners' (p 299).

[54] A Moffatt, *My Life with the Miners* (Lawrence & Wishart, London, 1965), p 77, cited by McIlroy and Campbell (n 12) p 57.

[55] McIlroy and Campbell (n 12) pp 58–59.

[56] Anarchist Federation (n 33) p 4.

[57] McIlroy and Campbell (n 12) p 62.

of Order 1508: conciliation and arbitration were the responsibility of the Ministry of Labour in Northern Ireland, led initially by John F Gordon. The prosecution of those engaged in illegal strikes in contrast was a matter in practice almost exclusively for the Northern Ireland Attorney General, the latter office occupied from 1941 by John MacDermott KC, a man of some distinction who had seen action in the First World War, and had been awarded the Military Cross in 1918. By the beginning of the Second World War, he was Unionist MP for Queen's University, a parliamentary seat being 'the almost obligatory route in those days to preferment'.[58] Enlisting again for military service at the start of the Second World War, MacDermott was 'released from the army at government request', serving initially as Minister of Public Security before being appointed as Attorney General.[59]

After serving as Attorney General for three years, MacDermott was appointed to the Northern Ireland High Court and, at the relatively young age of 51, subsequently elevated in 1947 to the House of Lords as a Lord of Appeal in Ordinary, where he would be joined by James Reid a year later.[60] Although remembered as a judge for having embraced ideas about matters such as 'the importance of the Rule of Law and the protection of human rights' and having done so 'long before they became fashionable',[61] MacDermott's tenure as Attorney General placed him on the other side of the fence: the rule of law was a weapon rather than a shield.[62] In this capacity MacDermott was much more prominent than his counterpart in England and Wales, where, as we have seen, Bevin had made an early intervention to ensure that the Ministry of Labour ultimately determined whether prosecutions should take place. The Northern Ireland files include a circular letter that had been sent to all Chief Constables in England and Wales by the Home Office, explaining that a dispute and any related strike would ordinarily be known to the Ministry of Labour, and that it would be 'for that Department to consider whether and at what stage proceedings should be instigated'.[63]

The position was very different in Northern Ireland, where the police took statements and even occasionally made recommendations on whether a case should be prosecuted or not. Royal Ulster Constabulary (RUC) reports would be sent to both the Ministry of Labour and the Ministry of Home Affairs, usually from the Inspector General's Office in Belfast, but often from police stations local to disputes outside the city. A final paragraph added to the police reports sent to the Ministry of Labour requested

[58] R Carswell, 'John Clarke MacDermott', *Dictionary of Irish Biography* (2009). MacDermott died in 1979. Robert Carswell was also a Lord of Appeal in Ordinary from 2004 to 2009.

[59] ibid.

[60] MacDermott was subsequently to become Lord Chief Justice of Northern Ireland in 1951, an office he occupied until 1971.

[61] Carswell (n 58).

[62] On these contrasting functions of the rule of law, see AW Bradley, KD Ewing and CJS Knight, *Constitutional and Administrative Law*, 18th edn (Pearson, Harlow, 2022), ch 6. For MacDermott on the rule of law, see Lord MacDermott, *Protection from Power under English Law* (Stevens, London, 1957).

[63] PRONI, CAB/9/C/22/1 ('Arbitration in Strikes and Industrial Disputes 1926–1942'). The circular issued to the Police, 'Trade Disputes – Strikes or Lock outs', 3 December 1941, is attached to 'Regional Industrial Relations Officers' Conference 16 January 1942, Notes on Item 1 'Trade Disputes – Proceedings in the Case of Illegal Strikes', as Appendix IV. The circular letter continued that complaints made to the police had to be reported to the Secretary at the Ministry of Labour in Whitehall, with 'no further investigation' to be made by the police 'unless a specific request is made by the Ministry'. The decision on whether to prosecute was said at that early stage 'to be one taken at Headquarters as the Minister wishes to be consulted in each case' (ibid).

officials to forward to the Chief Crown Solicitor any additional information that had a bearing on whether a prosecution would or would not be in the national interest.[64] Yet as far as we have been able to discover, the Ministry of Labour never recommended that a prosecution should be brought. In most instances, it stated in response simply that the Department had 'no knowledge of any other facts or circumstances' and 'had no views to offer' on whether a prosecution was in the national interest.[65] However, sometimes it might offer 'the opinion of the Department' that the national interest would not be prejudiced if proceedings were not taken in this case'.[66] Curiously, this paragraph in the police reports was omitted from the copy sent to Dawson Bates, the Minister for Home Affairs.

The RUC routinely reported very trivial matters as alleged violations of the Article 4 strike prohibition, some of which were clearly not even technical breaches of the Order. Stoppages as brief as 10 minutes drew their attention, and reports often betrayed a tendency to side with the employer.[67] They would 'talk up' sometimes tenuous links of the work in question to the war effort,[68] revealing an overriding desire to see proceedings brought, regardless of the likely damage to any settlement or to industrial relations. As in Scotland, there was thus perceived to be a pro-employer bias in the operation of the law, with the Belfast Shop Stewards complaining to the Home Secretary in London that the application of the Order in Northern Ireland was 'one sided',[69] a complaint that was refuted by Ministry of Labour officials in Belfast, to whom paradoxically the complaint was redirected. Thus, 'only two instances of an apparent breach of the Order by employers' had been brought to their notice and both were referred to the Law Officers. In one of these cases 'the decision was that the evidence did not warrant criminal proceedings', while in the other case 'proceedings were instituted and a fine imposed considerably heavier than any imposed on a worker'.[70]

Perhaps unsurprisingly, the robust approach of the police and the Law Officers to the use of the criminal law as the first option for dealing with strikes led eventually to a breakdown in relations between the Ministry of Labour and the Attorney General. The immediate cause of the breakdown was a police investigation of a three-day strike by

[64] The paragraph was omitted from the copy sent to Dawson Bates, the Minister for Home Affairs.

[65] PRONI, HSS 24/1 ('Conditions of Employment and Arbitration Order (NI) 1940, Policy in Regard to Operation of the Order') ('Ministry to CCS 4 November 1943 regarding a strike by office staff at Harland and Wolff on 21 and 29 October 1943').

[66] ibid ('Note to the CCS 29 September 1942 regarding a strike at a pottery during 9–23 August 1942').

[67] PRONI, HSS 24/1 ('Conditions of Employment and Arbitration Order (NI) 1940, Policy in Regard to Operation of the Order'). There were, however, exceptions, as in the case of a strike of 450 men at an aerodrome construction site during 21–23 November 1942. They were on strike because their pay had been withheld. The police inspector present reported that 'I am of the opinion that the firm has no right to stop any man's pay unless it can be proved in each individual case that the man was not working. I beg to recommend no police action in respect of this case'.

[68] As, for example, in the case of stoppages at a clothing firm, largely the result of sectarian differences, in Lurgan in March 1943. Despite the police reporting that the firm manufactured 'khaki trousers', the Ministry offered the opinion that a prosecution was inadvisable (ibid).

[69] PRONI, CAB/9/C/22/1 ('Arbitration in Strikes and Industrial Disputes 1926–1942') (letter dated 29 August 1942 which followed a resolution passed at an 'aggregate meeting of Shop Stewards, AEU and Confederated Trades' in Belfast). The AEU was not affiliated to the Confederation of Shipbuilding and Engineering Unions.

[70] ibid ('Ministry of Labour to the Cabinet Secretariat', 11 September 1942). We have not come across any record of either of the cases referred to by the Ministry of Labour.

plumbers in September 1942, the men involved said to have been given 'authority to strike' by their union. Asked by the police for their views about a prosecution, Ministry of Labour officials replied that 'in view of the existing industrial circumstances', a prosecution would not serve the national interest.[71] The Chief Crown Solicitor responded on behalf of the Attorney General with an expression of incredulity,[72] which appears to have infuriated the Minister of Labour. An official replied that the Minister had decided that in future, he would not offer opinions on whether to prosecute and that the letter containing the advice that MacDermott had questioned was to be withdrawn.[73] Addressing the matter subsequently in correspondence with John Andrews (the NI Prime Minister) on 2 November 1942, MacDermott served simply to underline the subordinate role of Gordon and his officials. According to the Attorney General, 'inviting' the Ministry to 'put before' the Attorney General 'its observations on each case of any importance' did not 'place on the Ministry any responsibility as to the institution of proceedings'.[74]

The disagreement with the Ministry of Labour was only one of the matters addressed by MacDermott in the foregoing correspondence with Andrews. In what was an important exchange, he also referred to the dispute over the provision of weekend overtime at the Shorts and Harland Balmoral Dispersal Factory which had led to two shop stewards being dismissed, the dispute escalating into a full-blown unofficial strike which spread rapidly to other establishments.[75] At the time of his letter, the dispute involving thousands of workers had only recently been settled, without any prosecutions having been brought. According to MacDermott:

> For even if the bulk of public opinion is behind the Order, it is now painfully evident that the punishment which may be imposed under it will not deter mass strikes. Indeed it may tend to protect them, for the strikers appreciate the safety in numbers. It is now impracticable and inexpedient to prosecute the 10,000 odd men who have just returned to work. They know it and the knowledge that numbers acting in concert will defeat the law is dangerous. This is so not only in relation to the particular law concerned but also because if one law can be publicly and repeatedly flouted with impunity the tendency is to bring the rule of law generally into contempt and to weaken the whole fabric of organized society.[76]

MacDermott was further troubled by a concern that while it was still practicable to enforce the law in the case of small isolated strikes, 'this can only be done by accepting the position that prosecution does not depend on the seriousness of the strike but on whether it can be "handled"'. This was 'obviously unsatisfactory'.[77]

[71] PRONI, HSS 24/1 ('Conditions of Employment and Arbitration Order (NI) 1940, Policy in Regard to Operation of the Order') ('Ministry to Chief Crown Solicitor', 27 October 1942).

[72] ibid ('CCS to Ministry', 28 October).

[73] ibid ('Ministry to CCS', 30 October). While the incidence of refusals to comment in the muted style cited above was even higher after this interdepartmental spat, the Ministry did nevertheless offer opinions, almost invariably taking the view that a prosecution would not be in the national interest.

[74] But he did concede that the Ministry's input was nevertheless 'often of considerable assistance': PRONI, CAB/9/C/22/1 ('Arbitration in Strikes and Industrial Disputes 1926–1942') ('Attorney General to the Prime Minister', 2 November 1942).

[75] On the significance of this strike, see B Black, 'A Triumph of Voluntarism? Industrial Relations and Strikes in Northern Ireland in World War Two' (2005) *Labour History* 5, especially p 12. See also Clegg (n 6) p 243.

[76] PRONI, CAB/9/C/22/1 ('Arbitration in Strikes and Industrial Disputes 1926–1942') ('Attorney General to the Prime Minister', 2 November 1942).

[77] ibid.

Complaining that 'the expediency of instituting proceedings had been made even more difficult' by the Ministry of Labour's refusal to co-operate in any decisions relating to prosecution,[78] MacDermott's solution was nevertheless a principled one. If the rule of law could not be enforced, then the law should be revoked: 'it would be better to have no penal provisions at all but to have them but only to be able to use them in the smaller and less important cases'.[79] He also argued in the same letter for reform of the conciliation and arbitration machinery, which in his view was too slow, and that there should be more regular resort to arbitration to settle disputes. When confronted about this by the Prime Minister, the Minister of Labour replied by saying that his approach had been to seek to resolve disputes rather than prosecute strikers, and to do so by using voluntary machinery, which in his view was 'capable of adjusting any differences that may arise'.[80] Although he had been 'assailed from time to time for failing to take immediate action' by critics who wanted him to transfer dispute resolution from the voluntary negotiating machinery to the National Arbitration Tribunal, if he did so, he would be a 'party to the weakening, if not the destruction' of the existing voluntary machinery. Dispute resolution along these lines would be 'bought at too heavy a price', which the trade unions would 'bitterly resent'.[81]

That apart, there was in any event no political option to revoke or amend Order 1508. As Gordon pointed out, it reflected the terms of the British Order 1305 which was made with the agreement of the British Employers' Confederation and the TUC, noting also the emphasis in the negotiations on the 'continuance of the existing negotiating machinery'.[82] Any amendment to Order 1508 or other change of direction would require TUC agreement, and he was sure that the TUC would insist on 'uniformity throughout the United Kingdom'.[83] The Minister further pointed out that it was 'generally admitted' that the British equivalent to Order 1508 had 'not done all that was hoped for': while disputes in 1940 and 1941 were of shorter duration, they were more frequent than in 1938 and 1939.[84] He also drew attention to the extraordinary difference in the extent to which the penal provisions of Order 1508 were invoked compared with the more restrained use of Order 1305 in Great Britain. Thus, during the two years it had been in force, there had 'only' been 30 prosecutions of 2,068 workers under Order 1305, including the 1,000 or so prosecuted following the Betteshanger strike. In Northern Ireland in contrast, a remarkable 2,271 workers had been prosecuted under Order 1508, a statistic which the Minister described with some understatement as being 'interesting', doubtless intended as a rebuke to the Attorney General.[85]

[78] ibid.

[79] ibid.

[80] ibid ('Minister of Labour to the Prime Minister', 5 November 1942).

[81] ibid.

[82] ibid.

[83] ibid.

[84] ibid. Gordon cited 2,847 for the two years in which Order 1305 had been in operation, and 1,815 for 1938–39.

[85] Very likely to emphasise the control exercised by his counterpart in Great Britain over decisions whether to prosecute, Gordon attached to his letter a lengthy extract from a recent report on the operation of Order 1305. This included a copy of the December 1941 Home Office circular instructing Chief Constables to pass on any reports of illegal strikes to the Ministry of Labour, requiring that 'no further investigations' be made 'unless a specific request is made by the Ministry'. See ch 2, p 20.

V. Harland & Wolff/Short & Harland and the Efficacy of the Criminal Law

The high numbers of prosecutions in Northern Ireland could be explained at least in part by the fact that there were more strikes in Northern Ireland than in Great Britain. From having been 'typically less strike prone' than Great Britain before 1939, Northern Ireland 'experienced a disproportionately severe level of industrial action during the War'.[86] Although precise data are hard to pin down, there were 947,570 strike days lost in Northern Ireland, compared with approximately 9,000,000 in Great Britain, which means that Northern Ireland had 10 per cent of the total strike days lost in Great Britain, despite the Province having only 2 per cent of the working population ('insured population'). According to Boyd Black in his illuminating study of industrial action during the Second World War, the figures suggest that the Province was four times more 'strike prone' than the national average, greatly exceeding levels of strike activity in all areas of the United Kingdom except Clydeside.[87] Providing a number of explanations for 'a remarkable strike activity', Philip Ollerenshaw has highlighted 'the expansion of large-scale production, the inexperience of management in dealing with rapid unionization, a resurgent Belfast Shop Stewards' Movement, and greater power for organised labour than had been experienced in a generation.[88]

These were not propitious conditions for the heavy-handed use of the criminal law, which, as we have seen, experience had revealed to be most effective when it was least needed – where workers were weak and disempowered, and the impact of any action on the war effort was comparatively insignificant. Thus, albeit with great regret on the part of the Law Officers, it was wisely decided in 1942 not to court conflict by invoking the law against the 10,000 and more workers who had walked out following the dismissals of shop stewards at aircraft manufacturers Short & Harland, mainly for reasons of practicability rather than a concern about provoking, inflaming or escalating an already tense situation. Yet although it was thus 'painfully evident' that Order 1508 was no deterrent against mass strikes, prosecutions nevertheless continued after 1942, despite the Prime Minister's concerns. As he explained in his response to the Minister of Labour on 5 November 1942, Andrews was unable to understand why Gordon did not deal with matters under Order 1508 'to the same extent that Mr Bevin does' under Order 1305.[89] That, however, would have required Andrews to have intervened, not to encourage Gordon to cooperate with MacDermott, but to insist on a radical change in the way alleged offences were investigated and prosecution decisions were made.

In other words, it would have required the police to be stripped of their investigatory role and for enforcement to have been transferred from the Law Officers to the Ministry of Labour. That step was not taken. On the contrary, the desire to enforce the law even in the case of mass strikes in key industries saw a change of tactics rather than

[86] P Ollerenshaw, 'War, Industrial Mobilisation and Society in Northern Ireland, 1939–1945' (2007) 16 *Contemporary European History* 169, p 188.

[87] Black (n 75).

[88] Ollerenshaw (n 86) p 188.

[89] PRONI, CAB/9/C/22/1 ('Arbitration in Strikes and Industrial Disputes 1926–1942') ('Prime Minister to Minister of Labour', 9 November 1942).

a change of strategy on the part of the Law Officers, which, as in Scotland, was to target the leadership of the strike rather than all the participants. But this too ended in failure. The occasion was a fresh dispute at Harland & Wolff, which in February 1944 led initially to a strike by some 1,300 fitters who had a longstanding and unresolved claim for parity with other shipyard workers.[90] The action soon escalated to involve other grades at what was 'one of the biggest shipyards in the world', which had 'expanded into armaments and tank production'.[91] On 14 March 1944, the Ministry of Labour informed the Chief Crown Solicitor that in accordance with Order 1508, the dispute had been reported, albeit after the stoppage had started, adding that negotiations instigated by the Minister were now underway with a view to reaching a settlement, and that 'the institution of proceedings would not be in the national interest'.[92]

Also on 14 March, however, workers at Short & Harland began to join the action, police reports indicating that some of those involved had similar grievances to those at Harland & Wolff, but that others had 'come out in sympathy with the men on strike in Belfast'.[93] It is estimated that some 36,000 workers were eventually participating in the action, with the involvement of Short & Harland now affecting combat aircraft production.[94] With the dispute unresolved by the beginning of April, there were growing demands for the government to intervene. These demands were made by a diverse range of individuals and organisations, including Harland and Wolff shop stewards,[95] as well as various branches of the Communist Party concerned that an 'immediate settlement [was] necessary in the interests of the war effort'.[96] Prospects for a settlement were dashed, however, when five men out of the thousands of workers who were on strike were selected for prosecution by the Law Officers. It is unlikely to have been a coincidence that four of the men were shop stewards from Short's main Belfast factory. Following their conviction by the city's magistrates on 3 April for action in breach of Order 1508, Article 4, all five were sentenced to three months with hard labour.[97] At which point, the government now had to face another problem, namely how to prevent the dispute escalating still further in sympathy with the five convicted men, who would inevitably be seen as martyrs.

[90] For fuller details of the strike and its context, see Black (n 75).

[91] Ollerenshaw (n 86) p 184.

[92] PRONI, HSS 24/1 ('Conditions of Employment and Arbitration Order (NI) 1940, Policy in regard to operation of the Order').

[93] ibid ('RUC Inspector General's Office, Reports to Ministry of Home Affairs and to Ministry of Labour', 14, 16 and 20 March 1944 about the strikes at various Short & Harland locations).

[94] Black (n 75) p 1. According to Black, some 450,000 working days were lost as a result of the dispute, which lasted from February until April.

[95] PRONI, CAB/9/C/22/2 ('Arbitration in Strikes and Industrial Disputes 1943–1947') ('Telegram from Production Committee Secretary and the Shop Stewards' Secretary at 'Harland and Wolff's Aircraft Depot to Prime Minister', 31 March 1943).

[96] ibid ('Telegram from Sloan South Branch Communist Party to Prime Minister', 3 April 1943). There is also a report of a telephone message from the North Belfast Branch of the Communist Party, the call probably made on the same day.

[97] ibid. On the evening of 4 April, the Ministry of Home Affairs Permanent Under Secretary was dispatched to the prison to report on the condition of the men. The men were facing three months' hard labour, yet the Permanent Under Secretary's chief concern was the men's garb: 'It is not new clothing … a man who has been having good wages and is accustomed to dress himself well would not feel particularly happy about his present get-up, but the clothing … is clean and it is the best that can be done in the present time, having regard to clothing restrictions.'

An obvious initial response was intimidation, with trade union leaders visited at home by the police in an effort to prevent the strike escalating.[98] Another was the spreading of disinformation, union leaders being told by Dawson Bates, Minister of Home Affairs, that an RUC informant had let it be known that the Shop Stewards' Movement was under the control of 'Roman Catholics from Eire'.[99] The Roman Catholic community would have been a convenient scapegoat, given the support for the war effort by the Communist Party. Unsurprisingly, the information was 'definitely incorrect', as a police 'investigation' was to confirm several months later. With the deployment of the criminal law thus in danger of backfiring spectacularly, the government was running out of options, ministers learning at the Cabinet meeting on 5 April of the need to 'face up to the possibility of a General Strike'.[100] In order to avert such a catastrophic escalation, at the same meeting the new Minister of Labour, William Grant, suggested that an anticipated petition for clemency for the five men being prepared by the Confederation of Shipbuilding and Engineering Unions (CSEU) should receive 'sympathetic consideration', telling ministers that the Confederation 'had exerted all their influence to keep their men at work', and that he was 'anxious that nothing should be done which would discourage this body at the present crucial juncture of the war'.[101]

On the following day (6 April), it was reported by the Prime Minister that the Minister of Labour had that morning attended a meeting organised by the Amalgamated Engineering Union and Harland & Wolff management, and that it was hoped that a settlement could be reached by extending the embrace of 'payment by results' to the fitters. Ministers also heard of the preparations being made to keep essential services running in the event of a General Strike, and they heard too from the Attorney General.[102] Far from penitent, MacDermott appeared to be prepared to dig the government into a still deeper hole. He told ministers that the five men had been prosecuted because there has been 'clear evidence' that they had been inciting colleagues to engage in an illegal strike, while his report that intelligence obtained about a 'large meeting' where workers were urged not to return to work unless the men were released indicated that more prosecutions were likely to follow.[103] The Minister of Labour warned that a return to work was very unlikely unless the men were released, and the Prime Minister told colleagues that the petition being prepared by the Confederation 'should not be lightly turned down'.[104] While it was agreed that ministers would wait until the petition was received, it must have been obvious to all present that the men had to be released and that no more arrests could be made.

[98] ibid ('Telegram from "a mass meeting" of "the people of Belfast" to the PM', 25 April 1944). The author of the telegram message protested 'in the strongest terms against the action of the Northern Irish Government in attempting to intimidate workers by sending the Police Force to visit their lawful representatives the shop stewards'. There is also a letter of protest on file sent by the Hon Secretary of the Short & Harland's Charge Hands' Association on 28 June informing the PM of the 'grave apprehension of our members, re the the recent raids by the the RUC on the homes of trusted trade union leaders in Belfast'.

[99] ibid ('Amalgamated Engineering Union to Prime Minister', 19 June 1944). The AEU had been told by the Minister of Home Affairs that this was the reason for the police visits.

[100] PRONI, CAB/9/C/22/2 (Cabinet Conclusions, 5 April 1944). See also Black (n 75) p 13.

[101] ibid.

[102] ibid.

[103] ibid.

[104] ibid.

In a fast-moving series of events, on 7 April, the men were released on bail pending appeal. Notably, this was done 'following intervention by the Belfast Trades Council'.[105] A settlement was secured between 8–10 April, and the strikers returned to work on 11 and 12 April. MacDermott nevertheless warned ministers that unless the men 'showed a change of heart', he would be unable to 'ask for the leniency of the Court'.[106] There was thus a concern that the men could be returned to prison, prompting Dawson Bates to suggest at a Cabinet meeting on 20 April that the newly minted Defence Regulation 1AA should be implemented in Northern Ireland as soon as possible.[107] The latter made it an offence to instigate or incite anyone to take part in a strike by workers engaged in the performance of essential services, and introduced severe penalties of up to five years and a fine of up to £500 for those found guilty.[108] Bates no doubt had in mind the wide definition of essential services for this purpose. Paradoxically, however, the Northern Ireland press had reported on 19 April that Regulation 1AA's 'drastic powers' did not apply in Northern Ireland[109] – paradoxical because of the suggestion that 'it was the militant activities of the Belfast Shop Stewards' Movement and the immediate threat of a regional general strike with the potential to the engineering industry nationally that provoked the introduction of the new Order [sic] 1AA'.[110]

While there is no reason to doubt the latter assessment, it is notable nevertheless that Bevin made no mention of Northern Ireland in the House of Commons debate on the new regulation in April 1944.[111] It is, however, pointless now trying to make sense of the political origins of Regulation 1AA, just as it is pointless trying to make sense of its territorial scope. If the drafting could give rise to an implication that it was not intended to apply to Northern Ireland by virtue of the omission of any reference to the Province, there was nevertheless no express exclusion to this effect in a text made under primary legislation which applied throughout the United Kingdom.[112] It is also the case that on 20 April 1944, correspondence from the Home Office in Whitehall to the Cabinet Secretary at Stormont indicated a clear intention that Defence Regulation 1AA would apply in Northern Ireland, despite the awkwardness in its drafting.[113] In the end, it did not matter, the fears of the shop stewards being returned to prison being misplaced. At the hearing before the Belfast Recorder on 8 June 1944, the men's counsel expressed regret on their behalf and confirmed that they had undertaken not to take part in any further strikes for the duration of the war. The appeals against sentence were allowed, the prison sentences

[105] Black (n 75) p 14.
[106] PRONI, CAB/9/C/22/2 (Cabinet Conclusions, 20 April 1944).
[107] ibid.
[108] See ch 2 above.
[109] *Belfast Newsletter*, 19 April 1944.
[110] Black (n 75) p 15.
[111] HC Debs, 28 April 1944, cols 1061–1158. There is no reference to Northern Ireland by any of the speakers in the debate.
[112] Defence (Emergency Powers) Act 1939, s 3. See also Defence (General) Regulations 1939, SR&O 1939 No 927, Reg 102 (Application to Northern Ireland).
[113] PRONI, CAB/9/C/22/2 ('Arbitration in Strikes and Industrial Disputes 1943–1947') ('Home Office to Gransden, Secretary to the Cabinet', 20 April 1944).

were commuted to probation orders, and the threat of renewed industrial action was thereby avoided.[114]

VI. Conclusion

In answer to the questions posed in the introduction to this chapter, the foregoing account prompts us to recall the point made in Chapter Two that while an appeal to the rule of law might suggest that the law should be enforced when the law is broken, the law itself must be capable of enforcement. As the Betteshanger dispute had shown in England and Wales in relation to Order 1305, so the dispute in Northern Ireland in 1942 in relation to Order 1508 demonstrated the impracticability of prosecuting, convicting and penalising thousands of strikers. The response of the state was thus in some cases to be selective: either to select in which strikes the law should be invoked, and/or to select which workers were to be prosecuted in those strikes where the law was to be invoked. But as Cardowan showed in Scotland in relation to Order 1305, so the dispute in Northern Ireland in 1944 in relation to Order 1508 confirmed that the victimisation of a handful of workers' leaders was an inappropriate way of dealing with the inadequacy of the law. At Cardowan, it led to 'mass defiance and solidarity',[115] which did not need to be displayed in Northern Ireland following the timely release of the five men. The latter also taught an important lesson that the selective prosecution of trade union activists in pursuit (and in breach) of the rule of law is likely to be counter-productive, a lesson that the post-war Attlee government had regrettably failed to learn.

This is not to deny the real dilemma facing ministers and the Law Officers when confronted with a failure on the part of thousands of people to comply with the law. We have seen in this and the previous chapter two different approaches to the rule of law in relation to Order 1305 and Order 1508. The first was the administrative approach adopted by Bevin, which was to enforce the law where possible and appropriate to do so. The other was the legal approach adopted by the Law Officers in Scotland and Northern Ireland, which was to enforce the law when it had been broken. While the former had the virtue of pragmatism and a realistic sense of what was possible, it was nevertheless difficult to justify from the perspective of constitutional principle for reasons explained by MacDermott in his correspondence with the Northern Ireland Prime Minister. And while the latter had the virtue of being consistent with constitutional principle, it was nevertheless difficult to justify from the perspective of the reality of social power ignored by those who made the law. The only solution to this dilemma was – as MacDermott proposed – to revoke the law and start again.[116] That said, it is difficult to see what realistically could have been done to make the criminal law more effective. But given the wartime experience, it is certainly not easy to understand what purpose could be served by retaining the penal provisions after the war.

[114] *Belfast Newsletter*, 9 June 1944.
[115] McIlroy and Campbell (n 12) p 59.
[116] PRONI, CAB/9/C/22/1, ('Arbitration in Strikes and Industrial Disputes 1926–1942') ('Note from Attorney General to the Prime Minister', 2 November 1942).

PART III

Retention of Order 1305: The Labour Government after the War

4

Creating the Legal Framework

Retention of Order 1305

I. Introduction

So what about the right to strike in the post-war era? It appears to have been widely assumed that Order 1305 would lapse and that there would be a return to the legal framework governing trade unions that had been established between 1871 and 1913. So far as the right to strike is concerned, that would mean back to the Conspiracy and Protection of Property Act 1875 and the Trade Disputes Act 1906 (reinforced by the *Crofter* decision),[1] the position to be consolidated by the Labour Party's electoral commitment to repeal the Trade Disputes and Trade Unions Act 1927.[2] This, however, is not what happened. It is true that while the 1927 Act was repealed and that various restrictions on the right to strike and other matters were removed as a result, it is also true that steps were taken to retain Order 1305. So although the pre-war statutory framework was to be restored, its operation would be held in abeyance until such time as the government determined that war-time powers were no longer necessary. Unfortunately, that is a call which the first Attlee administration never made: Order 1305 was to remain in force for the whole period of the Parliament elected in 1945, and was not revoked until 1951.

In this chapter we consider the wider context within which Order 1305 operated after the war, looking specifically at the different common law and statutory provisions relating to the right to strike. Following our consideration of the decision to retain Order 1305 and the means by which it was done, we highlight the inconsistency of retention with the government's electoral commitment to restore trade union freedom, which it fulfilled in part by repealing the Trade Disputes and Trade Unions Act 1927. This is followed by an analysis of the incoherence of retain and repeal, which as a result meant that the law appeared to criminalise conduct for which there was immunity from liability in tort, and which appeared to treat trade disputes more harshly than political disputes. Before concluding the chapter, we examine the limitations of Order 1305 in the face of what was perceived to be politically motivated action in the post-war era, and the proposals to take powers to deal with these limitations in the Overseas Operations (Security of Forces) Bill. The latter was vetoed by the TUC, which was unwilling to

[1] *Crofter Hand Woven Harris Tweed Co Ltd v Veitch* 1942 SC(HL) 1.
[2] On the electoral commitment, see p 76 below.

entertain any further restrictions on the right to strike at a time when Order 1305 was becoming particularly controversial.

II. A Constitutional Sleight of Hand

The story of Order 1305's retention is complex. It begins with a desire on the part of the Coalition government even before the war ended to retain Order 1305, Part III. The latter – the benign part – had addressed and implemented a longstanding TUC demand for the 'legalisation' of collective agreements,[3] which meant that as a matter of law, Joint Industrial Council agreements would apply to all workers and all employers in any sector to which an agreement operated. This would include those workers who were not members of the relevant trade unions, and those employers who were not members of the relevant employers' associations which were parties to the agreement in question. In the event of any allegation of non-compliance by an employer, as explained in Chapter One, a trade union could complain to the Ministry of Labour and National Service. The latter in turn could refer the question whether an employer was or was not observing the recognised terms and conditions in the relevant trade or industry to the National Arbitration Tribunal, which was authorised to vary the terms and conditions of employment of the workers to whom the application related.

Bevin as Minister of Labour in the Coalition government took the power to continue Order 1305, Part III in the Wages Councils Bill which he introduced at Second Reading on 16 January 1945.[4] Having 'worked so well throughout the war',[5] the Ministry of Labour thought it necessary to retain Order 1305, Part III in peace-time. The Wages Council Act 1945 thus not only renamed the trade boards and extended their powers, but also proposed to roll over until 31 December 1950 a simplified version of Order 1305, Part III.[6] During that time, employers would be 'under an obligation to observe no less favourable terms of employment than those settled by agreements between employer organisations and trade unions'.[7] In Bevin's words, there would be 'a complete national fair wages clause in order to maintain stability. That is really what it amounts to'.[8] The only major change anticipated was the dropping of the requirement that disputes about non-compliance with a collective agreement should be made in the first instance to the Ministry of Labour. Under the 1945 Act's procedures, it was anticipated that complaints would be made directly to the Industrial Court, which would perform the role of the National Arbitration Tribunal, which expected to be abolished with the anticipated revocation of Order 1305.[9]

[3] KD Ewing, 'The State and Industrial Relations: Collective Laissez Faire' Revisited' (1998) 5 *Historical Studies in Industrial Relations* 1.

[4] HC Debs, 16 January 1945, col 69.

[5] ibid col 110 (Malcolm McCorquodale, Joint Parliamentary Secretary to the Ministry of Labour). McCorquodale was a Conservative.

[6] Wages Council Act 1945, sch 3.

[7] HC Debs, 16 January 1945, col 76.

[8] ibid.

[9] The differences between the 1945 Act's provisions and Order 1305, Part III are explained by Bevin at HC Debs, 16 January 1945, col 82.

At some point during 1945, however, the newly elected Labour government had thus decided that Order 1305 should be retained. This was before the Cabinet debates discussed in section III below got underway, though it was a decision no doubt informed in part by a fear of industrial action once the legal brakes were released. But having decided to retain Order 1305, the next question was the means by which this was to be done. The obvious way to secure the necessary legal authority to retain Order 1305 would be to introduce primary legislation following the example of the Wages Councils Act 1945. Indeed, there was much to be said for using primary legislation to retain restrictions which had been made in war-time without any prior parliamentary consideration, never mind approval, particularly where the failure to comply with the restrictions in question could lead to imprisonment. There was, however, a chronic shortage of parliamentary time, not to mention the potential for acute embarrassment if the government was telling Parliament in one debate – on the Trade Disputes and Trade Unions Bill – about the need to remove restrictions on the right to strike,[10] and then announcing in another that the exercise of the right to strike had to be contained by the criminal law.

Albeit probably for the first (the shortage of parliamentary time) rather than the second (political embarrassment) of these reasons the government used other powers to retain Order 1305, thereby again denying Parliament a chance to approve what were far-reaching restrictions. The powers in question were provided by the Supplies and Services (Transitional Powers) Act 1945, which received the Royal Assent on 10 December 1945. It was introduced in anticipation of the expiry of the Emergency Powers (Defence) Acts 1939–40, which were due to lapse on 24 February 1946. The Defence Regulations made thereunder would automatically lapse as well, as would any powers to make Orders delegated to ministers by the Defence Regulations. These would include Defence Regulation 58AA, which had given the Minister of Labour the power by Order to take steps to deal with situations where work was interrupted by trade disputes. In enabling Order 1305 to be rolled over in this way with multiple other powers and restrictions, the 1945 Act reflected the view expressed in Cabinet that 'the Government should at once establish the principle that the next five years would be a period of transition in which the exercise of emergency powers by the Executive would be as necessary as it had been in the war'.[11]

Although far-reaching, the Supplies and Services (Transitional Powers) Act 1945 was not the only legislation designed to ensure the continuance of war-time powers. On 4 October 1945, shortly before the Second Reading of what became the latter Act, the Cabinet decided additionally to introduce an 'Emergency Laws (Transitional Provisions) Bill' to continue in force certain Defence Regulations' not covered by the Supplies and Services Bill.[12] The constitutional outrage could have been worse, the President of the Board of Trade, Stafford Cripps, looking for even more extensive emergency powers, expressing regret that the Supplies and Services (Transitional Powers) Act 1945 merely extended the life of the Defence Regulations, when 'it would be

[10] HC Debs, 12 February 1946, col 192.

[11] TNA, CAB 128/1/6 (Cabinet Conclusions, 16 August 1945).

[12] TNA, CAB 128/1 (Cabinet Conclusions, 4 October 1947). Introducing the Emergency Laws (Transitional Provisions) Bill on 7 November 1947, the Home Secretary Chuter Ede provided a useful recap of the legislative steps taken in 1945–47 (HC Debs, 7 November 1947, cols 2133–66).

convenient for the Government in carrying out their industrial policy to have power to introduce by Regulation various provisions which were not of major importance'.[13] But although the effect of the Supplies and Services (Transitional Powers) Act 1945 was that sub-delegated powers could continue to operate for the lifetime of the government without direct parliamentary approval, they did at least as an alternative have the approval of the clumsily named Joint Consultative Committee of the National Joint Advisory Council, the tripartite body established in 1939 as an embryonic Economic Parliament.[14]

The TUC had previously resolved that there must be an end to compulsory arbitration, but now accepted the prolongation of Order 1305 at a meeting of the General Council on 19 December 1945, on the strict understanding that the matter 'would be reviewed immediately either side wished it to be discontinued'.[15] Indeed, presumably as a face-saving measure, the TUC insisted that it be placed on record 'that the Minister of Labour has undertaken to make it possible for the General Council and the British Employers' Confederation to request the cancellation of the provisions for compulsory arbitration at any time in the future'.[16] In agreeing with the government's proposals to retain Order 1305, the TUC General Council had concluded – according to Hugh Clegg – that 'it was not in the interests of the Trade Union Movement or the nation as a whole to demand the abolition of compulsory arbitration at the present time'.[17] The General Council appears to have been concerned about releasing the power of the rank and file, anxious to 'curb' the 'extravagant and unreasonable claims by new elements with the least degree of responsibility'.[18] Just like the government, the TUC had already forgotten about the weakness of Order 1305 when faced with worker discontent.

In agreeing to the retention of compulsory arbitration, the TUC was also agreeing to its logical corollary, namely the prohibition of strikes and lock outs, with Article 4, making it a criminal offence to participate in either. This was a consequence which appeared to alarm Robert Gould, the Chief Industrial Commissioner, performing a role that had been performed by Sir Frederick Leggett and Sir Harold Emmerson during the war. Gould had warned Isaacs of what would now be regarded as rule of law concerns, pointing out that 'we should not lose sight of the fact that we are not at present in a position to apply the sanctions of the Order when an illegal strike occurs',[19] the Order having not been enforced to deal with two official strikes which were then in progress. In the same message to Isaacs, he also highlighted two other recent strikes that 'caught the public eye, the docks strike and the gas workers' strike', where 'the question of proceedings were similarly not considered'.[20] Here Gould was indicating that the invocation of

[13] TNA, CAB 128/1/7 (Cabinet Conclusions, 20 August 1945).
[14] See pp 84–85 below.
[15] TNA, LAB 10/581 ('Prolongation of DR58AA and its Subordinate Legislation Order 1305', Ministry of Labour and National Service, Joint Consultative Committee, 57th Meeting, 14 December 1945).
[16] ibid 'Vincent Tewson to RM Gould, 29 January 1946'. Tewson was then Assistant Secretary of the TUC. Tewson's reservation was duly noted by Gould in a letter on 1 February.
[17] HA Clegg, *A History of British Trade Unions since 1889: Vol 3 1934–1951* (Clarendon Press, Oxford, 1994), p 329.
[18] ibid.
[19] TNA LAB 10/ 581 ('Prolongation of DR58AA and its Subordinate Legislation Order 1305', Minute Note by RM Gould, Ministry of Labour, 15 December 1945). Gould was essentially attacking the proposal.
[20] ibid.

the penal provisions had always been selective,[21] and arguing that while this failure to enforce the Order was excusable 'when it seems apparent that the Order has ceased to have public support and its early revocation is expected', such inaction would be difficult to justify after a decision is taken deliberately to retain the law.[22]

Moreover, Gould warned that while a failure to enforce the Order had its pitfalls, enforcement would lead to industrial relations difficulties: 'In the large issues affecting important industries, such as the railways, the docks and the buses, there is no doubt that compulsory arbitration would not be accepted'.[23] Gould appears to have been suggesting that the numbers of workers involved and their reputation for militancy would mean that, aware of the impracticability of bringing large numbers of Order 1305 prosecutions, workers in those sectors could not be cowed by the strike prohibition. Fortunately, the post-war period was one of remarkably low levels of industrial conflict, with the number of working days lost annually falling almost every year from 1944 until it virtually flatlined in 1951.[24] The docks apart, this suggests a remarkable state of relative industrial harmony in a period of post-war wage restraint; or that trade unions were disinclined to embarrass their own government; or that the compulsory arbitration procedures of Order 1305, Part II were performing the role intended. Whatever the explanation, the relatively few official strikes meant that the limits of Order 1305 were not tested to the limits as Gould had feared. As we will see, however, the position was different in relation to unofficial action, where Order 1305 was to be deployed just as unsuccessfully as it had been during the war.

III. Retention and Repeal: A Political Contradiction

The retention of Order 1305 was obviously a surprise in light of the Labour Party's electoral commitment to restore freedom, including specifically trade union freedom.[25] It was all the more surprising for directly contradicting the steps being taken to repeal the Trade Disputes and Trade Unions Act 1927, which were well underway at the time the decision was taken to retain Order 1305. The general election having taken place on 5 July 1945, the Cabinet was told on 7 August that the TUC favoured the complete repeal of the 1927 Act, ministers accepting that 'the necessary Bill should be limited to this purpose'.[26] They also accepted that if repeal 'left the position unsatisfactory' for unspecified reasons, a further Bill could be introduced at a later date. A major trade union grievance for 20 years, the 1927 Act had been introduced as reparations demanded by the Conservative Party for the General Strike in 1926.[27] An attempt

[21] Although it suggests that he was unaware that Leggett had initiated a policy of only invoking the penal provisions in cases where there was subversive intent, which casts some doubt on how far that policy really reflected the practice of the Ministry.

[22] TNA LAB 10/ 581 TNA, ('Prolongation of DR58AA and its Subordinate Legislation Order 1305', Minute Note by RM Gould, Ministry of Labour, 15 December 1945).

[23] ibid.

[24] See H Pelling, *A History of British Trade Unionism* (Penguin, Harmondsworth, 1963), p 263.

[25] Labour Party, *Let Us Face the Future* (1945), discussed pp 76–77 below.

[26] TNA, CAB 128/1/1 (Cabinet Conclusions, 7 August 1945).

[27] A classic account of the General Strike is M Morris (ed), *The General Strike* (Penguin, Harmondsworth, 1976).

at repeal by the Labour government between 1929 and 1931 had been unsuccessful, Labour in a minority and unable to secure the necessary Liberal support for its proposals. With a large majority in 1945, the Labour government could now move quickly to keep its promise, able to resist what was at times a ferocious attack on multiple grounds from the Opposition benches in both the Commons and the Lords.

The principal purpose of the 1927 Act had been to declare the General Strike and strikes like it to be illegal, such activity condemned by the then Tory Attorney General, Sir Douglas Hogg KC, on the ground that the strike 'sets up a rival authority to the authority of the Government', and that it 'seeks, in the words of its authors, to substitute the dictatorship of the proletariat for the authority of Parliament'.[28] As explained in Chapter Two, industrial action was thus declared to be illegal if it met two conditions: (i) that it had any object other than or in addition to the furtherance of a trade dispute within the trade or industry within which the strikers (or employers locking out) were engaged; *and* (ii) that it was 'designed or calculated to coerce the Government either directly or by inflicting hardship on the community' (section 1(1)). Anyone who declared, instigated or incited others to take part in a strike or lock out declared by the Act to be illegal faced a fine or imprisonment, which could be two years if convicted on indictment. Otherwise, protection from civil liability provided by the Trade Disputes Act 1906 would not apply to any act done in contemplation or furtherance of a dispute declared illegal by the 1927 Act, with the result that the protection of trade union funds from liability in damages would cease to apply.

Although the foregoing restraints were resented for mainly symbolic reasons, the other parts of the 1927 Act were resented because of their more practical effects on trade union activity. These included the changes to the law of picketing as protected in the 1875 and 1906 Acts referred to above. Now the freedom to picket was heavily restricted, linked for the first time to the number of pickets attending. Thus, it was unlawful to 'attend in such numbers or otherwise in such manner as to be calculated to intimidate any person in that house or place, or to obstruct the approach thereto or egress therefrom' (section 3(1)).[29] Also significant were the restrictions on the freedom for unions to finance the Labour Party established by the Trade Union Act 1913,[30] with trade union members now required to contract in if they wanted to pay the political levy rather than contract out if they preferred not to do so, leading to a significant decline in trade union support for the Party. Other measures required civil service unions (including the post office unions at the time) to renounce affiliation to the TUC and the Labour Party, and while local authorities were prohibited from operating closed-shop arrangements, it was also an offence for public authority workers to strike 'knowing or having

[28] HC Debs, 2 May 1927, col 1310.

[29] Any such attendance was deemed to be watching and besetting for the purposes of the Conspiracy and Protection of Property Act 1875, s 7 which by virtue of the 1927 Act would be unlawful because of its lack of lawful authority. It was also provided separately that it 'shall not be lawful, for one or more persons for the purpose of inducing any person to work or abstain from working, to watch or beset a house or place where a person resides or the approach to such a place'. Breach of this provision was punishable by a fine or up to three months' imprisonment (s 2(4)). For a brief discussion of the operation of the 1927 Act's picketing provisions, see D Lyddon and P Smith, 'The 1906 Act: The First Fifty Years – Industrial Relations, Picketing and the Employers' Challenge', in KD Ewing (ed), *The Right to Strike: From the Trade Disputes Act 1906 to a Trade Union Bill 2006* (Institute of Employment Rights, Liverpool, 2007), ch 7.

[30] Following the judicial attack on political funding in *Osborne v Amalgamated Society of Railway Servants* [1910] AC 87.

reasonable cause to believe' that it would 'cause injury or grave inconvenience to the community'.

By mid-September, the Cabinet was considering a memorandum by the Lord Chancellor, William Jowitt, pointing out that the reversal of these restrictions was likely to arouse 'considerable political controversy' and that as a result, it should be introduced as soon as possible.[31] Jowitt was also concerned about the demands of the parliamentary process, reminding colleagues that when he was Attorney General between 1929 and 1931, he had no department to assist him and was left completely to his own resources. It was therefore imperative that while the 'main responsibility for the Bill in the House of Commons will undoubtedly rest with the Attorney-General', 'a Minister of Cabinet rank should be in general charge of it in the Commons'.[32] So when the Cabinet agreed that the Second Reading should be taken at an early date after Parliament had reassembled, it was thus also agreed that the Minister of Labour and National Service 'should be generally responsible for the Bill in the House of Commons' and that his Department should undertake any work connected with the preparation of briefs'.[33] The Minister of Labour was by now George Isaacs, who occupied a seat in the House of Commons and a place in the Cabinet while formally retaining his position as General Secretary of the National Society of Operative Printers and Assistants.[34]

Yet despite the initial haste, it was not until 12 February 1946 that the Trade Disputes and Trade Unions Bill was introduced by the Attorney General, Sir Hartley Shawcross, for its Second Reading,[35] by which time the government had decided with the TUC to retain Order 1305. Curiously, no mention was made of this latter decision, even though it appeared to contradict the restoration of civil liberties that repeal of the 1927 Act was intended to presage. The contradiction between the repeal of the 1927 Act and the retention of Order 1305 is made even more stark by the rhetoric of the government in its defence of the 1946 Bill. In countering the fierce Conservative criticism, the Attorney General argued that repeal of the 1927 Act would restore 'hard-won and important individual freedoms',[36] while claiming simultaneously that it would have 'no practical effect whatever on the exercise of the right to strike – not a scrap'.[37] Both of these statements were unlikely to have been correct. But given the retention of Order 1305, on balance the latter seemed closer to reality. Shawcross emphasised nevertheless the need to address 'the belief amongst workers that their hard-won right to withhold their labour if they chose, which, after all, is the inalienable right of every free man, had been whittled away'.[38]

Quite apart from these arguments rooted in what is ultimately a principled defence of the right to strike, there were also practical considerations reinforcing the

[31] TNA, CAB 129/1/49 ('Trade Disputes and Trade Unions Act Repeal Bill', Memorandum by the Lord Chancellor).

[32] ibid.

[33] TNA, CAB 128 (Cabinet Conclusions, 13 September 1945).

[34] He was given leave of absence by the union on his appointment to government, and only retired formally in 1948 on reaching the age of 65: GG Eastwood, *George Isaacs: Printer, Trade-Union Leader, Cabinet Minister* (Odhams Press, London, 1952), pp 84–85.

[35] HC Debs, 12 February 1946, col 192.

[36] ibid col 193.

[37] ibid col 194.

[38] ibid.

argument that the criminal law was not a suitable device for the resolution of industrial disputes. Taunted at Second Reading about a dock strike then in progress, the Attorney General replied by saying that the government had realised that because of the experience of unofficial strikes during the war, 'it is utterly impossible to prohibit strikes and prevent them by processes of the criminal law'.[39] For this reason, 'most people' appreciate that 'it is in the interests, not only of industry but of the State, to have strong and powerful trade unions of which all the workers in industry are members, and which are able to guide and to lead their members'.[40] But as the Attorney General also pointed out, it is not possible to deal with strikes, 'wrong and misguided as they may be', by 'putting a few people into prison', which 'only makes martyrs of those people'.[41] 'The way to stop strikes', it was claimed, is 'not by a policeman but by a conciliation officer, not by the assize courts but by the arbitration tribunals'.[42] Good points. So why retain Order 1305, to which these arguments applied with equal force?

Reference was also made to the prosecution in *R v Tearse*,[43] where – as we saw in Chapter Two – three appellants had been charged on indictment, convicted and sentenced to a period of imprisonment at Newcastle Assizes for, inter alia, acting in furtherance of a strike declared illegal under the 1927 Act. The trial judge rejected the argument that 'the words of the statute "in furtherance of" presupposed the existence of a strike, and that, therefore, the acts with which the appellants were charged, having been done before the commencement of the strike on March 28, 1944, could not be said to be in furtherance thereof'.[44] However, the argument was accepted by the Court of Appeal in upholding the appeal against conviction, Shawcross adding that the strikers were as a result able to go away and 'laugh at the law'.[45] This led the Attorney General to remind his audience that 'the maintenance and strengthening of the rule of law' depends 'in very large measure' on 'excluding from the Statute Book laws which are manifestly unenforceable, in the circumstances with which they purport to deal, and which at the same time cause resentment, rightly or wrongly, on the part of a large section of the population'.[46] These were words which were to return to haunt the Attorney General five years later; he was to become the victim of his own rhetoric.

Such considerations apart, the 1927 Act seemed rather anachronistic in the heady days after the war, a bequest from an era on which the curtains had drawn. No one was talking now of general strikes or of taking action 'to coerce the Government either directly or by inflicting hardship on the community'. For the TUC, the restoration of full trade union powers (such as they were) by the repeal of the 1927 Act was nevertheless a recognition of the important role of trade unions as a bulwark against those who would govern without consent.[47] Although it was not anticipated that trade unions would

[39] HC Debs, 12 February 1946, col 197.
[40] ibid.
[41] ibid col 203.
[42] ibid col 200. These are, of course, references to referrals for the purposes of compulsory arbitration under the terms of Order 1305 and arguably a reflection of the post-war view of the Order as a vehicle for settling disputes rather than prohibiting strikes.
[43] *R v Tearse* [1945] KB 1.
[44] ibid p 2.
[45] HC Debs, 12 February 1946, col 200.
[46] ibid col 204.
[47] LJ MacFarlane, *The Right to Strike* (Penguin, Harmondsworth, 1981), p 160.

need the restored powers, they were nevertheless justified by TUC General Secretary Sir Walter Citrine, according to whom 'only in the most exceptional circumstances, and when no other remedy appeared possible, would such a method be likely to be employed'.[48] Citrine's remarks perhaps unwittingly exposed a conflict between the traditional liberal and the evolving social democratic versions of constitutionalism, the latter to be seen in the growing space for the TUC and trade unions generally in the post-war economic governance of the country. It was certainly different from the more formal textbook version of constitutionalism that had been uttered from the Tory benches in 1926/1927 and again in 1946.

IV. Retention and Repeal: Incoherent Legal Consequences

So what was the effect of the retention of Order 1305 and the repeal of the 1927 Act for British labour law? Rather than a consistent if illiberal position as a result of Order 1305 and under the 1927 Act in which virtually all strikes would potentially give rise to criminal liability, the position was now somewhat incoherent:

- A strike in contemplation or furtherance of a trade dispute would be protected from criminal and tortious liability because of the Conspiracy and Protection of Property Act 1875 and the Trade Disputes Act 1906 respectively, but participating in a strike in connection with a trade dispute would be a criminal offence under Order 1305.
- A strike which was undertaken principally for political purposes would not be protected from criminal and tortious liability under the Conspiracy and Protection of Property Act 1875 and the Trade Disputes Act 1906 respectively, but participating in such a strike would not normally be a criminal offence under Order 1305.

So that which was protected from tort liability could give rise to criminal prosecution, but that which was actionable in tort would not be the subject of prosecution. Moreover, strikes for political purposes would be treated more favourably than strikes for industrial purposes. In practice, however, the position was not quite so straightforward.

Beginning with potential criminal liability, the starting point for this discussion is *R v Bunn* in 1872, where it was held that striking gas workers were guilty of a criminal conspiracy at common law.[49] The essence of the offence was the unlawful means of simultaneously breaking their contracts of service, for which the men were sentenced to imprisonment for 12 months.[50] In partially reversing the decision in 1875, Parliament provided that 'an agreement or combination by two or more persons to do or procure to be done any act in contemplation or furtherance of a trade dispute … shall not be

[48] HC Debs, 26 February 1946, col 1774. The point was raised by James Reid, former Lord Advocate in the war-time Coalition who we encountered in ch 3 above, to taunt Shawcross that by repealing the 1927 Act, the government was 'entrusting of the trade unions with a very great power to coerce Parliament, to upset the decisions of the democratically elected persons who sit in Parliament'.

[49] *R v Bunn* (1872) 12 Cox CC 316.

[50] For a good account, see S Webb and B Webb, *The History of Trade Unionism, 1666–1920* (Longmans Green, London, 1919 edn), pp 284–85.

indictable as a conspiracy if such act committed by one person would not be punishable as a crime'. Having gained in 1871 the right to organise, the 1875 Act secured for trade unions the right to strike, though, as suggested, *R v Bunn* was only partially reversed. Not only was the protection limited to actions in contemplation or furtherance of a trade dispute, but new offences were created, applying ironically to gas workers for maliciously breaking their contracts, and to others for wilfully breaking their contracts where the probable consequences of doing so would be to endanger human life, or cause serious bodily injury, or to expose valuable property (whether real or personal) to destruction or serious injury.

In limiting the statutory protection from criminal liability to 'trade disputes' (a term not defined until 1906), the legislation clearly set out the boundaries of legitimate trade union action. There would be no protection if the conspiracy was in contemplation or furtherance of a political dispute between the trade unions and the government, whether it be a dispute about extension of the franchise, the expansion of trade union rights, or the improvement of working conditions by means of an Act of Parliament. Nor would there be any protection for those who were using the cover of a strike to promote the objectives of a revolutionary political party. And just to make sure, a rider to what was section 3 of the 1875 Act provided that its provisions did not affect 'the law relating to riot, unlawful assembly, breach of the peace, or sedition, or any offence against the State or Sovereign'. This was not only a qualification, but also a revelation of a suspicion about the potential of trade unionism as a vehicle for unconstitutional action, a perception paradoxically to become prominent under the Attlee government, as it had been in earlier decades. It is a matter to which we return in the chapters that follow.

So despite the repeal of the 1927 Act, the Conspiracy and Protection of Property Act 1875 suggested that there was still continuing liability at common law for action which was not in contemplation or furtherance of a trade dispute, and suggested too that there was a continuing role for sedition – also an offence at common law, now abolished, but then second only to treason in the hierarchy of offences against the state – in the event of politically motivated industrial action. According to one contemporary account of the law:

> [T][he definition of sedition is wide enough to cover almost every act of disaffection or disloyalty whether to the State or the Established Church, but prosecutions for seditious offences, though they were frequent in the eighteenth century, are rare and juries are unwilling to convict for the expression of opinion relating to public affairs. In practice it is essential for a successful prosecution to prove a clear incitement to violence as well as the publication of defamatory words.[51]

Although a 'little used weapon',[52] the deployment of sedition remained an option in principle, having been used successfully by the Baldwin government against the Communist Party leadership in 1925,[53] and unsuccessfully by the Attlee government

[51] ECS Wade and GG Phillips, *Constitutional Law* (5th edn by ECS Wade) (Longmans, Green & Co, London, 1955), p 394.

[52] ibid.

[53] See KD Ewing and CA Gearty, *The Struggle for Civil Liberties: Political Freedom and the Rule of Law in Britain, 1914–1945* (Oxford University Press, Oxford, 2000), p 140.

against a newspaper proprietor in 1947 for publishing an article heavily laced with anti-semitism.[54] Yet despite the latter setback, as we mention in Chapter Six, there is evidence of Shawcross nevertheless looking for material on which to base a sedition prosecution against the organisers of unofficial strike action in the docks.

Sedition and the Labour Government

At a political level, it seems extraordinary that a charge of seditious conspiracy would be contemplated against trade unionists, no matter how strong the provocation. Although sedition (both statutory and common law forms of the offence) had been used against communist leaders in the past and famously against strikers following the Winnipeg General Strike in 1919,[55] it was necessary to go back to the days of the Chartists in the 1840s,[56] and the Tolpuddle Martyrs in the 1830s for examples of cases in which the political offences were used by state prosecutors against those who were contemplating the use of the strike as a political weapon, or for those who were simply engaged in other forms of trade union activity.

At a technical level, the problems of bringing a successful prosecution were revealed in the *Morecambe and Heysham Visitor* case, where a newspaper editor was charged with seditious libel following the publication of an article which tended expressly to advocate violence towards British Jews, following the killing of two British soldiers by Zionist partisans in Palestine. At the trial at Liverpool Assizes in November 1947, Mr Justice Coleridge emphasised the need to provoke disorder by promoting feelings of hostility and ill-will between different classes of the King's subjects. The editor denied he incited people to violence, his acquittal being celebrated by ECS Wade as a vindication of the jury system as the best way of protecting the 'full and free discussion of public affairs'.[57]

So far as the civil law is concerned, one effect of repealing the 1927 Act was to restore to the full the protection from liability in tort that had been established by the Trade Disputes Act 1906. Sometimes referred to as the 'Magna Carta of Labour',[58] the 1906 Act had been passed following a wave of House of Lords decisions in the early years of the twentieth century in which it had held that various forms of industrial action by workers was tortious, either on the grounds of conspiracy to injure or for inducing breach of the contracts of employment of the workers taking strike action.[59] It was also held that where the action was organised by a trade union, the latter would be liable not only to be restrained by an injunction, but also for unlimited damages caused by the

[54] ECS Wade, 'Seditious Libel and the Press' (1948) 64 *LQR* 203.

[55] *R v Russell* [1920] 1 WWR 624. See DH Brown, 'The Craftsmanship of Bias: Sedition and the Winnipeg General Strike 1919' (1984) 14 *Manitoba Law Journal* 1.

[56] *R v O'Connor* (1843) 4 St Tr (NS) 935; *R v Cooper* (1843) 4 St Tr (NS) 1249.

[57] Wade (n 54) p 204.

[58] See KO Morgan, '1906: Blissful Dawn' (2006) 51 *Journal of Liberal History* 32, at p 34.

[59] *Taff Vale Railway Co Ltd v Amalgamated Society of Railway Servants* [1901] AC 426; *Quinn v Leathem* [1901] AC 495; *South Wales Miners' Federation v Glamorgan Coal Co Ltd* [1905] AC 239.

action in question. In reversing this line of decisions, the 1906 Act provided that there would be no tortious liability for conspiracy to injure (section 1), inducing breach of contract of employment (section 3), or interference with trade, business or employment (also section 3). The protection from liability applied to acts done in contemplation or furtherance of a trade dispute, thereby extending to the civil law the formula used in 1875 for the purposes of the criminal law.

With the definition of a trade dispute limited to disputes between employers and workmen and workmen and workmen about terms and conditions of employment,[60] not all industrial action was covered by the protection, as indeed had been revealed during the General Strike, where the government argued forcefully and publicly that the action of the TUC in supporting the TUC was unconstitutional. In the words of the then Attorney General:

> The question really is whether the success of the General Strike, if it succeeded, does not necessarily involve a substitution of the strikers' will for the will of Parliament. That is the point. In this world, people have to be judged not by noble sentiments and strong sympathies but by the perfectly obvious consequences of what they deliberately do. If the strike really meant the substitution of the strikers' will for the will of Parliament, it would have meant the overthrow of constitutional government, and I should be doing no service to those whom I try to serve if I were for a moment to pretend that it meant anything else.[61]

Although Sir John Simon's view has been hotly disputed, niceties and fine distinctions are not likely to amount to very much in the heat of conflict, particularly in civil proceedings designed to restrain action by way of interlocutory injunction. The latter procedure in extreme cases empowers the court to weigh the defence that the action is lawful against wider considerations, such as the impact of the action on the public at large.[62]

It is thus unsurprising that the General Strike of 1926 should have been declared not to have been protected by the 1906 Act. In *National Sailors' and Firemen's Union v Reed*,[63] the union (which did not agree with the TUC call) sought an injunction to restrain its branches from supporting the strike. Granting the injunction, Astbury J said that the 'so-called general strike called by the Trades Union Congress Council is illegal, and persons inciting or taking part in it are not protected by the Trade Disputes Act 1906', adding that 'no trade dispute does or can exist between the Trades Union Congress on the one hand and the Government and the nation on the other'.[64] These remarks have since been exposed as being intended to assist the government and as having misrepresented the legal position;[65] while the 1906 Act did not protect a dispute between the TUC and the government,[66] the TUC's action was taken in furtherance of

[60] Trade Disputes Act 1906, s 5. This definition was applied also to the Conspiracy and Protection of Property Act 1875.

[61] Sir J Simon, *Three Speeches on The General Strike* (Macmillan, London, 1926), p 47 (from speech delivered in Clerkenwell Town Hall, 20 May 1926).

[62] See *NWL Ltd v Woods* [1979] ICR 867 (HL), pp 881–82 (Lord Diplock).

[63] *National Sailors' and Firemen's Union v Reed* [1926] Ch 536.

[64] ibid pp 539–40.

[65] See Ewing and Gearty (n 53) ch 4.

[66] Such a dispute would not be a dispute between employers and workmen or between workmen and workmen, as required by the Trade Disputes Act 1906, s 5(3). But TUC action in support of an affiliated trade union engaged in a trade dispute would be protected as being in furtherance of that dispute.

a trade dispute between the miners and the owners,[67] and consequently clearly within the scope of the 1906 Act. Nevertheless, the judicial intervention had the desired effect of helping to persuade the TUC to call off its action, leaving the miners to struggle on alone until December, when they were forced back to work on the employer's terms. It also helps to explain the 'declaratory' effect of the 1927 Act.

In taking the law back to the position operating immediately beforehand, the repeal of the 1927 Act would simply have removed criminal liability from action that was most likely to be held to be unlawful for other reasons. The injunction granted in the *NSFU* case to restrain the branches of a union which did not support the strike, raised converse questions about the possibility of injunctions being granted to trade union members to restrain their unions from supporting it, and to restrain the expulsion from the organization of those who refused to take part.[68] That apart, Astbury J's obiter dictum about the legal status of the General Strike in relation to the 1906 Act suggests that action of this kind would most likely be seen to be tortious, actionable at the suit of individual employers whose workmen were induced to break their contracts of employment to take part in the action (though admittedly not actionable by the Attorney General whose rights would not be directly affected). There would be no protection under the 1906 Act, the reason being that the action would most likely be held not to be in contemplation or furtherance of a trade dispute, but in contemplation or furtherance of a dispute between workmen, or a trade union, or trade unions, or the TUC on the one hand and the government on the other.[69]

'Sectarian, political, or purely mischievous'

It was not only overtly political strikes aimed at the government that were excluded from protection in tort. So too were covertly political strikes in the sense of strikes that were motivated by a political desire to cause disruption, or strikes that were using the cover of a trade dispute to promote a political cause. This is clearly established by the decision of the House of Lords in *Conway v Wade*,[70] to which we have already referred in Chapter Two. Although drafted in very wide terms, led by Lord Chancellor Loreburn, who had played a prominent part in drafting and navigating the Trade Disputes Bill through the House of Lords,[71] a bench of seven Law Lords took the opportunity within three years of the Bill's enactment to set

[67] See AL Goodhart, 'The Legality of the General Strike in England' (1927) 36 *Yale Law Journal* 464.

[68] According to Mr Justice Astbury: 'No member of the plaintiff union, or any other trade unionist in this country can lose his trade union benefits by refusing to obey unlawful orders': *National Sailors' and Firemen's Union v Reed* (n 63) p 540. This view found expression in the 1927 Act, s 2 which provided that individual workers who refused to strike, or who returned to work contrary to the union's instructions and were consequently subject to a detriment, could be awarded damages. Moreover, if the worker had been expelled, the union could be obliged to reinstate them, in lieu of which the union could be ordered to pay 'such sums by way of compensation or damages as the court thinks just'. Although these latter provisions went with the repeal of the 1927 Act, the repeal did not remove the common law constraints suggested by Mr Justice Astbury.

[69] For a recent example to this effect, see *Express Newspapers Ltd v Keys* [1980] IRLR 247 (strikes in support of a TUC Day of Action in protest against the Employment Bill 1980 were not protected).

[70] *Conway v Wade* [1909] AC 506.

[71] HL Debs, 4 December 1906, col 686.

boundaries around the scope of the Act and, in particular, what was meant by the phrase 'in contemplation or furtherance of a trade dispute'.[72] Of particular significance for the present purposes was the exclusion of action by a 'meddler' who used the trade dispute defence as a 'cloak beneath which to interfere with impunity in other people's work or business'.[73] Such behaviour would not be in contemplation or furtherance of a trade dispute, but of 'sectarian, political, or purely mischievous designs', as the case might be.

V. Cold War Politics and the Limits of Order 1305

The repeal of the 1927 Act would have been welcome across the trade union and labour movement for multiple reasons, removing several irritating restrictions. But because of the limitations of Order 1305, Shawcross came to regret its repeal, despite the fact that no one anticipated a repeat of the General Strike. In expressing this regret some four years later, Shawcross referred to the 'danger of strike action being used for political or subversive ends', which was said to have 'much increased since we repealed the Trades Disputes Act 1927 [sic]'.[74] The reason lay in the re-emergence of what was perceived to be a different kind of political strike following the beginning and then the intensification of the Cold War, which is widely accepted as starting in 1947 with major implications for domestic law and policy. As a result of the Cold War internationally, hostilities returned with the Communist Party domestically, the latter perceived to be involved in a campaign of subversion and mischief-making, as identified in Morrison's Memorandum referred to in Chapter Two.[75] These allegedly politically motivated strikes were associated with unofficial groups working in the trade unions, such as the Port Workers' Committee (PWC) in the docks which were said to be communist-dominated.

We return to the PWC in Chapter Six. In the meantime, these allegedly political strikes initially took two forms. The first were the Swift Scale-type strikes of the kind discussed in Chapter Two. These were ostensibly trade disputes which were said to be stirred up by political activists for political ends. And the second – which were never foreseeable – were the big dock strikes in 1949 – in solidarity with the communist-led Canadian Seamen's Union which was involved in a bitter inter-union dispute in its home country. It will be recalled that Order 1305 applied only to strikes in connection with a trade dispute which was defined to mean a dispute between employers and workmen or between workmen and workmen connected with terms and conditions of employment and related matters. It is conceivable that Order 1305 could have been used in the first type of case, as indeed it had been at Swift Scale, though that could by no means be guaranteed. As pointed out in the Box on pages 69 and 70, the definition of a trade dispute

[72] For a full discussion, see KD Ewing, 'The South Shields Case – Subverting the Trade Disputes Act 1906?', in Ewing (ed) (n 29) ch 5.

[73] *Conway v Wade* (n 70) p 512.

[74] TNA CAB 129/44/9 ('The Future of the Conditions of Employment and National Service Order', Memorandum by the Attorney General, 11 January 1951), para 5 (see ch 12 below).

[75] See also p 99 below.

did not apply to disputes which were motivated by sectarian, political or mischievous purposes. And as was indicated in Chapter Two, this important decision of the House of Lords was presumably not brought to FW Leggett's attention when devising Ministry prosecution policy during the war.[76]

The definition of a trade dispute was similar in Order 1305 to that in the 1906 Act, and it might have been assumed that although *Conway v Wade* (see above) was concerned with the latter, it had equal application to the former. If it was tortious because the action was not in contemplation or furtherance of a trade dispute, it could not simultaneously be an offence under Order 1305 as being connected with a trade dispute. In any event, the immediate concern was the activity of the PWC on the waterfront, in relation to which there were well-grounded doubts about the applicability of Order 1305 to the two most disruptive disputes in the post-war period. It is of course difficult to be definitive about the legal consequences of industrial action in the absence of all the facts that only litigation can reveal. Nevertheless, at least on one interpretation of events, the first dispute was a dispute between a Canadian employer and a Canadian trade union about the de-recognition and replacement of the union, while the second was a dispute between a union and some of its members about the discipline and expulsion of activists who had taken a leading role in the first strike. The former was arguably not a trade dispute as defined by Order 1305, Article 5 (because of the subject matter), while the latter was almost certainly not a trade dispute as so defined (because of the parties).

That said, there was no need to regret the repeal of the 1927 Act in these latter cases: it is unlikely to have been capable of deployment had it still been in force. It will be recalled that the 1927 Act prohibited action that had an object other than or in addition to: (i) the furtherance of a trade dispute within the trade or industry within which the strikers (or employers in the case of a lock out) were engaged; *and* (ii) was 'designed or calculated to coerce the Government either directly or by inflicting hardship on the community' (section 1(1)). It is unlikely that these requirements were satisfied in the case of either of the docks disputes. It is true that the action in both dock strikes may have inflicted hardship on the community. Indeed, it was necessary to declare a state of emergency under the Emergency Powers Act 1920 in the case of the first of these strikes.[77] Assuming for argument's sake that the action was for a purpose in addition to the furtherance of a trade dispute, it would nevertheless be difficult to argue that it was designed or calculated to coerce the government. In the first dispute, the action was designed to put pressure on the Canadian owners of the vessels which were blacked, while in the second dispute, it was to put pressure on their own union (the TGWU) to reinstate expelled members.

The dock strikes will be considered more fully in Chapters Seven and Eight. In the meantime, the concern about political strikes was to take a new turn following the start of the Korean War in June 1950, when action of a different kind was feared. This was the concern that the dockers would frustrate the war effort by imposing an embargo on goods and materials destined for war-related purposes. Here again, Order 1305 was of little use, simply because any strike action would not be connected with a trade dispute

[76] See p 22, above.

[77] On which, see GS Morris, 'The Emergency Powers Act 1920' [1979] *PL* 317.

on the ground that this was not a dispute between employers and workmen or workmen and workmen, but between an unofficial group of trade unionists and the government. It is at this point that Shawcross had plausible cause to regret the repeal of the 1927 Act. Although the action anticipated by the dockers may not have inflicted hardship on the community, it would arguably have had an object other than or in addition to the furtherance of a trade dispute, in the sense that it was a protest against the war, while also being designed or calculated directly to coerce the government, in the sense of being designed to put pressure on the Cabinet. That said, nothing could be taken for granted, as revealed by the war-time prosecution of the RCP activists for inciting strikes against the industrial conscription of apprentices.[78]

It will be recalled that in *R v Tearse*, the government was wrong-footed by the Court of Appeal's interpretation of the 1927 Act, as a result of which the appellants' convictions were quashed. But although Shawcross had concluded that the law was 'manifestly unenforceable', such considerations did not stop the Cabinet proceeding four years later with proposals to restore some of the powers that had been lost by the repeal of the 1927 Act. Home Office concerns were laid bare in a memorandum circulated by the Home Secretary on 18 July 1950,[79] the Home Secretary advising the Cabinet two days later that if 'dockers refused to handle supplies destined for Korea, there was nothing that could be done under the existing law to deal with them, or with the people who may have incited them to withdraw their labour'.[80] In what was a clear recognition of the limited utility of Order 1305 at the time, the Home Secretary was supported in his call for legislation by Shawcross, the Attorney General proposing to make it an offence for 'any person to perform any act which was designed to interfere with the movement of supplies destined for use by units of His Majesty's forces engaged in any active operations, or was calculated to assist the forces opposed to His Majesty's forces in those operations'.[81]

It took two days to prepare the Overseas Operations (Security of Forces) Bill for circulation to ministers together with an accompanying memorandum by the Home Secretary.[82] The Bill proposed to give to the government the power by Order in Council to invoke its provisions 'if at any time it appears to His Majesty that any of His Majesty's forces or any forces acting in association with His Majesty are engaged, or may shortly be engaged, in operations outside the United Kingdom involving the use of force'.[83] Once invoked, Clause 2 provided that:

> If any person does any act with intent to interfere with or impede the operations or movements of any of His Majesty's forces or of any associated forces, or the provision of supplies or services for any such forces, he shall be guilty of an offence.

It was then proposed that these provisions would not apply to those engaged in a lawful strike arising out of a dispute between employers and workers. Although it would thus be an offence to engage in an unlawful strike for the prohibited purpose in the Bill, it

[78] *R v Tearse* (n 43).

[79] TNA, CAB/129/41/174 ('Subversive Activities in Connection with the Fulfilment of His Majesty's Obligations in Pursuance of the United Nations Charter', Memorandum by the Home Secretary, 18 July 1950).

[80] TNA, CAB 128/18/8 (Cabinet Conclusions, 20 July 1950).

[81] ibid.

[82] TNA, CAB 129/41/183 ('Overseas Operations (Security of Forces) Bill', Memorandum by the Home Secretary, 22 July 1950).

[83] Overseas Operations (Security of Forces) Bill, cl 1.

is not clear on what ground a strike for the prohibited purpose would be unlawful, or why fresh legislation of this kind was necessary if the strike was already unlawful. But for multiple reasons, the Bill failed to make any progress, not least because of caution on the part of the Prime Minister, who did not want to 'raise old bogies of the 1927 Act' or 'give the impression that Order 1305 was likely to be permanent'.[84]

Although the Bill 'would be of little value if it did not penalise those who incited or took part in unofficial strikes which were aimed at impeding military operations', there was concern about how this would be received in Parliament, which would 'look closely at any provision discriminating in this way between lawful and unlawful industrial action'.[85] An even greater concern was how the proposed legislation would be received by the TUC, whose views the Cabinet thought it 'wise to ascertain' before proceeding any further. The Lord President (Herbert Morrison), the Minister of Labour (George Isaacs), the Attorney General (Shawcross), and the Lord Advocate (John Wheatley) were duly dispatched to consult the TUC 'urgently and in confidence' on the question whether legislation along the lines of Clause 2(4) would be 'acceptable to organised labour'.[86] With other provisions of the Bill relating to restrictions on press freedom already giving rise to serious reservations by ministers about proceeding further, the deputation to the TUC delivered more bad news for its supporters on the following day. The Lord Advocate reported to the Cabinet that the TUC would want specific safeguards regarding industrial action to be included in the legislation. For all practical purposes, that was the end of the Bill, the Cabinet agreeing that the type of guarantee demanded by the TUC 'would deprive the Bill of its usefulness'.[87]

Tort on the Waterfront

The potential of tort law – albeit on different grounds from those referred to in the text – was revealed in *Canadian Pacific Railway v Gaud*,[88] which arose on the eve of the most important of the many unofficial and allegedly communist-inspired dock strikes in the post-war period.[89] According to the law report, the strikers were members of the Canadian Seamen's Union (CSU), unhappy that the ship owners were 'negotiating another agreement with the Seafarers' International Union, said to be an American concern'.[90] The striking crew members were discharged by the master, but remained on the vessel (the *Beaverbrae*), causing the owners to bring proceedings to have them removed.

Although not referred to in the law report, government ministers alleged that the CSU was communist-dominated and that the solidarity action by British dockers was communist-led, with the purpose of undermining the Marshall Plan, by which

[84] TNA, CAB 195/8/22 (Cabinet Secretary's Notebook, 24 July 1950).
[85] TNA, CAB 128/18/9 (Cabinet Conclusions, 24 July 1950).
[86] ibid.
[87] TNA, CAB/128/18/10 (Cabinet Conclusions, 25 July 1950).
[88] *Canadian Pacific Railway v Gaud* [1949] 2 KB 239.
[89] For a full account, see pp 125–129 below.
[90] *Canadian Pacific Railway v Gaud* (n 88) p 241.

the US agreed to finance much of the rebuilding of post-war Europe. In other words, it was claimed that the action was politically motivated and subversive in intent, despite presenting itself as a response to the hostile action of an employer challenging a fundamental trade union principle that workers should be free to choose their own union. These claims would have been fuelled by the identity of the lawyers for the respondents.[91]

An injunction granted by Mr Justice Sellars on 5 May 1949 was upheld by the Court of Appeal a week later, despite the claim by the defence that the remedy was 'oppressive': 'these seamen are all Canadian citizens and the effect of the injunction is to uproot them from Canadian soil, represented by this Canadian ship, and forcing them into exile in this country'.[92] On the contrary, it was held that by choosing to remain on board, the striking crew members were trespassers. The court was unwilling to say that they should be allowed to continue their trespass to the prejudice not only of the owners, but also of the Port of London Authority and those seeking to be supplied with the food which the ship was bringing to this country.[93]

VI. Conclusion

The restrictions on the right to strike were almost certainly incidental to the main reasons for the retention of Order 1305, which, as we discuss in the next chapter, was important in helping the Treasury to deal with post-war economic problems. It is nevertheless to be seen in the context of one of a number of civil law and criminal law tools available to the government to deal with strikes. Notably, however, the civil law liabilities highlighted in Cabinet meetings were in contract rather than tort. Apart from dismissal, the remedy being pushed by Shawcross was damages for breach of employment contracts. Such a claim was not implausible in principle, with the Court of Appeal having held in *Ebbw Vale Steel, Iron and Coal Co Ltd v Tew* that workers who took industrial action in breach of contract were liable in damages for the loss of profit arising as a result.[94] But although there was some discussion of tort-based liabilities and remedies, as we will see below, these were not actively promoted, despite the shipowner's success in the *Gaud* case (see Box above). Such action would not be free of risk if taken against dockers rather than crew. How would an injunction be enforced, and what could sensibly be done if it was ignored?

As Attorney General, Shawcross appeared to prefer the criminal law. But Order 1305 was designed principally to reinforce the requirement of compulsory arbitration for

[91] Gaster and Turner were solicitors for the defendants, who were represented in court by Dudley Collard. All three were members of the Communist Party Lawyers' Group. See KD Ewing, J Mahoney and A Moretta, *MI5, the Cold War and the Rule of Law* (Oxford University Press, Oxford, 2020), ch 7.

[92] [1949] 2 KB 239, at p 242.

[93] ibid pp 248–9 (Cohen LJ).

[94] *Ebbw Vale Steel, Iron and Coal Co Ltd v Tew* (1935) 79 Sol Jo 593. See subsequently *Fife Coal Company v MacBain* (1936) 52 Sh Ct Rep 84; *National Coal Board v Galley* [1958] 1 WLR 16.

disputes about wages and working condition, in relation to which it was to be used successfully against striking gas workers. In contrast, Order 1305 was not designed to deal with what was perceived to be politically motivated discontent, and it was not capable of being easily adapted for this purpose. Had it been retained, the same would have been true of the 1927 Act, which was intended for political activity of a kind never to be repeated and very different from that experienced on the waterfront. In that sense, the repeal of the 1927 Act changed little, at least in relation to the government's capacity to deal with post-war strikes. It does not follow, however, that the government was ill-equipped by the criminal law to deal with what was perceived to be Cold War subversion. Shawcross had hoped to bring a prosecution for seditious conspiracy, but in the absence of any evidence to justify such a charge, he eventually resorted to reviving common law criminal conspiracy, and to taking a gamble on Order 1305. We return to these charges and the trial in Chapter Thirteen.

5

Containing Trade Union Power

Collective Bargaining and the Wage Restraint Bargain

I. Introduction

The war-time Coalition was replaced by the Labour government elected with an overall majority of 146 seats on 5 July 1945. The Labour Party had campaigned on a manifesto openly declaring that its 'ultimate purpose' was 'the establishment of the Socialist Commonwealth of Great Britain – free, democratic, efficient, progressive, public-spirited, its material resources organised in the service of the British people'.[1] This strong commitment to freedom included the removal of restraints on trade unions by the repeal of the Trade Disputes and Trade Unions Act 1927,[2] though no mention was made of the revocation of Order 1305. And in asserting that it was the party of freedom, Labour made it clear that this did not include the 'freedom to exploit other people; freedom to pay poor wages and to push up prices for selfish profit; [or] freedom to deprive the people of the means of living full, happy, healthy lives'.[3] On the contrary, in an echo of the International Labour Organization (ILO) Declaration of Philadelphia,[4] Labour made a commitment to 'full employment', making 'fair shares' and 'good wages' the 'national rule'.[5]

Although there was no explanation of how these objectives would be met, this was not likely to be a problem, even if the foregoing commitments might have sounded rather hollow if read by some trade unionists five years later. To the extent that improvements to living standards would take place under a Labour government through better pay and working conditions, this would be by existing institutions as they had developed during the war under Bevin's guidance. As a result of these developments, there was now in place a comprehensive system of economic democracy, with high levels of trade union membership and virtually saturation collective bargaining (or equivalent)

[1] Labour Party, *Let Us Face the Future* (1945).
[2] ibid.
[3] ibid.
[4] The ILO Declaration of Philadelphia 1944 includes a commitment of the ILO to further among the nations of the world programmes that will achieve 'policies in regard to wages and earnings, hours and other conditions of work calculated to ensure a just share of the fruits of progress to all' (Part III(e)).
[5] Labour Party (n 1).

coverage through multi-employer procedures. There was no need for major institutional reforms as on later occasions when the Labour Party came to office following long periods of Conservative rule.[6] And there was no doubt either about Labour's support for trade unions, the manifesto announcing that the Labour Party stood with 'the great Trade Union and co-operative movements' for 'the wise organisation and use of the economic assets of the nation for the public good'.[7]

II. The Debate Begins

The main issue for the Labour government after the war was thus not the extension of trade union freedom and collective bargaining procedures, but how to manage worker expectations in what was an obviously difficult economic climate. If nothing else, the management of these expectations would shed some light on what a government 'proudly' proclaiming itself to be socialist meant by being 'free, democratic, efficient, progressive, [and] public-spirited'.[8] So far as workers were concerned, it meant not only an aspiration in principle to improve working conditions, but also a commitment to govern with their trade unions. The trade union role in democracy had both an economic and a political dimension. Trade unions had not only acquired a regulatory role in sectoral collective bargaining, but by now also expected to be consulted about major political decisions affecting their interests, and in some instances for government to proceed only with their agreement.[9]

An important issue in the early years of the new government was wages. There were labour shortages and problems of low pay in some sectors, as well as the need to close wage differentials. But concerns were also to emerge about wage inflation and the perceived need to control wage settlements by the better paid. So the challenge for the government was how to increase the wages of some while restricting increases to others, without resorting to coercive legal restraints. The first consideration of these questions at Cabinet level appeared to take place fortuitously on 14 March 1946 when two unconnected disputes were on the agenda for ministers.[10] One was at the Ford automobile works at Dagenham, Essex, which now seemed to be under control, the Cabinet informed that the parties to the dispute had agreed to discuss their problems under the chairmanship of the Chief Industrial Commissioner, Robert Gould.

The second dispute, however, had led to an unofficial strike at the Humber automobile works in Coventry, which was still ongoing, though it was favourably reported that 'there had been little response to the strikers' appeal that other engineering workers in Coventry should also suspend work'.[11] Some comfort was taken from the fact that 'the Amalgamated Engineering Union had taken prompt and firm action in advising their

[6] Notably 1974 and 1997.

[7] Labour Party (n 1).

[8] ibid.

[9] The Ministry of Labour regarded the TUC as being 'free, unfettered, and uncontrolled as Parliament itself. It is the Parliament of Labour, and in that way it will carry on its good work': HC Debs, 19 November 1946, col 760 (George Isaacs, Minister of Labour).

[10] TNA, CAB 128/5/24 (Cabinet Conclusions, 14 March 1946).

[11] ibid.

members to ignore the invitation of the unofficial strikers; and the present position in Coventry seemed to imply local confidence in the Union and in the normal machinery for the settlement of industrial disputes'.[12] There was no mention of Order 1305, and no suggestion that proceedings had even been contemplated (in either case). There was, however, an apparently unanticipated consideration of wages generally, beginning with wage rates in the engineering industry, leading in turn to an exchange of views about the role of government in wage-setting.[13]

The initial concern was with the implications for other sectors if demands for higher wages in engineering were conceded: there was already difficulty in recruiting workers for agriculture because of low pay, while a wage increase in engineering would be likely to provoke demands by coal miners. This led in turn to suggestions by ministers that in order to prevent an upward spiral in wages, the government should formulate and announce a wages policy, which 'without pegging wages by a rigid formula' would 'establish some principles which would help to prevent an unregulated spiral movement'.[14] With this in mind, some thought was given to 'consultation with the Trades Union Congress, who were already concerned about this problem',[15] while George Isaacs (the new Minister of Labour, replacing Bevin, who had become Foreign Secretary) thought 'it might be expedient to appoint a Royal Commission to investigate the wages structure as a whole'.[16] Although the latter suggestion was not accepted, the discussion set in motion an internal Cabinet debate that took two years before a decision was reached in April 1948.

The discussion on 14 March appears to have been dominated by Bevin, who – informed by long experience before the war as an effective trade union general secretary, and by more recent experience as an accomplished Minister of Labour in the Coalition government – was 'strongly opposed to any system by which the State attempted to regulate industrial wages'.[17] He argued that 'if the State took a hand in fixing industrial wages, it would become a party to every industrial dispute', which would be 'fraught with grave danger to the Government'.[18] According to Bevin, the main problem was the need to improve wages and conditions in the less well-paid and more unpleasant industries, 'such as brick works, tanning, gas works, etc'.[19] However, this affected only a relatively small number of workers (about 600,000), so that together with agriculture, the total of low-paid workers was unlikely to exceed one million by much. In Bevin's view, the aim should be to make improvement in these fields, without thereby creating 'a startling change in the total wages bill of the country'.[20]

For Bevin, therefore, 'there was no serious risk in allowing wages to continue to be settled by the traditional procedure of collective bargaining', and that on the contrary the 'introduction of undue rigidity in the wages structure would prejudice the continuing

[12] ibid.
[13] ibid.
[14] ibid.
[15] ibid.
[16] TNA, CAB 195/4/12 (Cabinet Secretary's Notebook, 14 March 1946).
[17] ibid.
[18] TNA, CAB 128/5/24 (14 March 1946).
[19] ibid.
[20] ibid.

development of industrial efficiency'.[21] Bevin's position is recorded more frankly in the Cabinet Secretary's Notebook, where he is reported as saying that once the state starts fixing wages, it is necessary to have sanctions to enforce the limits, and crucially 'you can't use the sanctions'.[22] Moreover, in a 'hybrid industrial system with state fixing wages, every dispute is a dispute with the State. Playing with fire'.[23] But although he was a powerful presence, Bevin's was not the dominant view, the Cabinet Conclusions recording that others thought that it would be difficult to apply the government's policy of planning for full employment 'while leaving industrial wages to be determined, without any guidance from the Government, by the free process of collective bargaining between employers and workers'.[24]

Until Herbert Morrison (then Lord President of the Council) intervened at the end of the discussion, it was only Bevin's views that were specifically identified in the minutes. Nevertheless, the Conclusions record that it was pointed out in discussion that:

> The Government had not consistently applied the principle of leaving these matters wholly to collective bargaining; but they had not clearly defined the principles determining the extent and method of Government intervention in these matters. What was needed was that the Government should review their attitude towards wages questions in the light of the economic policies to which they were committed; and should endeavour to formulate a considered wages policy which could be publicly announced and made the basis of consistent action in relation to the successive claims for wage increases which were likely to be put forward by different industries.[25]

At this point, Morrison is recorded as having announced that because of the need for the government to formulate a wages policy, he had taken the liberty in advance of the meeting of already arranging for a working party of officials to consider the matter, and that he expected to receive their report sometime soon.[26]

Once the working party report had been received and considered by the Lord President, Morrison suggested that recommendations based on the report could be presented to the Cabinet. This was duly done, with a memo from Morrison dated 3 April on wages policy (to which the working party report was conveniently attached) being considered by the Cabinet on 11 April.[27] Both the Working Party and the Lord President's Committee (which modified some of the Working Party's proposals) struck a conciliatory note, carefully navigating a path between the need to respect the autonomy of existing collective bargaining and dispute resolution procedures on the one hand, and the need to address low pay and the need for wage restraint on the other. But in seeking to navigate that path in a way not very far from where government policy eventually landed, the Lord President had to overcome the

[21] ibid.
[22] TNA, CAB 195/4/12 (Cabinet Secretary's Notebook, 14 March 1946).
[23] ibid.
[24] TNA, CAB 128/5/24 (Cabinet Conclusions, 14 March 1946).
[25] ibid.
[26] ibid.
[27] TNA, CAB 129/8/30 ('Wages Policy', Memorandum by the Lord President of the Council, 3 April 1946); TNA, CAB 128/5/33 (Cabinet Conclusions, 11 April 1946).

ultra-laissez-faire Foreign Secretary, and the ultra-interventionist Minister for Fuel and Power, Emanuel Shinwell.

III. The Lord President's Working Party

The Working Party report began by setting out the industrial relations framework inherited by the new government. Informed no doubt by data provided by the Ministry of Labour, the Working Party explained that:

> The system of collective bargaining, by which terms and conditions of employment are settled by means of voluntary collective agreement between employers and trade unions, has been supported for many years by employers and workers and by Governments. By 1914 most of the big staple industries were covered by this machinery. During the war of 1914–1918 special war-time measures were introduced, but the membership of Trade Unions greatly increased and the extension of collective bargaining was maintained. In 1917 the Whitley Committee urged a continuance of the existing system whereby industries made their own agreements and settled their differences themselves, with resort where necessary (and by mutual agreement of both sides) to voluntary arbitration. This policy was enacted in the Industrial Courts Act 1919. In the inter-war period, voluntary collective bargaining was further developed with the approval of successive Governments and of industrial organisations. By 1939 the number of work-people covered by joint voluntary agreements was 10 million.[28]

This explanation very much under-estimates the role of the Ministry of Labour in the construction of the system outlined: the system was not merely developed with the approval or consent of the government, but with its active encouragement bordering on insistence.[29]

It was also acknowledged by the Working Party that the system continued to expand during the war, bringing the number of JICs to 103, 'covering industries that in 1939 had 12 million workers'.[30] The system was further strengthened by the less controversial 'benign elements' of Order 1305, Part III which as explained in Chapter One were offered to the TUC as a sweetener for acceptance of compulsory arbitration, these elements providing for the mandatory application of 'recognised' standard minimum terms and conditions of employment by all employers in a particular sector.[31] By giving *erga omnes* effect to

[28] TNA, CAB 129/8/30 ('Wages Policy', Memorandum by the Lord President of the Council, 3 April 1946, Annex, Official Working Party on Wages Policy, First Report, 26 March 1946, para 5).

[29] See KD Ewing, 'The State and Industrial Relations: Collective Laissez Faire' Revisited' (1998) 5 *Historical Studies in Industrial Relations* 1.

[30] TNA, CAB 129/8/30 ('Wages Policy', Memorandum by the Lord President of the Council, Annex, Official Working Party on Wages Policy, First Report, 26 March 1946, para 6).

[31] An interesting and pioneering article published shortly before Order 1305 was made which draws on the ILO's international survey to compare labour law in Great Britain with Italy, France, Germany and the United States, and makes clear by implication the significance of Part III. There, the unidentifiable author draws attention to the development of collective bargaining as tending more and more to replace individual contracts, a tendency with which 'the State is content to rest, giving to 'the respective associations of employers and workers a free hand to draw up and operate their own collective agreements': J G L, 'Collective Agreements and Collective Labour Disputes' (1930) 55 *Scottish Law Review* 45. However, these agreements did not give rise to binding legal effects (*Downie v James Cowie & Son* (1935) 51 Sh Ct Reps 212), despite TUC policy since 1925 in favour of their 'legalisation' in the form eventually adopted in Order 1305.

sectoral agreements, in the words of the Working Party, the system was designed specifically to provide 'statutory support to joint agreements between employers and Trade Unions, representing substantial numbers in the industries concerned'.[32] In addition, there were 'several enactments which [provided] for the establishment of statutory Wages Boards or Councils with powers to make proposals to the Minister concerned for fixing *minimum* remuneration and holidays with pay'. And as the Working Party further pointed out, 'such proposals when made effective by Statutory Order become legally enforceable', while there were now also 'separate enactments providing for the fixing of statutory minimum remuneration in the case of agriculture, road haulage and the catering industry'.[33]

Wages Councils were of course tripartite bodies which could now be established 'where there is no adequate voluntary machinery for the regulation of wages and conditions, or where any such voluntary machinery is likely to cease to exist or be adequate and a reasonable standard of remuneration will not be maintained'.[34] Although Wages Council orders were legally binding, they were nevertheless made by a process of joint regulation with many of the features of collective bargaining. By 1945, the number of workers covered by statutory minimum wage legislation had risen to three million, and by 1946 the effect of both collective bargaining and statutory minimum wage regulation by Wages Council and similar bodies was to rise to 86 per cent of the workforce, a density level that was to remain roughly constant for 35 years or so. The role of these different arrangements as instruments of government policy was explained by the Working Party in the following terms:

> The underlying object of the Government's approach to wages has been to safeguard industrial peace and maintain stability of the wages structure while preserving flexibility in the treatment of individual wages questions. Effect has been given to this policy by:
>
> (a) Entrusting responsibility for wage regulation to the experienced machinery of joint voluntary negotiation.
> (b) Giving help by way of conciliation or voluntary arbitration in the event of a dispute.
> (c) Continuing to stimulate and assist the setting up of machinery for voluntary negotiation and for the prevention and settlement of disputes.
> (d) Setting up statutory minimum wage fixing machinery.[35]

The purpose of the Working Party's report, however, was not simply to review the existing arrangements, but to recommend greater government involvement in how they might be used. As such, it was part of a government response to the problems identified above: how do they get people into the right jobs and how do they prevent inflationary wage rises? In other words, what can government do in a planned economy directly or indirectly to regulate wages in a system where there was widespread coverage of collective bargaining and collective agreements? The dilemma was nicely expressed by the Working Party as follows:

> There can be no compromise between a democratic and an authoritarian system, and the practical problem must be cast in terms of how our industrial democracy can be persuaded to

[32] TNA, CAB 129/8/30 ('Wages Policy', Memorandum by the Lord President of the Council, Annex, Official Working Party on Wages Policy, First Report, 26 March 1946, para 6).
[33] ibid para 7.
[34] ibid.
[35] ibid para 8.

> understand and accept the new responsibilities imposed upon it by the very different conditions of full employment. A fuller measure of self-discipline on the part of both workers and employers is the price which must be paid if everybody is to have a job and industry is to be consistently prosperous. Education will not eliminate the sectional considerations which underlie the determination of the earnings of labour, nor will it make collective bargaining a perfect or tidy instrument of economic policy. But given the right leadership, there is good cause to expect that a real and vigorous industrial democracy can be combined with the essential requirements of a full employment era.[36]

In addressing the pay problem, the Working Party thus expressly rejected the 'direct fixing of wages by the State' as being 'out of the question'.[37] Quite apart from extreme administrative difficulties, 'such a step would destroy the whole fabric of harmonious industrial relations, the Government would become the focus for workers' claims and strike action, and every major wage issue would be subject to strong political pressure and dangerous sectional passions'.[38] The Working Party was no more sanguine about some kind of hybrid system of 'compulsory limits imposed by the Government within which collective bargaining would be free to operate'.[39] So although the Working Party had no hesitation in concluding that 'the constitutional machinery for joint wage negotiation by organisations of employers and employed remains of fundamental value and should continue to be developed in accordance with established policy', there were nevertheless concerns that in the conditions of full employment:

- 'When negotiating wages it is difficult for organisations of employers or workers in one section of industry to see beyond their immediate interests, or to appreciate the significance of their decisions in relation to the general economic background'.
- 'The system does not at present provide adequate means of adjusting relative levels of wages according to national needs'; and
- 'Left to themselves, wages in general will tend to rise faster than output, which will push prices up and unbalance foreign trade'.[40]

It was thus proposed that there must be a better 'channel of communication to keep the individual employer and worker informed about Government plans and the economic position of the country'.[41] This would require the development of 'regular constitutional channels of consultation between the Government and employers' organisations and Trade Unions on problems affecting the use of labour in connection with economic planning'.[42] In this way the government would not be setting wages, but enabling the institutional structures it promoted for the regulation of terms and conditions of employment to exercise their powers consistently with government policy. The strategy was quite explicit, Morrison pointing out to the Cabinet on 11 April 1946 that the aim was for intermediaries who 'would indirectly influence wages negotiations in particular industries so as to ensure that the results did not run counter to the general

[36] ibid para 22.
[37] ibid para 19.
[38] ibid.
[39] ibid para 20.
[40] ibid para 23.
[41] ibid para 23.
[42] ibid para 24(d).

economic policy of the Government'.[43] To this end, Morrison endorsed a Working Party proposal for some institutional innovation in the form of a tripartite National Industrial Conference, which despite the title would be a permanent body with which the government would consult in the hope that the other two parties (TUC and employers) would give effect to government economic policy.[44]

Although there was strong support from ministers (including the Chancellor of the Exchequer) when Morrison's report was considered by the Cabinet on 11 April 1946, it was opposed by Bevin (who had previously circulated his objections in a separate memo) and by Isaacs. Bevin's memo reinforced the points he had made in Cabinet on 14 March,[45] and was circulated in advance of the meeting on 11 April, at which Morrison's paper was considered. According to Bevin, Morrison's proposals for a wages policy 'if adopted will cause the Government considerable difficulties',[46] objecting to the proposed role of the TUC and the Employers' Confederation in relation to wages and working conditions, as cutting across the democratic mandates and responsibilities of individual trade unions. Bevin continued by attacking the 'second proposal in the paper', that is to say, the proposal for a National Industrial Conference 'to debate these problems without any executive authority or without means of application of the decisions afterwards'.[47] According to Bevin, this would:

> [O]nly create another piece of machinery which will prevent settlement and not aid it. All this was done at the end of the last war by Mr Lloyd George and it turned out a complete fiasco. Not a single trade in the country adopted any of the reports and the executives of either side took little notice. It became a place where people went to make speeches which in the main had a disturbing effect and provided no solution. The body which is established for dealing with what are described as common problems between the State and the industry is the Joint Consultative Committee of the National Joint Advisory Council and is, in my view, sufficient. It represents the Confederation of Employers and the TUC and they work within a very limited but important reference and at no point do they impinge upon the executive authority of the Employers' Associations or the unions. On the other hand, the very voluntary nature of the body causes far more attention to be given to its conclusions and in my view this body has proved that it clearly meets the situation.[48]

Despite the well-judged nature of the Working Party's proposals, the Cabinet discussion on 11 April nevertheless ended inconclusively, with Morrison and Isaacs being sent off by Attlee to resolve their differences about a National Industrial Conference. In a joint report subsequently by Isaacs and Morrison, it was agreed on 30 April that:

> The function of the Conference would be to provide an effective channel through which the Government could discuss economic prospects and policy confidentially with both sides of industry, and a basis upon which they could give their considered views for the guidance of industry, so helping to ensure that the collective bargaining system operated with the fullest measures of independence and efficiency. The Conference would play no part in the joint

[43] TNA, CAB 128/5/33 (Cabinet Conclusions, 11 April 1946).
[44] TNA, CAB 129/8/30 ('Wages Policy', Memorandum by the Lord President of the Council, Annex, Official Working Party on Wages Policy, First Report, 26 March 1946, paras 26–28).
[45] TNA, CAB 129/9/48 ('Wages Policy', Memorandum by the Secretary of State for Foreign Affairs, 10 April 1946).
[46] ibid.
[47] ibid.
[48] ibid.

> negotiating machinery of particular industries, by which wage agreements must continue to be reached. Its purpose would, in fact, be to reinforce the voluntary democratic character of industrial relations by disseminating the fullest understanding among both employers and trade unions of the new problems and responsibilities inherent in a policy of planned full employment.[49]

Although approved by the Cabinet on 6 May, this nevertheless appears to have killed off the initiative, for what was proposed here is a pale shadow of that proposed earlier by the Lord President's Working Party.[50] There is little discussion thereafter of the National Industrial Conference ever having been appointed or having met.[51] This is not to say that the ideas it represented were killed off, other institutional structures being wheeled into place, and another strategy being adopted to render it unnecessary.

Trade Union Voice in Government

Trade unions were now embedded in government in different ways. Several ministers had been trade union officials. Bevin had only recently relinquished his role as TGWU General Secretary, to be replaced by George Isaacs as Minister of Labour. Although an altogether different character from Bevin, Isaacs had been General Secretary of the National Society of Operative Printers and Assistants since 1909, a position which – as discussed in Chapter Four – he retained until 1948. Since 1939, trade unions also had a formal consultative role on the NJAC, which had been established by the government during the war as 'permanent formal machinery' through which 'matters of common interest to employers, workers and the Government could be discussed'.[52] The NJAC consisted of 15 representatives of the TUC and the British Employers' Confederation respectively, under the chairmanship of the Minister of Labour and National Service. A smaller body – the Joint Consultative Committee – of seven representatives from each side took over the NJAC's functions and was credited with having 'contributed greatly to the success of the manpower and general industrial policy on which the country's war-effort was based'.[53]

This procedure was formally renewed after the war in preference to Morrison's proposal for a standing National Industrial Conference, it being 'obvious that regular consultation with the two sides of industry would have an equally important

[49] TNA, CAB 129/9/29 ('Constitution of a National Industrial Conference', Memorandum by the Lord President of the Council and the Minister of Labour and National Service, 30 April 1946), para 2.

[50] TNA, CAB 128/5/42 (Cabinet Conclusions, 6 May 1946).

[51] It is referred to by Shinwell in his Memorandum for the Lord President's Committee, 'A National Wages Policy', Memorandum by the Minister of Fuel and Power, 30 June 1947 (22 October 1946): 'It is not enough, in my view, to set up machinery merely for *discussing* the problems, as envisaged in the recently established National Industrial Conference. This will no doubt fulfil a valuable educative function, but in addition to this there is a judicial or executive job to be done' (para 11). The memorandum is attached to a later Cabinet Memorandum by Shinwell (TNA, CAB 129/19/39, 'A National Wages Policy', Memorandum by the Minister of Fuel and Power, 30 June 1947).

[52] Ministry of Labour, *Industrial Relations Handbook* (HMSO, London, 1961), p 16. First published in 1944, over 100,000 copies of the first and second editions were sold. It was a superb account of the British economic constitution.

[53] ibid.

role in peacetime'.[54] Renewal of the NJAC was agreed with the TUC and the British Employers' Confederation, before being announced to the House of Commons by Ness Edwards on behalf of Isaacs on 30 July 1946. With representatives from local authorities and the nationalised industries augmenting the TUC and British Employers' Confederation (BEC) nominees, the renewed NJAC met thereafter on a quarterly basis, the first meeting taking place on 31 July 1946. Isaacs invited Morrison to attend, along with the Chancellor of the Exchequer (Hugh Dalton) and the President of the Board of Trade (Cripps). The latter was concerned that the NJAC was intruding into his National Production Advisory Council's territory,[55] though as the Ministry of Labour's Ness Edwards pointed out in an Adjournment Debate several months later, these were complementary rather than contradictory initiatives.[56]

The new NJAC took its place alongside other formal and informal methods of consultation between the government and government departments on the one hand, and the TUC and individual trade unions on the other. These other methods were alluded to in correspondence from Tewson to Isaacs on 2 July in anticipation of the 15 July meeting, Tewson stating that the TUC General Council 'have agreed to appoint fifteen members to [their] Side of the Council on the distinct understanding that the existence of the body will not interfere with the present channels of negotiation and consultation between the General Council and other Government Departments'.[57] Evidence of the latter is to be found in the Cabinet Conclusions which are peppered with references to bilateral meetings with the TUC. These covered a wide range of issues affecting trade unions and their the most notable example being the intense bilateral discussions on wages policy leading to the agreement in 1948, which is discussed later in this chapter. As the Cold War intensified, it is clear that the relationship between the government and the TUC extended to national security as well as economic and political questions.

IV. The Cabinet Divided

Subsequent Cabinet discussions reveal that Bevin and Isaacs were not Morrison's only critics. The Lord President effectively occupied the middle ground, flanked on either

[54] ibid. A Ministry of Labour file confirms that the initial proposal for an NIC evolved into the NJAC taking on a wider role: TNA, LAB 10/662 ('Establishment of a National Industrial Conference or National Joint Advisory Council Regarding Arrangements for Consultation between the Government and the Two Sides of Industry on Matters of Common Interest to Employers and Working People').

[55] TNA, LAB 10/662 ('Establishment of a National Industrial Conference or National Joint Advisory Council Regarding Arrangements for Consultation between the Government and the Two Sides of Industry on Matters of Common Interest to Employers and Working People') ('Internal Ministry of Labour Note', 27 November 1946).

[56] HC Debs, 13 November 1946, col 231.

[57] TNA, LAB 10/662 ('Establishment of a National Industrial Conference or National Joint Advisory Council Regarding Arrangements for Consultation between the Government and the Two Sides of Industry on Matters of Common Interest to Employers and Working People').

side by the voluntarists (Bevin and Isaacs) and the interventionists (Emanuel Shinwell and Bevan) respectively. At the far end of the interventionist scale, Shinwell (Minister of Fuel and Power) had argued that a highly centralised wages policy was required, and at the Cabinet meeting on 6 May, he told colleagues that he 'doubted whether the existing methods of piecemeal negotiations in individual industries would work satisfactorily in conditions of full employment now that the discipline imposed by war conditions had been removed'.[58] Apparently supporting Shinwell, Bevan said that the government frequently had to intervene when negotiations had failed – 'after the harm had been done' – and that in any event, with responsibility for maintaining full employment, government intervention was inevitable.[59] The debate occupied the Cabinet's attention for the next 12 months and although it tugged towards Bevin and Isaacs rather than Shinwell and Bevan, it was nevertheless vigorously contested.

In June 1947 Shinwell circulated a paper on the need for a centralised and co-ordinated policy on wages and terms and conditions of employment to be supervised by a tripartite body he variously termed a 'National Wages Authority', 'Central Arbitral Committee', 'Central Advisory Wages Council' or 'Central Advisory Council'.[60] This was a diluted version of more radical proposals that had been circulated on 22 October 1946 (and which was appended to his new submission).[61] There he had suggested the creation of a centralised National Wages Authority to (a) ensure that changes made in wages were not incompatible with price stability, and (b) to develop a structure of relative wages that would help to promote a flow of labour into areas of labour shortage.[62] Although the National Wages Authority would be tripartite and its 'whole purpose' would be 'to ensure that wage changes should be in conformity with the requirements of the Government's general economic policy',[63] the final say on 'so important a function as actually determining wages' should lie with the government, to which the National Wages Authority would make non-binding recommendations.[64]

In revisiting his proposals over a year later, Shinwell emphasised that a satisfactory system of wage-fixing should ensure the following:

(a) All wages should be at least sufficient to provide the wage-earner with a minimum standard of living, covering all the essential needs of life.
(b) This minimum should broadly apply to men and women alike; to meet the greater needs of workers with families to support, the existing system of family allowances should be augmented, by increasing the weekly payments and providing for their further increase if conditions warrant.
(c) Above this minimum, actual wages in different occupations should not vary one from another erratically on account of factors like the bargaining strength of different negotiating parties. They should bear a consistent relationship, depending on the

[58] TNA, CAB 128/5/42 (Cabinet Conclusions, 6 May 1946).
[59] ibid.
[60] TNA, CAB 129/19/39 ('A National Wages Policy', Memorandum by the Minister of Fuel and Power, 30 June 1947).
[61] ibid ('A Proposed Wages Policy', Memorandum by the Minister of Fuel and Power, 22 October 1946).
[62] ibid para 17.
[63] ibid para 13.
[64] ibid para 15.

> different degrees of skill required in different occupations, 'and – especially important in our current manpower situation – the comparative reluctance or readiness of workers to engage in particular occupations; we must, in short, be able to use wage relations towards solving the problem of the vital but undermanned industries'.[65]

As Shinwell pointed out, 'these results were not consistently achieved by the prevailing methods of wage-fixing'. And as he also pointed out, 'wages vary from industry to industry, and even within a single industry, for reasons quite unrelated to differences of skill and to relative shortages of labour in different occupations. One main cause of variation is the strength or weakness of the trade unions concerned'.[66]

Shinwell's initial plans were not dissimilar to the highly regulated system of conciliation and arbitration operating in Australia, albeit with overtly political oversight rather than the judicial oversight there. As such, it would have dramatically changed the role of trade unions in British industrial relations, and it is one which trade unions were unlikely to accept. Yet there could be no change without trade union support, and perhaps for this reason, Shinwell adapted his proposals so as not 'in any way' to prejudice the position of the trade unions. In the later iteration of his proposals, the National Wages Authority would no longer be tripartite, but would be composed of 'men of broad knowledge and experience of industrial relations'. All wage claims would be referred to the Authority, which would be required to report on each claim, taking into account the wider economic and social issues raised. A report would be handed down by the Authority and then the claim would – so Shinwell proposed – be negotiated in the normal way, with an expectation that the negotiating parties would 'be fully appraised of the economic and social factors involved in changing particular wage rates'.[67]

These proposals (in both forms) were anathema to Isaacs, who replied to Shinwell's paper on 3 July 1947.[68] Isaacs had wholly rejected the idea of a 'central arbitral body' in 1946, when Shinwell had initially aired his proposals, and he reiterated his objections in his 1947 paper, where in paragraph 20 he concluded that:

> (1) I have very carefully considered the proposal to focus arbitration authority in a central body, but I have come to the conclusion that the risk to the established machinery involved in anything that might impair general confidence in its independence is too great to be taken. We cannot afford it.
>
> (2) As an alternative to the proposal in (1) we should continue the policy of:
>
> (a) Drawing arbitrators from a select body of men who will have a knowledge of a number of industries and can be depended upon to have a broad and statesmanlike outlook.

[65] TNA, CAB 129/19/39 ('A National Wages Policy', Memorandum by the Minister of Fuel and Power, 30 June 1947), para 14. On the contemporary significance of Shinwell's ideas, see KD Ewing, '"A Just Share of the Fruits of Progress": The Role of Collective Bargaining' in K Arabadjieva, N Countouris, B Luna Fabris and W Zwysen (eds), *Transformative Ideas: Ensuring a Just Share of Progress for All* (European University Institute, Brussels, 2023).

[66] TNA, CAB 129/19/39 ('A National Wages Policy', Memorandum by the Minister of Fuel and Power, 30 June 1947), para 5.

[67] ibid para 7.

[68] TNA, CAB 129/19/40 ('Development of National Arbitration Machinery', Memorandum by the Minister of Labour and National Service, 3 July 1947).

(b) Employing the same individual as Chairman of a number of Wages Councils or Wages Boards, and adopting the same policy in regard to the independent members of such Councils and Boards. This, I am satisfied, is the best way of achieving the two important objectives of—

(i) ensuring that in making awards proper regard is paid to the general economic position of the country;

(ii) a reasonable relativity is maintained between the awards made to different classes of workers.

(3) Consideration should be given to the possibility of making appointments to bodies like the Burnham Committee on teachers' remuneration and the Rushcliffe Committee on nurses' remuneration, which would have the effect of applying the same principles to those Committees.

(4) With a view to bringing home to the workers and the public as a whole the dangers of unrestrained claims for improved remuneration we should take steps to make the facts of our economic position more widely known, and for this purpose we should—

(a) press on, in association with the two sides of industry, with the establishment of Joint Production Committees or their equivalent;

(b) take full advantage of the co-operation of the National Joint Advisory Council in disseminating information relating to our economic position.

(5) The results to date of the working of the existing system have been most satisfactory. There seems to be danger of an upward trend in prices that may affect wages, but the change-over to the new interim index of retail prices should prove a stabilising influence.[69]

At the bottom of it, however, a centralised system would be contrary to Isaacs' unyielding commitment to the existing structures. He had warned earlier of the danger that rulings on wages 'could be debated in Parliament'. Making wage-setting a 'political matter' would be 'disastrous to our whole system of industrial relations'.[70] Maintaining that the detail of wage rates had to be determined 'by discussion at shop level',[71] Isaacs was backed by Morrison, who re-entered the debate on 14 July 1947.[72] That said, Morrison introduced a little scepticism, noting in a fresh memorandum that 'there appears to be a wish in some Trade Union quarters and even among some ministers to adopt a *laissez faire* attitude and to assert that everything will quickly come right in the wash of industrial adaption'.[73] Remarkably, Morrison questioned whether the government could go on attacking the laissez-faire inclinations of the opposition and private industry (no doubt he did not need to remind colleagues that they were overseeing the implementation of an interventionist 'planned' economic

[69] ibid para 20.

[70] TNA, CAB/129/19/45 ('National Wages Policy', Memorandum by the Minister of Labour and National Service, 29 October 1946), para 3. The Memorandum was drafted for the Lord President's Committee in response to Shinwell's 1946 proposals for a central wage setting body. Isaac's text is appended to a memo dated 8 July 1947 written in response to Shinwell's revival of these proposals, hence the odd reference to a 1946 document in a 1947 file.

[71] ibid para 5.

[72] TNA, CAB 129/20/2 ('National Wages Policy', Memorandum by the Lord President, 14 July 1947).

[73] ibid para 3.

programme), yet 'adopt a Manchester School attitude where our own friends and our own "interests" are concerned'.[74] He added:

> In all these matters, Socialists should apply only one test – the public interest, which in the not very long run is also the interest of the workers. As I said in my Margate speech (which was approved by the Prime Minister and well received by the delegates), we stand for the worker's right to his full share of production, but we are in danger of overdrawing on our overdrafts. The reception of this speech at Margate, my contacts with the Parliamentary Labour Party and my experience at public meetings convince me that the workers are ready to face the facts if our Trade Union colleagues and ourselves are ready to state them courageously and fully. The workers must be persuaded to abandon the mentality of nineteenth century capitalism, to realise the social consequences of the blessings of full employment, and to recognise that in our fairly advanced stage of transition to a new social order, the first economic duty of each man and woman is to the nation as a whole.[75]

Morrison nevertheless endorsed Isaacs' paragraph 20 (referred to above) in paragraph 10 of his own memorandum, albeit with additional bells and whistles. It was paragraph 10 of the Morrison memo that was then approved by the Cabinet on 17 July, the Cabinet thus indirectly endorsing Isaacs.[76] It should be pointed out, however, that Isaacs had moved closer to Morrison than Morrison had moved to Isaacs. The key element of Morrison's original position was a subtle strategy whereby 'without directly intervening' government would 'promote reasonable settlements'.[77] This is not any less a repudiation of collective laissez-faire than was the more formally interventionist position of Shinwell. It is true that by this stage, there was no reference to the National Industrial Conference (NIC), but as paragraph 20 of the Isaacs memo made clear, the NIC was largely unnecessary. As Bevin had pointed out, there was already in existence a much less grandly titled National Joint Advisory Council on which employers and trade unions were represented,[78] well able – as paragraph 20(4)(b) of Isaacs' memo made clear – to perform the role anticipated by Morrison for the NIC.

Government policy appeared to be settled at the Cabinet meeting on 17 July 1947 as being one of interference through control of wage-determining bodies on the one hand and 'education' on the other – interference nevertheless, and interference designed to prevent the free operation of 'Manchester school' principles. Summing up on 17 July, Attlee stated that it was clear that a positive wages policy was necessary. However, he warned that 'in countries where the government had intervened directly', the results 'had not always been satisfactory', and consequently 'it would be unwise to adopt' Shinwell's proposals 'at least at any rate for the present'.[79] The Conclusions for 17 July 1947 record that Isaacs' paragraph 20 (in the form of Morrison's paragraph 10) 'should be followed up', adding that 'there should be an enquiry into what special new machinery ought to be set up in order to deal with claims by workers in socialised industries'. It is also recorded that it would be helpful 'if a few of the ministers mainly concerned were to

[74] ibid para 4.
[75] ibid.
[76] TNA, CAB 128/10/13 (Cabinet Conclusions, 17 July 1947).
[77] TNA, CAB 128/2/1 (Cabinet Conclusions, 1 November 1945).
[78] See Ministry of Labour (n 52) pp 16–17.
[79] TNA, CAB 128/10/13 (Cabinet Conclusions, 17 July 1947).

have a preliminary informal talk with the representatives of the trade unions'.[80] The Cabinet evidently saw Morrison and Isaacs as the men who should talk to the unions for this purpose.[81]

V. The Importance of the TUC

Yet despite the foregoing, it was not long before the position had to be looked at again as 'the economic situation darkened'.[82] A meeting of the Cabinet on 13 November 1947 revealed tension between Cripps (then Minister for Economic Affairs) and Isaacs, the former arguing that a government statement should be issued to the effect that the traditional differentials between wages levels in different industries must be abandoned in favour of new differentials more relevant to the national interest.[83] The statement would set out the principles to which, in the government's view, those engaged in wage negotiations should have regard. He also proposed the establishment of a central tribunal to which appeals from existing arbitral bodies might be taken by either side, and to which decisions arrived at by such bodies could be referred by the Minister of Labour, after consultation with the NJAC, 'if he considered that the national interest had not been taken into full account'.[84] Isaacs' objection was predictable, on the ground that it would 'undermine the position of the executive councils of the trade unions and destroy the authority of the existing arbitral bodies', adding that 'there was no way of enforcing a limitation of wage payments to individual workers'.

Although arguments swung both ways in the ensuing discussion, it was said that 'Government intervention in the negotiation of wages settlements was in principle undesirable and would in the end lead to a clash between the workers and the Government'. The Cabinet was urged to 'think twice before abandoning, in order to meet a temporary emergency, the principle of collective bargaining, subject to independent arbitration, on which the strength of the trade union movement had been founded'. Unsurprisingly, ministers appeared to accept Isaacs' suggestion that 'before the Cabinet reached any firm decisions, the Trades Union Congress, who were now conscious of the need to devise some means of preventing wage increases which would injure the national interest, should be allowed to make their own suggestions to the Government'.[85] Although the Prime Minister was due to meet the TUC a few days later, it was accepted that the government was not in a position to formulate proposals in time for the meeting. As a result, ministers should merely take note of what the TUC had to say. In the meantime, Isaacs was invited to prepare and circulate proposals for a 'more positive', but limited wages policy dealing with 'cases where claims for increased wages were made

[80] ibid.
[81] They also requested that Bevan work with the Committee on the Socialisation of Industries to consider what measures were necessary to deal with pay in the nationalised industries, as well as industries dependent on government subsidies and workers employed by local authorities.
[82] SH Beer, *Modern British Politics* (Faber & Faber, London, 1965), p 203.
[83] TNA, CAB 128/10/39 (Cabinet Conclusions, 13 November 1947).
[84] ibid.
[85] ibid.

by employees of public boards and local authorities, or where the grant of a wages claim would involve an additional charge on the Exchequer'.[86]

It was not until 23 January 1948 that Isaacs produced the proposals that had been requested at the Cabinet meeting on 13 November, by which time the TUC had issued on 31 December 1947 its Interim Report on the Economic Situation.[87] According to Isaacs, the TUC in this latter report had displayed 'considerable courage, enjoining as they do upon members and leaders of trade unions that they should show caution, restraint and a sense of responsibility in wages negotiations'. But at the same time, he pointed out that 'the TUC express themselves as completely opposed to the imposition of specific limits and restrictions on wage increases and to the establishment of machinery for the purpose of controlling wages'. The attitude of the TUC on this question was in his view 'conclusive'.[88] By now, however, the economic situation had become even more grave, and Cripps – appointed Chancellor of the Exchequer following the resignation of Hugh Dalton coincidentally on 13 November – had produced a draft government statement on the need for wage restraint, an approach which seemed to unite the Cabinet, winning the support of Isaacs, who saw it as a way of reconciling the competing shades of opinion. The Chancellor's proposals are acknowledged by Isaacs in his memorandum of 23 January, and his response thereto is worth repeating in full:

> 3. Within the last few days the Secretary of State for Foreign Affairs has proposed that in our foreign publicity we should go over to the offensive against Communism and that the main feature of such action on our part should be to show that the way of life of a social-democratic State is far superior to life in a communistic or authoritarian State. I cannot help feeling that the force of this argument would be seriously weakened if, at the same time, we introduced a measure of State control, under whatever disguise, in that sphere in which more than almost any other our people are attached to the principles of free discussion and negotiation – namely, the determination of wages and conditions of employment.
>
> 4. Nevertheless I am very conscious that the Government, having deliberately adopted the policy of a planned economy, including the socialisation of a number of the most important industries and services, should face up to the full implications of that policy. In particular I agree that the Government cannot stand aside in face of movements which not only by their inflationary effect threaten the standards of life in this country but by raising prices above a competitive level might seriously prejudice the export policy upon the success of which our whole future depends. In the field of wages this means, in my view, that the Government should take all steps in their power by way of guidance, exhortation and appeal to persuade both employers and trade unions to exercise restraint in negotiations relating to wages and to keep before them as an overriding consideration the wellbeing of the country as a whole. I am, therefore, attracted by the idea, which was tentatively put forward by the Chancellor of the Exchequer himself in our discussion on 13th November, that the Government should issue a statement on wages policy which would set out the principal economic considerations to be borne in mind in wages negotiations and, if an agreed and suitable form of words can be found,

[86] ibid.

[87] TNA, CAB 129/23/28 ('Wages Policy', Memorandum by the Minister of Labour and National Service, 23 January 1948).

[88] ibid para 2.

> the principles which in the Government's view should govern wage movements at the present time.[89]

Isaacs appended to his document a suggested draft statement, based largely on a text that had been circulated previously by Cripps.[90] The document was discussed by the Cabinet on 23 January, where Isaacs explained that 'the reference to a Central Appeal Tribunal had been omitted' and that 'additional paragraphs had been inserted to emphasise the importance of strict adherence to the terms of wage agreements', with a passage warning also that 'the Government would not automatically increase grants or subsidies, or concur in increased prices, in order to compensate for additional costs resulting from increases in wages'.[91] Isaacs also insisted that the TUC should be 'fully consulted' before the statement was made public. With consensus breaking out, it was agreed that a revised draft tabled by Cripps should be examined in detail by Cripps, Morrison and Isaacs before being presented to the Cabinet at its next meeting on 3 February. Recognising the importance of the initiative, ministers thought it appropriate that 'special steps' should be taken to emphasise its significance, with a parliamentary statement by the Prime Minister to be 'supported and amplified by the fullest publicity campaign'.[92] After further revisions and ministerial discussions,[93] it was agreed by the Cabinet on 2 February that Attlee, Morrison and Cripps would make the final touches to the text, which would be published as a White Paper (*Personal Incomes, Costs and Prices*, Cmd 7321, 1948).[94]

As agreed by the Cabinet, the Prime Minister made a lengthy parliamentary statement on 4 February.[95] The statement gave a very full and at times a verbatim account of the contents of the White Paper, including the purpose of the policy it contained, which was to impose tight controls on wages, prices and profits. As such, it purported to be governed by three (contradictory) principles: freedom of contract between individual workers and employers; strict adherence to the terms of collective agreements (which would be mandatory by virtue of Order 1305, though this was not referred to by Attlee); and no bargaining by individual employers beyond the terms of collective agreements, the government unable to 'stress too highly the importance which they attach to this [third] principle'.[96] There would be, however, a measure of flexibility: wage restraint did not mean that there could not be wage increases at all, Attlee noting that it would not be right 'to stabilize all incomes as they stand today', and that there might be cases where increases could be justified in the national interest, 'to man up a particular undermanned industry' where 'only an increase in wages will attract the necessary labour'. But each claim would have to be considered on its merits in the national interest and not on the basis of 'maintaining a former relativity'.[97]

[89] ibid.

[90] TNA, CAB 129/22/14 ('Wages Policy', Memorandum by the Minister of Labour and National Service, 11 November 1947).

[91] TNA, CAB 128/12/9 (Cabinet Conclusions, 2 February 1948).

[92] ibid.

[93] TNA, CAB 129/24/38 ('Statement on Personal Incomes, Costs and Profits', 30 January 1948).

[94] TNA, CAB 128/12/9 (Cabinet Conclusions, 2 February 1948).

[95] See HC Debs, 4 February 1948, col 1821.

[96] ibid col; 1823; see also *Personal Incomes, Costs and Prices*, Cmd 7321, 1948, para 7.

[97] HC Debs, 4 February 1948, cols 1823–24; see also *Personal Incomes, Costs and Prices* (n 96).

The Prime Minister having addressed the House of Commons, the matter was before the Cabinet briefly on the following day, when ministers were made aware of the TUC's displeasure, not so much because of its content but because of what was regarded as a discourtesy.[98] With not a little pomposity, the TUC thought that it should have been consulted before the statement to Parliament, about which Attlee put them right. At this stage, however, the TUC had not agreed to the policy, and tensions were aroused again when Isaacs wrote to various Wages Boards and Wages Councils on 9 March in the following terms:

> As was made clear in the subsequent debate in Parliament on Thursday, 12th February, the present economic situation in the country calls for the utmost co-operation throughout industry and the Minister trusts, therefore, that when considering any matter likely to affect personal incomes, costs and prices, Wages Boards and Wages Councils will have full regard to the principles of the White Paper, a copy of which is enclosed for information. As Wages Boards and Councils will appreciate, the Minister will be under a duty henceforward when considering wages regulation proposals, to be satisfied that in reaching the proposals full regard has been had to the principles of the White Paper. For this purpose I am to request that any proposals submitted should now be accompanied by a memorandum explaining the considerations that have led the Board or Council to form the opinion that its proposals are in accordance with those principles.[99]

It appears, however, that the TUC had objected to this letter because it 'might be interpreted as meaning that the Government regarded the principles indicated in the White Paper as being in the nature of a directive imposed by the Government rather than proposals for which the voluntary support of trade unions was being sought in the national interest'.[100] Following a meeting between the Prime Minister and a TUC deputation on 23 March, it was agreed to 'withdraw the letter and to substitute another document which would express more clearly the Government's intention'.[101] A replacement letter was drafted to be sent to the Wages Boards and Wages Councils, and this was approved by the Cabinet on 25 March, on the understanding that the additional precaution would be taken to consult the TUC and the British Employers' Confederation before it was issued.[102] The new letter set an altogether different tone:

> As was made clear in the subsequent debate in Parliament on Thursday, 12th February, the present economic situation in the country calls for the utmost co-operation throughout industry and the Minister trusts, therefore, that when considering any matter likely to affect personal incomes, costs and prices, Wages Boards and Wages Councils will have full regard to the principles of the White Paper, a copy of which is enclosed for information.
>
> As is emphasised in the White Paper itself, the Government regard it as of first importance to maintain unimpaired the full responsibility of voluntary joint negotiating machinery for determining the terms and conditions of employment of workers so covered. Equally, where

[98] TNA, CAB 128/12/11 (Cabinet Conclusions, 5 February 1948).
[99] TNA, CAB 129/25/76 ('Statement on Personal Incomes, Costs and Profits: Follow-up Action', 9 March 1948).
[100] TNA, CAB 128/12/25 (Cabinet Conclusions, 25 March 1948).
[101] ibid.
[102] TNA, CAB 129/26/97 ('Statement on Personal Incomes, Costs and Profits: Follow-up Action', 24 March 1948).

> Wages Boards and Councils are concerned the Government do not wish in any way to derogate from their authority as the bodies charged with considering and negotiating proposals relating to the terms and conditions of employment of workers covered by the respective Boards and Councils.
>
> The legal provisions under which Wages Boards and Councils operate are not affected by the White Paper which should not be regarded as being in the nature of a legal pronouncement or directive by the Government; it sets out principles for which the Government seek the support of industry. As an administrative measure however to assist him in the discharge of his statutory responsibility for confirming proposals, the Minister will need to be informed that in their deliberations, Councils and Boards have taken the White Paper into full account. For this purpose I am to request that proposals should now be accompanied by a memorandum for the Minister's information, showing that this has been done.[103]

The Government's decision to withdraw the letter of 9 March 'had been an important factor' in securing trade union approval for the White Paper at a special conference of TUC affiliates in London on 24 March.[104] The Cabinet was informed on 25 March that the TUC-convened special conference 'had endorsed by a majority of over 3 million votes the report of the General Council urging support for the Government's policy on wages and prices'.[105] As the Cabinet Conclusions also record, however, 'the speeches at the conference had shown that there was much opposition to the Governments policy', especially from the group of engineering unions, the shop workers and civil servants. It was soon clear that although endorsed by the TUC, this agreement was not going to be observed by all unions in all circumstances. The Cabinet was told on 6 April of a vehicle builders' dispute in which an *official strike* had been called *after* the dispute had been referred by Isaacs to the National Arbitration Tribunal under Order 1305.[106] So even if a large number of individual unions voted to support the policy, it did not follow that all workers in all workplaces would necessarily agree to be bound by it, raising the spectre of unofficial action, and 'a clash between the workers and the Government', a prescient fear raised at the Cabinet meeting on 13 November 1947. As Isaacs had pointed out, 'there was no way of enforcing a limitation of wage payments to individual workers'.[107]

The Wage Restraint Bargain of 1948

The 'Wage Restraint Bargain of 1948' was an important initiative for multiple reasons,[108] with Samuel Beer, the Harvard-based British historian, drawing attention to the constitutional significance of the agreement 'as a kind of extra-governmental regulation'.[109] This of course directly contradicts Isaacs' claim in his revised letter written to the wages councils and wages boards following the TUC's complaint

[103] TNA, CAB 129/26/97 ('Statement on Personal Incomes, Costs and Profits: Follow-up Action', Annex II, 'Proposed Letter to Wages Boards and Wages Councils', 24 March 1948).
[104] TNA, CAB 128/12/25 (Cabinet Conclusions, 25 March 1948).
[105] ibid.
[106] TNA, CAB 128/12/26 (Cabinet Conclusions, 5 April 1948).
[107] TNA, CAB 128/10/38 (Cabinet Conclusions, 13 November 1947).
[108] The 'Wage Restraint Bargain' is the term used by Beer (n 82) p 205.
[109] ibid.

in March 1948. Subsequent developments nevertheless reveal that in practice, the policy was treated by the Cabinet as if it was something in the nature of the legal pronouncement or a government directive that it was expressly proclaimed not to be. An early sign of this was at the Cabinet meeting on 15 April 1948, when Isaacs was reminded of his obligation to find information about public sector wage claims, which he had been reluctant to do because of what he had understood to be government policy of not interfering in the administration of these bodies. Isaacs had been specifically instructed to obtain this information at the Cabinet meeting on 19 February,[110] an instruction repeated on 15 April:

> *The Government had a special responsibility for ensuring that unjustifiable claims for higher wages or shorter hours made by public employees were not granted and it was impossible to accept a state of affairs in which they would know less about claims by these employees than about claims by workers in private industry. It had been agreed that the Minister of Labour should be responsible for questions of wages or conditions of work which arose in socialised industries, and there seemed to be no reason why he should not make a direct request to the boards of these industries and to local authorities to supply him with the information asked for by the Cabinet at their meeting on 19th February.*[111]

A better illustration of the Wage Restraint Bargain 'as a kind of extra-governmental regulation' is illustrated by the Cabinet meeting on 11 June 1948, where there was discussion of the procedure that 'ought to be followed by the Minister of Labour when one party to wage negotiations, within either the public or the private sector, had reported to him that the negotiations had broken down, or had applied for arbitration'.[112] The Cabinet was not now developing policy, but determining how existing policy should be interpreted and implemented. In dealing with such cases, Isaacs revealed that his department's aim was 'to help the parties to reach agreement by negotiation', without suggesting 'what should be the terms of the settlement', though sometimes it was 'possible and desirable to exercise informal influence on one or both of the parties, but in doing this they had regard to the principles set out in the White Paper'. A robust intervention by Cripps proposed that 'no action ought to be taken by the Ministry of Labour which might be interpreted by the employers concerned as an invitation by the Government to make concessions on a disputed wages claim which would be at variance with the principles set out in the White Paper'. Although this was agreed, ministers appeared willing to cut Isaacs more slack than Cripps had appeared to propose, the Cabinet taking note that:

> *[I]t was the policy of the Minister of Labour to refrain from taking any action on any wage dispute, within either the public or the private sector of employment, which might encourage the employers concerned to suppose that the Government expected them to grant an increase of wages, unless the increase could be justified as being in accordance with the principles set out in the White Paper on Personal Incomes, Costs and Prices; and agreed that*

[110] TNA, CAB 128/12/15 (Cabinet Conclusions, 19 February 1948).
[111] TNA, CAB 128/12/28 (Cabinet Conclusions, 15 April 1948).
[112] TNA, CAB 128/12/38 (Cabinet Conclusions, 11 June 1948).

> *the Chancellor of the Exchequer and the Minister of Labour should discuss with officials of the Ministry of Labour the best means of giving effect to this policy.*

From the perspective of both constitutional law and labour law, it is thus difficult to under-estimate the importance of the Wage Restraint Bargain of 1948. For labour lawyers in particular, it is important not only because of what it tells us about the historic role of the state in labour law and industrial relations institutions, but also about the changing role of institutional actors. As pointed out by Vic Allen, the Bargain was 'the beginning of a new phase of trade union behaviour in relation to the state', the first time that trade unions had made concessions to government since the First World War when they had been made to assist with the prosecution of the war. He continued:

> *Now in 1948, not only members of the General Council but rank-and-file members of union executives, agreed to exercise wage restraint. Although it could be argued that by their action they were helping to stabilize prices and were therefore maintaining real-wage levels, their decision was equivalent to a suspension of the basic function of unions. The determination of money wages had always been regarded as the raison d'etre of union activity; real wages and prices fell outside its scope.*[113]

As we will see, however, it is doubtful that trade union leaders or trade union executives were speaking for their rank-and-file members, and indeed it was the failure to take trade union members with them that led ultimately to the end of the experiment. An early sign of trouble was the continuing unofficial action on the docks where there were longstanding grievances, raising questions about the ability of all trade unions to deliver an implicit yet key part of the White Paper, namely the government's insistence that collective agreements should be followed as if they were legal instruments. The disputes on the waterfront also raised questions about the steps available to government to enforce the White Paper's expectations against those unwilling to be bound.

VI. Conclusion

The challenge for labour law after the war was thus not how to build or rebuild institutional structures that war had destroyed, but, on the contrary, how to contain and control the operation of structures that the war had preserved. As such, the main problem for government was how to manage expectations and, in particular, demands for higher wages, while responding to the related problem of getting people into jobs where labour was scarce. This provoked a fascinating discussion between ministers which raised questions about how socialist beliefs and ambitions would affect the operation of collective bargaining procedures. Just as importantly, it raised important constitutional questions about economic decision making in the post-war government, highlighting

[113] V L Allen, *Trade Unions and the Government* (Longmans, London, 1960), p 286.

in particular the role of the TUC as a political institution the consent of which should be actively sought. There was, however, very little discussion in Cabinet about either the risk of strikes or the laws to deal with the risk. True, Order 1305 was referred to by both the Lord President on 3 April 1946[114] and the Minister of Labour on 3 July 1947.[115] But the instrument was mentioned only in passing, with the caveat that it had been introduced in 1940 at the request of the industrial parties, and had survived with their continuing agreement. According to Isaacs, moreover, the government had 'no intention under present circumstances of retaining this form of machinery as a permanent feature of our industrial legislation'.[116]

Indeed, although 'penalties are provided for breach of [Order 1305]', Isaacs appeared to reinforce its perceived marginal significance by referring to 'experience during the war', which was said to have 'shown that they are quite ineffective if required to deal with any large numbers of men'.[117] And yet, Order 1305 fitted nicely with post-war wages policy in a highly developed system of centralised collective bargaining in which it was likely to have been an integral and essential part. This is because under Order 1305, any disputes could be referred by the Ministry of Labour to one of various forms of dispute resolution provided in Articles 2 and 3, those taking part in dispute resolution no doubt responsible individuals who would have due regard to government policy on wages in the manner provided by the White paper. The blind spot, however, was unofficial action and the grievances of workers which this very highly centralised system did not fully accommodate. There was no reason in principle why unofficial disputes could not be reported to the Ministry under Order 1305, Article 2, as some had done during the war, albeit invariably with the co-operation of a Regional Industrial Relations Officer. But as we will discuss more fully in Chapters Eleven and Twelve, Isaacs refused to accept referrals from non-official sources, perhaps on the basis that the resolution of these matters was for the unions themselves to address internally. The only option for workers whose union was unresponsive to their grievances was to take industrial action and to risk prosecution under Order 1305 as a result.

[114] TNA, CAB 129/8/30 ('Wages Policy', Memorandum by the Lord President of the Council, 3 April 1946, Annex, Official Working Party on Wages Policy), para 6.
[115] TNA, CAB 129/19/40 ('Development of National Arbitration Machinery', Memorandum by the Minister of Labour and National Service), paras 2–8.
[116] ibid para 5.
[117] ibid.

6

Controlling Trade Union Activists

MI5 and Special Branch

I. Introduction

As we saw in Chapters Four and Five, the state played a prominent role in post-war industrial relations, adjusting the legal foundations of trade union freedom, and developing a framework of economic democracy that had its origins in the 1930s, if not before. The system was very highly centralised with high levels of government oversight and intervention. Industrial disputes were to be dealt with peacefully under the procedures established by Order 1305, a system of compulsory arbitration which, as we will discuss, was weakened in practice by the absence of any settled procedure for dealing with unofficial industrial action. In this chapter we are concerned with another role of the state: the work of government agencies in the monitoring and surveillance of trade unions and trade union activists with a view to ensuring that the system was not subverted for political purposes, and more specifically, that trade unions were not subverted for political ends. The alleged source of this potential subversion was the Communist Party of Great Britain, which it was claimed existed to serve the interests of a foreign power.

Although the Communist Party supported the war effort (sometimes with embarrassing fervour),[1] even during the war suspicions remained in government about its intentions. Citing extensively from well-placed sources, an assessment prepared in 1943 concluded as follows:

> These quotations are given to show that the Communist Party in this country believes that a revolutionary situation may develop in the comparatively near future, and has taken steps to see that its leaders are in a position to take advantage of it, if it should occur. It is not suggested that every member of the Communist Party is aware of the Party's revolutionary programme, but the Party itself believes that its leaders, properly instructed, will be able to carry the rank and file with them far down the road to revolution.[2]

[1] See especially J McIlroy and A Campbell, 'Beyond Betteshanger: 'Order 1305 in the Scottish Coalfields during the Second World War, Part 2: The Cardowan Story' (2003) 16 *Historical Studies in Industrial Relations* 39.

[2] TNA, CAB 66/35/9 ('Communist Party of Great Britain', Memorandum by the Home Secretary, 13 March 1943).

Here we consider how the security and intelligence services were used to (i) monitor trade unions to ensure that they did not stray from the path prescribed for them, and (ii) search for information to justify prosecutions where subversive activity was allegedly taking place. 'Subversion' is used not only in the formal sense of sedition (political subversion), but also in the informal sense of unofficial action (subverting the industrial relations system as it had been constructed). The adverse impact of each on UK politics and industrial relations was believed to be compounded by the simultaneous presence of both; they could be said to have been thought by elements in government and in the security services to have enjoyed something of a symbiotic relationship.

II. Subversion, the Communist Party and Trade Unions

As we have written elsewhere, the post-war Labour government had effectively declared war on the Communist Party. Party members and supporters were excluded from the Labour Party.[3] They were also removed from employment by the civil service and government contractors,[4] with Attlee announcing to Parliament on 15 March 1948 the civil service 'purge' of Communists engaged in secret work.[5] The existence of a Communist conspiracy on the home front became thereafter a defining feature of trade disputes for the Attlee government. Alongside the penetration of the official trade union structures, there was concern about the Communist Party's role in instigating unofficial action by trade unionists, a concern previously highlighted by the Lord President of the Council in the 'most secret' memorandum about the Communist Party referred to above, which he had circulated to colleagues when Home Secretary in the Coalition government.[6] According to the Morrison memorandum – focusing mainly on the engineering industry and almost certainly written with input from MI5 – one of the tactics of the Party before it changed its mind about the war was to 'exploit existing grievances in the factories' rather than openly foment strikes: 'there was not a factory in which there was not a grievance which could be turned into a strike'.[7]

The perception that the Communist Party was responsible for fomenting strikes persisted after the war, as relations between Soviet Russia and the Allies began to chill, and as reports of industrial action began to make their way to ministers and to be discussed in Cabinet. An indication of these concerns is revealed by a Cabinet meeting on 17 November 1947, where the Home Secretary and the Minister of Labour reported on a strike at the Savoy Hotel in London, a dispute it was claimed was being exploited by unnamed people acting under the directions of the Communist Party.[8] It was thought

[3] J Mahoney, 'Civil Liberties in Britain during the Cold War' (1989) 33 *American Journal of Legal History* 53.

[4] On the origins of the purge and the impact of the announcement, see KD Ewing, J Mahoney and A Moretta, *MI5, the Cold War and the Rule of Law* (Oxford University Press, Oxford, 2020), pp 230–51. On vetting and purging the civil service and industry, see chs 9–12.

[5] HC Debs, 15 March 1948, col 1703.

[6] TNA, CAB 66/35/9 ('Communist Party of Great Britain', Memorandum by the Home Secretary, 13 March 1943). Morrison was a noted red-baiter. See William Gallacher, *The Case for Communism* (Penguin, Harmondsworth, 1949), p 195.

[7] ibid.

[8] TNA, CAB 128/10/39 (Cabinet Conclusions, 17 November 1947).

that one of the objects of the Communists was to cause inconvenience 'by continuing this strike throughout the week of the Royal Wedding'.[9] Some 16 months later, a sudden stoppage of work at Barking Power Station was said by the Minister of Labour as having 'not been justified by the ostensible grounds of dispute', as well as being 'in breach of the men's contract of service'.[10] Stoppages had been threatened at other power stations on 'equally trivial and unjustified grounds', Communists said to be 'responsible for these occurrences'.[11] It was no surprise then that the government should highlight the role of the Communist Party in the dock strike of 1949.

Allegations of Communist instigation in the dock strike –which had been organised in support of the Canadian Seamen's Union in dispute with their Canadian employer about being replaced by the Seafarers' International Union (SIU), a rival US-based organisation – were made by Isaacs in parliamentary statements on a number of occasions in 1949. On 28 June, he claimed that it was 'intolerable that our trade and our recovery should be interfered with [by strikes] in this way', and that it was 'abundantly clear that the Communists, in their support of the Canadian Seamen's Union, are completely indifferent to the loss and hardship that may be occasioned to our dockers and their families and the rest of the community'.[12] Returning to the theme a week later, the Minister added that 'the men [were] in breach of their agreements and of the provisions of the Dock Labour Scheme',[13] claiming that the action was 'nothing but a Communist manoeuvre'.[14] This predictably drew derision from the two Communist MPs, one of whom asserted that the strike was 'an exhibition of working-class loyalty on the part of the dockers', asking Isaacs why he repeated this 'childish plea about Communism'.[15]

Some time after the dispute was resolved and the men returned to work, a White Paper was published on behalf of the Ministry of Labour. With no indication of its authorship or the sources relied upon in its 46 pages (including appendices),[16] the document was presumably drafted by civil servants. Isaacs wrote in the preface that the industrial action had 'one aim and one aim only – to restore the fortunes of the Communist dominated Canadian Seamen's Union'.[17] He also wrote about British trade union leaders opposed to the action being 'assailed and abused by the Communists in this country who were supporting the strikes'.[18] It was claimed in the body of the text that there was 'evidence of a plan carefully prepared by the CSU before the strike in Canada had begun, to pursue their quarrel with the Canadian shipowners and the SIU in British ports and involve British dockers in it'.[19] But predictably, none of the 'evidence' was produced. It was also claimed that 'the campaign in this country was founded upon

[9] ibid.
[10] TNA, CAB 128/15/21 (Cabinet Conclusions, 21 March 1949).
[11] ibid.
[12] HC Debs, 28 June 1949, col 982.
[13] On the Dock Labour Scheme, see pp 119, 125, 129, 133, 245 and 285 below.
[14] HC Debs, 4 July 1949, col 1789.
[15] HC Debs, 28 June 1949, col 983 (William Gallacher MP).
[16] Review of the British Dock Strikes, Cmd 7851, 1949.
[17] ibid p 3.
[18] ibid.
[19] ibid para 87.

the support mainly of members of the Communist party and their sympathisers'.[20] The evidence to support this latter claim (in only two paragraphs of the report) was notably very thin.[21]

It was not only the Labour government that saw Communist conspiracies everywhere. So too did the TUC which, as we have shown with Joan Mahoney in work published elsewhere, appeared to enjoy an informal relationship with both MI5 and the Information Research Department, another shadowy organisation which operated in the intelligence sphere.[22] That said, the TUC was unlikely to have needed much encouragement in its attempt to purge the Movement of communist influence. This began formally with the drafting of a statement, *Trade Unions and Communism*, in what was the opening shot in the TUC's anti-Communist onslaught.[23] *Trade Unions and Communism* was expanded and published in December 1948 as *Defend Democracy*,[24] with TUC affiliates invited to consider whether Communists should be barred from holding office in individual unions. This was on the ground that Communist Party members were not only engaged in subversive activities, but allegedly were being directed from outside the trade union movement.[25] If that was not enough, in January 1949 the TUC followed up with *The Tactics of Disruption; Communist Methods Exposed*. The latter dealt with alleged Communist Party methods for infiltrating trade unions and trades councils.[26]

Shortly thereafter, a number of unions changed their rules to exclude Communists from office. These included the TGWU, where General Secretary Arthur Deakin had been working to rid himself of the Communist contingent on the union's General Executive Council after they had doubled in number to comprise eight of the 34 members,[27] of whom three were said to sit on the 'powerful' Finance and General Purposes Committee.[28] On 19 August 1949, the TGWU Biennial Delegate Conference amended the union's rule book to deny members of the Communist Party or a fascist party the right to hold any official position in the union. Deakin wrote later, in response to criticism of this decision as being an interference with the liberty of the individual, that 'it is a measure of self protection against those who openly and unashamedly seek to use our organisation as an instrument for subversive propaganda and policy'. He justified his actions in orchestrating this purge on the additional ground that other unions had 'also found it necessary to curtail, by various means, the activities of the

[20] ibid.

[21] ibid paras 42–44.

[22] See Ewing, Mahoney and Moretta (n 4) pp 87–88.

[23] On the TUC and Communism, see TUC, *The TUC and Communism* (TUC, 1955).

[24] J Phillips, 'Labour and the Cold War: The Politics of Anti-communism, 1945–55' (1999) 64 *Labour History Review* 48.

[25] H Pelling, *The British Communist Party* (A&C Black, London, 1975), p 154.

[26] ibid. Apart from the documents published in 1948 and 1949, a statement by the TUC General Council (which included one known member of the Communist Party) claimed that the Party was seeking to sabotage the European Recovery Programme. It was also alleged that 'Communist influences are everywhere at work to frame industrial demands for purposes of industrial agitation; to magnify industrial grievances; and to bring about stoppages in industry': TUC Report 1949, p 274, quoted in Pelling (n 25) p 154.

[27] Bert Papworth, Bill Jones, Jim Sloan, Charles McKerrow, Bert Slack, Alex Grant, John Trotter and Muriel Rayment (listed by Graham Stevenson in his *Communist Biographies*: www.grahamstevenson.me.uk).

[28] Pelling (n 25) p 154.

communists in their midst, by denying or depriving them of office, or by disciplinary procedure in various forms'.[29]

But Deakin was concerned not only about Communist penetration of the official structure of the union. He was just as concerned by unofficial groups, a practice that had been identified in the Morrison memorandum.[30] Deakin's immediate concern was the unofficial committees in the union and the platform they allegedly provided for the Communist Party.[31] His strong hostility was expressed in the pages of the *Record*, the union's journal, where he wrote to condemn the Party and the tactics of its members, in one notable article referring to the 1949 dock strike in support of the Canadian Seamen's Union as an attempt:

> [T]o interfere with the flow of trade with this country [as] merely another facet of the attempt that is being made on the part of international communism to prevent our economic recovery, and especially the flow of American aid to Europe. For a very long time a drive has been going on by the Communists to gain a foothold in those unions on the waterfront having a membership amongst dockers. In France, Italy, Australia, Finland and Belgium there has been a determined effort to get a foothold in this important industry. The communists recognize that it is the vital lifeline of the country, and that if they can interfere with transport, then they can make very difficult the effort which is being made to effect economic recovery.[32]

Although the body to become known as the 'Port Workers Committee' is not mentioned by name, it is clear to whom Deakin's remarks were directed. That said, the forerunner of the PWC was not the only source of torment, with the 'Committee for Trade Union Democracy' also being singled out.[33] According to Deakin, they were a 'fifth column within our midst', who pledged to use any means at their disposal to make the democratic decision to exclude Communists and fascists from holding office ineffective.[34]

These unofficial groups within the TGWU were denounced for violating the formal structures of the union: 'any attempts to discuss the business of the union through the medium of an organization which is not part of the union is an offence against the rules'. Members were warned by the union's General Executive Council that it would 'regard very seriously any connection with [the Committee for Trade Union

[29] A Deakin, 'British Trade Unions and the Communist Conspiracy' (1952) 139 *National & English Review* 337, at p 339. Deakin also dealt with the purging of Communist influence in the trades councils, leading to a number having 'their registration withdrawn'.

[30] Morrison had referred to the Party 'in some cases sheltering behind its auxiliary, the Engineering and Allied Trades Shop Stewards National Committee': TNA, CAB 66/35/9 ('Communist Party of Great Britain', Memorandum by the Home Secretary, 13 March 1943).

[31] Many of the problems in the TGWU were laid bare in a devastating critique of the union by an American chronicler: Joseph Goldstein, *The Government of British Trade Union: A Study of Apathy and the Democratic Process in the Transport and General Workers Union* (George Allen & Unwin, London, 1952). Goldstein noted Deakin's complacent satisfaction that 'the rank and file member is being heard', and his expectation that members engaged with the union at Branch meetings. That is how it should have been. However, during one of the many dock strikes in the 1940s, Goldstein had attended three Branch meetings held for the dockers and had seen that the attendance for all three meetings was smaller than the numbers who were attracted to any one of the major unofficial events (pp 62–63). Credit to Deakin, however, for writing a foreword to the book (which was dedicated to Harold Laski).

[32] A Deakin, 'Trade Unionism v Communism: The Gloves are off!', *Transport and General Workers' Union Record*, July 1949.

[33] A Deakin, 'A Challenge to Democracy! – And Our Answer', *Transport and General Workers' Union Record*, January 1950.

[34] ibid.

Democracy], or any attempt to discuss the business of the Union, except through the constitutional procedure'.[35] It is unlikely, however, that the emergence, development and effectiveness of unofficial groups within the union agitating for improved working conditions was due principally to the persuasive powers of the Communist Party alone. As the Morrison memorandum had unwittingly revealed in 1943, a more likely explanation was union failure, no matter how convenient a target the Communist Party might have been. Deakin was not only the successor of one Cabinet member (Bevin); he was also the friend of another (Isaacs), and was believed to be serving the interests of the government rather than his members. Dockers were especially resentful of the union's failure under his leadership to address their concerns.[36]

III. The Security Service

In April 1946, Attlee appointed Sir Percy Sillitoe – an ex-policeman – as the new Director General of MI5, to the dismay of most MI5 officers. The Prime Minister had been keen to ensure that intrusions by MI5 into the private lives of citizens of whatever political stripe were to be permitted only as far as was necessary for *the Defence of the Realm*. The appointment of a police officer to the top job at MI5 was an element of this break with the past. Much more significant, however, was the 'Attlee Directive' issued to Sillitoe shortly after his appointment. Drawing heavily on a report compiled by Sir Samuel Findlater Stewart, the purpose of the Attlee Directive was to clarify the status of MI5, by setting out the limits of its responsibilities and, as far as possible, reconciling its activities with civil liberties to ensure that it concentrated its efforts on catching spies rather than spying on law-abiding citizens with left-wing sympathies.[37] Written by the Prime Minister in collaboration with the then Cabinet Secretary, Sir Edward Bridges, this was the Security Service's first Charter, operating until 1952 when it was re-issued by the then Home Secretary in an amended and significantly diluted form to become known as the 'Maxwell-Fyfe Directive'.[38]

It is a striking feature of these arrangements that they were made without any apparent consideration of their legal basis. There was no statutory authority for the creation in 1909 of what became the Security Service, and no parliamentary approval of its Charter in 1946 with its reference to the purpose, powers, and procedures of the Service. Nor was there any express parliamentary approval of its annual budget. Not only that: the Charter was not published, so that by 1949, even the Attorney General is recorded by the Deputy Director of MI5 as being unaware of 'the organisation which

[35] ibid.

[36] See Phillips (n 24).

[37] On the Stewart Report of 1945, see Ewing, Mahoney and Moretta (n 4) ch 2, and on the Attlee Directive, MI5's dilution of the strictures of that original charter and the resulting Maxwell Fyfe Directive, see ch 5.

[38] Details of the Maxwell Fyfe Directive were made public for the first time in Lord Denning's Report, Cmnd 2152, 1963, para 238. The Denning Report was published in the wake of the Profumo scandal in September 1963. See also David Williams' excellent *Not in the Public Interest: The Problem of Security in Democracy* (Hutchinson, London, 1965), pp 129–30. On Profumo and the security services, see Ewing, Mahoney and Moretta (n 4) ch 14.

was directed to countering subversive movements'.[39] Readers can choose whether this was an expression of the maturity or the immaturity of the United Kingdom's constitutional arrangements, whether it was a vindication or weakness of the United Kingdom's political constitution, or whether it matters: do different constitutional forms really make any difference to the role, methods and accountability of security and intelligence services? Whatever the answers, the Attlee Directive sought to impose restraints on the Service in the post-war era, and to that extent, it was a step in the right direction.

The Attlee Directive made it clear that the Director General was responsible to the Prime Minister, to whom he had the right of direct access. It also made clear that the Director General was responsible for keeping the Prime Minister 'constantly informed of subversive activities likely to endanger the security of the State' (paragraph 1). Beyond that, the Directive provided:

> The Security Service is part of the Defence Forces of the country and has no concern with the enforcement of the criminal law. Its task is the Defence of the Realm as a whole, from external and internal dangers arising from attempts at espionage and sabotage, or from actions of persons and organisations, whether directed from within or without the country, which may be judged to be subversive of the security of the state. (paragraph 2)

For these purposes, subversion was not defined, though Findlater Stewart had referred to it in his report as meaning 'the promotion of political aims by unconstitutional methods'. It should be noted that unlike 'espionage' and 'sabotage', which would normally involve the commission of a common law or statutory offence, subversive activity was not necessarily unlawful, despite being deemed to be 'unconstitutional'.

Apart from setting out the responsibilities of the Security Service, the Attlee Directive also imposed a number of constraints. First was the principle of necessity: it was the duty of the Director General to take 'special care' to ensure that the work of the Service was 'strictly limited to what is necessary' in the discharge of its tasks. Second was the principle of political neutrality: it was 'essential' that the Service 'should be kept free of any political bias or influence', the Director General required to impress on his staff that they have no connection whatever with any matters of a party political character'. Third was the principle of operational independence: no enquiry was to be carried out on behalf of a government department unless 'an important public interest bearing on the Defence of the Realm as defined in paragraph 2 [of the Directive] is at stake'. Fourth was the principle of confidentiality: records were to be destroyed when no longer needed for the Defence of the Realm, and ministers were not to be provided with detailed information, but only with such information as may be necessary for the determination of any issue on which the Service's guidance was sought. And finally there was the principle of accountability: the Director General was responsible to the Prime Minister.

In practice, the reference to subversive activity was quickly taken to include the Communist Party, partly in the mistaken belief that by the investigation of those associated with progressive political views, the Service would be led to those who did pose a genuine threat to the Defence of the Realm – that is to say, to Eastern Bloc espionage

[39] TNA, KV4/471 (Liddell Diary, 4 July, 1949).

networks.[40] Meanwhile, the monitoring of trade unions – a prima facie breach of the Service's new Charter – was ostensibly reconciled with the terms of the Attlee Directive by adapting the familiar argument that the Party was infiltrating the unions with the intention of stirring up industrial unrest: according to the Morrison memorandum, this was a key element in preparing for revolution, which in turn would involve shooting army officers and getting 'rid of the police'.[41] These arguments were informed in part by an understanding that a number of trade unions were now, in Henry Pelling's words, either 'communist controlled' or 'communist penetrated',[42] and by the presence of a number of Communist activists in the powerful unofficial groups working within trade unions, to which we have referred in the case of the TGWU. These activists were also to take a leading part in the unofficial action that plagued the government.

Such conduct could plausibly be said to constitute 'the promotion of political aims by unconstitutional methods', as could the belief that the Party sought to place its people in key roles in the unions so that Communist Party supporters would be able to disrupt the British rearmament programme, and subsequently the conflict in Korea from 1950.[43] But whatever the justification, it is clear that the trade union movement was deeply infiltrated by MI5 in the post-war era, as illustrated by the revealing diary entries made by Guy Liddell (MI5's Deputy Director) during the dock strike in support of the Canadian Seamen's Union in 1949.[44] Here it is recorded that the Attorney General was looking for evidence to bring sedition charges against the strike leaders following the example of similar charges brought against the Communist Party leadership in 1925.[45] According to Liddell, the Attorney General had written to Attlee complaining about a lack of co-ordination with regard to Communist matters, apparently 'searching around for something in the nature of the Zinoviev letter which would show that on the direction of Moscow strikes are being started in Canada, Australia and the UK with the object of wrecking the Marshall Plan'.[46] An MI5 official drafted a reply for Attlee to send

[40] The surveillance of those on the left of the political spectrum (so-called counter-subversion operations) could thus be presented as counter-espionage work. See Ewing, Mahoney and Moretta (n 4) pp 40, 50, 453 and 459–60. This argument reflected Findlater Stewart's observation in 1945 that MI5 took the view that 'most of the persons concerned with the promotion of political aims by unconstitutional methods are members of the Communist party' and that 'many of its members are exposed to, and some succumb to, pressure to engage in espionage on behalf of the international Communism'.

[41] TNA, CAB 66/35/9 ('Communist Party of Great Britain', Memorandum by the Home Secretary, 13 March 1943).

[42] Pelling (n 25) p 227.

[43] See C Andrew, *The Defence of the Realm: The Authorised History of MI5* (Penguin, London, 2010), pp 406–08.

[44] Liddell was MI5's Deputy Director General from 1946 to 1953.

[45] On which, see KD Ewing and CA Gearty, *The Struggle for Civil Liberties: Political Freedom and the Rule of Law in Britain, 1914–1945* (Oxford University Press, Oxford, 2000), ch 3.

[46] TNA, KV4/471 (Liddell Diary, 4 July, 1949). The Zinoviev letter refers to a letter purportedly written by Grigori Zinoviev and others to British Communists encouraging them to mobilise the Labour Party in support of an Anglo-Soviet treaty and to promote subversive activities in the army. Zinoviev was the President of the Moscow-based Communist International, and the letter was leaked to the *Daily Mail* on the eve of the general election in 1924, at which the incumbent minority Labour government was heavily defeated, though its impact on the election is contested. It is widely believed that the letter was a forgery and that its publication by the *Daily Mail* was designed to help the Conservative Party at the election. An official historical inquiry subsequently concluded that the letter had been leaked by an MI6 official who was unlikely to have thought it to have been genuine. See *The Guardian*, 4 February 1999; and G Bennett, *The Zinoviev Letter: The Conspiracy That Never Dies*

to Shawcross, in which the role of the Service was made crystal clear, it being explained that:

> [T]he Security Service is really the focal point for information on these matters and that information from their sources is closely co-ordinated with that of the police throughout the country. [Shawcross] was also told that the general picture with regard to the dock strike was fairly clear. The Communist Party had not been involved at the outset, but had since done all they could to give support to the strikers. Although Barrett, the union leader was indirectly encouraging the strikes, he could not do so officially by virtue of his position. As regards directives from Moscow, it is extremely unlikely that any exist, since the days of Zinoviev letters were over and guidance and direction came through the open press and the radio.[47]

According to Liddell, Shawcross 'sent a somewhat apologetic reply'.[48] Nevertheless, 'if there was any information which showed that the Communists were deliberately inciting people to sabotage the Marshall Plan he would be prepared to mount a case'.[49]

There were two issues here: one was the possibility of bringing charges against unknown persons for sedition; and the other was whether there was any evidence of Moscow involvement. The former was not dependent on the latter, which would have been sensational and – if the experience of the Zinoviev letter in 1924 is any guide – not necessarily in the Labour Party's interests to expose. Liddell was of the view, however, that prosecution for sedition would be impossible 'unless there was some incitement to a breach of the peace',[50] a position confirmed when he saw someone from the DPP's office a few days later.[51] Liddell explained to Gerald Paling from the DPP's office about 'the situation as we saw it', Paling 'entirely' agreeing with him that 'in the circumstances there was not likely to be any evidence upon which to stage a prosecution'.[52] As to the suggestion of directives from Moscow specifically, this was scotched a week later when Liddell and Bernard Hill (the MI5 Legal Officer) met the DPP 'regarding Sir Hartley Shawcross's suggestion to the PM that a case might be mounted against the Communists if it could be proved that on directions from Moscow they were deliberately trying to create trouble in the dock strikes in order to wreck the Marshall Plan'.[53]

Apart from exposing the willingness of Shawcross to raise the temperature with what have been a very provocative prosecution, Guy Liddell's diary entries are notable for revealing the influential role of MI5 in prosecution decisions, despite the provisions in its Charter stating expressly that it was not concerned with the enforcement of the criminal law. More importantly, the entries are notable also for suggesting on MI5's part a deep knowledge of the Communist Party's role in the dock dispute, as well

(Oxford University Press, Oxford, 2018). It is to be hoped that Shawcross was looking for a genuine and not a fake directive from Moscow.

[47] TNA, KV4/471 (Liddell Diary, 4 July, 1949).

[48] ibid.

[49] ibid.

[50] ibid.

[51] The DPP had been asked by Shawcross for an assurance that Special Branch and the Security Service 'were doing all they could in connection with the dock strike': TNA, KV4/471 (Liddell Diary, 7 July, 1949).

[52] TNA, KV4/471 (Liddell Diary, 4 July, 1949).

[53] ibid 15 July 1949. The DPP also agreed that there was no possibility of a prosecution unless there was definite evidence of an incitement to cause a breach of the peace, to which Liddell replied that 'if we did ever have anything from a usable source which showed that there had been incitement to commit a breach of the peace, we would let him have it'.

as a deep knowledge of the Communist Party's links with Moscow. Such knowledge would require in turn a deep knowledge of the trade union movement and the unofficial bodies operating within it. Such knowledge would include a knowledge of personnel, networks and tactics, obtained by a wide range of information-gathering techniques, including the use of informers, the infiltration of organisations, the attendance at meetings, and the use of other forms of surveillance such as the interception of mail and the tapping of phones, as well as the use of electronic bugging devices. While some of this activity would have been undertaken by MI5 officers directly, as discussed below, MI5 also received information from other sources, most notably Special Branch, which used similar surveillance techniques.

MI5, Special Branch, and Labour Law

The role of MI5 and Special Branch is obviously a matter of concern to constitutional lawyers and civil liberties lawyers respectively, raising questions about legality and the rule of law. Thus, how were these agencies created? What is the source of their legal powers? Who authorised the use of the different surveillance techniques employed? To whom were they accountable?[54] But they are also of concern to labour lawyers, particularly in relation to freedom of association, the activities of MI5 and Special Branch covered in this book being all the more poignant for the fact that they coincided with the making of ILO Convention 87 (the Freedom of Association and Right to Organise Convention, 1948). The latter provides, inter alia, that workers' and employers' organisations have the right to 'draw up their constitutions and rules, to elect their representatives in full freedom, to organise their administration and activities and to formulate their programmes'. Critically, it also provides that the 'public authorities shall refrain from any interference which would restrict this right or impede the exercise thereof' (Article 3). Note also that while ILO Convention 87, Article 8(1) provides that workers' organisations are expected to obey the law of the land, it is also provided that the latter should not be such as to impair the guarantees provided for in the Convention (Article 8(2)).

The infiltration and surveillance of trade unions and trade unionists by agents of the state and the sharing of information about trade unionists is not compatible with these obligations. First, it undermines trade union integrity. Infiltrators who take part in a trade union's activities – perhaps as *agents provocateurs* – are secretly serving the interests of a third party and not the interests of the membership. The same applies where officials are exchanging information with, acting under instruction from, or otherwise colluding with state authorities. Second, infiltration and surveillance undermine the effectiveness of the organisation, particularly if the latter's negotiating positions and operational plans are made available in advance to adversaries, whether these be employers with whom the union is engaged in collective bargaining, or the state preparing a response to a union's demands or activities. And third, infiltration and surveillance expose trade union activists – individually

[54] See Ewing, Mahoney and Moretta (n 4) for a full discussion of these questions.

and collectively – to the risk of blacklisting, victimisation and discrimination when information obtained by the state is shared with employers. The same applies where the information about activists is shared with a trade union leadership, as in the examples discussed in this chapter. There is presumably a special place in hell reserved for trade union officials and others who collude with the repressive agents of the state.

IV. Special Branch

Formed in 1883 without any statutory authority or accountability,[55] the Metropolitan Police Special Branch was said by Lord Denning in 1963 to have several tasks, including collecting intelligence on subversive organisations: 'one of its duties is to obtain information regarding them and pass it on to the Security Service'.[56] But in addition, it was 'also concerned with offences against the security of the State, such as treason, espionage, offences against the Official Secrets Act and the Public Order Act'.[57] Quite why offences against the Public Order Act 1936 should be offences against the state is difficult to fathom: the Act was concerned with the control of meetings and demonstrations, the very essence of the democracy which the agencies of the state should be straining to preserve. But if marches and demonstrations were within the purview of Special Branch, it was likely that at least some strikes would be too, though the mandate is far from clear. Lord Denning did not explain what the opaquely phrased 'concerned with' offences against the state involved, though it appears to have included multiple forms of monitoring and surveillance, none of which – as in the case of MI5 – had any formal legal authority for the dubious reason that none of the methods employed was necessarily unlawful.[58]

Legend has it that MI5 merely collated information and that Special Branch were the 'executive arm' of the security and intelligence services. That erroneous belief would appear to derive from what Lord Denning was told by the security services in 1963 when investigating the Profumo debacle,[59] which was in turn dictated by the facts that arrests or *lawful* searches of premises had to be made by the police,[60] and that for the previous 30 or so years, the Branch had, as a matter of practice, passed information on subversion, as well as anything relating to espionage or national security more generally, to the Security Service.[61] A subversive was defined by Denning as one

[55] For a brief account, see AW Bradley, KD Ewing and CJS Knight, *Constitutional and Administrative Law*, 18th edn (Pearson, Harlow, 2022), pp 597–98.

[56] Lord Denning's Report, Cmnd 2152, 1963, para 76.

[57] ibid.

[58] On the contrary, *Thomas v Sawkins* [1935] 2 KB 249 authorised Special Branch presence at a meeting against the wishes of the organisers where this was necessary to prevent a breach of the peace or the commission of an offence (such as sedition).

[59] Lord Denning's Report, Cmnd 2152, 1963, paras 76 and 273.

[60] The Security Service Act 1989 first allowed for MI5 to obtain 'property warrants' and thus enter premises lawfully.

[61] Lord Denning's Report, Cmnd 2152, 1963, para 76.

who 'would contemplate the overthrow of the Government by unlawful means',[62] which was narrower than the term used by Findlater Stewart to the extent that in the British system at the time, unconstitutional means could be lawful.[63] The reality in contrast was that although Security Service officers were, as Lord Denning put it, 'in the eye of law, ordinary citizens with no powers greater than anyone else',[64] in practice both organisations engaged in much the same activities, with the result that Special Branch might better have been described as the executive arm of the Home Office.[65]

By the 1940s, both MI5 and Special Branch operated independently of each other. This is not to say that there was no co-operation, which despite the rivalry was probably at its peak in the post-war era during the years 1945–51. Guy Liddell was not only an ex-Special Branch officer, but was also a friend of the new head of Special Branch, Leonard Burt, who had been appointed in 1946.[66] Burt had been seconded to MI5 by the Metropolitan Police during the war and Liddell had recommended Burt for his new role. Liddell also enjoyed excellent relations with Sir Harold Scott, appointed Commissioner of the Metropolitan Police in 1945.[67] Nevertheless, Special Branch ran its own agents and enjoyed the fruits of physical surveillance ('watchers' following targets, and officers breaking into premises to gather information and evidence), as well as mail interceptions, telephone 'taps' and electronic eavesdropping devices to inform their investigations.[68] Additional information on political targets was provided by the 'ordinary' police – Chief Constables were encouraged by Special Branch to pass on information, and many provincial forces had officers who either partially or wholly concerned themselves with what was called 'Special Branch work'.[69]

Throughout this book, we see the results of this web of surveillance, the source often explicitly or implicitly acknowledged. However, perhaps just as often, we can only make an educated guess as to how, and by which organisation, the intelligence in question had been gathered. So far as Special Branch is concerned, however, its political surveillance work was well known. As early as 1924, two Special Branch officers were found hidden in a secret room under the stage of the Rehearsal Theatre in Bedford Square, London where a meeting of the London District Congress of the Communist Party was being held.[70] In the confusion that ensued, officers Gil and Hopley left behind three notebooks which revealed that the officers had been 'continually employed spying at all Communist meetings, and sneaking into hotels to watch and listen to Communist delegates to conferences'.[71] One of the books recorded the movement of the people being watched, together with the names and addresses of delegates to these conferences. Photographs of the notebooks as well as extracts therefrom were reproduced in the

[62] Lord Denning's Report, Cmnd 2152, 1963, para 76.

[63] It is of course difficult to say what is or is not unconstitutional. But assuming that a General Strike would be regarded as an unconstitutional means of securing a political end, on at least one view, this would not be unlawful following the repeal of the Trade Disputes and Trade Unions Act 1927. See ch 4 above.

[64] Lord Denning's Report, Cmnd 2152, 1963, para 273.

[65] Although MI5 officers, unlike police officers, are thought not to have had powers of arrest, at least one MI5 officer is recorded as making an arrest – see Ewing, Mahoney and Moretta (n 4) p 18.

[66] ibid pp 78–79. On Burt, see pp 137, 149 and 247.

[67] See TNA, KV4/196 (Liddell Diary, 29 May 1945).

[68] Ewing, Mahoney and Moretta (n 4) ch 8.

[69] ibid pp 94–95.

[70] Ewing and Gearty (n 45) pp 114–15.

[71] ibid p 115.

Workers' Weekly and were retained by persons unknown in the hope that they might be handed over to a Committee of Inquiry, which predictably never took place.[72]

Very few Special Branch files relating to the post-war era have been released to the National Archives, though sufficient material has come to light to indicate that Special Branch made great efforts to monitor political parties and other organisations on both sides of the political divide.[73] Here reference might be made to Special Branch reports of a Christmas reunion of those interned under Regulation 18B,[74] held in 1945 at the Royal Hotel on Woburn Place in Central London. Admission to the event – attended by Oswald Mosley and his wife – was strictly by ticket only, with the result that the police were unable to gain admission. But ever resourceful and with the consent of the hotel manager, a Special Branch officer 'climbed by way of a fire escape onto the roof', where he was 'able to see all and hear most of what went on in the dance hall below'.[75] According to the Special Branch report, there were about 1,000 people present, with Mosley arriving to a 'tremendous ovation', the 'crowd cheering and chanting M-O-S-L-E-Y', for 'several minutes', many with arms raised 'to give the old fascist salute'.[76] Much of the rest of the report is an account of Mosley's speech,[77] which followed a number of presentations to stalwarts of the 18b Detainees (British) Aid Fund.[78]

Given the monitoring of the Communist Party in the 1920s,[79] the National Unemployed Workers' Movement in the 1930s,[80] and the British Union of Fascists in the 1940s, it has long been implausible to believe that Special Branch were not also monitoring the activities of trade unionists, and we will show in the pages that follow that trade unions and trade unionists were indeed the subject of close surveillance. Multiple surveillance techniques were used, though in the case of trade unions, the material we have seen indicates that it would typically take the form of physical surveillance and/or the use of informers.[81] Much of the surveillance involved attending meetings and reporting in detail on the proceedings: who was present, who said what, and what was the outcome. Meetings attended would be both official meetings and unofficial meetings, Special Branch officers unwilling to discriminate between the two, and certainly unwilling to embrace Bevin's arresting view of the trade union meeting to which he gave legal protection from liability under Defence Regulation 1AA for things said or done on the ground that:

> I regard the trade union branch jealously as a place of assembly, where no one but those entitled to attend can be present. Whatever is said in that branch is as sacrosanct to me as what a man says in his own home and I am against detectives, police or anybody having the right

[72] ibid.

[73] Ewing, Mahoney and Moretta (n 4) pp 73–82.

[74] Defence Regulation 18B allowed for the detention of people of 'hostile origin or associations' and gave rise to one of the most notorious examples of judicial deference in English law: *Liversidge v Anderson* [1942] AC 206.

[75] TNA, HO 45/24467 ('DISTURBANCES: Fascist organisations: renewal of activities after Second World War) (Special Branch Report, '18b Detainees (British) Aid', 16 December 1945).

[76] ibid.

[77] Another report from someone at the meeting refers to Mosley as the 'cynosure of all eyes': ibid (Special Branch Report by DAC, 21 December 1945).

[78] ibid.

[79] On which, see Ewing and Gearty (n 45).

[80] See *Elias v Pasmore* [1934] 2 KB 164.

[81] TNA, KV4/472 (Liddell Diary, 5 October 1950). See ch 8 for more details.

> to go into a branch and use anything that is said, however wise or however foolish, in a police court as evidence against a man.[82]

Special Branch surveillance could be overt or covert. In the former case, the surveillance would be made known to the press and used as an instrument of intimidation, as in the example of the dockers' leaders discussed in Chapter Eight below.[83] More usually, however, it would be covert, with officers at a large gathering hidden in plain sight or, as in the Rehearsal Theatre example, concealed on the premises. It has been claimed that an example of the latter form of surveillance in the specific context of trade unions is provided by Special Branch surveillance of the inaugural meeting of the Port Workers' Committee on 7 August 1949. Here Tony Bunyan in his pioneering work on the political police referred to a 'ploy to discredit one of the organisers', stating that 'officers hid in the vicinity of a meeting room in Canning Town and recorded a speech by the organiser in question'.[84] Although he does not cite any evidence to support these claims, and although there is a slightly different version of events told by Colin J Davies,[85] Bunyan's version is nevertheless highly plausible, given what is known about the conduct of Special Branch at the time and the methods of surveillance used by it. As Guy Liddell subsequently makes clear, these included the use of electronic eavesdropping equipment, albeit not as sophisticated as the gear used by MI5.[86]

Bunyan's more controversial claim is that Special Branch records of the Canning Town meeting 'were used by Arthur Deakin' to 'expel the man from his union'.[87] Although again no evidence is cited to support this claim, some corroboration is provided in a TGWU file dealing with the proceedings of the Special Committee appointed by the TGWU Executive Council in December 1949 to investigate allegations against members of the London Central Lock-out Committee, as the PWC was initially known.[88] The file is particularly notable for containing very detailed typed accounts of the speeches given by three of the members who had been charged with disciplinary offences following the Canning Town meeting (including Ted Dickens, who was recommended for expulsion).[89] Although this makes clear that the meeting had been under surveillance, it does not tell us whether the surveillance was by Special Branch. It is not impossible

[82] HC Debs, 28 April 1944, cols 1129–30.

[83] See especially pp 147–151.

[84] T Bunyan, *The History and Practice of the Political Police in Britain* (Quartet Books, London, 1977), pp 124–25.

[85] CJ Davies, *Waterfront Revolts: New York and London Dockworkers 1946–61* (University of Illinois Press, Champaign, 2003), p 196.

[86] TNA, KV4/473 (Liddell Diary, 15 February 1951). Here Liddell records that his friend, Commander Leonard Burt, the head of Special Branch, had told him that his force had used hidden microphones to listen in to PWC meetings, which by Burt's account was one of the *least* dubious means by which the police had obtained information on the dockers.

[87] Bunyan (n 84), p 125.

[88] For the report of the investigation, see TGWU, Unofficial London Docks Strike 1949, Report of the Special Committee appointed under the terms of the decision recorded in Minute No 1125 of the General Executive Committee, dated 15 December 1949 (1950). The report can be found in Warwick Modern Records Centre, TGWU Archive, File MSS.126/TG/44724/3.

[89] Warwick Modern Records Centre, TGWU Archive, File MSS.126/TG/44724/4. The two others (VF Marney and J Blomberg) whose speeches feature in the file were recommended for prohibition from holding union office. The file contains 'Extract[s] from Notes of a Meeting of the London Central Lock-out Committee held at Canning Town Public Hall, on Sunday, 7th August, 1949'.

that it could have been undertaken by the union itself, though the style of the reports is not unlike Special Branch reports of trade union and Communist Party meetings to be found in files held by the National Archives. If as Bunyan claims the surveillance was conducted by Special Branch, it is difficult to understand how anyone other than a Special Branch or government source could have supplied the reports to the union.

V. Special Branch and the TGWU

Further suspicions of a link between Special Branch surveillance and the protection of the TGWU leadership are indicated by the example of the surveillance of the Smithfield Meat Workers during a trade dispute in June–July 1950 (the dispute is considered more fully in Chapter Seven).[90] It is clear from the files that the local strike committee (it was an unofficial strike) was the subject of intense Special Branch surveillance. Although the strike was likely to have been unlawful, with Shawcross offering to prosecute a few strikers, presumably under Order 1305, there was no evidence in the files of Communist instigation that would justify bringing a prosecution for reasons relating to sedition. To that extent, the surveillance operation drew a blank, with ministers obviously disappointed. It is clear, however, that the surveillance was not conducted solely for the purpose of securing evidence to mount a prosecution. On the contrary, it was being undertaken as part of an ongoing process of surveillance of activists within the TGWU, which on this occasion provided a wealth of information about the conduct and tactics of the strike committee and its relationship with the union hierarchy.

The dispute was considered by the Cabinet, coincidentally only a few hours before the strike ended. At the meeting on 10 July 1950, ministers raised concerns about the failings of the union, these concerns informed by a report 'suggesting that the local machinery of the Transport and General Workers' Union at Smithfield was being used to assist the unofficial strike'. Attlee proposed that he, Chuter Ede (Home Secretary), George Isaacs (Minister of Labour and National Pensions) and Alfred Barnes (Minister of Transport) meet Deakin 'to discuss with him some of the issues which were troubling Ministers'.[91] Two days later, Shawcross wrote to Attlee to say that there would be no prosecutions,[92] regretting that 'the necessary evidence on which to prosecute was not forthcoming'.[93] This seems odd, given that many workers took part in the strike apparently in breach of Order 1305, though it is true, as we discuss below, that there was some doubt for unspecified reasons as to whether those taking part in related action were involved in a trade dispute as defined by Order 1305. As we also discuss below, however, what Shawcross appeared to suggest was that there was insufficient evidence to prosecute the right people. In the meantime, although the strike was over, the dispute had yet to be resolved.

[90] See pp 134–138 below.

[91] TNA CAB 128/18/4 (Cabinet Conclusions, 10 July 1950); see also pp 114–115 below. It is not known if the meeting took place.

[92] TNA, PREM 8/1538 ('1951 Strikes and Industrial Disputes') (Shawcross to Attlee, 12 July 1950).

[93] ibid.

Thus, in the redacted copy of his extraordinary letter now held on file at the National Archives, Shawcross referred to a Special Branch report which indicated that the unofficial strike committee was to continue in operation, 'with a view to giving 21 days' notice of further strike action' if the men were unhappy with the outcome of the procedures agreed for the resolution of the dispute,[94] a strategy which other activists – including the striking gas workers we encounter in Chapter Nine – thought they too could deploy. But Shawcross was to reveal a lot more than a threat about further industrial action. Highlighting 'a very strong and general hostility to Mr Deakin', he referred to a Special Branch report that expressed the view of union activists that 'the unofficial strike action had achieved a considerable victory over him'.[95] Shawcross continued by telling Attlee that while '[t]he Union has lost all control', the unofficial organisation was becoming stronger, and one Spencer Henry Tribe, TGWU organiser at Smithfield, was '[a]t the back of all this activity'.[96] The latter was 'well known to Special Branch, [and] has been a member of the Communist Party since 1931'.[97] At this point, the letter moves to questions of discipline within the unofficial committee, Shawcross quoting at length from an earlier Special Branch report in a passage that unfortunately has been completely redacted.

A few paragraphs later, however, the letter resumes and we are allowed to read that 'there is no doubt that a good deal of intimidation took place' during the recent strike.[98] This was a claim supported by evidence of the experience of a few named individuals, who allegedly had been on the receiving end of what Shawcross evidently thought to have been rough justice. One shop steward, who had initially advised members against striking, was 'interrogated' at Smithfield Canteen (apparently run by Spencer Henry Tribe and his brother) on 28 June 1950 by the strike committee, 'a Mr Farquhar' ('Dixie' Farquhar, who re-appears in Chapter Eight below) taking the notes. The steward in question was then issued with the 'much dreaded' 'white card' summoning him to an unofficial disciplinary meeting.[99] These 'white cards', apparently signed by a man named Pope and stamped with the union rubber stamp, could lead to disciplinary expulsion from the union. Another man received similar treatment. 'The methods of obtaining strike funds' were said 'to be similarly objectionable', with those refusing to contribute being told that colleagues would refuse to work with them when the strike was over. Shawcross concluded:

> I do not know what steps can be taken by the Union or by Government Departments, but it seems evident that trouble will continue at Smithfield so long as the men are served by individuals like Tribe. I am assured by the Police that Tribe is the *fons et origo* of all the troubles. I am sending a copy of this letter to the Home Secretary.
>
> PS. I should have added that the Police heard that Tribe is protected by some high influence in the Union.[100]

[94] ibid.
[95] ibid.
[96] ibid.
[97] ibid.
[98] ibid.
[99] ibid.
[100] ibid.

In raising the possibility that unspecified steps might be taken by government departments, the latter passage suggests that having stumbled on information disagreeable to ministers (but insufficiently disagreeable to justify a prosecution), surveillance material was now being used by ministers to interfere in the internal affairs of the union. Shawcross had been particularly interested in the tactics employed by the Smithfield activists when raising money for the strike fund, and in prosecuting them for 'demanding money with menaces', or 'intimidation'.[101] However, because no violence had been threatened, it could not be said that any demand for financial support had been made either with menaces or with intimidation.[102] But although advising the Home Secretary that he could not use the criminal law 'for the purpose of enforcing Trade Union discipline and for dealing with *matters which the Trade Union ought to consider its urgent domestic concern*',[103] Shawcross nevertheless made it clear that the issues uncovered by the Special Branch reports would make it impossible for the government to avoid 'before long' being involved 'in similar trouble of an even graver kind'.[104]

If the latter passage is slightly enigmatic as to what Shawcross had in mind, the words in italics in the earlier passage are crystal clear: this was an internal problem that the union needed to sort out, Shawcross suggesting further that the problem was deep-rooted and not confined to the raising of money for the strike fund:

> There are all sorts of stories going about that things are wrong in the Union and there is talk even of criminal offences. Indeed, the current gossip there is that Tribe has great personal influence with Mr Deakin, and these rumours are naturally reinforced by the fact that so far no action has been taken against Tribe or the Strike Committee although Tribe's activities should have been known to Mr Deakin for a long time. The Police feel that if Tribe and his gang were removed there would be such a feeling of relief amongst the good men at Smithfield and of fear amongst the evil ones that peace would be produced.[105]

Putting to one side the reliance on 'stories', gossip' and 'rumour', this would make uncomfortable reading for Deakin if it were to be shared with him. In Shawcross' view, however, it was his job and not the government's to sort out, the job being to remove and replace what Shawcross believed to be were toxic elements within the union organisation.

Nevertheless, the question for Shawcross was how to ensure that the information obtained by Special Branch could now be used successfully to bring down Tribe and the unofficial committee. By this stage, the material had been shared not only with the Prime Minister but also with a number of government departments, the Home Secretary suggesting in reply that the case for prosecutions should be reconsidered without any indication as to why. This led Shawcross to consult the DPP and the police before concluding again that for reasons unexplained, prosecutions would be 'inadvisable'.[106] That being the case, if Deakin were to address the Attorney General's concerns, he

[101] It was apparently not now 'appropriate to prosecute for taking part in an illegal strike': ibid.
[102] See ch 11 below for similar proposals to prosecute the Park Royal Vehicles' workers over fundraising for the Duple Motors' strikers.
[103] TNA, PREM 8/1538 ('1951 Strikes and Industrial Disputes') (Shawcross to Chuter Ede, 20 July 1950), emphasis added.
[104] ibid.
[105] TNA, PREM 8/1538 ('1951 Strikes and Industrial Disputes') (Shawcross to Chuter Ede, 20 July 1950).
[106] ibid.

would need to know at least the gist of these concerns. Presumably with this in mind, Shawcross also wrote to the Minister of Labour, drawing attention to 'the latest Special Branch Report in regard to the Smithfield labour situation' (which he assumed Isaacs had seen), adding that 'it seems clear that matters are being kept simmering and just off the boil'.[107] At the very least, the letter to Isaacs is significant for indicating that the Ministry of Labour was regularly supplied with Special Branch intelligence about trade unions and trade union activists, as part of what had become a persistent and institutionalised surveillance culture.

The letter to Isaacs is significant also because of the Minister of Labour's evident sympathy for Arthur Deakin, whom he frequently defended in the presence of ministers from what he perceived were Communist-inspired personal attacks. The suspicion is that in writing to Isaacs, Shawcross was indirectly seeking to ensure that the contents of the Special Branch report were communicated to Deakin, though it must be emphasised that there is nothing in the file to confirm that this was done. Nevertheless, given the climate of the time, the absence of clear rules governing the sharing of intelligence material with third parties, the close relationship between ministers and senior trade unionists, and the personal standing of the beleaguered Deakin, it is not unlikely that this information would have been communicated to him by one means or another. As Shawcross makes clear, there would be adequate justification for doing so, which would serve the interests of the government as well as the union. Deakin needed to be alerted to the full extent of the problem; he needed to understand the government's concerns; and he needed to do something about it, in preference to the government having to act directly. As with the ban on Communists holding union office, self-regulation was to be preferred to legislation.

VI. Conclusion

Trade unions were the subject of surveillance at two different levels by at least two different state organisations, neither of which was established by Parliament, neither of which had parliamentary approval to engage in the surveillance of trade unions, and neither of which had parliamentary authority to engage in the different forms of surveillance which were undertaken. The first kind of surveillance was of the Communist Party which was closely watched, so that information would be obtained and recorded about its strategies and tactics, and about anyone it had dealings with. The second kind of surveillance was of trade unions and trade union activists, which would involve the surveillance of bodies such as the PWC to monitor activities and to gather information about personnel, movements, relationships, conduct, and plans. This might help to inform prosecution decisions, as well as to warn about future flashpoints. In the case of the Smithfield meat workers, for example, Special Branch activity revealed that Farquhar and Howell told their colleagues of an impending meeting with the TGWU disciplinary committee.[108] According to Shawcross, 'the ground was evidently being laid for action

[107] TNA, PREM 8/1538 ('1951 Strikes and Industrial Disputes') (Shawcross to Isaacs, 4 August 1950).
[108] On Farquhar and Howell, see p 153 below.

which might be taken if the union took any effective steps against them'.[109] The government and the employers could prepare accordingly.

Very little of this was about obtaining information that would be necessary for the purposes of a prosecution either for seditious conspiracy or a breach of Order 1305. As Guy Liddell made clear in 1949, there was no evidence that would justify a prosecution under the former, and as Hartley Shawcross made clear subsequently, it would not have been in the public interest to prosecute under the latter. The surveillance nevertheless continued in different forms, the nature of the surveillance raising a number of concerns. One was the question of reliability, with the references to 'stories', gossip', and 'rumour' already highlighted. The second was the nature and extent of the information obtained, recorded and relied on, going well beyond anything necessary for a prosecution that would never take place. And the third was the opportunity for the information to be shared with the TGWU leadership, and the possibility if not the likelihood that this may well have occurred. The latter may have been hard to avoid when trade unions were dependent on the state, and when their activities and personnel were closely intertwined with the interests of the state. Trade unions were not only instruments of government but also instruments through which state administrations governed. Such practices were nevertheless at best of doubtful propriety and questionable legitimacy.

[109] TNA, PREM 8/1538 ('1951 Strikes and Industrial Disputes') (Shawcross to Isaacs, 4 August 1949).

PART IV

Revival of Order 1305: Unofficial Action as Economic and Political Subversion

7

The Re-emergence of Order 1305

I. Introduction

In this chapter we are concerned with the re-emergence of Order 1305 as a restraint on the right to strike, despite initial expectations that the law would never be used. Although industrial action operated at relatively low levels after the war, the government was nevertheless confronted by an outbreak of unofficial action, particularly in the ports. An attempt to address grievances about casualisation and poor working conditions by the creation of the National Dock Labour Scheme was not enough to deal with the dockers' longstanding concerns, which crystallised around the 'Dockers' Charter'. The latter embraced demands adopted at the TGWU's National Docks Delegate Conference in 1945: an increase in the daily minimum wage from sixteen shillings to twenty-five shillings; two weeks' paid annual leave; payment for statutory holidays; a reduction in the working week to 40 hours; retirement allowances; and the provision of medical services.[1] Unofficial strike action taken in support of these demands in 1945 was said to involve 'the majority of the national workforce' and to 'cost the industry 1,107,000 working days', in what was also said to be the 'largest single industrial dispute of the period'.[2] It was, however, to be followed by other disputes leading to more unofficial industrial action, particularly in 1948, 1949, and 1950, all of it a likely consequence of – albeit not always directly related to – these grievances.

The problem for the government was not just a problem of unofficial action but also a problem of *organised* unofficial action, the organisation being undertaken by what evolved into what was perceived to be the powerful London-based Port Workers' Committee, which we encountered in Chapter Six. Operating unofficially within the TGWU, the Committee was very hostile to the union leadership generally and to its General Secretary (Arthur Deakin) in particular. And as was also pointed out in Chapter Six, the influence of the PWC was to spread beyond the ports to include the Smithfield meat workers, as well as those engaged in road haulage. The action of the unofficial groups was seen to be subversive of the union leadership, subversive of the industrial relations procedures which were then in place, and subversive of the government, being undertaken in the interests of a political party believed to be serving the interests of a foreign enemy during the Cold War. In this chapter we

[1] J Phillips, *The Great Alliance: Economic Recovery and the Problems of Power 1945–1951* (Pluto Press, London, 1996), p 50. Also important is Colin J Davis, *Waterfront Revolts: New York and London Dockworkers, 1946–61* (University of Illinois Press, Urbana, 2003).

[2] Phillips (n 1) pp 49–59.

consider how the strike restrictions in Order 1305 were taken out and dusted down to deal mainly (though not exclusively) with the unofficial committees and the unofficial action for which the committees were thought to be responsible. In doing so, we highlight the frustration of ministers, law officers, and officials, who were to discover the limits of Order 1305, as well as its unsuitability for dealing with the problems it was now being used to address.

Strikes after the War

To the extent that there was a strike problem after the war, it was a problem largely of unofficial action and, if the government was to be believed, unofficial action that was largely politically motivated. The nature of the problem should not be exaggerated, with numbers of days lost to strikes declining every year between 1944 and 1950, with the exception of 1946, when there was a temporary reversal in the downward trend. It is also the case that although 1949 was a year of bitter conflict on the waterfront, this activity obscures the fact that the 1.8 million days lost to stoppages was lower than in any year since 1942. So while the government was fretting about strikes, it was doing so in the context of relatively low and declining levels of industrial action.

This is not to say that the industrial action that did take place is to be underestimated, with dockworkers occupying a strategically important role in the post-war period with a power to disrupt which is greatly overlooked today. Although working arrangements had changed, dockworkers retained a capacity seriously to interfere with not only the flow of trade but also the supply of arms to battle zones. As pointed out by Jim Phillips, the docks 'witnessed a disproportionate level of strike activity', adding that 'the average docker was on strike six times more often than the average coal miner'. According to Phillips, 2.8 million of the 14.27 million working days lost to strike action between 1945 and 1951 were attributable to the docks, with a workforce of only 80,000.[3]

II. The Re-emergence of Order 1305

The big dock strike ended on 5 November 1945 with the port workers' demands only partially addressed.[4] But unofficial action was to persist periodically, becoming a matter of acute political concern, the Prime Minister being pressed in the House of Commons as early as April 1946 to set up a Royal Commission to investigate its cause.[5] In the following year, unofficial action by dockers to protest against redundancies on the Clyde was supported by colleagues in London, leading to ships laden with food and coal being

[3] ibid p 26.
[4] ibid.
[5] HC Debs, 8 October 1946, col 24.

left idle. On the same day that Isaacs made a statement in Parliament to condemn the action (29 April 1947),[6] we find the first suggestion in the Cabinet Conclusions that the criminal law might be deployed against striking dock workers. Without revealing the real cause of the strike in question, the Minister of Labour told the Cabinet that:

> The Glasgow [dock] strike had been called by a Scottish Union which was not affiliated to the Transport and General Workers Union; and the London stevedores and lightermen who had suspended work in support of the Glasgow dockers had been influenced by a desire to embarrass the latter union.[7] These strikes are symptomatic of growing tendency to ignore the advice of responsible union leaders.[8]

Two days later, Isaacs informed the Cabinet Emergencies Committee that the dockers in both cities appeared to be on the verge of returning to work.[9] Nevertheless, the Committee considered an agenda item on the 'Prosecution of Ring Leaders of Illegal Strikes',[10] the Home Secretary telling his colleagues that some Glasgow strikers, 'names known', had visited other ports with the intention of spreading the strike, and that while proceedings might prove difficult in the current case, the Committee ought to consider what should be done in future.

Although Order 1305 was not specifically mentioned, there was general agreement that the law could not be 'flouted', that prosecutions must ultimately be brought, and that TUC support should be sought before doing so. Addressing the question of prosecution, the youthful Attorney General, Hartley Shawcross, at that stage urged restraint on the ground that if the government acted against the instigators of unofficial strikes, 'it would be difficult to ignore similar action by responsible officials of trade unions who might be responsible for official but illegal strikes'. This uncharacteristic caution notwithstanding, the penal provisions of Order 1305 were now beginning to be recognised as part of the government's arsenal for dealing with strikes. It appears too that some thought was being given to the process of enforcing the law, in terms of who would initiate a prosecution, and in what circumstances. It will be recalled that during the war, Bevin was able to insist that prosecution would not be a matter for the law officers, but for the Ministry of Labour, which would use the power only in limited circumstances. What was emerging now in contrast was a suggestion that prosecution would be a matter to be determined collectively by the Cabinet Emergencies Committee advised by Shawcross,[11] who would become much less cautious as he became more confident in his role in the face of a rising tide of unofficial action.

[6] HC Debs, 29 April 1947, cols 1731–34.

[7] The only union mentioned at the CEC was the 'stevedores' union', presumably the National Amalgamated Stevedores and Dockers (NASD).

[8] TNA, CAB 128/9/42 (Cabinet Conclusions, 29 April 1947).

[9] TNA, CAB 134/175 (Cabinet Emergencies Committee, 1 May 1947). At that point the Glasgow dockers were still out pending a secret ballot and the London men had largely returned to work, although there were concerns that dissident elements might continue to hold out.

[10] Those present included Chuter Ede, the Secretary of State for Scotland (Hector McNeil), the Minister of Defence (Albert Alexander), the Attorney General (Hartley Shawcross), the Home Office Permanent Under Secretary (Frank Newsam), and Baker of the Home Office's F3 industrial policing division.

[11] This is because prosecution would be used only where there was a political element in the dispute, that is to say, where there was a smell of Communist engagement. Order 1305 was to be used as a weapon of counter-subversion, not as a weapon to deal with what was a minor industrial offence, which may help to explain why the role of the Ministry of Labour was being diminished if not sidelined.

The marginal role of the Ministry of Labour in this process was to be seen again when use of the penal provisions in Order 1305 was considered by the Cabinet Emergencies Committee in 1948 on the occasion of another dispute in London docks, a strike about the unloading of white oxide explored in great detail by Colin J Davis.[12] Despite the TGWU leadership claiming that the unofficial action was politically motivated,[13] 'Scotland Yard was of the opinion that the strike was not being fomented by Communists', albeit that 'there was some indication that the Communist Party was beginning to take an interest in it for political purposes'.[14] Noting that on 1 May 1947 the Cabinet Emergencies Committee agreed in principle to prosecute the instigators of illegal strikes (albeit without explicitly referring to Order 1305), it was considered that 'the present case might be a suitable one on which to take action'.[15] Shawcross again seemed cautious, warning colleagues 'that there were questions of policy to be decided before legal action was taken in cases of this kind, but that he would undertake to examine the legal points with the Parliamentary Secretary, Ministry of Labour [Ness Edwards]',[16] who had previously expressed scepticism about whether the dispute (between the workers and the dock labour board rather than their employers) was a trade dispute within the meaning of Order 1305.[17]

Deciding not to prosecute, the government instead chose to declare a state of emergency under the Emergency Powers Act 1920.[18] This was the first time since the General Strike in 1926 that the Emergency Powers Act 1920 had been invoked.[19] It was a grave step for any government to use such powers when faced with industrial action, and a grave step for a Labour government in particular. The Act – which was repealed and replaced in 2004 – could only be invoked where 'any action' had been taken or was immediately threatened 'by any body of persons of such a nature and on so extensive a scale as to be calculated, by interfering with the supply and distribution of food, water, fuel, or light, or with the means of locomotion, to deprive the community or any substantial portion of the community, of the essentials of life'.[20] The proclamation of a state of emergency was said by Jim Phillips to have been 'entirely disingenuous' and 'entirely symbolic',[21] an assessment reinforced by the fact that the government had other statutory powers to call in the troops without the need to deploy the 1920 Act.[22] Nevertheless, Attlee broadcast to the nation on 28 and again on 29 June 1948, explaining why the 1920 Act had been used, asking the men to return

[12] Davis (n 1) ch 5.

[13] TNA, CAB 134/175 (Cabinet Emergencies Committee, 21 June 1948).

[14] ibid.

[15] ibid.

[16] ibid. See also N Fishman, '"A Vital Element in British Industrial Relations': A Reassessment of Order 1305, 1940–51' (1999) 8 *Historical Studies in Industrial Relations* 43.

[17] Davis (n 1) p 119.

[18] HC Debs, 1 July 1948, col 2385.

[19] For a full account of the deployment of the 1920 Act, see GS Morris, 'The Emergency Powers Act 1920' [1980] *PL* 317.

[20] Emergency Powers Act 1920, s 1(1). The Act was repealed and replaced by the Civil Contingencies Act 2004.

[21] Phillips (n 1) p 65.

[22] These were replaced by the Emergency Powers Act 1964. The Cabinet was fully aware of them: see Cabinet Secretary's Notebook, 29 June 1948.

to work, claiming that they had been duped by political agitators to act against their own people and their own interests, while pointing out that:

> We have built up in this country a system of collective bargaining without parallel in the world. Under this system, agreements are made and machinery set up for settling disputes. Whether the employers are private firms or public bodies the same principles hold good. The success of this system depends on agreements being honoured on both sides.[23]

The men voted to return on 30 June. But Order 1305 was back on the agenda within the year. On this occasion, the National Amalgamated Stevedores and Dockers (NASD) called an official strike after a number of elderly London dockers had been effectively dismissed by the National Dock Labour Board.[24] Essentially, the dispute – 'the first official illegal strike since the end of the war' – was about the lack of any provision under the Dock Labour Scheme for illness or retirement, the NASD being joined by many TGWU men who came out in support, against the wishes of their union. The Cabinet, noting that the NASD was 'under communist influence', understood that the strike 'was aimed at dislocating essential services and impeding the delivery of the Marshall Plan'.[25] Ministers were also told by the Attorney General that the strike was illegal due to its failure to comply with the procedures in Order 1305, in what appears to be the first occasion on which Order 1305 is expressly referred to in full Cabinet proceedings in relation to any post-war industrial action. The Cabinet Emergencies Committee had already considered whether legal proceedings could be brought against the strikers or their organisers, inclining in favour of 'civil proceedings being brought by the National Dock Labour Board' in the apparently mistaken belief that the Board was 'the employer of the men concerned'.[26]

In a very full briefing to the Cabinet, Shawcross reported that it was impracticable 'to contemplate proceedings, either civil or criminal, against the general mass of the strikers'.[27] He continued:

> It would, however, be practicable for the National Dock Labour Board to take civil proceedings against individual strike leaders, if it could be shown that they were continuing to incite the men to break their contract of service. Alternatively, an attempt might perhaps be made to secure an injunction to prevent the Stevedores' Union from giving strike pay in respect of an illegal strike. A third possibility was that the Attorney-General himself should seek an injunction against individual strike leaders on the ground that their action was causing injury to the public interest. On the whole, he was doubtful about the value of civil proceedings, unless it was thought that a decision by a court that the strike was illegal might impress the strikers

[23] GG Eastwood, *George Isaacs: Printer, Trade-union Leader, Cabinet Minister* (Odhams Press, London, 1952), This contains a verbatim account of much of Attlee's address at pp 179–85. Attlee made it clear that the government could not recognise or deal with those who were leading an unofficial strike: 'To do so would cut at the whole basis of collective bargaining and the scheme for the regulation of working conditions' (at p 180).

[24] The NASD was a small occupational union, much more inclined to defend the interests of its members than the TGWU. The men, some of them very elderly, were taken off the register kept under the Dock Labour Scheme, and consequently they were no longer able to work. On the Dock Labour Scheme, see p 285 below.

[25] TNA, CAB 128/15/27 (Cabinet Conclusions, 13 April 1949). According to Isaacs, there was 'a deliberate attempt by Communists to create trouble for political reasons': TNA CAB 195/7/24 (Cabinet Secretary's Notebook, 13 April 1949).

[26] On civil liability more generally, see ch 4.

[27] TNA, CAB 128/15/27 (Cabinet Conclusions, 13 April 1949).

> and induce them to return to work. If proceedings were to be taken, he favoured summary criminal proceedings under the Defence Regulations for counselling and procuring a breach of the Conditions of Employment and National Arbitration Order, 1940. He assumed that it would be possible to collect evidence showing that individual strike leaders had incited their members to break the Order. A charge of criminal conspiracy, which would be taken on indictment, would be more difficult to sustain. The decision whether to take criminal proceedings would rest with him; but he would welcome an expression of view by Ministers on the question whether the prosecution of the leaders would be likely to stiffen or to weaken the resolution of the strikers.[28]

Shawcross' confidence was surprising. As in the case of the white oxide dispute above, this was a dispute between the union and the Board. Not being a dispute with employers it is difficult to see how Order 1305 could have applied. Nevertheless, in accordance with established practice at the time, it was appropriate that he should consult the Cabinet in advance.[29] On this occasion, he was advised that the strike was on the brink of collapse and that any premature action by the Attorney General might 'have the effect of stiffening the attitude of the rank and file'.[30] On the other hand, 'the Government could not appear to condone illegal action by a Trade Union', it being observed further that it 'would be more difficult to prosecute in any later case if proceedings were not taken in this case where the breach of the law had been wanton and so clearly based on political motives'. Trapped between industrial relations pragmatism and constitutional principle, the Cabinet dithered, unable to 'express a final view on the desirability of a prosecution at that juncture', but did want it to be made known publicly that 'the question of taking proceedings was being looked into'. To that end, evidence was to be gathered so that if the strike continued, 'the way would be clear to launch prosecutions about the time when military assistance was brought into the docks'.[31]

Shawcross nevertheless appears to have cleared Isaacs to threaten the NASD with the penal provisions of the Order, at which point Isaacs spoke to the General Secretary on the telephone, also making a broadcast on the BBC urging the men to return to work. On the day following the broadcast, the NASD held a mass meeting at which the General Secretary, Dick Barrett, told members that the union could not risk prosecution, and the men voted to go back to work. Significantly, Order 1305 was back in business, apparently deployed against the NASD unusually in the context of an official dispute, albeit one with what was claimed to have an underlying political element. Significantly too, the re-emergence of Order 1305 was distorting the government's vision on other matters, including paradoxically ILO Convention 87, which was the subject of a preliminary discussion by the Cabinet on the same day that Shawcross gave his legal advice on the NASD dispute (13 April 1949). As the Conclusions record, 'some anxiety was expressed

[28] ibid. According to the Cabinet Secretary, Shawcross had said: 'This is not a case in which I would prosecute without being assured by my colleagues there is no political objection to prosecution': TNA, CAB 195/7/24 (Cabinet Secretary's Notebook, 13 April 1949).

[29] See KD Ewing and CA Gearty, *The Struggle for Civil Liberties: Political Freedom and the Rule of Law in Britain, 1914–1945* (Oxford University Press, Oxford, 2000), pp 122–27 on the controversy around political interference in prosecutions that brought down the MacDonald government in 1924; and pp 137–38 on the restatement of principle by Douglas Hogg subsequently in relation to the prosecution of leading Communists for sedition.

[30] TNA, CAB 128/15/27 (Cabinet Conclusions, 13 April 1949).

[31] ibid.

at the possible consequences of ratifying the Convention on Freedom of Association and the Right to Organise'. This was because the Convention 'had been drafted in very general terms, and it might be found that it unduly restricted the Government's freedom of action in dealing with illegal strikes inspired by political, rather than industrial, objectives'.[32]

III. The Limitations of Order 1305 Reinforced

As the NASD strike was ending, another strike was brewing. By far the most notable industrial action taken at the time was the official solidarity action by the NASD on the one hand, and the unofficial solidarity action by members of the TGWU on the other, in support of the Canadian Seamen's Union (CSU) in a recognition dispute with Canadian ship-owners. This was notable because it was probably the most vivid example of international solidarity action in defence of freedom of association ever undertaken by British trade unionists, and notable too for the expulsion of several of the strike leaders from the TGWU in a muscular response by the union's General Secretary, a response which was to backfire spectacularly as the expulsions were met by a further prolonged period of unofficial industrial action by TGWU members on the docks, as will be discussed in section IV below. The action in support of the CSU lasted from 1 May until 23 July 1949 and involved at least eight vessels in five ports, causing a loss of 400,000 working days in total. It was brought to the Cabinet's attention for the first time on 26 May 1949, the dispute having been the subject of litigation between the owners and the crew earlier in the year.[33]

As explained subsequently by the government,[34] the dispute presented in three phases. The first, beginning on 1 May 1949, was confined initially to the Bristol Channel ports where the Avonmouth lock-gate-men and tugboat-men refused to facilitate the departure of the *Gulfside*. It was, however, some time before the matter was brought to the attention of the Cabinet, with the Home Secretary (not the Minister of Labour) referring on 26 May to 'the serious situation which was arising as a result of the action of the Canadian Seamen's Union in calling a strike affecting ocean-going vessels trading from the eastern seaboard of Canada', while observing that the ever-loyal Arthur Deakin was willing to allow 'volunteers' to be enlisted to unload the ships in question in order to bring an end to the dispute.[35] A notable feature of the Cabinet meeting on 26 May was the immediate jump to the conclusion that the whole thing was being stoked by the Communists for political reasons, which is presumably why it was a Home Office rather than a Ministry of Labour matter. And notable also that

[32] ibid. Ministers were right to anticipate its application to the right to strike generally, though the recognition of the right was not unlimited, and is still contested. For a seminal account, see Tonia Novitz, *International and European Protection of the Right to Strike* (Oxford University Press, Oxford, 2004). The UK was the first country to ratify the Convention, and Isaacs attended the ILO Conference in San Francisco when it was adopted. Indeed, his biographer reports that he attended all the annual ILO Conferences while Minister of Labour: Eastwood (n 23) pp 170–71.

[33] *Canadian Pacific Railway v Gaud* [1949] 2 KB 239. See pp 73–74 above.

[34] Review of the British Dock Strikes, Cmd 7851, 1949, para 3.

[35] TNA, CAB/128/15/38 (Cabinet Conclusions, 26 May 1949).

ministers felt that 'more effective steps should be taken to bring home to the dockers in the United Kingdom ports mainly affected the true facts and significance of this strike of Canadian seamen'.[36]

The first phase of the dispute continued until 15 June, having extended from Avonmouth to Liverpool, where 6,000 dockers had come out in sympathy with 45 men suspended for refusing to unload a ship diverted from Avonmouth.[37] But discontinuation of the action brought only brief respite, the Cabinet being informed by Isaacs about a second phase of the dispute on 20 June, NASD members having declined to unload two Canadian ships in London Docks (the *Beaverbrae* and the *Argomont*), with the result that '300 men had been suspended from employment in the port'.[38] As explained by Shawcross (writing over two weeks later), they had done so in support of 'the seamen on two Canadian ships, berthing respectively in the Surrey and Royal Groups of Docks', who had gone on strike 'believing, rightly or wrongly, that on their return to Canada they would not be re-engaged unless they joined the Seamen's International Union instead of the Canadian Seamen's Union'.[39] This second wave of industrial action ended on 24 June, but only after the Cabinet had been told that the NASD General Secretary, 'who was reported to have favoured the course taken by these men', was 'being seen at the Ministry of Labour that day'.[40] Dick Barrett appears again to have backed down in the face of undisclosed threats.

The third and much more bitter phase began only three days later, following 'an alleged' and hotly disputed 'breach of undertaking by the Canadian shipowners'.[41] This time members of *both* the NASD and the TGWU stopped work on the ships currently being unloaded in London, to be joined by dockers employed at other ports. Problems escalated quickly, with almost 14,000 workers and 132 vessels 'idle' by 13 July.[42] The steps taken to educate dockers about the menace of Communism had clearly failed, attention by now being focused on less benign methods to bring matters under control. These included Order 1305, which the government was being assailed by the Opposition to invoke. No doubt to his acute embarrassment, Shawcross was reminded about remarks made during the debates on the Trade Disputes and Trade Unions Act 1946, where he had used extravagant rhetoric to explain the need to sweep 'forever from the law of this country' what 'was bastard product of narrow legalism and craven politics'.[43] According to Quintin Hogg (a future Lord Chancellor), Shawcross had been 'utterly irresponsible and mischievous' and by his words as Attorney General of England and Wales had 'tended to bring the law into contempt'.[44] On 13 July 1949, Shawcross explained

[36] ibid. With this in mind, it was suggested by Attlee that 'it would be helpful if the true facts of the situation could be explained to the Avonmouth dockers by some trade unionist with an established local reputation in an address broadcast on the [BBC] West Regional Programme'.

[37] TNA, CAB/128/15/40 (Cabinet Conclusions, 2 June 1949).

[38] TNA, CAB/128/15/41 (Cabinet Conclusions, 20 June 1949).

[39] TNA, CAB 129/35/38 ('The London Dock Strike', Memorandum by the Attorney General, 8 July 1949).

[40] TNA, CAB/128/15/41 (Cabinet Conclusions, 20 June 1949).

[41] HC Debs, 13 July 1949, cols 441–42 (Prime Minister).

[42] Review of the British Dock Strikes (n 34) Appendix VIII.

[43] HC Debs, 2 April 1946, col 1214 (Third Reading).

[44] HC Debs, 13 July 1949, col 468.

nevertheless that Order 1305 could not be used in the Canadian seafarers' dispute, pointing out that:

> We cannot settle the dispute on the Canadian ships by any action which we can take in this country, and even if the matter had been referred to the Minister, it is very difficult to see that he could have referred it to the arbitration tribunal. I cannot speak for my right hon. Friend, of course, but I can say that when this wartime legislation was introduced, it contemplated very different circumstances from those existing here.[45]

But not everyone was convinced, the sceptics including Sir David Maxwell Fyfe, who had served briefly as Attorney General under Churchill during the war and was later to become Home Secretary in 1951, before being appointed Lord Chancellor in 1954 (sitting as Viscount Kilmuir). In reply to Shawcross, Maxwell Fyfe argued that 'this is a strike in connection with which none of the steps under Order 1305 had been taken'. In his view, therefore, 'there is *prima facie* illegality'.[46] But in a sense, that was not Shawcross' point, which was rather different. He was not disputing that the industrial action fell within the definition of a trade dispute for the purposes of Order 1305. Nor was he denying that Order 1305 did not apply *in principle* to disputes taking place overseas. Rather, he was saying that because it was a dispute between a Canadian employer and a Canadian trade union about de-recognition and the recognition of an American rival,[47] there was nothing *in practice* that the NAT could do to resolve the dispute. That being the case, the implication was that although the strike action by the dockers may have been in breach of Order 1305, Part II, it would not be appropriate to prosecute in circumstances where the dispute could not otherwise be resolved by the arbitration machinery established in Part I. This is a matter to which we will return in Chapter Twelve.

Apart from raising questions about the applicability of Order 1305, Shawcross also explained that while he was keen to prosecute the instigators of the action, he was 'very reluctant' to 'use the Order against ordinary individual strikers' who were 'loyal and sincere citizens who have been misled into this action by a misconception of the true facts'.[48] He made it clear nevertheless that 'if legally appropriate evidence were available of the commission of criminal offences on the part of those people upon whom the real responsibility for this stoppage lies, there would not be any hesitation in applying the law in the ordinary course', adding that 'the position in regard to other individuals is being carefully watched'.[49] The law being contemplated here included seditious conspiracy, for which Shawcross was making determined efforts to find evidence, as revealed by the diary of Guy Liddell, MI5's Deputy Director General.[50]

[45] ibid col 481.
[46] ibid col 558.
[47] As made clear in *Canadian Pacific Railway v Gaud* [1949] 2 KB 239, at p 241. Shawcross himself was to express the view 18 months later that Order 1305 applied to recognition disputes (TNA, CAB 129/44/9 ('The Future of the Conditions of Employment and National Arbitration Order', Memorandum by the Attorney General, 11 January 1951, para 6). This view was not shared by the Ministry of Labour, the position of which was subsequently vindicated by the decision in *R v Minister of Labour and National Service, ex parte Manning* (1951) Sol Jo 238. See ch 12 below.
[48] HC Debs, 13 July 1949, col 481.
[49] ibid col 480.
[50] For a fuller account, see KD Ewing, J Mahoney and A Moretta, *MI5, the Cold War and the Rule of Law* (Oxford University Press, Oxford, 2020).

As pointed out in Chapter Six, an entry for 7 July 1949 records a meeting between Liddell and an official from the DPP's office, who had been 'asked by Shawcross for an assurance that Special Branch and the Security Service were doing all they could in connection with the dock strike'.[51] On the same day as the latter diary entry, the Cabinet were informed that:

> [T]he police had little evidence about the activities of Communists in fomenting the various dock strikes, though strikers were being advised by persons with legal experience who had Communist sympathies. The Secretary of State for Commonwealth Relations had already suggested to various Commonwealth Governments that they should collect and pool information about the ramifications of the organisation which was causing disputes in ships and docks, and it would be useful if further enquiries could be made into this point in this country.[52]

It is clear from the foregoing that ministers believed that there was an international conspiracy behind the dock strikes, despite the inability of the security services to provide any evidence to justify this belief. But it is also clear that despite equivocation on Shawcross' part,[53] Order 1305 was not a reliable instrument for bringing the strikes to an end whether by arbitration or prosecution.[54] Apart from genuine doubts about Order 1305's scope, there was an understandable hesitation about prosecuting 14,000 strikers or a selection thereof in light of war-time experience (including Betteshanger, Cardowan, and Harland & Wolff. More importantly perhaps, there is a suggestion that the 'complicated' facts may also have acted as a restraining influence. Thus, in his memorandum to the Cabinet on 8 July, Shawcross explained that when the industrial action resumed on 27 June, 'the Port employers announced that, while work would continue on ships then in the course of loading or unloading, no labour would be requisitioned in respect of ships on which work had not begun'.[55] As Shawcross pointed out, 'this amounted in effect to an announcement of a lock out in respect of future ships', adding pointedly that 'neither employers nor workers gave notice under the Conditions of Employment and Arbitration Order'. It followed that 'there is a strike in relation to certain of the ships and a lockout in relation to others'.[56]

It was thus 'not possible in law to give unqualified support to the view that the present stoppage is a strike'. In these circumstances – which were not disclosed to Parliament during the debate on 13 July – it would have been difficult to prosecute strikers under Order 1305 without also prosecuting employers for the lock outs. This would be another good reason for focusing on sedition and the alleged Communist subversion, and for deciding again to fall back on the Emergency Powers Act 1920, the use of which did not depend on whether 'the present stoppage is a strike'.[57] It was enough that the action in

[51] TNA, KV4/471 (Liddell Diary, 7 July 1949).

[52] TNA, CAB/128/16/1 (Cabinet Conclusions, 7 July 1949).

[53] Note that Shawcross conceded in the Commons that he was 'far from saying that the Order could in no circumstances be applied in the present case': HC Debs, 13 July 1949, col 481.

[54] This is a point to which Shawcross returned some time later, expressing the view that the industrial action was beyond the reach of Order 1305 because it was in support of an overseas dispute: TNA, CAB/129/44/9 ('The Future of the Conditions of Employment and National Arbitration Order 1940', Memorandum by the Attorney General, 11 January 1951, para 6(iv)).

[55] TNA, CAB 129/3/38 ('The London Dock Strike', Memorandum by the Attorney General, 8 July 1949), para 9(d).

[56] ibid para 9(h).

[57] ibid.

question was calculated to deprive the community of the essentials of life.[58] But although a state of emergency was duly proclaimed on 11 July 1949, section 2(1) of the 1920 Act expressly prohibited the making of regulations empowering ministers to (i) stop the industrial action, or (ii) conscript workers to do work affected by the dispute. Yet, as indicated in the following box, Shawcross had cooked up a plan whereby the Emergency Regulations would not only allow for the better management of the dispute, but would also enable workers to be coerced to work despite the provisions of the 1920 Act and Shawcross' own admission that his plans might be unlawful. The state of emergency lasted until 26 July, three days after the dispute ended; the Emergency Regulations were then revoked accordingly.

The State of Emergency and the Rule of Law

In proposing that His Majesty should be invited to declare a state of emergency, Shawcross explained in a Memorandum of 8 July 1949 that there was no power under the ordinary law or under the Emergency Powers Act 1920 to introduce anything in the nature of industrial conscription by compelling men to work, adding that there was a power of direction under Defence Regulation 58A which was still in force. But Articles 16 and 17 of the Dock Labour Scheme enabled local dock labour boards to suspend or dismiss a registered dock worker for misconduct. Moreover, wrote Shawcross, 'under the ordinary law an action for damages would lie in the County Court against a dock worker who broke his contract of employment'. Although he was aware that local boards had been reluctant to use these powers, Shawcross was not as squeamish, having regard to the 'calamitous consequences' of the employers' decision on 27 June to institute a lock out'.[59]

Shawcross' plan was that following a state of emergency being declared, an independent port emergency committee should be established and that it should be directed to instruct the local dock labour boards to operate Articles 16 and 17 or to sue for damages, in the curious belief that the adverse repercussions would not be as acute as they would be if the action was taken at the initiative of the local dock labour boards.[60] Shawcross was to admit to his Cabinet colleagues that it was doubtful whether any such instruction would be 'legally enforceable', while other steps proposed 'may not be strictly intra vires'. But the risk should be taken nevertheless, ministers being advised not to have 'undue regard to the niceties of the law'. In an emergency, he continued, in what was extraordinary advice from a Law Officer, 'the Government may have, in matters admitting of legal doubt, to act first and argue about the doubts later, if necessary obtaining an indemnification Act'.[61]

[58] Emergency Powers Act 1920, s 1.
[59] TNA, CAB 129/3/38 ('The London Dock Strike', Memorandum by the Attorney General, 8 July 1949), para 3.
[60] ibid para 4.
[61] ibid para 5.

IV. The Limitations of Order 1305 Revealed Again

After several months' respite (and the holding of a general election on 23 February 1950), industrial action by dockers was resumed on 9 March 1950. On this occasion, the action was taken by the strikers in protest at the discipline of three of their colleagues, Harry Constable, Ted Dickens and Bert Saunders, who were expelled from the TGWU for their role in the London dock strike in 1949, with lesser sanctions being imposed on another five. At the same time as the London dockers were protesting about the expulsion of their unofficial leaders, there was a threat of strike action in a separate dispute between the NASD and the shipping company Shaw, Savill & Albion about working practices. Both disputes were likely to affect food distribution if they were prolonged, and both raised questions about the application of Order 1305. In bringing these matters to the attention of the Cabinet on 20 April 1950, Isaacs said that:

> [T]he unofficial Port Workers' Defence Committee had organised a stoppage of work in some of the London docks as a protest against the action of the Transport and General Workers' Union in expelling three men from the Union on account of their activities in connection with the London dock strike in 1949. This was independent of the current dispute between the Stevedores' Union and a shipping company which wished to engage some gangs of stevedores on weekly wages instead of by the day. Efforts to extend the stoppage of work had not so far been very successful; and, as it seemed unlikely that the unloading of any perishable cargoes would be delayed, the Minister thought that the Government should not be in a hurry to introduce emergency measures, such as the use of troops to unload ships.[62]

In addressing the troubles on the docks yet again in a statement to Parliament on the same day, Isaacs repeated that the strike by TGWU members was a response to the expulsion of three officials from the TGWU who had been blamed for the 1949 strike in support of the Canadian seamen, adding that:

> [T]he strike last summer resulted from the deliberate planning of Communist agitators in another country, supported by Communist sympathisers in this country. The cases of the three men expelled, one of whom is a well-known Communist, were dealt with as a domestic matter within the union and under its constitutional rules that govern such proceedings. Appeals were heard and the expulsion confirmed by a duly constituted committee consisting entirely of rank and file members of the union.[63]

According to Isaacs, the new unofficial strike by dockers was part of a continuing conspiracy and was 'in no way connected with any dispute with the employers regarding rates and conditions of employment'.[64] Throwing in a fresh allegation, Isaacs told the House that the dockers' action demonstrated 'once again the lengths to which the Communists are prepared to go in their attempt – and I am glad to say their losing attempt – to gain control of the trade union movement'.[65]

On the following day (21 April), the Attorney General circulated a memorandum to Cabinet colleagues on the legal issues surrounding both disputes. Dealing mainly

[62] TNA, CAB 128/17/22 (Cabinet Conclusions, 20 April 1950). The final sentence is a reference to the first but not the second dispute.
[63] HC Debs, 20 April 1950, col 331.
[64] ibid cols 330–31.
[65] ibid.

with criminal liability in the dispute involving TGWU members, Shawcross' initial focus was the anti-strike provisions in Order 1305. According to the Attorney General in relation to the strike by TGWU members:

> The present stoppage is not a 'trade dispute' within the meaning of the Trade Disputes Act, 1906, or of [Order 1305], nor is it a 'strike' within the meaning of the last named Order. It is in effect an attempt by a section of Dock workmen to compel their Trade Union to reverse a decision come to in accordance with the Union's rules and in the meantime to hold up work in the Docks in the hope that thereby pressure will be brought to bear on the Executive of the Union. It is clear from reports of speeches I have seen that the movement is directed against the leadership of the Union. It is therefore manifest that the stoppage relates to a domestic matter within the Union.[66]

It therefore followed that criminal proceedings could not be taken under Order 1305. According to Shawcross, however, 'as it is not a trade dispute within the meaning of the Trade Disputes Act, 1906, any conspiracy on the part, for instance, of the members of the Strike Committee to induce a breach of contract or of the Dock Labour Scheme by the Dock workers would, if it could be established by evidence, constitute an indictable offence at common law'.[67]

Turning to civil liabilities, Shawcross drew attention to the distinction between the National Dock Labour Board and the men's employers, clarifying the implications of this distinction that had been missed by ministers in the earlier disputes referred to above. He argued that the most obvious remedy was 'of course' that which was expressly provided by the disciplinary machinery set up by the Dock Workers (Regulation of Employment) Order 1947. This, however, was a matter for the National Dock Labour Board, the government having no legal power whatsoever to give directions to the Board in a matter such as this, 'since (subject to such influence as the Government may see fit to exercise on particular members) the decision is one solely within the domestic competence of the Board'.[68] Otherwise, dockers who had stopped work during the currency of an engagement 'whether for the week, or, more usually, for the day, committed a breach of the contract of employment existing between them and their employers'.[69] 'For this breach', continued Shawcross, 'their employers could, if so advised, claim damages either by a civil action in the County Court or, under the Employers and Workmen Act 1875, in the Magistrates' Courts. In the latter case the amount claimable is limited to £10 exclusive of costs'.[70]

So far as the dispute between the NASD and Shaw, Savill & Albion was concerned, Shawcross indicated clearly that his advice about Order 1305 referred to above about the TGWU members did not conceal any reluctance on his part to prosecute. On the

[66] TNA, CAB 129/39/27 ('Stoppage in the London Docks', Memorandum by the Attorney General, 21 April, 1950).

[67] ibid. This was presumably because the definition of a trade dispute in the 1906 Act was the same as the definition for the purposes of the Conspiracy and Protection of Property Act 1875, s 3.

[68] ibid.

[69] ibid.

[70] ibid. However, 'in order to obtain judgment for more than nominal damages (a shilling or a penny) the employers would have to prove actual damage. This, I think, they would probably be able to do but only in a small amount' (ibid).

contrary, it was by now obvious that he was itching for a fight, advising the Cabinet as follows:

> I take the opportunity of referring to the application of [Order 1305] to other disputes which may occur in the future. The threatened strike by stevedores in the London Docks would clearly be illegal. So might a strike by engineers following the ballot now being taken. It is my duty as Attorney-General to consider whether or not prosecutions ought to be brought under this Order and I must accept full responsibility. I am, however, entitled to seek the advice of my colleagues whether they are aware of any special grounds which might lead me to consider such prosecutions inexpedient in the public interest. I have hitherto refrained from proceeding under the Order owing to the fear that action might simply exacerbate the strike situation. I think it has to be recognised that the ordinary processes of the criminal law are ineffective to stop large-scale strike action, but while this very explicit Order remains in existence I find it increasingly difficult to refrain from operating it, since it is impossible to allow the law to be consistently and contemptuously flouted. As at present advised I am inclined to direct prosecutions in the next suitable case, which might be the threatened stevedores strike, in which evidence is available. While, however, in no way seeking to abdicate my responsibility I should be grateful for the advice of my colleagues if any particular reasons are known to them affecting the public interest which I might take into account in arriving at my decision. It is indeed for consideration whether it is desirable to maintain the Order in existence at all if it is to be broken with impunity.[71]

The Cabinet considered Shawcross' memorandum on the same day it was circulated (21 April), Isaacs reporting in relation to the NASD dispute that the union 'had on the previous evening rejected a suggestion that the matter should be handled by the conciliation machinery of the industry, and had declined to go to arbitration. If the employers agreed, it would probably be desirable to refer the matter to the National Arbitration Tribunal'.[72] Shawcross repeated his claim that strike action 'would probably be illegal within the terms of [Order 1305]' and 'he felt that it would be difficult for him to refrain from prosecutions since the Order, so long as it remained in force, could not be allowed to become a dead letter'.[73] On again requesting the views of ministers on the political and other repercussions of any prosecutions,[74] Shawcross received advice which was most probably unwelcome. The Cabinet agreed 'to postpone for consideration at a later meeting the question whether Ministers should express a view on the possible repercussions of a prosecution of stevedores, if they engaged in an illegal strike, for breach of [Order 1305]'.[75]

That comes pretty close to a Cabinet veto rather than the expression of an opinion, and one that constitutionally Shawcross probably ought not to have entertained. He may of course have ignored the foregoing, and decided not to proceed under Order 1305 for wholly unrelated reasons. Curiously, there is no entry in Norman Brook's Notebook covering this crucial meeting, the Notebook jumping from 20 April to 24 April (and notably in the case of the meeting on 20 April, Brook was absent from the room for 15 minutes while the dock strike was being discussed).[76] So we are denied the opportunity

[71] ibid.
[72] TNA, CAB 128/17/23 (Cabinet Conclusions, 21 April 1950).
[73] ibid.
[74] ibid.
[75] ibid.
[76] TNA, CAB 195/7/85 (Cabinet Secretary's Notebook, 20 April 1950).

of a fuller account of what was said on 21 April, which would have been especially important in relation to 'advice' given to Shawcross. There was, however, no need for advice in relation to the dispute involving TGWU members, Shawcross repeating his opinion that the stoppage 'was not a "trade dispute" and was not, therefore, illegal within the terms of [Order 1305]'.[77] In the absence of criminal liability, Shawcross returned to the question of dismissal of the strikers:

> [T]he disciplinary code under the Dock Workers (Regulation of Employment) Order, 1947, had, however, been infringed; and it would be open to the Dock Labour Board to suspend men for a period not exceeding seven days, or to discharge them from the scheme. Since the men were already suspending themselves from the scheme, suspension as distinct from discharge did not appear to be an effective remedy. Employers could probably institute civil proceedings in the county court or police court for breach of contract, where men engaged on daily or longer contracts had stopped work in the middle of the day. It would, of course, be difficult to assess the amount of the damages and those awarded against individual dockers might be of the order of £1 or less.[78]

Picking up the Attorney-General's last point, ministers 'with experience of the practice of bringing civil proceedings against miners who came out on strike in breach of contract' quite remarkably favoured civil proceedings for breach of contract. This would be against 2,000 dockers mainly in the Royal Docks who were believed to have broken their contracts by stopping work in the middle of the day:

> In the long run civil penalties were likely to be more effective in discouraging Communist-inspired stoppages than attempts to enforce the disciplinary code against large numbers of workers. The unions could undertake the defence of the men in court and could endeavour to compound with the employers on the amounts which had eventually to be paid; and this would help to strengthen the position of the unions. Other Ministers were doubtful whether it was expedient for the Government to encourage employers to take civil proceedings; and *The Minister of Transport* said that, while the employers might be prepared to take proceedings, they would undoubtedly argue that the proper course was for the Dock Labour Board to take action under the disciplinary code.[79]

There appears, however, to have been little or no support for the option of dismissal by the National Dock Labour Board of what were said to be over 7,000 dockers who had stopped work: 'this might lead to a wide extension of the stoppage and it would be necessary to employ troops in place of the dockers for a period the length of which could not be predicted'.[80] But it was accepted that dismissal was a decision for the Board, not the government, though the 'Minister of Labour would doubtless be given an opportunity of seeing the terms of any notice which the London Board proposed to put up'. At the Cabinet meeting on 27 April, those present were told about plans by the London Dock Labour Board to consult the National Dock Labour Board for approval to dismiss the strikers.[81] Ministers were alarmed because it was believed that

[77] This would be because the dispute was between the workmen and their union, not between workmen and an employer, or between workmen and workmen, as Order 1305 required. This was to be the central issue in the 1951 trial considered in ch 13 below.
[78] TNA, CAB 128/17/23 (Cabinet Conclusions, 21 April 1950).
[79] ibid.
[80] ibid.
[81] TNA, CAB 128/17/26 (Cabinet Conclusions, 27 April 1950).

the National Board would sanction the move, the Cabinet believing it to be 'inexpedient to threaten dismissal at the present time'.[82] Isaacs was told to ensure that the plan was aborted,[83] a wise decision that avoided further trouble at a time when the disputes were being brought under control. They were considered by the Cabinet for the last time on 1 May 1950.[84]

V. The Re-activation of Order 1305

Two more disputes in the docks were thus brought to an end without a prosecution, though the decisions about prosecutions were notable for revealing high levels of political interference in prosecution decisions. Predictably, however, the problems were to continue, as the influence of the port workers spread, and with it the willingness of workers in other sectors to indulge in unofficial action. On 23 June 1950, lorry drivers serving the Smithfield Meat Market took strike action in a dispute about wages, without the authority of their union, which again was the TGWU. Reflecting his growing frustration with unofficial action, the Attorney General told the Cabinet Emergencies Committee on 26 June that 'the stage was rapidly being reached at which, if the law were not to be brought into contempt, its enforcement against unofficial strikers would have to be considered'.[85] On the following day, the same Committee heard that Deakin 'had quite failed to persuade the men to go back to work', Deakin telling Isaacs that 'in his view the strike had been organised in advance and he hoped the Government would stand firm'. The Committee also heard, presumably from Special Branch, that 'the unofficial Port Workers Committee' had 'issued instructions that if the troops were used for handling meat at the docks and cold stores all the workers there were to strike'. Ministers nevertheless took the view that they should not hesitate to use the military,[86] though the government was loath to risk provoking the dockers by having the troops attempt to collect meat from the docks.

On 28 June, Shawcross made his frustrations known to the Cabinet, noting in a fresh memorandum on the legal position that the government had 'deliberately continued [Order 1305] in operation', yet so far had 'refrained from taking any criminal proceedings'.[87] With 'the law about illegal strikes to be flouted', Shawcross was apparently now worried by the prospect of 'strong criticism' if he continued 'to treat the Order as a dead letter'.[88] The Attorney General therefore wished to seek the view of ministers again in relation to the question of instituting criminal proceedings should the necessary

[82] ibid.
[83] ibid. Isaacs was told to 'arrange for the London Dock Labour Board to be informed that, in the view of the Government, it would be untimely for them to approach the National Dock Labour Board for advice on the handling of the situation'.
[84] TNA, CAB 128/17/27 (Cabinet Conclusions, 1 May 1950).
[85] TNA, CAB 134/177 (Cabinet Emergencies Committee, 26 June 1950). There were two meetings of the CEC on that day.
[86] TNA, CAB 134/177 (Cabinet Emergencies Committee, 27 June 1950). As pointed out in the discussion (Isaacs, Robert Gould, and Shawcross were in attendance), the employers were free to report the dispute: 'It would then be open to the Minister of Labour to refer the matter for compulsory arbitration.'
[87] TNA, CAB 129/40/43 ('Illegal Strikes', Memorandum by the Attorney General, 28 June 1950).
[88] ibid.

evidence be available. Shawcross was careful to explain the constitutional basis for his decision to consult colleagues. In a more assertive recitation than previously, the Attorney wrote that:

> I think the true doctrine is that it is the duty of the Attorney-General in deciding whether or not to authorize a particular prosecution to acquaint himself with all relevant facts including, for instance, the effect which a prosecution, successful or unsuccessful (as the case might be) would have upon public morale and order, and with any other considerations affecting public policy. In order so to inform himself he may, but he is not obliged to, consult with any of his colleagues or with the Cabinet but their assistance must be confined to informing him of particular considerations which may influence his own decision and must not consist in recommending what that decision should be. The responsibility for the eventual decision lies solely upon the Attorney-General and he is not to be put under pressure by his colleagues in the matter nor is he entitled to ask them directly for, nor ought they to give, their opinion as to what his decision ought to be.[89]

With that out of the way, the Attorney General formally asked colleagues 'whether any circumstances are known to them which they think [he] ought to take into account in deciding whether or not to prosecute in the case of the present strike in the event of the police having adequate evidence on which such a prosecution might be founded'.[90]

In addressing these matters, Shawcross made clear that he was contemplating such action with hesitation, being unconvinced that 'the prosecution of a handful of individuals in the course of a strike is likely to have any particularly useful effect', having 'never favoured the use of the police court for the purpose of breaking strikes, unless indeed something in the nature of a seditious conspiracy is involved'.[91] But so long as the government 'see fit to maintain the existing law', he could not 'continuously shut [his] eyes to its existence'.[92] Following a detailed discussion of the dispute at Cabinet on 29 June,[93] Shawcross presented his paper. The official record of the discussion – which must have been led by Shawcross and Isaacs – highlighted the problems faced by the government if no one reported the dispute to the Minister of Labour:

> The dispute could not be taken to arbitration under the Conditions of Employment and National Arbitration Order, 1940, because neither the employers nor the Union had asked that the dispute should be taken to arbitration and the Minister could not be satisfied that the resources of the ordinary negotiating machinery had been exhausted. It was suggested that there ought on such occasions to be some means of ensuring reference to arbitration: but on the other side it was pointed out that this would undermine the authority of the Trade Union and imply recognition of those who had organized an unofficial strike. On the present occasion this would be specially unfortunate if the Tribunal were to make an award which was in excess of the employers' offer or made it impossible to apply the conditions regarding restrictive practices which would be a valuable feature of the settlement which the employers were endeavouring to reach.[94]

[89] ibid.
[90] ibid.
[91] ibid.
[92] ibid.
[93] TNA, CAB 128/17/40 (Cabinet Conclusions, 29 June 1950).
[94] ibid.

This is a matter to which we return, raising as it does important questions about how workers dissatisfied with their union could have their grievances addressed without taking action that was a one-way ticket to the criminal courts. Ignoring any such concerns, Shawcross was given a green light to proceed, but against the dockers as well as the drivers, the Port Workers' Committee having allegedly infiltrated the unofficial drivers' group:

> In discussion Ministers expressed serious disquiet at the action taken by members of the Port Workers' Committee in actively fomenting an unofficial strike in an industry with which they were not themselves concerned. If the leading members of the Committee could be shown to have been responsible for this, their action would appear to amount to a conspiracy which public opinion would regard as meriting imprisonment. The leaders of the meat drivers' stoppage might not be thought to deserve imprisonment, but, if they were convicted and fined, the effect might be salutary.
>
> *The Attorney-General* said that, in reaching his decision on the question whether any criminal proceedings should be instituted, he would take account of the considerations of public policy to which reference had been made in the Cabinet's discussion.[95]

Note that the Cabinet Conclusion was not that PWC members should be prosecuted, but that they should be imprisoned, which speaks volumes for the confidence the Cabinet had about judicial proceedings. It is surely unusual for the Cabinet to contemplate the imprisonment of anyone, as if it could be secured as a matter of routine, in complete disregard for the legal process.[96]

But while ministers agreed that PWC members were to be prosecuted, the exchanges revealed by the Cabinet Secretary's more detailed account of the meeting suggest that some had in mind prosecutions for seditious conspiracy and others for prosecutions based on Order 1305.[97] The evidence of the Port Workers' Committee's involvement had been supplied by the Home Secretary, who was able give the Cabinet the news conveyed to the Cabinet Emergencies Committee a few days earlier (presumably supplied by Special Branch), that the PWC were 'intervening from outside to foment an illegal strike'. Isaacs reminded his colleagues of Betteshanger, and it was agreed as result to go for the instigators and leave the rank and file alone. He also chipped in to claim that the drivers' action was political: 'Object is to embarrass Government not to improve conditions. They got a substantial rise in August "49"'. Morrison – evidently a conspiracy theorist as well as a pragmatic politician – told his Cabinet colleagues '[t]here is a subtle brain behind this', and that 'housewives are getting tired of [the] Smithfield business'. But as ministers rushed to jail the PWC's leaders, the Home Secretary highlighted one snag: while there were trade disputes and unlawful strikes, there was no evidence of any seditious conspiracies.

The search for evidence nevertheless continued. In the meantime, on 6 July – just 11 days after the beginning of the Korean War – a tug boatmen's strike was briefly discussed in Cabinet, the strikers also being TGWU members. Attlee asked Isaacs whether the action was 'Communist inspired?'[98] Isaacs replied in the affirmative, telling the Prime Minister and the other ministers present: 'Yes. Related to Korea.'[99] The Home

[95] ibid.

[96] Hugh Dalton is reported by Norman Brook as saying: 'Go for Port Committee and get them in jail. Korea would help you. Leave the others alone': TNA, CAB 129/8/14 (Cabinet Secretary's Notebook, 29 June 1950).

[97] ibid, on which the rest of this paragraph draws.

[98] TNA, CAB/195/8/17 (Cabinet Secretary's Notebook, 6 July 1950).

[99] ibid.

Secretary, no doubt aware as a result of the information reaching him from Special Branch that the strikers were motivated by dissatisfaction with their terms and conditions of employment and with their union, observed that there was an 'increasing implication that the TGWU have no disciplinary control over their men'.[100] Isaacs stood up for the union leader: 'Communists are out to get Deakin, who is spearhead of TU attack on Communism',[101] also pointing out Deakin's attitude of 'no compromise' and 'no concession to unofficial strikers'.[102] Attlee, apparently addressing both Isaacs and Chuter Ede,[103] asked the question that the Cabinet Secretary Norman Brook was to put to senior MI5 officers on the following day: 'Can't you find out who is behind these strikes?'[104] Both the Prime Minister and the Cabinet Secretary were essentially asking to be reassured that the strikes were being directed by the Communist Party.

Isaacs was, however, obliged to acknowledge that: 'Home Office have found nothing, save Port Workers' Committee'. The Home Secretary clarified his colleague's statement: 'No evidence of Communist inspiration.'[105] Shawcross' only contribution to the discussion was to state that the 'Police are looking for evidence for criminal proceedings',[106] and to ask his colleagues whether the employers of the lorry drivers in the Smithfield strike had 'considered proceedings for damages', presumably against the strikers individually.[107] He had at some point in the previous few days spoken to Leonard Burt, head of Special Branch, MI5's Guy Liddell recording in his diary on 5 July that:

> Burt tells me that he was sent for by Shawcross, who wishes to institute prosecutions for conspiracy against the Smithfield strikers. Miss Nunn [Principal Private Secretary to Chuter Ede and his Tory successor Maxwell Fyfe], whom I saw subsequently at the Home Office, told me that this was a question which had come up frequently but it had always failed, owing to a lack of evidence, or at any rate evidence that could be used. The prosecutions (sic) for a breach of contract in not giving sufficient notice before strike action were generally cumbersome and ineffective.[108]

By 10 July, the police had given up looking for evidence of political motivation amongst the Smithfield men.[109] According to the Home Secretary:

> No evidence of any political motive in this strike, though we have tried hard to find some. Special Branch report to DPP names a man called Tribe whom [Bob] Mellish believes to be at bottom of it all. Paid organiser for TGWU in Smithfield.[110]

[100] ibid.
[101] ibid.
[102] ibid. (Deakin's position was set out very clearly in A Deakin, 'Trade Unionism v Communism: The Gloves are off!', *TGWU Record*, July 1949, pp 7–8).
[103] ibid.
[104] TNA, CAB 301/20 ('Interviews at Leconfield House', 7 July 1950). Brook's handwriting is unmistakable.
[105] TNA, CAB/195/8/17 (Cabinet Secretary's Notebook, 6 July 1950).
[106] ibid.
[107] ibid.
[108] TNA, KV4/472 (Liddell Diary, 5 July 1950). It seems likely that the last sentence was a muddled reference to the fact that while strikes were technically breaches of contract it was impractical for an employer to sue all of its own workers. If it was a reference to the possibility of criminal proceedings under the Conspiracy and Protection of Property Act 1875, s 5, there was no known precedent.
[109] TNA, CAB/195/8/18 (Cabinet Secretary's Notebook, 10 July 1950).
[110] ibid. Bob Mellish was MP for Rotherhithe. Born in Bermondsey, he was said by Tam Dalyell MP to have been 'the authentic voice of working class dockland London': 'Obituary: Lord Mellish', *The Independent*, 11 May 1998.

The Cabinet was by now agonising over the dispute. Meat supplies ashore were dwindling and it was increasingly looking as if they would have to authorise the use of troops to attempt to collect meat from the docks.[111] This in turn could trigger not only a walk out of dockers but also of petrol tanker drivers. Shawcross continued to press in Cabinet for prosecutions in order to bring the situation under control. But now the focus was on strikers, not instigators, the Attorney General reporting to ministers that:

> Saw DPP this morning. Raised difficulties re proceedings, including the Minister of Labour's view that stoppages in other parts of road haulage industry are not '[trade] disputes'. No evidence of anyone inciting others to strike. Could prosecute a few men for striking. Have told DPP that members of the strike committee should be asked by police whether they are members.[112]

Shawcross' order (or suggestion) that the DPP instruct the police to question members of the unofficial drivers' group (the Road Haulage Workers and Allied Trades Committee) might well have been a veiled instruction to 'lean on' the members of the group, although neither the Attorney General nor the DPP had any constitutional authority to direct the police. The dispute was, however, very rapidly brought to an end when the matter was referred to arbitration, the problems highlighted in Cabinet on 29 June by Isaacs and Shawcross apparently having been overcome.[113] Here was proof if any were needed that the strike arose because of a grievance over low pay, together with TGWU and Ministry of Labour inaction. The Cabinet's obsession with Communist plots had distracted ministers when they should have been addressing the real but comparatively simple problems they faced.

VI. Conclusion

Beset by unofficial industrial action on the docks and in the TGWU more widely, the government responded initially by using troops as strike-breakers, before moving on to the use of the Emergency Powers Act 1920, while contemplating also the use of the law to punish those who organised strikes. But although Order 1305 was closely examined and could be and was used as a threat against the NASD, it proved to be of limited utility against the participants and organisers of the contemporary unofficial strikes. This is because fortuitously it did not apply to strikes which were not connected to trade disputes as defined, an exclusion which appeared to rule out its use in the Canadian seafarers' dispute and the subsequent dispute following the expulsion of the three PWC activists. And even in disputes to which Order 1305 did apply, there was a caution about using it, with growing ambitions to do so tempered by realism and the long-term damage

[111] There were fears not only that such a step would cause the dockers to walk out, but that it might also lead to maintenance men in cold stores in the London area going on strike. Ministers and officials contemplated restricting service personnel to one group of docks or to increasing the amount of meat loaded directly from ships onto trains in dockside sidings (see TNA, CAB 134/177 (Cabinet Emergencies Committee, 4 July 1950)), although the latter idea was ultimately dismissed on the ground that the dockers would realise what was going on, and that it might even lead to rail strikes.

[112] TNA, CAB/195/8/18 (Cabinet Secretary's Notebook, 10 July 1950). The brackets indicate that a guess has been made where the writing is indecipherable.

[113] See pp 135–136 above.

to industrial relations that could be caused by steps taken in response to short-term frustrations. Nevertheless, the limitations of the law were to be revealed again, just as the Smithfield strike was coming to an end, with the Home Secretary circulating the memorandum to colleagues referred to in Chapter Four expressing concern about the conduct of the war in Korea which had started on 25 June 1950, and the possibility of it being frustrated by the subversive activities of politically motivated trade unionists and others.[114]

Apparently worried that attempts would be made, as in Australia and France, to induce workers to interfere with supplies, it was at this point that the Home Secretary introduced his proposals to deal with the potential for strike action by dock workers.[115] As we saw in Chapter Four, he was 'disturbed' to discover that if 'dockers refused to handle supplies destined for Korea, there was nothing that could be done under the existing law to deal with them, or with the people who may have incited them to withdraw their labour'.[116] Although – again as we have already seen – Ede was supported in his call for legislation by Shawcross, these proposals never bore fruit.[117] As discussed in Chapter Four, it would have been a remarkable irony if having repealed the Trade Disputes and Trade Unions Act 1927 early in its first term, the Attlee government were to introduce similar albeit much narrower restrictions at the beginning of its second, particularly as experience would suggest that the Home Secretary had over-reacted to the threat of politically inspired action designed to frustrate the war effort. Whatever the dockers and their official and unofficial leaders may have thought about the hostilities, we are unaware of any industrial action designed specifically to disrupt military or other supplies for troops in Korea. There was no need for legislation, though, as we will discuss in the next chapter, the port workers continued to cause real concern.

[114] See pp 72–73 above.
[115] TNA, CAB 128/18/8 (Cabinet Conclusions, 20 July 1950).
[116] ibid.
[117] See pp 72–73 above.

8

Preparing for Prosecution

Surveillance and Co-ordination

I. Introduction

Ministerial concern about unofficial action continued into September 1950, and no doubt increased when the TUC Annual Congress rejected the continuation of the government's pay freeze. Delegates did so despite a personal plea from the Prime Minister who had addressed Congress to ask for the help of 'the mass of steady sober British trade unionists' in defeating what he called the 'fanaticism of the Communists', a struggle which needed 'in every member of the great Labour Movement a constant realisation of the ideals for which we stand'.[1] The rejection of wage restraint did not mean that the TUC had turned against 'their' government: a resolution demanding an end to Order 1305 and 'compulsory arbitration' was defeated at the same Conference. Nevertheless, the rejection of the wages policy was a blow to the authority of the administration, and a personal defeat for Attlee. The fact that the wages policy resolution had been tabled by a Communist will have done nothing to assuage the paranoia of the Cabinet. If ministers were to be believed, the country was on the brink of a September Revolution.

Thirteen days in September 1950 witnessed a peak in anxiety levels about unofficial industrial action, and in particular the influence of the PWC and other unofficial bodies. Ministers were convinced that the latter provided a platform for Communist-inspired industrial action designed to disrupt essential services at a time of international conflict involving British troops in Korea. This conviction continued to lack evidence, an essential ingredient which, as we saw in previous chapters, was in short supply. In this chapter we consider the Cabinet meeting of 14 September, which marks the high water mark of collective ministerial alarm, and thereafter the steps taken to deal with it. The latter are significant notably for recognising the powerlessness of the government in terms of dealing with the problem, leading to a determination by ministers and officials – led by the Home Office – to co-ordinate efforts to find evidence to sustain a prosecution finally to crush the leaders of the unofficial dockers' movement in particular.

[1] TUC, *Annual Report 1950* (1950), p 354.

II. 'On the Eve of Revolution'

More bad news was to follow the TUC's rejection of wage restraint, with the threat of industrial action by the busmen and the dockers making the news on the next day.[2] Thereafter, headlines in *The Times* referred to 'Threat to Union Authority' and 'Members' Discontent'.[3] The union in question was, of course, the TGWU. During the summer, a new 'Dockers' Charter' had been drawn up, highlighting the depth of the dockers' grievances, with their modest demands being much the same as they had been in 1945. It will be recalled from Chapter Seven that the latter had included an increase in the basic rate of pay from sixteen to twenty-five shillings per day, two weeks' annual holiday with pay, and pensions for old and infirm port workers. These demands were now reinforced by the not unreasonable claim that '*ten* hours per day, four times a week, eight hours on another day, and four hours on a Saturday are *NOT* just and proper hours of work', particularly when the arduous nature of the work was considered. There were also complaints about the 'heavy sick and accident rate', caused by 'excessive overtime'.[4] Needless to say, information about the dockers' concerns made its way to the government from various sources, with a copy of the Charter on deposit in a Home Office file.

The Times' coverage was followed two days later by a provocative report in the Labour-supporting *Daily Herald*. On the front page, next to a column about the first British serviceman to be killed in Korea,[5] was a story headlined:

> **Wave of strikes plotted in docks**
>
> Communists and their stooges are trying to promote another outbreak of dock strikes in British and West European ports this autumn … part of a plot to cripple recovery this side of the Iron Curtain. Behind the plot in this country is the unofficial Port Workers Defence Committee … Three members of the London committee have just returned from a Warsaw conference … one purpose was to see that the coming campaign in Britain is closely co-ordinated with similar activity on the Continent.[6]

The author, George Thomas, went on to warn his readers that Communist-inspired strikes were indistinguishable from unofficial strikes brought by workers demanding improved terms and conditions of employment:

> The technique followed is this: The men are urged to demand more pay, longer holidays and pensions, but are told – and this is the key point – that only 'militant action' preferably on a national scale, will get results.
>
> This follows strictly the policy of the Cominform, which is to engineer strikes, not to promote improvements for the men.

[2] *The Times*, 9 September 1950.
[3] *The Times*, 12 September 1950.
[4] TNA, HO 45/25546 ('Disturbances: strikes in industry: communist instigated subversion') (Home Office F3 file 827723/331, 'Unofficial Strikes (Communist Instigation')).
[5] Reg Streeter, who was due to have been demobbed in October. One of the other major stories was 'TIGHT GRIP ON PRICES' about Hugh Gaitskell's pledge 'to prevent prices from soaring and profiteers from gaining as a result of the three year £3,600,000,000 rearmament programme', which Jowitt promised 'will not cause any cuts in the social services. If they were slashed it would only lead to a seething discontent which a small but active group would exploit to the uttermost'.
[6] *Daily Herald*, 14 September 1950.

> They sidestep the fact that dockers have a democratic organisation for making claims and for negotiating on them.[7]

It is not known who fed this story to the *Daily Herald*. But Isaacs and Deakin, as well as the Foreign Office's Information Research Department, would head any list of suspects.

George Isaacs took a copy of the *Daily Herald* with him to the Cabinet meeting on the same day. Together with the earlier piece in *The Times*, it no doubt helped to inform the discussion which was dominated by an agenda item on 'Industrial Disputes – Communist Incitement'.[8] The Conclusions from that meeting are extraordinary, recording a lurid analysis of Communist influence at a time when the recent general election revealed support for the Communist Party to be in freefall.[9] Nevertheless, it was claimed by the Minister of Labour that:

> [T]he Communist Party appeared to be actively engaged in an attempt to disrupt transport in this country, and had formed a rail and road transport section for this purpose. There seemed to be no adequate grounds for the present strike of London busmen, who had already obtained substantial concessions, but appeared to be adopting the tactics of submitting further claims as soon as outstanding claims were settled. As regards the docks three Communist members of the unofficial London port-workers defence committee had recently returned from a Warsaw conference convened by the Polish dockers' union, and they doubtless had been given a plan of campaign. In Liverpool a dock strike committee had been formed which might provoke a strike in the Liverpool docks on the following day. Unofficial port-workers' committees had been formed in Manchester and Hull. The aim at all the ports was to put forward claims on behalf of the dockers for increased wages, a shorter working week and pensions schemes. Information had been received which suggested that an attempt might be made to interfere with the sailing of two ships which were loaded with goods for Korea. An article in a publication of the Czechoslovak Ministry of Foreign Trade, signed by an official in the Polish Ministry of Transport, stated openly that it was hoped to capture for Gdynia the trans-shipment trade now done in London and other European ports.[10]

Isaacs went on to suggest that 'early discussions should be held with the General Council of the Trades Union Congress on the steps which could be taken to counter this Communist campaign'. He also pointed out that 'the General Secretary of the Transport and General Workers' Union was pressing for action to be taken against the Communist Party'.

A very full discussion is then reported in the Conclusions, in which a number of notable points were made. The first related to an assessment of the Communist Party's political strategy, undoubtedly briefed by MI5. According to the report, the Communists were said to have 'embarked upon a campaign of political warfare, which they would intensify as the Government defence programme got under way'. Having tried to obtain representation in Parliament and to secure control of the trade unions, 'they had now abandoned parliamentary action and were concentrating on fomenting industrial troubles', and would doubtless 'continue their efforts to capture control of the key unions'.

[7] ibid.

[8] TNA, CAB 128/18/18 (Cabinet Conclusions, 14 September 1950).

[9] The Communist Party lost its only two MPs – William Gallacher and Phil Piratin – at the general election on 23 February 1950.

[10] TNA, CAB 128/18/18 (Cabinet Conclusions, 14 September 1950).

The second point related to the role of the law, which it was acknowledged to be hopeless in dealing with the perceived Communist threat:

> The criminal law could not be invoked effectively against these efforts to cause industrial strife. The promotion of a series of strikes was not in itself an offence; and, when it came to proof of seditious intention in any charge of conspiracy, it would be difficult to establish that an accused person had not been moved by a desire to improve the conditions of the workers who were being asked to strike. The Cabinet would shortly be considering the draft of an Overseas Operations (Security of Forces) Bill, but the mischief at which this Bill aimed was narrower than a Communist attempt to disrupt the economic life of the country, and some ministers felt doubtful whether criminal proceedings against individuals could play an effective part in dealing with the Communist threat.[11]

There is notably no reference to Order 1305, despite the fact that it was an offence to conspire to commit an offence under Article 4 (that is, to take part in an illegal strike). For all practical purposes, at this stage, after the interest taken in the invocation of its penal provisions in 1949,[12] it seems that Order 1305 had become redundant and was thought to be no answer to what was believed to be a politically inspired campaign to promote industrial unrest, using the cover of industrial grievances for subversive purposes.

In terms of what could be done, a number of steps were proposed, beginning with Isaacs' suggestion that 'there should be an early meeting of ministers with the General Council of the Trades Union Congress to plan the measures required to prevent the Communist Party from securing leadership in the trade unions'. The fact that there were now no Communists on the TUC General Council was thought to be helpful with a view to facilitating these discussions. This is another small but revealing example of how the TUC had been drawn into the process of government and had become an instrument of the government to contain worker power. In the United States, Congress had in 1947 banned Communists from holding trade union office. Legislation would not be necessary in the United Kingdom: the same result was to be achieved so far as possible by the actions of the TUC at the request of the government, with 'full use [to] be made of the regional councils of the Labour Party'.[13] This would reinforce the steps already taken in 1948 and 1949, which are discussed in Chapter Six above and which had already seen some unions (including the TGWU) changing their rules in order formally to exclude Communists from office. As events in the Electrical Trades Union were subsequently to reveal, however, the purge was not entirely effective.

More immediately, the Cabinet agreed that Isaacs should on the following day make a parliamentary statement 'on the evidence of a Communist conspiracy to promote industrial stoppages' and make a broadcast within the next few days telling dockers not to be led astray.[14] It should highlight foreign interference so that workers were informed that they were being 'used for furthering international Communist policies', though 'charges of foreign intervention should not, however, be made unless they could be fully

[11] ibid.
[12] See ch 5 above.
[13] TNA, CAB 128/18/18 (Cabinet Conclusions, 14 September 1950).
[14] ibid.

substantiated'. It was also proposed to adopt 'enemy' tactics by publicly denouncing the ringleaders:

> It might also be desirable to refer by name to individual Communists in this country who were prominent in fomenting industrial strife for political purposes; but here again no statement or allegation should be made which could not be fully substantiated.[15]

Ominously, it was proposed further that a 'small group of Ministers should review the action required to counter this Communist campaign', with Morrison invited to consult the Home Secretary and the Minister of Labour on 'what further steps could be taken to counter Communist endeavours to cause industrial unrest'.[16] This was ominous because the intervention of the Home Office would obviously give further encouragement to the police, further legitimising and intensifying their surveillance activities.

As will be explained below, Isaacs had wildly exaggerated both the nature and the immediacy of the threat. Nevertheless, he made a statement to the House of Commons on 15 September as agreed, highlighting a series of meetings of the workers in dispute that were to take place that weekend. According to Isaacs:

> Evidence is accumulating that an organisation is being created chiefly by men prominent in previous unofficial strikes, including some who were expelled from their union because of their anti-union activities and others who have just returned from a meeting with their Comintern friends in Warsaw. These men are going about the country with promises and proposals that are impossible of fulfilment. This weekend a number of meetings are being held purporting to represent dockers, road transport workers, and workers concerned with our meat supplies.[17]

Isaacs accepted that the men 'no doubt feel that they have a grievance', but told the House that these grievances should be dealt with through the union rather than through 'Communist agitators who have been expelled from office in their unions'.[18] None of the 'agitators' was named. Isaacs also stated that the government was 'keeping a close watch on these activities and will not hesitate to take all necessary action',[19] which drew a response from Anthony Eden, who thought Isaacs' statement to be 'one of the gravest made to us in the House in recent years in time of peace'.[20] When asked by Eden whether 'all necessary action' would include legislation to which Eden committed the Conservative Party's support, Isaacs stumbled by agreeing that it did, 'if such should be necessary'.[21]

Isaacs was corrected by Morrison as Leader of the House, who thanked Eden for his offer, but made it clear that the government was not committed to legislation, though it reserved 'all rights to proceed that way if we think it right'.[22] This of course begs the question what 'all necessary action' the government had it in mind to take.

[15] ibid.
[16] ibid.
[17] HC Debs, 15 September 1950, col 1405.
[18] ibid col 1407.
[19] ibid col 1406.
[20] ibid.
[21] ibid.
[22] ibid.

Isaacs' statement was otherwise followed by questions and interventions by only half a dozen backbenchers, mainly adding to the sense of gravity. Indeed, Leslie Hale from the Labour benches urged Isaacs 'who is highly esteemed throughout the whole trade union movement', to 'make a statement on the radio to the nation, giving some of the facts on which he based his serious statement today, and take the nation into his confidence and give it full information'. Today, we would suspect that Hale had been put up to this by the government. But not all those who spoke in the debate were convinced, with a sceptical Emrys Hughes asking the Minister if he was 'aware that there is a threatened strike of chemists in Scotland, and has he any information whether it is due to the instigation of Communists?'[23] Hughes was not alone in his scepticism, the Deputy Director General of MI5 recording in his diary that: 'Isaacs, the Minister of Labour, has made a stupid speech about Communist plots. It is likely to recoil on our heads. He had little or no evidence on which to base his statement.'[24]

Cabinet Meeting, 14 September 1950

More detail about the Cabinet Meeting on 14 September 1950 is provided by the Cabinet Secretary's Notebook,[25] which suggests that the discussion had been led by Isaacs, who also told his colleagues of the demands of the busmen, and of plans for unofficial Sunday meetings of the Dockers and 'meat market … and meat transport' men, warning those present that strike action in these vital industries was imminent.[26] Isaacs acknowledged that much of this information came from the beleaguered Deakin, and told his colleagues that Deakin had advised him that the government should consult with the TUC 'at once' with a view to proscribing the Communist Party. The reactions of Isaacs' colleagues to his briefing on the burgeoning September Revolution – a stellar cast of twentieth-century Labour politicians – are of interest. They are recounted by the Cabinet Secretary (Norman Brook) as follows:

> Harold Wilson, President of the Board of Trade, suggested that 'If we could say in advance of the strike that this was communist organised, it would help to keep sensible people out of the strike'.[27]
>
> Herbert Morrison considered these events to be 'organised political warfare' and insisted that the 'Labour Party must get a counter organisation. Broadcast to the

[23] ibid col 1408. Hughes was from Tonypandy in South Wales, and was Labour MP for South Ayrshire. On the left of the party, he was married to Keir Hardie's daughter.

[24] TNA, KV 4/472 (Liddell Diary, 18 September 1950).

[25] TNA, CAB 195/8/29 (Cabinet Secretary's Notebook, 14 September 1950).

[26] The Smithfield Meat Market was the hub of the British meat trade, while disruption on the buses would be potentially very damaging for London. As a result, these sectors were seen as providing essential services. See TNA, CAB 129/41/158 ('The Smithfield Strike', Memorandum by Home Secretary, 5 July 1950).

[27] Harold Wilson, MP for Huyton, boasted that he had heard of the proposed strike at the Liverpool docks the week before.

> workers. Put our cards on the table. Get at the rank and file and stop them being sheepish'.
>
> Emmanuel Shinwell: 'Communists will run organised sabotage. We must go for them'.
>
> Hugh Dalton: 'Slack, Dickens, Jones.[28] Are these men capable of being arrested for conspiracy? Jail them. *Plus* full publicity'.
>
> Isaacs: '... no evidence for charge. Maybe there is now'.
>
> Jim Griffths: 'Struggle for leadership of trade unions. We must find means of winning this fight. Favour early consultation with TUC and perhaps Labour Party Executive. Regulatory councils might be called and told of situation, mobilise our supporters, with agreement of General Council of TUC'.
>
> Jowitt: 'Existing law won't do. Agitation to promote strikes isn't an offence – you will have to prove seditious intent. Must either strengthen law on basis of emergency or ... [sic]'.
>
> Nye Bevan: 'Don't panic. This is a revolving drum tactic, practised in France for some time.
>
> First: tell our people the facts. Put it over via BBC announcer.
>
> Start active propaganda. Facts v Communist Russia. No use proscribing Communist Party or dealing with this by strengthening law – will draw them underground. They have gone to ground by deciding to support the Labour Party'.

Shawcross was noticeably absent from the meeting, presumably because the Attorney General is not a minister and because the issues raised were of a political nature which did not require his legal input. It is hard to believe that he would not have taken a similarly robust line had he been present.

III. Surveillance as Intimidation

Isaacs' reference to the meetings due to take place at the weekend, and his general observation that the government was keeping a 'close watch on these activities' was a clear warning that the security services were taking a keen interest in events. By now there were three agencies involved: the Security Service (MI5), Special Branch, and the Home Office.[29] All would have been interested in trade unions for decades. As we show with Joan Mahoney in *MI5, Civil Liberties and the Cold War*, however, the material released to the National Archives on the surveillance of trade unionists (usually having escaped censorship by accident, we suspect) is but the very tip of a very large iceberg.[30] However, a rare insight into the world of trade union surveillance is provided by File 827723/331 'Unofficial Strikes (Communist Instigation)', which was opened on 18 September 1950 by F3, the Home Office division tasked

[28] Leading members of the London PWC. Bert Slack was a road haulage official on the TGWU executive. None of them had gone to Poland, but Dickens had visited Birkenhead to speak to his colleagues there (see below, pp 147, 247.).

[29] On the surveillance of trade unionists and the work of F3, see also KD Ewing, J Mahoney and A Moretta, *MI5, Civil Liberties and the Cold War,* (Oxford University Press, Oxford, 2020), pp 77–80.

[30] ibid pp 72–82.

with overseeing the policing of industrial disputes. The cover of the file indicates that it was added and referred to on numerous occasions until 29 October 1950 by the F3 team and by the Home Office Permanent Under Secretary, Sir Frank Newsam. Containing numerous wholly unexpurgated Special Branch reports, the file reveals an intensification of surveillance from mid-September, as well as references which make it very obvious that the surveillance of trade unionists had long been taking place as a matter of routine.[31]

The opening of the file coincided with the alarm in government following the TUC's rejection of pay restraint and the fresh demands of the dockers and bus workers. According to a notable Minute on 'The Threatened Dock Strike' by Mr RR Pittam of F3, dated 14 September 1950:

> There has been a suggestion originating with MI5 who had it from a 'delicate source' [a commonly used Security Service euphemism for electronic eavesdropping or a well-placed informant] that a dock strike would be started on Merseyside on 15 September, 1950, and would then be spread to London and might involve road haulage.[32]

Pittam also explained that MI5 were aware of 'recent contacts between the Dockers of London and Merseyside',[33] and that the Chief Constable of Birkenhead had been visited by an MI5 officer 'who knew of the threatened strike'. But although 'very careful enquiries had been made from all possible sources', 'no indication of immediate trouble' could be found. Indeed, Pittam's memo went on to say that Deakin had told Isaacs on 14 September that he 'did not expect any immediate strike, though he regarded the troublemaking in London and Liverpool very seriously and thought it might cause a strike before very long'. He continued:

> The aim seems to be to concert action to compel the TGWU to press for the implementation of what the trouble makers call the 'Dockers Charter' … On the question of relationships between Dockers and the Road Haulage Workers, see the last two reports on [File] 823988/59.

It is very likely that the latter were Special Branch reports on the Road Haulage Workers and Allied Trades Committee; the Home Secretary appeared to have been well briefed on the collaboration between the drivers and the PWC.[34]

Despite such an inconclusive search for corroboration that a strike was about to take place in the ports, as we have seen, the Cabinet nevertheless worked itself into a lather on 14 September and Isaacs went ahead with his parliamentary statement the following day. But having made the statement and undertaken at some stage to make a broadcast to the nation, Isaacs now needed information to justify both. For this purpose, it would be useful to find out what was said at the trade union meetings to be held on Sunday, 17 September, to which Isaacs had referred in the House of Commons. So Diack from the Ministry of Labour telephoned Hughes at the Home Office on the afternoon

[31] TNA, HO 45/25546 ('Disturbances: strikes in the industry: communist instigated subversion') (Home Office F3 file 827723/331, 'Unofficial Strikes (Communist Instigation')).

[32] Like everything else in the rest of this and the next section which is not otherwise attributed, the Minute by Pittam is to be found in TNA, HO 45/25546 ('Disturbances: strikes in industry: communist instigated subversion) (Home Office file 827723/331, 'Unofficial Strikes (Communist Instigation')).

[33] Ted Dickens and Albert Timothy of the London PWC had addressed the Birkenhead Dockers.

[34] See ch 5 above.

of 15 September, following Isaacs' address. Like Pittam, Hughes was employed in F3, worked very closely with Special Branch, and was in regular contact with MI5. Diack told Hughes that 'if the industrial situation warranted it the Minister of Labour was likely to make a broadcast speech to the nation early next week'. Diack mentioned meetings of the Port Workers' Committee and Smithfield drivers due to take place on 17 September, and told him that Isaacs 'was wondering if Special Branch could cover those meetings for the purpose of finding out what the results of the meetings were, and the repercussions of them likely to be'.[35]

In a carefully composed note to his superior, Hughes understood this to mean that 'the information was required before the Minister made his broadcast, since it might well have some influence on what he has to say'. And in an observation which makes it apparent not only that Hughes knew that the police had been monitoring the trade unionists in question, but that F3 routinely received intelligence on the activities of trade unions, their members, and officials, he also said:

> I may be wrong, but it [appears] to me that such procedure might well be dangerous and likely to jeopardise the delicate relations which exist between Special Branch and their informants, and possibly lead to a cessation of the supply of information which proves of great value to us. I therefore informed Mr Diack that it was not the normal function of the already hard pressed Special Branch to make special arrangements to cover meetings of this nature, and we would hesitate asking them to do so. Occasionally, however, we were fortunate enough to obtain certain information which, if we considered of any value to the Ministry of Labour, would of course, be passed on to them. Mr Diack accepted this position and said that he would telephone on Monday to see if we had any knowledge of what had transpired at the meetings.[36]

As we will discuss below, Special Branch did 'cover' the meetings. To the profound regret of F3, however, the press was fully briefed that it would do so, presumably to discourage workers from attending or to intimidate those who did attend. In other words, someone unknown was evidently weaponising surveillance by openly acknowledging that it was taking place, in order to halt strikes believed to be imminent, and by advertising that the organisers risked prosecution. Even one of the most sober newspaper accounts suggested not only that there had been a press briefing, but also that those who had been briefed had been told that the security services had been keeping the government appraised of the activities of the PWC for at least the past two or three weeks. Thus, Margaret Stewart, the highly respected Industrial Correspondent of the *News Chronicle*, was able to report that 'Isaacs will follow up his warning on industrial troubles, given in the House of Commons yesterday, with a broadcast to the nation', that 'information about disruptive activities and plans to hamper Korean supplies has been reaching the government since the end of August', and that the government 'has information about a number of unofficial committees originally set up to organise strikes, which have been turned into semi-permanent bodies'.[37]

[35] Internal Home Office note by KE Hughes to WH Cornish reporting the telephone conversation with Diack, 15 September 1950.
[36] ibid.
[37] *News Chronicle*, 16 September 1950.

Not everyone was so subtle or restrained. The Tory press went along with the talk of Communist plots, having obviously been given very comprehensive briefings by sources in government about Special Branch surveillance targets and methods:

> *Daily Telegraph*, 16 September 1950:
>
> YARD WATCH ON AGITATORS: COMMUNISTS' FILES
>
> Scotland Yard Special Branch would be ready to make instant arrests of agitators trying to cause industrial unrest if effect were given to legislation hinted at by Mr Isaacs … Close watch has been kept for years on the activities of members of the Communist Party. As a result, clear cut legislation would be welcomed by the Special Branch. In the files at Scotland Yard agitators are listed under categories ranging from 'very dangerous' to 'mildly dangerous.' Thick dossiers record the activities of prominent agitators over a period of years.
>
> *Daily Express*, 16 September 1950:
>
> SECRET AGENTS TACKLE PLOT
>
> In several parts of the country tomorrow conspirators will meet to fill in details of the Great Strike Plot, exposed by Mr George Isaacs … But Government secret agents have been briefed. They know where the meetings are to be held who is to attend and what will be discussed … The plot is for workers in the docks, road transport, meat carrying and the markets to strike in key places.

Here we learn that secret agents were spying on workers and keeping thick dossiers of personal information. It is surprising that such activity should be so openly discussed, given the condemnation of similar behaviour by state authorities in other parts of the world at the time. And surprising also to learn of Special Branch support for coercive legislation, presumably to extend their powers still further.

The popular left-leaning *Daily Herald* added its support to Isaacs. But to the dismay of the Cabinet, the Home Office and Special Branch, it was even less restrained than either the *Daily Telegraph* or the *Daily Express*, revealing more information about Special Branch targets and methods, in this case the PWC and the role of informers respectively. The *Daily Herald* reported that:

> PLOT CHIEFS ARE KNOWN: WATCH THIS WEEKEND
>
> The men operating the Communist plot … are not mystery men to the Government. The Cabinet has exact information about them. It knows the part they are playing in the present London bus strike and their plans for creating trouble this autumn in the docks, in the building trades, on the railways. Regular reports from Commander Leonard Burt, chief of Scotland Yard's Special Branch, have set out their activities in detail.
>
> Yard Has Agent
>
> A committee of eight, the 'secret eight' is directing the disruptive operations. The members meet alternately in London's East End and in Islington. No minutes are kept at these meetings. But Commander Burt knows all about the discussions *because the Special Branch has an informant inside the organisation.*[38]

Here we have additional information about how these thick dossiers were fed, in the case of the PWC by at least one informant on the inside, information incidentally corroborated by Guy Liddell's Diary, which provides a rare glimpse of trade union

[38] Emphasis by the *Daily Herald*. This passage was marked by the Home Office.

surveillance missed by those tasked with removing such material from the often heavily censored texts. In recording an anecdote about how careful Special Branch had to be about the sensitivities of other police forces, Liddell revealed that a Special Branch informer on the London PWC was 'run' by a Special Branch sergeant. As told by Liddell, the latter would pass on at least some of the information he received to the Port of London Authority via an Admiralty 'Dock Police' officer.[39]

But although the presence of informers may not have been surprising, F3's Hughes no doubt would have preferred that it was not made public. It is to be hoped one day in the interests of transparency that the names of the individuals may yet be revealed. Obviously aware of the existence of at least one informer, Hughes considered that the *Daily Herald* piece was 'likely to lead to a purge within the Port Workers Committee [and] may well lead to a total cessation of the valuable information which we have been getting. This is most regrettable'.[40] Worse, however, was the revelation in the downmarket *Daily Graphic*, announcing under provocative headlines ('Now Name the Traitors! Anyone Who Goes on Strike Now Will Do So Knowing That He is Helping Traitors') that 'Special Branch Officers will be present at three important meetings of dockers, meat porters and lorry drivers planned in London tomorrow'.[41] This had been met with particular dismay at the Home Office, Hughes considering that the piece 'will doubtless result in Sunday's meetings being generally closed to the press and certainly to the police, so we shall probably be able to give Isaacs no help with his broadcast!'.[42] The events went ahead, nevertheless, despite the unwanted publicity.

IV. A Poor Surveillance Harvest

Special Branch was able to cover in one way or another four meetings held on the weekend. These were (i) the London Port Workers' Mass Meeting at the Old Council Chambers, Poplar, (ii) the meeting of the TGWU Smithfield Branch at Holborn Hall, (iii) a second meat workers' meeting at Poplar Town Hall, and (iv) an unofficial building workers' wages campaign committee meeting, interest in which was no doubt heightened by concerns that the Festival of Britain, scheduled for the summer of 1951, might be postponed or disrupted.[43] Brief initial reports on the meetings, very likely rushed over to the Home Office on the same day, remain on the Home Office file along with the more usual formal and lengthy Special Branch reports. Unfortunately for the government, however, the main themes of the meetings provided little evidence that the trade unionists were 'plotting' or 'conspiring' for political rather than economic ends. Just as Liddell had predicted, Isaacs' ridiculous claims – as well as his announcement that

[39] TNA, KV4/472 (Liddell Diary, 5 October 1950).

[40] Internal Home Office handwritten note from Hughes to Cornish, 16 September 1950.

[41] *Daily Graphic*, 16 September 1950.

[42] Internal Home Office handwritten note from Hughes to Cornish, 16 September 1950.

[43] On 18 September, Newsam asked Hughes to find out who had booked the Halls for the various meetings, perhaps hoping it had been Harry Pollitt or Joseph Stalin. It had been the PWC and Farquhar respectively. His interest may have been triggered by the report that Farquhar had announced at the close of the Poplar Town Hall meeting that he had paid the £20 fee for the hire of the hall and had requested that the men contribute to a fund to cover the cost as they left the meeting.

the unofficial strikers were being monitored – were indeed backfiring on the security services, as trade unionists expressed outrage at being spied upon by the British political police.

The flyer for the Port Workers' meeting made it clear that their dispute was an attempt to improve terms and conditions of employment and to express dissatisfaction with the TGWU. It announced that:

> [B]rother Trade Unionists in the ports of LIVERPOOL, BIRKENHEAD and HULL have taken up the campaign for the 25/- a day, a fortnight's paid holiday and pensions at 65. Our brothers in the Road Haulage and Road Passenger sections of the Transport industry are pressing for wage increases. Like us they are determined to shake into action or shake free of, leaders who sit on our backs, but refuse to fight for our just demands … they cling to views on wages policy as shown at this year's TUC which are discredited by a majority of the Trade Union Movement. Ever since 1947, our representatives in the Branches, Divisional committees, London Docks Trade Group and the National Docks Trade Group have pressed the GEC [General Executive Council of the TGWU] to place our claim for 25/- a day before the employers. But the GEC refused [and] barred our path protecting the employers from being reached with our claims.

The flyer called upon 'Dockers, Stevedores, Lightermen and Clerks' to elect spokesmen to the PWC and 'Plaster the Port' with their demands. It was filed with the five-page Special Branch Report dated 17 September 1950, presumably having been picked up by the Special Branch officer present.[44]

Only 50 or so men attended the meeting, the very low turnout a source of relieved amusement at the Home Office, though the officials in question might have reflected with greater justification on whether the attendance vindicated the surveillance effort which they had organised. According to Special Branch reports, Albert Timothy told the meeting that the working conditions at the Birkenhead docks were 'deplorable', and that the Merseyside men were:

> [R]eady to have a go. Our committee alone has prevented a stoppage in Birkenhead. They were thinking of marching on London; we were able to persuade them to hold their action. Yet these things are printed for the public to read as Communist plots.[45]

In contrast, Timothy (whose visit to Poland earlier in September had been publicised by the *Daily Herald* on 14 September) had been favourably impressed by the conditions enjoyed by the Polish dockers. He had not, however, been to any secret meetings:

> I am the man who went to Poland to conspire with the Cominform, yet I state that not one night in Poland did I go to any meeting of any kind except on the last night when I attended a social of Polish dockers their wives and children. If we conspired there it was a conspiracy to uphold world peace – and no more.[46]

Special Branch noted every word he had to say on the matter. Later on in the meeting, Timothy decided to say a few more words on what he described as 'Mr Isaacs'

[44] 'The press' were admitted and it is possible that a police officer was among them. It is of course also possible that Special Branch were provided with a transcript by a journalist.

[45] Special Branch Report, 17 September 1950.

[46] ibid.

accusations that he – TIMOTHY – had gone to Poland on a conspiracy against the Government':

> As a matter of fact we went over to see the re-construction of a country not in receipt of Marshall Aid. What I saw there amazed me. If only we could do the same here it would be a better thing for everybody. In Poland the Docker gets two weeks' annual holiday with pay, and his pay for that holiday is based on his last three months earnings. His fares from home to his holiday camp are paid by the Government. When he arrives at his destination two thirds of the holiday expenses are met by the Government. In three years they have got something that we shall take five years from now to get – unless we take drastic strike action.[47]

Ted Dickens, who had been accorded the honour of being denounced in Cabinet on 14 September by Hugh Dalton, was reported by Special Branch as referring again to 'the recent Press Red Bogey smear and said that it was a big laugh. He didn't care if MI5 came to his meetings. There was nothing they would learn. The Red Bogey plot was brought out every time the government had a question put to them that they couldn't answer'.[48]

Meanwhile, over at Holborn Hall, the Smithfield porters and drivers drew an impressive 450–500 of the men who had been on strike in the summer for an extra £1 per week. The 'Top Secret' Special Branch report tells us that the men were concerned on this occasion primarily with the suspension of two of their officials, 'Dixie' Howell and Jeff Farquhar from the TGWU's General Executive Committee, following the recent Smithfield strike referred to in Chapters Six and Seven above.[49] The resolution moved was that no disciplinary action should be taken against the two, and that a failure of the GEC to comply with the meeting's wishes would mean that those present would have to consider whether the TGWU 'can represent our interests any further'.[50] A little friction was recorded about the Communist presence on the unofficial Road Haulage and Allied Trades Committee, whose membership included docker Ted Dickens. Otherwise, similarly innocuous material is recorded in relation to the meeting of 200 or so at Poplar Town Hall later the same day. Open to the TGWU general haulage drivers who had a wages claim pending, the meeting was attended by some of those who had been present at Holborn Hall earlier, and was addressed by some of the same speakers. However, unlike the PWC meeting, entry required the production of a union card, which would have added to the problems of police surveillance.

The Special Branch report of the latter meeting is signed by a sergeant by Chief Superintendent Thompson, and described as 'information received'. Appended to the

[47] ibid.

[48] ibid. However, Vic Marney – one of the organisers, rather than a speaker – was recorded by Special Branch as having made the modest suggestion that 'in view of the fact that secret agents were expected to be at their gatherings, writing shorthand notes of everything they said, a check on credentials would not be out of place': ibid.

[49] Both men were lay activists in the TGWU based at Smithfield Market. Dixie Howell was a shop steward who later became a member of the union's Executive Committee and a member of the TUC General Council. An obituary is to be found in TUC Annual Report 1976, p 354. Jeff Farquhar was later described by the editor of *Socialist Review* as a 'responsible and militant socialist who has served the labour movement long and well': *Socialist Review*, 1 September 1958, p 2. It is unknown whether either man was or had been a member of the CPGB, though it is to be noted that the *Socialist Review* was not a Communist Party journal.

[50] According to the Special Branch report, 'the chairman put the resolution to the meeting and it was carried with only a few against'.

report is a verbatim record (no doubt with a potential prosecution in mind) of all that was said ('Dixie Howell said "---" etc). It is evident that a bare unedited record provided the basis of the subsequent report by the unnamed author, and it seems very likely indeed that the meeting had been 'bugged', whether by a police stenographer in a neighbouring room, or by more sophisticated means (the same probably being true of the Smithfield men's meeting at Holborn Hall). Although strongly critical of the union's handling of the wages' claim, chairman Jeff Farquar is reported as having stated at the outset that the meeting's purpose 'was not in any way concerned with strike action'. The report is otherwise notable for recording that the resolution objecting to the disciplinary proceedings against Howell and Farquhar (Howell was a speaker) was carried unanimously, and that Deakin was 'attacked' by all speakers as someone who 'was no longer on the side of the employees but was, in fact, a servant of the Government'. One speaker described him as a 'traitor', while another demanded he 'should go', no doubt reflecting the views of those present.[51]

So far as the last of the meetings is concerned, Special Branch reported that there were 102 delegates present. Unlike the other three meetings which were dominated by TGWU members, the building workers were members of the National Federation of Building Trades Operatives. As such, they had established their own Wages' Campaign Committee 'as a natural expression of the indignation of the Building Workers at the failure of their Executive Committee' to 'carry out the proper functions of our Trade Union i.e. to defend our wage standards in the face of rising costs'.[52] The Committee ('Communist-controlled' according to Special Branch) regarded the TUC rejection of the wage freeze and the adoption by their union of their demands as a vindication, but cautioned that: 'It is clear from recent statements that while they formally accept the demands of the rank and file, many of the trade union leaders are still opposed to wage demands.' The builders wanted an extra sixpence an hour: 'We want the Tanner! Now!'[53] Unlike the other three meetings on 17 September, Special Branch had to rely on an informant (even though it was in the same building as the Smithfield porters and drivers meeting earlier in the day),[54] according to whom the CPGB Executive had ordered the Committee to be 'disbanded' by the oddly specific time of 10 am on that day.

Whether that claim was true or not, the Committee was dissolved, the motion in favour of doing so having 'received almost unanimous support'.[55] But as in the case

[51] Special Branch Report, 18 September 1950.

[52] From a circular issued to members of the NFBTO by the chairman and secretary of the Building Workers' Wages Campaign Committee, Frank Stone and Jeff Mildwater.

[53] ibid.

[54] Special Branch Report, 'Building Workers Wages Campaign Committee', 18 September 1950. According to the report, the informant knew those involved very well and had reported that 'Steve LONSDALE checked the credentials of those attending the meeting'. The press were invited but only after a vote (72 to 10) was taken. One of the committee members, Jock Currie, objected to the presence of the press, his suspicions no doubt aroused by the fact that 'MI5 had visited his home last week'. Whoever had provided the information had been able not only to name the man who checked the men's credentials on the door, but also report that members had been issued with a policy statement as a guide for discussion prior to the meeting, 'copy attached'. The impression given is that the Special Branch informant was one of the delegates present; no doubt there were informers present at the other larger meetings although the relevant reports rely almost wholly on transcripts of the proceedings.

[55] Special Branch Report, 'Building Workers Wages Campaign Committee', 18 September 1950.

of the other three meetings on 17 September, there was very little here that could be used by Isaacs in his proposed broadcast which, as we will discuss in Chapter Nine, was delayed until 25 September. Nor did it produce much to corroborate the allegations of Communist agitation. On the contrary, what Special Branch coyly referred to as 'information received' had revealed to them not only that the Building Workers' Wages Campaign Committee had disbanded, on the instructions of the CPGB, but also that those present agreed to engage with the National Federation of Building Trades Operatives as well as to 'to work in a constitutional manner for their demands for a wage increase'.[56] Moreover, it was reported that Jock Currie, a Communist Party member, who earlier in the meeting mentioned that MI5 had recently visited him at home (for purposes not explained), had been able to calm the assembled delegates 'by his eloquence' and that he 'read a poem he had specially written for the occasion'. Yet the government ploughed on regardless, ignoring the causes of worker discontent rooted in economic hardship and a compromised union leadership. It appears that ministers preferred to believe that these grievances were the manufactured product of Communist Party subversion, preying on what it presumably also believed to be gullible and vulnerable workers.

V. MI5–Special Branch Co-operation

While Special Branch officers were busy infiltrating and recording the four meetings by the use of different forms of surveillance (physical attendance, recording by stenograph or electronically, and the use of what are referred to now as human intelligence sources (informers)), Hughes was working at Whitehall on 17 September. He telephoned the Chief Constables of Birkenhead, Bristol, Cardiff, Glasgow, Hull, Liverpool, Newcastle upon Tyne, Portsmouth, and Southampton to discuss any 'subversive activities which were taking or were to take place particularly in the docks or transport industries'.[57] Nothing of note was reported. He also wrote to constabularies on 17 and 18 September, referring to what the Portsmouth City Police called 'the alleged Communist plot to hold up public services'.[58] The general response in their prompt replies was along the lines that 'no information has been received', to suggest that there was any 'such attempt to foment unrest locally'.[59] The Newcastle City Police told Hughes that 'in this area it is believed that the Communist Party does not exercise much influence in the sphere of Industrial Trade Union activity'.[60]

Also on 17 September, Chief Superintendent Thompson of Special Branch (who had ultimately signed off the reports of the various meetings referred to above) was summoned to Whitehall to meet Hughes and Newsam, although little evidence

[56] ibid.

[57] Hughes was working on the instruction of Cornish. Sir Frank Newsam had requested that the calls be made.

[58] Letter from DI Atkins, Portsmouth City Police, to Hughes, 17 September 1950.

[59] These phrases were used by the Detective Inspector who took Hughes' call and suggest that the Home Office man really did believe that a Communist plot was coming to fruition.

[60] Supt JG Barrett CID to Hughes, 17 September 1950.

remains of what was said, and there is nothing to indicate who else was present. There is, however, a record of Hughes suggesting to Sir Frank on 18 September that: '*A propos* yesterday's meeting in the Secretary of State's room [with Thompson on the previous day], the Secretary of State may, if there is time … wish to inform the Cabinet that Dixie Howell and Jeff Farquhar … are to be disciplined by the TGWU on Wednesday of this week, and that expulsion of these two individuals from the union may well lead to further troubles in the market, and possibly the docks.'[61] Although there is no evidence that this information was conveyed formally to the Cabinet, it may well have been done so informally. Not everything that takes place in Cabinet appears to be recorded in the Conclusions. Either way, Hughes' suggestion reveals an unhealthy interest in the internal affairs of trade unions by civil servants, and an expectation that there would be a similar interest on the part of ministers, reinforcing in turn the suggestion made in Chapter Six of a remarkable penetration of trade unions by the state.

All present at the Cabinet meeting on Monday, 18 September would have been aware that the hapless Deakin had spoken to the press over the weekend, the *Manchester Guardian* informing readers that morning that: 'MR DEAKIN DEMANDS ACTION AGAINST COMMUNIST PARTY: "DAILY WORKER" SHOULD BE SUPPRESSED'.[62] Deakin may have known that the Overseas Operations (Security of Forces) Bill was back on the Cabinet agenda on 18 September after having been vetoed by the TUC in July, his intervention designed presumably to stiffen ministerial resolve. Perhaps unsurprisingly, the discussion on the Bill focused not only on the possibility of its restoration, but also on whether it should be amended to deal with Communist activities that had been the subject of Cabinet discussions four days earlier.[63] The Conclusions record that:

> The draft Bill was intended to prevent interference with the operation of United Nations forces in Korea and was designed to penalise action, whether by sabotage, strikes or propaganda, calculated to impede active operations undertaken in time of peace by His Majesty's Forces or by forces associated with them. The Cabinet discussion turned mainly on the question whether the Bill should be so amended as to cover such Communist attempts to disrupt the national economy as had been described at the Cabinet's meeting on 14th September and had been the subject of the statement made by the Minister of Labour in the House of Commons on 15th September. These Communist activities were likely to take the form of attempts to disrupt communications; and they could be covered, so long as United Nations forces were operating in Korea, by extending Clause 2 of the Bill to actions likely to prejudice the maintenance of services essential to the life of the community.[64]

[61] Hughes to Newsam, 18 September 1950. The phrase 'and possibly the docks' had been added to the note in long hand by Newsam. Howell had mentioned this at the Poplar meeting. In fact, the findings of the enquiry into their conduct would not be known until the following meeting of the TGWU General Executive Council – scheduled for November – so the Home Office group need not have worried. It seems likely that Hughes had picked up the news he had been so keen to pass on to the Home Secretary from the interim Special Branch reports and was consequently unaware of this detail.

[62] *Manchester Guardian*, 18 September 1950.

[63] TNA, CAB 128/18/18 (Cabinet Conclusions, 14 September 1950).

[64] TNA, CAB 128/18/20 (Cabinet Conclusions, 18 September 1950).

Ministers decided in favour of legislation in principle, but agreed that further work needed to be done. A principled impasse had been reached. In the meantime, it was clear from the inconclusive discussion that the Home Secretary was at least as concerned about the amount of publicity that had been given to the Special Branch operations.

These concerns do not appear in the Cabinet Conclusions, but only in the note kept by the Cabinet Secretary, Norman Brook. Thus, the Home Secretary reported that there had been a 'Statement in the press that police knew what was going on at a meeting of the Dockers. Such disclosures may damage the work of Special Branch'.[65] As we have seen, there was more than one statement, the matter being well covered by various newspapers on 16 September suggesting that the press had been briefed either by ministers or officials, or by Special Branch or rogue officers operating therein. The last of these options cannot be discounted in light of another Liddell Diary entry in which the MI5 man recorded a conversation some time later with Leonard Burt, head of Special Branch, the latter expressing concern about the leaking of information, with CID as well as 200 Special Branch officers having access to the Special Branch (though not MI5) files.[66] Returning to the Cabinet meeting on 18 September, Norman Brook records only Herbert Morrison's response, which was 'Let the Home Secretary speak to the Editor of *the Daily Herald*',[67] presumably to warn him to take greater care with sensitive information. The implication is that the other coverage and the threats it carried appear to have been thought acceptable.

The Overseas Operations (Security of Forces) Bill

The Cabinet meeting on 18 September again decided effectively to postpone further consideration of the Overseas Operations (Security of Forces) Bill, which as we saw in Chapter Four had already been postponed in the light of TUC objections earlier in the year. Although a relatively full account is given in the formal Cabinet Conclusions of this second bout of indecision, a fuller account still is provided in Norman Brook's Notebook. The latter records that the Attorney General had complained at the start of the meeting that the Bill as it had been brought back to the Cabinet did not 'purport to cover Isaacs' statement of last week'.[68] Sir Hartley had insisted that the Bill should be extended to 'cover any action likely to interfere with essential services. Would cover bus strike etc, as now'.[69] Isaacs liked Shawcross' idea. But Jowitt was sceptical about whether it would ever be possible to use the criminal law if workers were not deterred by the threat of criminal sanctions. Similarly, Bevan expressed the view that the situation was 'not so serious as to warrant panic action', and that the 'Communist leadership can be broken if exposed'.[70] Although the introduction of legislation was nevertheless approved in principle, it was agreed

[65] TNA, CAB 195/8/30 (Cabinet Secretary's Notebook, 18 September 1950).
[66] TNA, KV4/472 (Liddell Diary, 15 February 1951).
[67] TNA, CAB 195/8/30 (Cabinet Secretary's Notebook, 18 September 1950).
[68] TNA, CAB 195/8/30 (Cabinet Secretary's Notebook, 18 September 1950).
[69] ibid.
[70] ibid.

> that the Lord President would examine whether 'the criminal law could with advantage be strengthened for the purpose of countering a Communist conspiracy to foment industrial unrest in this country'.[71]

Evidently disappointed not only by the surveillance of the four meetings on 17 September, and by the response to Hughes' call for reports from the police forces on 17 and 18 September, on 19 September, Sir Frank Newsam, Permanent Under Secretary at the Home Office, convened the first of two high-level meetings with a view to improving co-operation between the surveillance agencies. Sir Theobald Mathew, the DPP, was present, as were Sir Percy Sillitoe and Graham Mitchell of MI5. The police were represented by Sir Harold Scott, Metropolitan Police Commissioner, and Assistant Commissioner Ronald Howe, who was in charge of the Criminal Investigation Department.[72] Pittam of F3 was also there. Despite the failure of the intelligence operations to date, the Home Office appeared to believe that the problem was not a lack of evidence. On the contrary, the evidence was not being found, or where it was found, it was not being shared as circumstances required. In the clear belief that there must be evidence available, Sir Frank wanted it to be unearthed to increase the chance of prosecutions, whether under existing or proposed new powers. So did the DPP, who was particularly anxious for 'any evidence which could be produced in court if necessary'. This was to be done by better co-operation between the different agencies, designed to enhance the role of Special Branch in relation to alleged Communist activity on the docks in particular.

Surveillance straddled a fault line between Home Office, the police and MI5,[73] with MI5 by virtue of its Charter being primarily responsible for the surveillance of Communists and others. But MI5 was very jealous of this role, and generally secretive and possessive about its information, seeing itself as the receiver rather than the provider of intelligence, which it was unwilling to share with other agencies. In proposing an enhanced role for Special Branch in relation to Communism in the docks (presumably because the police would be more pliable than the Security Service to Home Office requests and instructions), Newsam was effectively proposing that MI5 should hand over data to Special Branch. Although Newsam claimed that his initiative did not infringe upon 'Security Service general responsibility for intelligence work',[74] from MI5's position, such an impact was inevitable. A particular anxiety was that MI5 already worked closely with chief constables in monitoring Communists and others, as Hughes had learned when he communicated with the police on 17 and 18 September. Senior MI5 officers were concerned that these arrangements would be disrupted and the flow of information diverted by Newsam's plan for a new focus on the Metropolitan Police as

[71] ibid.

[72] Commander Burt had taken a day's leave, and when back on duty was due to 'visit the continent' with Chief Superintendent Thompson.

[73] On the constitutional position of the Home Office and the police, see Sir Frank Newsam, *The Home Office* (Allen & Unwin, London, 1954), p 45.

[74] Note of a meeting held in Sir Frank Newsam's Room on 17 September 1950.

the body with responsibility for collecting and processing information about subversive activities.

Liddell had made considerable efforts – not always successfully – to win over the police and to overcome suspicions of MI5 and its methods held by some police officers.[75] He made it a practice to speak at police events to discuss the role of the Security Service and to invite senior police officers from the provincial forces – usually Chief Constables – to MI5's headquarters for lunch and to let them see how the Service functioned. His diaries are peppered with brief accounts of such occasions. It was no surprise then that Hughes had learned from the Portsmouth Chief Constable that MI5's Director General, Percy Sillitoe, had already circulated a request to various police forces requesting 'any information' about 'Communist participation in any dock or transport strikes occurring in the near future'. He was to learn as well that Kingston-upon-Hull CID had informed MI5 of a recent visit from a member of the Merseyside PWC to the city,[76] and that a report had been sent to Mr Osmond at B.1.D, the MI5 counter-subversion section with responsibility for the trade unions.[77] The Chief Constable, following his telephone conversation with Hughes, sent him a copy of the latter report, with a covering letter assuring him that his officers were 'in touch with informants and with reliable leaders of the Transport and Dock Workers' Unions and also with railway representatives and bus operators'.[78]

It was nevertheless agreed that the Metropolitan Police should collate information provided by the provincial forces, and that a meeting of the Chief Constables of the port cities would be convened on 26 September. MI5 agreed to help, although the lack of enthusiasm in doing so is palpable: Sillitoe said that the Security Service would have no objection to the proposed arrangement and, in reply to a question from Assistant Commissioner Howe, said that he saw no reason why the Security Service should not supply Special Branch with any of the information in their possession which would help them in 'formulating the background and assessing the importance of the evidence they were collecting'.[79] Liddell was obliged on at least two occasions thereafter to reassure MI5 officers who expressed concern that the police were usurping the Security Service, that the new arrangements were temporary, confined to dock and transport workers, and intended to provide evidence for a limited number of prosecutions.[80] Sillitoe, the ex-Chief Constable of Kent, personally appointed by Attlee, could perhaps have been expected to go along with this politically inspired witch-hunt co-ordinated from the heart of government, no matter what his private

[75] Not all were convinced that there was a need to maintain lists of citizens who had come to the attention of their forces in connection with Communism. See, for example, the Chief Constable of Berkshire's 1949 exchange with the Director General of MI5 (Ewing, Mahoney and Moretta (n 29) pp 149–50). On the role of provincial forces see ibid pp 11–12, 79–80, 94–95, and 149–50.

[76] Hughes was also to learn a good deal of information on the visitor's host, paradoxically a trade unionist known for his anti-communist views. The police informer supplied a copy of the 'Dockers' Charter' referred to above. So few of these were in circulation that a copy was taken, and the original returned to the informer. The visitor was identified as one Bill Johnson.

[77] The 'your ref' slot at the head of the letter SF 452-13/B 1 D/PAO tells us its recipient was at MI5. 'SF' here stands for 'special file'.

[78] Letter to Hughes from Sydney Lawrence, Chief Constable, Kingston upon Hull, 17 September 1950.

[79] Note of a meeting held in Sir Frank Newsam's Room on 17 September 1950.

[80] TNA, KV4/472 (Liddell Diary, 22 September 1950; 12 October 1950).

thoughts may have been. Indeed, by 1963, Lord Denning was able to wax lyrical about the 'excellent co-operation between the Security Service and the police forces', both in the 'metropolis' and in the 'country'.[81]

VI. Conclusion

The response of the government during a period of 13 days in 1950 (7–19 September) was barely credible. The year 1950 was one of historically low levels of industrial action, despite workers being frustrated by poor working conditions in an era of austerity and pay restraint. Ministers were nevertheless determined to prosecute, convict and imprison, with the existing law providing a few options to enable them to do so. As the *Manchester Guardian* pointed out on the day of the press frenzy in response to Isaacs' suggestion that the government might legislate:

> [T]he Government already possesses great powers. Some of the public utilities are protected by legislation. The Conspiracy and Protection of Property Act 1875 and the Electricity Supply Act 1919, make an employee liable to civil prosecution if he breaks his contract knowing that such action will deprive customers of their supply. The Conditions of Employment and National Arbitration Order, 1940 [Order 1305], in effect makes all strikes illegal unless a dispute has been reported to the Minister of Labour and three weeks' notice has been given. (The existence of this order has not prevented many unofficial strikes from occurring recent months).[82]

All three of the measures referred to by the *Manchester Guardian* made it an offence to participate in a strike, not to organise one. But they would also have enabled prosecutions to have been brought against 'ringleaders', 'instigators' and 'conspirators', particularly where the latter were politically motivated, if such people could be found.

The 13 days in September are important also for revealing the extent to which the surveillance of trade unionists in the ports was intensified, used initially as an instrument of intimidation and then more systematically to find evidence that could be used as a basis for prosecution, the *Manchester Guardian* having noted pointedly in response to Isaacs' statement on 15 September that it understood that 'the Government possesses no evidence in a legal sense which could form the basis of a prosecution under existing law'. Having decided for the time being not to change the law, the government decided instead to streamline intelligence-gathering procedures to find the evidence that would allow a prosecution to be mounted most probably for seditious conspiracy. A few weeks after the dispute between Newsam and Sillitoe on 19 September, however, Guy Liddell recorded a lunch engagement with an unidentified American – 'Dan' – who 'talked to [him] about Isaacs' statement on communist plots'.[83] Liddell clearly could not confirm Isaacs' tales because he

[81] Lord Denning's Report, Cmnd 2152, 1963, paras 274 and 275.
[82] *Manchester Guardian*, 16 September 1950.
[83] TNA, KV4/472 (Liddell Diary, 12 October 1950).

knew them to be at best unsubstantiated. But as MI5's Deputy Director General, he could not explicitly tell the American that the British government was treating unofficial industrial action as subversion and that the Cabinet had directed the Home Office to oversee a search for non-existent evidence of non-existent subversion.[84] Nevertheless, by directing the American to MI5's monthly summary of UK security, Liddell was most likely indicating to the American that there were no Communist plotters.

[84] ibid: 'I had lunch with Dan [surname redacted]. He asked me for a list of Israeli officials in this country which I promised to let him have. He also talked to me about Isaacs' statement on Communist plots; this had caused a good deal of anxiety in the US and naturally they wanted to know the truth. I said that in a way I was in rather an embarrassing position, but as he received our regular monthly summary he would know the real position.'

9

London Gas Workers

An Unexpected Prosecution

I. Introduction

The 'September Revolution' was of course a fiction of only the most fertile ministerial imagination. Nevertheless, the conflation of unofficial industrial action with Communist Party instigation for destabilising political ends was important, and led inexorably to the deployment of the criminal law against supposed political activists. However, opportunities to use the criminal law are not always in the gift of the government and depend to a large extent on circumstances: who is on strike and what evidence is available to condemn them? Here we find that the first dispute to lead to prosecution was perhaps the least propitious for the purposes of government strategy. This was the unofficial action by London gas workers who had legitimate grievances, and who also had been failed by the official structures in their union, but in relation to whom there was little evidence of Communist instigation. Indeed, as we will see below, quite the opposite is the case, in the sense that Claude Berridge – the leading Communist in the drama – was thought initially by Special Branch (though, as we will point out in Chapter Ten, not by Shawcross) to have played a restraining role rather than that of *agent provocateur*. The other issue revealed by the gas strike was the continuing uncertainty about the utility of Order 1305, the government deciding initially to use the Conspiracy and Protection of Property Act (CPPA) 1875, section 4, with Order 1305 operating only as a fall-back.

The use of the 1875 Act in the context of a gas strike would not be without irony. As we saw in Chapter Four, the Act had been passed following *R v Bunn*, where the Beckton gas strikers were convicted of common law conspiracy in 1872 and sentenced to 12 months' imprisonment.[1] But although the 1875 Act (section 3) largely removed the risk of criminal conspiracy from strikers in most cases, the same Act paradoxically introduced new statutory restrictions for gas and water workers (later extended to electricity supply workers in 1919).[2] As a result, the strike that led to a prosecution that in turn produced a change in the law, albeit after much 'political agitation',[3]

[1] *R v Bunn* (1972) 12 Cox CC 316. The sentences of 12 months with hard labour were commuted to four months with hard labour: D Brodie, *A History of British Labour Law, 1877–1945* (Hart Publishing, Oxford, 2003), p 16.

[2] Electricity Supply Act 1919, s 31.

[3] S Webb and B Webb, *The History of Trade Unionism, 1666–1920* (Longmans Green, London), p 285.

nevertheless might well still have attracted criminal sanctions. It was now an offence by virtue of section 4 'wilfully and maliciously' to break a contract of service, 'knowing or having reasonable cause to believe' that 'the probable consequence' of doing so would be to deprive the local inhabitants of their gas (or water or subsequently electricity) supply. Conviction under section 4 could lead to a fine of £20 or a term of imprisonment of up to three months, admittedly not as harsh an outcome as the 12 months to which the London gas-stokers had been sentenced under the common law in 1872. In this chapter we consider, inter alia, what is believed to be the only industrial dispute in which the CPPA 1875, section 4 was invoked (albeit unsuccessfully) before its repeal in 1971.

II. The Gas Workers' Strike

Work in the gas industry was hard, dirty and poorly paid, but also 'essential'. It was work which the Cabinet had long recognised had to be made less unattractive by improving the terms and conditions of employment.[4] Gas workers' wages had nevertheless fallen behind,[5] and their concerns had been before the Cabinet on several occasions in 1950.[6] On 6 April, in what was the main item of business in the second of the two meetings convened that day, the Cabinet considered a memorandum by the Minister of Fuel and Power concerned with union claims for a minimum wage of £5 per week for labourers in the gas industry (£5 and five shillings in some parts of the country). Apparently, the unions involved thought there was 'an exceptionally strong case for an increase of wage rates' on the grounds of 'increased productivity' and 'the lack of any general wage increase in the industry since early in 1948'.[7] A notable feature of the discussion was the revelation that the employers (the Gas Council) were anxious to keep the matter away from arbitration, indicating clearly that the gas workers had a good case: 'if the claim went to arbitration, manual workers might be awarded more than could be agreed as a result of negotiation'.[8]

Ministers were also keen to keep the dispute away from arbitration because of the effect a significant wage rise would have on other industries, where similar demands were likely to be made if the gas workers prevailed. According to the Cabinet Conclusions, 'while it would clearly be undesirable that the good relations which had existed in the gas industry should be impaired', it was more important to 'hold back the large number of other claims which would be strongly pressed if the gas workers secured an increase in wages'.[9] So although the Minister for Fuel and Power conceded in Cabinet that there was 'a strong case for increasing the wages of manual workers in this industry, which were very low in some areas',[10] the legitimate claims of gas workers were to be sacrificed

[4] See TNA, CAB 128/5/24 (Cabinet Conclusions, 14 March 1946).
[5] See TNA, CAB 128/17/24 (Cabinet Conclusions, 24 April 1950).
[6] See TNA, CAB 128/17/20 (Cabinet Conclusions, 6 April 1950); TNA, CAB 128/17/20 (Cabinet Conclusions, 24 April 1950); TNA, CAB 128/17/20 (Cabinet Conclusions, 18 May 1950).
[7] TNA, CAB 128/17/20 (Cabinet Conclusions, 6 April 1950).
[8] ibid.
[9] ibid.
[10] TNA, CAB 128/17/24 (Cabinet Conclusions, 24 April 1950).

on the altar of national economic interest, with employers to be instructed to adjust regional anomalies rather than concede a national minimum wage.[11] At the same time, it was said also to be 'important to preserve the authority of those trade union leaders who had supported the Government in the policy of wages stabilization'.[12] As a result, the grievances of gas workers remained unresolved throughout the summer of 1950, despite their claim having been submitted in November 1948.[13]

The dispute was being handled on the workers' side by the Confederation of Shipbuilding and Engineering Unions (CSEU), an umbrella organisation embracing the unions to which the gas workers belonged, primarily the AEU, the ETU, and the Boilermakers' Union. Experiencing similar problems to the Smithfield drivers, the gas workers felt that they had no option but to take unofficial action. Only by doing so would they provoke the CSEU to address their demands. A walk out thus took take place on 1 September 1950. In a bid to get the men back to work, the CSEU revealed that they were due to discuss the gas workers' claim with the employers on 14 September, a meeting which had not previously been disclosed to union members.[14] Nevertheless, on the evening of their walk out on 1 September, the striking gas workers heard from Claude Berridge at a meeting in Central London. Berridge was an officer of both the AEU and the Confederation. He was also 'a known Communist'. After hearing Berridge, the men returned to work the following day, having according to Special Branch sources, managed tacitly to agree between themselves that they would renew the strike if their claim was not met in full.[15]

Perhaps predictably, the promised meeting between the Gas Council and CSEU on 14 September ended unsatisfactorily, with an agreement for an extra one-and-a-half penny per hour falling well short of the workers' demands.[16] As news of the settlement spread across the capital,[17] the men walked out, evidently as disgusted with their unions as with the gas boards. At the Cabinet meeting on 18 September, when ministers were considering the Overseas Operations (Security of Forces) Bill, Isaacs told them that the men were demanding 'an exorbitant rate', and misled those present by saying that the workers had rejected the 'small award at arbitration'.[18] There had been no arbitration; it was a settlement negotiated by the CSEU. This exchange does not feature in the Cabinet Conclusions, but only in the record kept by the Cabinet Secretary, which also reveals that Isaacs had told ministers that the extended Overseas Operations (Security of Forces) Bill suggested by the Attorney

[11] ibid; TNA CAB 128/17/32 (Cabinet Conclusions 18 May 1950).
[12] TNA, CAB 128/17/20 (Cabinet Conclusions, 6 April 1950).
[13] TNA, HO 45/25546 ('Disturbances: strikes in industry communist instigated subversion') (Home Office F3 file 827723/325, formerly 823996/8, 'London Gas Strike. Prosecution of Certain Strikers') (Special Branch Report of the Trial at the Magistrates' Court, 5 October 1950). The police recorded that the date of the claim was mentioned by counsel for the defence.
[14] ibid, Special Branch Report, 21 September 1950.
[15] ibid, Special Branch Reports, 21 and 29 September 1950.
[16] They met on 14 September and as the news of the settlement spread across the capital, the men walked out, evidently as disgusted with their union as with the gas boards.
[17] The men learned about the outcome from press and radio reports rather than from the Confederation, their respective unions, or their employers: TNA, HO 45/25546 ('Disturbances: strikes in industry communist instigated subversion') (Home Office F3 file 827723/325, formerly 823996/8, 'London Gas Strike. Prosecution of Certain Strikers') (Special Branch Reports 21, 29 September 1950).
[18] TNA, CAB 195/8/30 (Cabinet Secretary's Notebook, 18 September 1950).

General would be 'very valuable'.[19] Isaacs perhaps saw the hand of the Communist Party in the gas strike, the issue before the Cabinet being whether the Overseas Operations (Security of Forces) Bill 'could with advantage be strengthened for the purpose of countering a Communist conspiracy to foment industrial unrest in this country'.[20]

On the day after Isaacs' Cabinet intervention, shop stewards from various unions met officers from the Confederation. Also present were full-time officials from the individual unions: Haskell of the ETU, Williams of the Boilermakers' Union, and Claude Berridge. Information about that meeting is helpfully provided by Special Branch, which made arrangements to 'cover' it, though the arrangements had to be altered when the venue was changed at the last minute. We can only speculate what forms of surveillance were in place for the initial location. But with the location changed, Special Branch now had to rely on informants present at the meeting, who reported that the shop stewards:

> [W]ere sore (a) at the fact that they had not been told officially by their unions the exact terms of the settlement, but had only heard 'second hand' either through press statements or from wireless bulletins and (b) that the unions had settled for 1 and a half pence … without consulting the men.[21]

It was also reported that the shop stewards demanded that the full claim was met, and passed a resolution stating that the strike would continue until 'the further 3d per hour is granted'. Additionally, the informant was able to provide the police with names and workplaces of the six shop stewards who spoke in favour of the resolution,[22] though the Chief Inspector who signed the report noted that the initial strike had been spontaneous, and that he 'could get no evidence that individuals have been prominent in inciting the men to strike'. While 'there are Communists among the stewards', 'it cannot be said that at this stage that they are more prominent than the others in their determination to continue the strike'.[23] Indeed, it was noted that the Communist AEU official Claude Berridge had 'urged' the men to return to work.

With the gas workers' shop stewards unexpectedly thrust into the limelight, they now became new targets for persecution. A list of 20 shop stewards on the 'Central Strike Committee' was drawn up by the police, eventually whittled down without explanation to 10.[24] The 'Central Strike Committee' appears to have existed largely in

[19] ibid.

[20] TNA, CAB 128/18/20 (Cabinet Conclusions, 18 September, 1950).

[21] TNA, HO 45/25546 ('Disturbances: strikes in industry communist instigated subversion') (Home Office F3 file 827723/325, formerly 823996/8, 'London Gas Strike. Prosecution of Certain Strikers') (Special Branch Report, 21 September 1950).

[22] ibid. These were Lambert, Spencer, Simpson, Chase, Foley, and Broadbent. Lambert and Broadbent were identified as Communists by the informer and their Special Branch file numbers were added to the report (PF 400/43/27 and PF 402/44/1513). All six were subsequently selected along with four others for prosecution. See below, pp 174–176.

[23] TNA, HO 45/25546 ('Disturbances: strikes in industry communist instigated subversion') (Home Office F3 file 827723/325 formerly 823996/8, 'London Gas Strike. Prosecution of Certain Strikers') (Special Branch Report, 21 September 1950). As for the strength of the strike, while noting that 'discreet enquiries' indicated that the men might be persuaded to return to work, the information provided suggested that the 'position is still deteriorating, 18 plants now being affected with a total of about 1,500 tradesmen on strike': ibid.

[24] ibid.

the orderly thoughts of those police officers, politicians and civil servants who had hoped to uncover a Communist plot.[25] With the latter in mind, Shawcross had sent Phillip Noel-Baker, the Minister of Fuel and Power, the list of alleged Committee members, noting that:

> [T]here is no evidence that these men are in fact engaged in a conspiracy which I could put before the Court, but insofar as they are themselves on strike they are guilty of an individual offence and in the event of their being convicted, the Court could be informed that they are understood to be amongst the ringleaders of the illegal strike action.[26]

Here was an acknowledgement that there could be no prosecution for seditious conspiracy as had been proposed in relation to the dockers, and that attention was turning to unspecified offences elsewhere, the use of the word 'strike' pointing to Order 1305.

The Conspiracy and Protection of Property Act 1875

The Conspiracy and Protection of Property Act 1875, section 4 had not featured in the Shawcross memorandums or in previous Cabinet discussions. It had, however, been raised by ex-TUC General Secretary Walter Citrine in his new role as chair of the British Electricity Authority. In 1949 Citrine had suggested that section 4 of the 1875 Act should be invoked to prosecute power station workers who break their contracts knowing that the public would be deprived of electricity,[27] while former Cabinet Secretary Edward Bridges was to argue the same a few months later.[28] And when commenting on Isaacs' conduct on 16 September 1950, the *Manchester Guardian* had reminded readers that 'some of the public utilities are protected by legislation', though adding confusingly that they 'make an employee liable to civil prosecution if he breaks his contract knowing that such action will deprive customers of their supply'.[29]

That said, section 4 did not impose a total ban on strikes by gas workers, but banned only strikes by employed persons who in the course of their action 'wilfully and maliciously' broke a contract of service with a municipal authority, company or contractor.[30] A strike during the currency of a contract of employment would of

[25] According to Special Branch, apparently conferring order on what was in reality a fluid organisation taking instruction from the members, rather than the Politburo, there was an 'East' Committee and a 'West' Committee (relating to areas of London), believed to amount to 50 people in all: ibid.

[26] TNA, HO 45/25546 ('Disturbances: strikes in industry communist instigated subversion') (Home Office F3 file 827723/325, formerly 823996/8, 'London Gas Strike. Prosecution of Certain Strikers') (Letter to Noel-Baker from Shawcross, 25 September 1950).

[27] Citrine had suggested Isaacs use the 1875 Act, as extended to the electricity generating industry in 1919. See TNA, PREM 8/1082 ('Minister of Labour to make an oral statement to Cabinet on danger of strikes which threaten the supply of electricity. Question of enforced contracts of service in essential industries'). See also N Fishman, '"A Vital Element in Industrial Relations": A Reassessment of Order 1305, 1940–51' (1999) 6 *Historical Studies in Industrial Relations* 43, pp 56–57.

[28] ibid, at p.57.

[29] See pp 159, 161–162 above. The matter was also raised in a letter to *The Times* from Henry Strauss (Tory MP) on 25 September 1950.

[30] Questions were raised about whether the offence in s 4 survived the nationalisation of the gas industry in 1948. Section 4 applied to persons employed by 'a municipal authority or by any person or contractor upon

course be a breach of contract. But as the Donovan Royal Commission pointed out in 1968, it was 'no offence under this section for an employee to terminate his contract of service with a gas or water undertaking by proper notice'.[31] For much of the period when section 4 was in force, the notice period was unlikely to have been very long, and in the absence of an express term to the contrary, the notice period required by statute to terminate the contract (but only since the Contracts of Employment Act 1963) was one week.[32]

Section 4 also required employers to post a copy of the 1875 Act, section 4 in a conspicuous place at the workplace so that it could be read by employees. It was the duty of the employer to ensure that copies were reposted to deal with defacement, obliteration or destruction. It is not clear what would be the consequences for criminal liability if this obligation was not complied with, and whether a failure to post or replace a notice would be a defence to any prosecution. We will never know: section 4 was never successfully deployed in the 96 years it was on the statute book. Unlike the CPPA, section 5,[33] it was not re-enacted following its repeal.[34] In the 1950 gas workers' strike, however, the point may have been moot: the files show that the relevant notices had been put up in North Thames Gas Board workplaces by the old Gas Light and Coke Company,[35] though this does not mean that the full extent of the law was complied with.

III. Isaacs' Broadcast

While the government's legal strategy for dealing with the gas workers was evolving, some ministers continued to be concerned with the aftermath of the dockers' and meat workers' disputes. Although by now it had become apparent that there was not going to be a 'September Revolution', the concern about unofficial action was nonetheless still acute. As we saw in Chapter Eight, it had been decided in Cabinet on 14 September that Isaacs should make a wireless broadcast on 16 or 17 September.[36] In fact, Isaacs' broadcast was

whom is imposed by Act of Parliament the duty [of supplying gas]'. Did this apply to the new gas boards? See TNA, HO 45/25546 ('Disturbances: strikes in industry communist instigated subversion') (Home Office F3 file 827723/325, formerly 823996/8, 'London Gas Strike. Prosecution of Certain Strikers') (Note of telephone call to Home Office by Mr Turner of the Ministry of Fuel and Power, 21 September 1950).

[31] Royal Commission on Trade Unions and Employers' Associations, 1965–1968, Report, Cmnd 3623, 1968, para 832.

[32] Nevertheless, the Donovan Commission heard that the section had 'a useful restraining influence by imposing, in effect, a short period of delay equal to the length of the period of notice required to terminate the contract of employment'. Donovan recommended section 4's retention, persuaded that it served a useful purpose for giving both employers and the public prior notice of impending action: ibid para 838.

[33] Section 5 made it an offence wilfully and maliciously to break a contract of employment knowing or having reasonable cause to believe that in doing so human life will be endangered, serious bodily injury will be caused, or valuable property will be exposed to destruction or serious injury.

[34] Trade Union and Labour Relations (Consolidation) Act 1992, s 241.

[35] TNA, HO 45/25546 ('Disturbances: strikes in industry communist instigated subversion') (Home Office F3 file 827723/325, formerly 823996/8, 'London Gas Strike. Prosecution of Certain Strikers') (Note of telephone call to Home Office by Mr Turner of the Ministry of Fuel and Power', 21 September 1950).

[36] TNA, CAB 128/18/18 (Cabinet Conclusions, 14 September, 1950).

delayed until 21 September, and then again until the evening of 25 September. There was nothing unusual about making such an address: we have seen in earlier chapters that ministers had used the medium in the case of dock strikes.[37] This one seemed different in the sense that it was more overtly partisan, conflating recent strikes with Communist Party tactics, before launching a strong attack on the Communist Party, which seemed out of all proportion to its role or influence. Needless to say, there was no question of the Communist Party being give a right to reply on the BBC.

A leader in *The Times* on the morning of 25 September considered both the gas strike and Isaacs' imminent broadcast. The assessment was telling, advising Isaacs not to be obsessed by the Communist Party at the expense of addressing the underlying problems which were responsible for the unofficial action now taking place:

> Mr Isaacs is to broadcast tonight on the menace of unofficial strikes. It is much to be hoped he will not devote all his attention to the evidence of agitation and conspiracy in industry to which he has already rightly pointed. He should also have something important to say about the structure and attitude of trade unions and the present unsatisfactory methods of solving disputes. It is on these shortcomings that agitation feeds.[38]

This advice evidently fell on stony ground at least so far as can be judged by the draft script, which the record suggests was a joint effort from the Ministry of Labour under the supervision of Gould (the Chief Industrial Commissioner), with early input from Newsam (Home Office), and perhaps Attlee and Morrison, with later advice from other interested ministers.

Having been instructed by Attlee to make the broadcast, Isaacs told the Nation that he was responding to an expectation from the people that he should address them. But despite the best efforts of *The Times*, the broadcast was principally not only an attack on the Communist Party, but also the strike leaders:

> As a nation we are able to assess at their true value the glib promises and allurements held out by people like the communists and their fellow travellers. That is why at the last Parliamentary Election the Communist Party were utterly routed. What we are now faced with is their effort to gain ground in the industrial field having completely failed in the political field. In March last year communists held a National Industrial Conference in pursuance of their publicly declared policy of concentrating their activities on industry. On March 6th, after this Conference, *The Times* reported Mr Harry Pollitt, General Secretary of the Communist Party in this country as follows – and here I quote – 'the great issues would be settled not in the areas of this reactionary Parliament, but by workers mass struggles in the factories and streets'. This no doubt sounds extravagant to you and you would probably be prepared to dismiss it as the usual hot air, but developments since that date show that we cannot take this threat lightly. The great majority of workers in this country, certainly in our vital industries, are organized in their trade unions and the Trade Union Movement can be the surest bulwark against Communism and must be kept so. That is why the attack now being launched is designed to weaken the trade unions. Take away the workers' loyalty to his union, destroy the spirit of discipline, and chaos will follow. The result to workers would be disastrous.[39]

[37] For earlier broadcasts, see pp 122–124, 126, 143–146, and 148 above.
[38] *The Times*, 25 September 1950.
[39] TNA, HO 45/25546 ('Disturbances: strikes in industry communist instigated subversion') (Home Office F3 file 823980/33 formerly 827723/331, 'Unofficial Strikes (Communist Instigation)) (Draft of Isaacs's address, 25 September 1950).

Isaacs cited the dock strike of the previous year, as a 'sordid story' of 'Communist intrigue and plotting',[40] and identified the leaders of that strike as the London Port Workers' Committee. He claimed that the Committee had appointed 'liaison officers' tasked with establishing similar committees in other ports – finding 'the few individuals required who will undertake the tasks allotted to them'.[41] Reference was made to the Road Haulage and Allied Workers' Committee (on which sat PWC representatives), and the other unofficial 'workers' committees' associated with the trade disputes at Smithfield, while Isaacs also attempted to justify his dramatic warning in Parliament on 15 September, on the grounds that there had been meetings in 'London, Liverpool, Birkenhead and Salford'.[42] In a passage very reminiscent of the *Daily Herald* article he had presented to the Cabinet on 14 September, Isaacs claimed further to have detected a familiar pattern in recent unofficial strikes – dissatisfaction with pay and conditions, or solidarity action with workers elsewhere, were the 'plausible pretext' for industrial action:

> [T]he deep sense of loyalty of the worker to his fellow worker is exploited and continued with intimidation to spread the strike,[43] a list of demands is then prepared which the strikers are told will be the conditions for the return to work, and when the strike fails – as fail it must when the community are determined to resist – there is usually some face saving formula to conceal the failure.[44]

The draft indicates that Isaacs warned that the government was prepared to legislate to deal with the continuing threat of unofficial industrial action,[45] though the references to statutory intervention were both vague and guarded: 'Some may say that legislation is necessary if we are to deal with this threat effectively'.[46] However, the trouble with legislation is that 'inevitably you must restrict the freedom of the individual. We do not want to be forced to that kind of action'.[47] But if 'such legislation should unfortunately prove necessary, there would be no hesitation in telling the country so and inviting Parliament to pass the necessary law'.[48] That said:

> If the workers in the industries that serve the public and on whose services and work the public depend for vital supplies, refuse to take any part in an activity that is not sponsored officially by the union, the danger will cease to exist. I do not want to express any opinion as to what the unions should do.[49]

[40] ibid.
[41] ibid.
[42] ibid.
[43] The reference to intimidation appears to have been omitted from the broadcast on the advice of Newsam: 'If there had been any evidence of intimidation it would have been possible to prosecute those responsible': TNA, HO 45/25546 ('Disturbances: strikes in industry: communist instigated subversion') (Home Office F3 file 823980/33, formerly 827723/331, 'Unofficial Strikes (Communist Instigation)') (Newsam to Gould at Ministry of Labour, 21 September 1950).
[44] ibid, draft of Isaacs's address, 25 September 1950.
[45] ibid, Newsam to Gould at Ministry of Labour, 21 September 1950. The word 'threat' was substituted for 'attack' (see p 167 above) at the suggestion of Frank Newsam on the advice of F3.
[46] ibid, draft of Isaacs's address, 25 September 1950.
[47] ibid.
[48] ibid.
[49] ibid.

The minister's muted appeal to the unions is understandable. It was likely to be far less politically damaging if the trade unions rather than the government acted to rein in unofficial industrial action.

Newsam had also commented that 'action by the Trade Unions is not merely simpler but is also preferable'.[50] But neither ministers nor senior civil servants had any idea what the unions should do. Isaacs' only answer was to address workers and their families directly. The central theme of the broadcast was thus to *persuade* trade unionists not to support unofficial industrial action. He was not afraid to labour the point, exhorting his listeners to be trade union activists rather than trade union card holders, urging members to attend Branch meetings, to express their views, and 'not allow mischief makers to inflame feelings'. He continued:

> It is not right that out of a Branch of, say, 1,000 members, only 50 should turn up at a meeting and perhaps 40 out of that 50, knowing that you will not be there, should pass a resolution which they say is on behalf of 1,000 members. There is a remedy for all this mischief which is injuring the country, causing inconvenience to the community and (what is important also to us trade unionists), damaging the name of the trade union movement. It is simply this: remain alert; remain loyal to your union; follow official union advice; and ignore these unofficial elements. In this way you can more effectively prevent planned disturbances of our supplies and services than any legislation can do.[51]

Although these were well-meaning and admirable sentiments, following 'official union advice' had done little to advance the gas workers' cause. The union had been secretive, ineffective, and authoritarian; union officials were remote, unaccountable, and conflicted.

There was, however, no direct reference to the gas strike in Isaacs' address, though it is impossible not to make the connection to that dispute in the passages of the address referred to above. The key points that stand out are Communist agitation, provoking a pattern of unofficial action, in which workers were being duped for political ends to take action that was 'injuring the country' and 'causing inconvenience to the community'. As already suggested, the draft of the speech thus did what *The Times* had urged Isaacs not to do, which was to 'devote all his attention to the evidence of agitation and conspiracy in industry', when what was needed was something 'important' to say on the 'unsatisfactory methods of solving disputes'. At the very least, this would have required a less superficial attempt to discover why the unofficial action in the gas industry and elsewhere was taking place. He might also have explained why the disputes had not been brought to a speedy conclusion by referring them to arbitration under Order 1305. Although the government could not initiate the procedure, it could put pressure on both the employers and the trade unions to do so. In the case of employers, it would have been fairly straightforward in the nationalised and state-controlled industries for the Ministry of Labour to insist that any such disputes should be reported.

At the heart of this, however, was Isaacs himself, and his refusal to permit unofficial groups of workers to report disputes on their own behalf. It will be recalled that a strike would be lawful under Order 1305 only if a dispute had first been reported

[50] ibid, Newsam to Gould at Ministry of Labour, 21 September 1950.
[51] ibid.

to the Minister, and then only if the Minister slept on the report for 21 days. But by virtue of Ministry of Labour policy adopted since the war, reports from unofficial sources were not accepted nor referred to arbitration, presumably to force workers to pursue the resolution of disputes through official channels. Although the policy was understandable, its legitimacy (if not its legality) depended on trade unions properly representing the interests of their members rather than giving effect to the wishes of the government. Workers were at the mercy of union officials, with no option but to strike (and thereby risk prosecution) if their interests were being compromised or sacrificed. As the gas workers case vividly demonstrated, the policy was manifestly inappropriate and invited an explanation as to how workers neglected by their union were otherwise expected to redress their grievances. This is not the practice that had been followed during the war, and it was a matter of great surprise to Isaacs when he was eventually told by Shawcross that the policy was unlawful and had to be discontinued, a matter which we will deal with in Chapter Eleven.

IV. The Decision to Prosecute

When delivering his address, Isaacs would of course have known that the gas strike was the first item on the Cabinet agenda the next morning, making even more implausible any suggestion that the gas workers were not at least partially in his sights as he was speaking. Rather than confront the causes of the dispute, the stage was now being set for prosecution, the brief Cabinet Conclusions reflecting Isaacs' conspiratorial assessment:

> *The Minister of Labour* reported the latest developments in the unofficial strike of maintenance men employed by the North Thames Gas Board.[52] The Confederation of Shipbuilding and Engineering Unions, who represented these men, had presented on their behalf a claim for a wage increase of 4.5d per hour and had accepted a settlement of 1.5d an hour [bringing the hourly rate up to 3s 6d]: the men had staged this unofficial strike in an attempt to secure their full claim. The Confederation had asked that efforts at conciliation should be conducted through them; but the London District Committee of the Confederation, through which the Confederation itself and the Ministry of Labour would then have to work, was dominated by Communists. The Ministry were now in direct touch with the Amalgamated Engineering Union and other constituent unions: they were also asking the Gas Board whether Service men could carry on the maintenance work at the gas works and what risk there was that their introduction would lead to a sympathetic strike by the men engaged on the production of gas.[53]

The fuller account of the proceedings in Norman Brook's Notebook suggests, however, that Isaacs was unhappy with by-passing the Confederation, and was claiming that the 'local' unions were 'in London dominated by Communists', and that the 'main trouble

[52] Many strikers were employed by other gas boards, but all ten prosecuted worked for the North Thames Gas Board.

[53] TNA, CAB 128/18/21 (Cabinet Conclusions, 26 September 1950).

is ETU is Communist dominated'.[54] What a dilemma: Communists appeared to be everywhere.

More notable perhaps is a statement to colleagues at the same meeting by the Attorney General, who said that:

> [H]e was considering whether proceedings could be brought against those members of the unofficial Strike committee who had themselves broken their contracts of employment by coming out on strike. He would wish to know whether there were any political and other considerations which he should bear in mind before taking a decision; and he was in touch with the Home Secretary and Minister of Labour on this point.[55]

By focusing on the breach of contracts, Shawcross now appears to have been contemplating proceedings under the 1875 Act, though the Cabinet Secretary's Notebook records that Shawcross had written to his colleagues earlier regarding the prosecution of leaders to say that the prosecution would be under the 'compulsory arbitration Order' (that is to say, Order 1305).[56] Isaacs expressed no doubts, telling his colleagues 'I feel bold'.[57] Attlee and Chuter Ede (Home Secretary) counselled restraint, insisting that the question go to the Cabinet Emergencies Committee, and that the latter's decision be referred back to the Cabinet.[58] This would give the full ministerial team an opportunity to bring to the Attorney General's attention 'any factors which he should bear in mind before taking a final decision'.[59] Separately, however, Philip Noel-Baker, the Minister of Fuel and Power, told Shawcross that a prosecution would be a mistake,[60] having been warned by the chairman of the Gas Council that it would spread the strike and strengthen the resolve of the workers.

Following the Cabinet's instruction, the possibility of prosecution was considered by the Cabinet Emergencies Committee on 27 September.[61] With the Home Secretary in the chair, the Committee comprised Isaacs, Noel-Baker, Shawcross, the Ministers of Transport and Food, and the Secretary of State for Scotland, Hector McNeil. Frank Newsam and Robert Gould were among the officials present. They had before them Newsam's note on the conclusions that his Official Committee (which had met the previous day) had reached on the gas strike:

> THE HOME SECRETARY drew attention to the serious situation disclosed in the report- the hardship to many householders, the prospect of heavy unemployment and the partial breakdown of bakeries and catering establishments; hospitals had been able to carry on reasonably well. The report advised against bringing Service labour and concluded that overt action to replace the strikers would spread the strike.[62]

[54] TNA, CAB 195/8/31 (Cabinet Secretary's Notebook, 26 September 1950).
[55] TNA, CAB 128/18/21 (Cabinet Conclusions, 26 September 1950).
[56] ibid. Presumably this is a reference to the note sent on 25 September, referred to at n 79 below.
[57] TNA, CAB 195/8/31 (Cabinet Secretary's Notebook, 26 September 1950).
[58] ibid.
[59] TNA, CAB 128/18/21 (Cabinet Conclusions, 26 September 1950).
[60] TNA, HO 45/25546 ('Disturbances: strikes in industry: communist instigated subversion') (Home Office F3 file 827723/325, formerly 823996/8, London Gas Strike. Prosecution of Certain Strikers) (Letter from Noel-Baker to Shawcross, 26 September, 1950).
[61] TNA, CAB 134/177 (Cabinet Emergencies Committee, 8th Meeting, 27 September 1950).
[62] ibid.

Isaacs argued that the attempts of the CSEU to communicate with the workers over their pay claim 'had been frustrated by the shop stewards who had, among other things, failed to pass on to the men instructions to attend a mass meeting summoned by the Confederation',[63] Noel-Baker concurring 'that the unofficial strike committee were anxious to keep the unions and their members apart'.[64] Ministers on the Cabinet Emergencies Committee expressed their faith that the men's unions (the AEU, the Boilermakers' Union, and the ETU) would secure an end to the strike, despite Isaacs having told the Cabinet on 26 September that the ETU was 'dominated by Communists'. Should the unions fail and the strike continue, then according to Shawcross, 'it would be difficult to refrain from operating the ordinary processes of the law. The strikers would probably be fined and not imprisoned'.[65]

The focus it seems was now on the 1875 Act, section 4. Unlike Order 1305, which at least had been used during the war, the former had never been deployed in the 75 years since its enactment. Although determined for some time to invoke the criminal law, Shawcross was thus sailing into uncharted waters and understandably seemed keen to ensure that others shouldered as much responsibility as possible. He claimed to regret that the Gas Boards had failed to bring a civil action against the strikers for breach of contract, and he would no doubt have noted that the Cabinet Emergencies Committee apparently shared his supposed concern that criminal proceedings might hinder attempts by the union to return to work. However, Shawcross would have been satisfied that the Committee took the view nevertheless that if the men were not back at work by 30 September, then if sufficient evidence was available, the Committee 'would not wish to represent to the Attorney General that criminal proceedings were inadvisable'.[66] At the risk of reading too much into the use of the double negative, it seems likely that the Committee, like Shawcross, were conscious that the prosecutions could ultimately prove to be a mistake, particularly in view of the uncertainties associated with dated legislation.[67]

The gas strike was back on the Cabinet agenda the next day – only two days after ministers had first discussed it. Introducing the item on 28 September, the Home Secretary revealed that it was a Communist conspiracy after all, that Isaacs and Gould were hoping to use Jack Tanner, General Secretary of the AEU, as an intermediary to broker a deal, and that employer opposition to a prosecution was beginning to fade, as the Conclusions make clear:

> *The Home Secretary* said that the Emergencies Committee had met on the previous evening and reviewed the latest developments in the London gas strike. The London branches of the Unions mainly concerned were dominated by Communists and were unwilling to summon meetings at which the workers could express their views. The President of the Amalgamated Engineering Union was therefore being asked to establish direct contact

[63] Remarkably the Cabinet Emergencies Committee minutes reveal that Isaacs was to make another broadcast on the BBC: 'The hands of the unions should be strengthened by the broadcast which the Minister of Labour was to make later that evening, in the course of which he had been authorized to say that the Government would use all its powers, should it be necessary to safeguard essential services' (ibid).

[64] TNA, CAB 134/177 (Cabinet Emergencies Committee, 8th Meeting, 27 September 1950).

[65] ibid.

[66] ibid.

[67] See the box on pp 165–166 above.

> with the men. Meanwhile, supervisory staff were carrying out a certain amount of essential maintenance work at gas works and the workers engaged on production had not so far objected to this. It seemed wiser to continue on these lines than to call in Service men, especially as the Services would not be able to provide enough technicians to meet the needs of the situation which would arise if recourse to the Services provoked an extension of the strike. The North Thames Gas Board had originally feared that the prosecution of ringleaders under the Conspiracy and Protection of Property Act, 1875, might lead to an extension of the strike, but they had now withdrawn their opposition; and the Emergencies Committee were of the opinion that, if the strike had not ended by the following day and if the Attorney-General was then satisfied that there was evidence on which to base a criminal charge against the ringleaders, there were no political or industrial reasons why he should not commence proceedings against them.[68]

In the discussion that followed the Home Secretary's introduction, it is clear that ministers were nevertheless concerned that 'serious dislocation and unemployment were likely if the strike continued'.[69] But it appears that the threat of escalating industrial action in a 'vital service' was not a sufficient reason for prosecutorial restraint in the public interest.

Notably, the concern here was only with the impact of the strike and the consequences of the proposed legal action – no attention appears to have been paid to the chances of its success, the risks of its failure, or the implications of a trial collapsing. It is perhaps a measure of ministers' desire to make an example of a group of workers – any group of workers – that Shawcross should be authorised to prosecute the strike leaders while the Ministry was still attempting to broker a deal, and when the strike was on the verge of collapsing.[70] The more detailed account of Cabinet proceedings on 28 September in Norman Brook's Notebooks emphasises the political undercurrents behind the prosecution, with Shawcross regretting that Isaacs' 'public statements' had now made it 'increasingly difficult to refrain from operating the criminal law – especially the Act of 1875'.[71] Less explicitly, Phillip Noel-Baker, Minister for Fuel and Power, revealed that he had changed his mind and now favoured a prosecution.[72] Although evidently hopeful that Tanner might persuade the men to return to work (begging the question of how much Tanner knew of plans to prosecute and why he did not report the dispute under Order 1305), Noel-Baker conceded that 'some day we must prosecute someone. This is as good a case as we are likely to get'.[73]

Norman Brook's Notebooks also reveal that Shawcross had told the Cabinet that the Gas Board should bring actions for breach of contract: 'If men go back, the Boards can settle.'[74] This was a reprise of a position he had advocated earlier in the year in one of his legal memorandums, on the basis that it would (i) be understood by the workers involved as a consequence of breach of contract, (ii) be appreciated publicly, (iii) have

[68] TNA, CAB 128/18/22 (Cabinet Conclusions, 28 September 1950).
[69] ibid.
[70] It was nevertheless impressive that the strike lasted as long as it did, given the pressure and intimidation the strikers were required to endure, not least from government and the police.
[71] TNA, CAB 195/8/32 (Cabinet Secretary's Notebook, 28 September 1950).
[72] ibid. Previously he had sided with the chairman of the Gas Boards in opposing a prosecution. See note 103 below.
[73] ibid.
[74] ibid.

a salutary effect, (iv) put the party bringing the case more in control of the proceedings, and (v) put the unions in a good light as honest brokers in dealing with the aftermath. The suggestion was well received, though there is no suggestion in the Conclusions or in Norman Brook's more detailed account that this expedient should be actively pursued in the gas strike. However, at the suggestion of Aneurin Bevan no less,[75] a new Cabinet edict on 28 September insisted that as a general principle 'the boards of socialised industries ought, during a period when there were no major strikes in progress, to issue leaflets to their workers pointing out that they were under contracts of service and that, if they broke these contracts without reasonable cause, the Board would consider the institution of civil proceedings against them in the county courts for the recovery of damages'.[76]

In terms of prosecution, it should be emphasised that at the Cabinet meeting on 28 September, Shawcross was given authority to proceed only under the 1875 Act if the strike had not ended by the following day.[77] There was no reference to or approval for proceedings under Order 1305. It is clear from ministerial correspondence, however, that Shawcross was 'considering with the Director of Public Prosecutions' the possibility of invoking Order 1305 for what would be the first time since the war even before the Cabinet meeting on 26 September.[78] He had raised the possibility of such proceedings in correspondence with Chuter Ede, Isaacs, and Noel-Baker on 25 September (the day before the Cabinet considered the strike for the first time).[79] And according to the Cabinet Secretary, Shawcross had raised Order 1305 at the Cabinet meeting on 26 September, even though the point is not recorded in the formal Conclusions.[80] But given the care the Attorney General normally took about such matters, it is nevertheless surprising that there is no evidence that the Cabinet had formally approved proceedings under Order 1305. Approval to prosecute under the 1875 Act appears nevertheless to have been taken as a licence to prosecute on other grounds as well.

V. The Gas Workers' Strike and Order 1305

Ten men were selected for prosecution under both the CPPA, section 4, and Order 1305, Article 4. The basis of the prosecution was that they had each taken part in a strike in breach of these particular measures. Those selected were the ringleaders listed in the Special Branch Report of 21 September referred to above.[81] All worked

[75] ibid.

[76] ibid. The boards were already required to post a copy of the 1875 Act, s 4 in a conspicuous place at workplaces so that it could be read by employees. See the box on p 166 above.

[77] It was also noted that the employers had withdrawn their objections to prosecution.

[78] TNA, CAB 128/18/22 (Cabinet Conclusions, 28 September 1950).

[79] See TNA, HO 45/25546 ('Disturbances: strikes in industry communist instigated subversion') (Home Office F3 file 823980/33, formerly 827723/33, 'Unofficial Strikes (Communist Instigation')) (Note from Shawcross to Home Secretary and Ministers of Labour and Fuel and Power, 25 September 1950). It is recorded that Shawcross again repeated the constitutional position that 'the ultimate responsibility of deciding whether there should be a prosecution rests with me'.

[80] TNA, CAB 195/8/31 (Cabinet Secretary's Notebook, 26 September 1950).

[81] TNA, HO 45/25546 ('Disturbances: strikes in industry: communist instigated subversion') (Home Office F3 file 827723/325, formerly 823996/8, 'London Gas Strike. Prosecution of Certain Strikers') (Special Branch Report, 29 September 1950).

for the North Thames Gas Board (NTGB). One of the 10 men, Fred Lambert, was reported by a Special Branch informer as having told his colleagues that his selection for prosecution was 'a mystery', as was that of his friend Charlie Broadbent.[82] In fact, the pair had been identified by Special Branch as the only two known Communists (Special Branch already having files on them) among the six most vocal proponents of the strike spotted among 100 or so shop stewards present at a meeting on 19 September. All six of the men singled out that evening were in the group of 10 prosecuted, highlighting the importance of Special Branch and its methods, not only in relation to this particular dispute, but probably also more generally.

Summonses were issued by the Chief Magistrate at Bow Street on 2 October 1950. Clerical officers and managers of the NTGB were ready to testify that the defendants had gone on strike, while the police confirmed that a certificate of failure to report the dispute would be issued by the Ministry for the purposes of the prosecution – that failure apparently seen as an essential element of the Order 1305 offence.[83] Such a certificate was of course a pointless formality, given departmental policy that would have prevented any such report to have been accepted even if it had been made.[84] Nevertheless, the certificate was duly issued by the Ministry, 'GIVEN UNDER THE OFFICIAL SEAL OF THE MINISTER OF LABOUR', listing the names of the 10 shop stewards and stating that they 'are charged with taking part in a strike, [which] was not reported to the Minister by either party to the dispute in accordance with the provisions of Article 2 of the said Order'.[85] Each of the 10 was charged not only with a breach of Order 1305, but also the Conspiracy and Protection of Property Act 1875, section 4 (despite having provided a clear month's notice of their action) and (according to Special Branch) to which the foregoing Order 1305 formalities would not be relevant.

The prosecution claimed that the 10 shop stewards had been carefully selected as representatives of the 1,500 strikers working for the North Thames, Eastern and South Eastern Gas Boards, though, as we have seen, they all worked for the first of these employers only. Summonses were served the same day by a Special Branch Chief Inspector ('as instructed by the Attorney General'), each of the men being asked:

- Are you the person named?
- Are you employed by the North Thames Gas Board?
- Are you on strike?
- Are you a member of the Strike Committee?

[82] ibid: Special Branch Report, Meeting at Beckton Gas Works on 13 October, 20 October 1950.

[83] War-time experience suggests that a certificate essentially guaranteed a conviction, and it is likely that it was for that reason so much emphasis was placed on the failure to report the dispute.

[84] See p 97 above. See also chs 11 and 12 below, especially pp 213–216, 219, 237, 238 and 241.

[85] TNA, HO 45/25546 ('Disturbances: strikes in industry: communist instigated subversion') (Home Office F3 file 827723/325, formerly 823996/8, 'London Gas Strike. Prosecution of Certain Strikers') (Certificate signed by Godfrey H Ince, Secretary, Ministry of Labour and National Service, 3 October 1950).

The answers served as witness statements. Two claimed to have done no more than take telephone messages. A third had denied that there had been a committee, telling the police that: 'It really is a representation of a big body [sic]. I don't think it is called a strike committee.' A fourth man, Broadbent, later denied being on any committee and believed that he had been targeted for producing what the police described as the 'Strike Committee Bulletin'.[86] Not that it made any difference for the purposes of a prosecution under either Order 1305 or the 1875 Act. Any of the 1,500 strikers would have fitted the bill.

Despite a prediction he made to the Cabinet Emergencies Committee about fines being the most likely outcome, Shawcross may well have wanted the men to be imprisoned. Newsam told the Home Secretary on 4 October that: 'The Attorney General has decided to ask for a *remand* when the strikers who are being prosecuted appear tomorrow.'[87] It is also possible of course that Shawcross simply wanted the defendants to taste jail before being given a lesser sentence. On the same day, a well-attended meeting of the London and South East Regional Board for Industry saw employers' representatives voice 'sympathy with work people' on the issue of summonses 'which appeared to have been unfortunately timed', while workers' representatives at the same meeting 'alleged that but for [the] issue of summonses men would have quite probably have been back at work today'. Recognising the unfortunate nature of the prosecution, the Board's chairman agreed to organise an 'off the record' meeting between the gas shop stewards and Robert Gould at the Ministry of Labour.[88] The intention was clearly to bring about a 'relaxation of the present tension', by persuading the government to instruct the DPP to drop the case.[89]

But the matter was out of Gould's hands and the prosecution went ahead the next day – 5 October 1950 – at Bow Street Magistrates' Court. Christmas Humphreys KC appeared for the prosecution, having appeared for the Crown in the Klaus Fuchs official secrets case earlier in the year.[90] The pleas were not guilty to the offence under the 1875 Act, but guilty under Order 1305. The not guilty plea was accepted by the prosecution, indicating perhaps that there was still doubt as to whether the 1875 Act, section 4 had continued to apply in the gas industry after nationalisation. So far as Order 1305 is concerned, however, Humphreys chose to claim that:

> The law is not only clear, but is perfectly well known to these men and the whole of the trade union movement. There is no question of taking out a moribund prosecution as a weapon for political prosecution [sic].[91]

Counsel for the defendants Eric Falk (Special Branch checked to see if they had a file on him and no doubt opened one when they found they had not) pointed out the iniquity

[86] ibid, Metropolitan Police Statement of Witness, 3 October 1950.
[87] ibid, Newsam to Chuter Ede, 4 October 1950, emphasis added.
[88] ibid. Gould was Chief Industrial Commissioner in the Ministry of Labour.
[89] ibid, extract from message from Mr Searle, Ministry of Transport on 5 October 1950, following a meeting of the London and SE Regional Board for Industry.
[90] He appeared with Donal Barry from the office of the DPP.
[91] Humphreys did come to regret these claims. See Fishman (n 27) pp 59–60.

of prosecuting 10 men out of 1,500 strikers,[92] and of mounting a prosecution after the very many unofficial strikes that had taken place with impunity since 1945:

> It must be within your knowledge that hundreds of thousands, if not millions, have been out on unofficial strikes, on illegal strikes, from 1945 to 1950.[93]

Falk told the court that he had tried to get the figures from the Ministry of Labour, but had found that the statistics failed to distinguish between unofficial and official strikes. The reality, however, was that there had been very few official strikes, and that the overwhelming majority of strikes must have been unofficial.

Such was the continuing confusion over Order 1305 that the court – Falk included – appeared to have taken official strikes to be, by definition, lawful and unofficial strikes by definition to be unlawful.[94] Worse still, the Chief Magistrate, Sir Laurence Dunne, interrupted Falk after the latter had stated the normal practice would have been for union officials to have reported the dispute to the Ministry of Labour under Order 1305, Article 2. According to Dunne, the men themselves could have made the report,[95] evidently unaware of departmental policy not to accept or refer reports of disputes except from trade unions or employers, of which regrettably no one appeared to inform him.[96] It was an intervention that tended to contradict another contestable statement by the Chief Magistrate. Thus, the prosecution was 'intended to affirm a principle'. 'That principle', Dunne continued, is that 'we are still under the rule of law', before adding 'This is a perfectly ordinary prosecution', and that 'There is nothing political about it'.[97] But perhaps anticipating the possibility that the prosecution was politically motivated, it was apparently necessary for Dunne to insist that the role of the court was to deal with the cases brought before it, not to choose who to prosecute and who to ignore.

That said, the Chief Magistrate also revealed a measure of sympathy for the defendants, confessing that he felt it 'distasteful for a magistrate' to deal with men 'who have not committed a crime in the ordinary sense'.[98] But any sympathy Dunne might have had was not reflected in the one-month jail sentence imposed on each of the defendants,

[92] TNA, HO 45/25546 ('Disturbances: strikes in industry: communist instigated subversion') (Home Office F3 file 827723/325, formerly 823996/8, 'London Gas Strike. Prosecution of Certain Strikers') ('Mr Eric Victor FALK, of counsel, of whom there is no record in Special Branch, appeared for the defence').

[93] TNA, HO 45/25546 ('Disturbances: strikes in industry: communist instigated subversion') (Home Office F3 file 827723/325, formerly 823996/8, 'London Gas Strike. Prosecution of Certain Strikers') (Special Branch Report, 5 October 1950).

[94] In addition, it seems that many had previously taken the view that unofficial strikes were not affected by Order 1305 probably because unofficial strikes had taken place with apparent impunity since the war.

[95] 'If the men were dissatisfied it would be for them to raise the matter, and if the employer wished to alter the terms of service it would be the employer': TNA, HO 45/25546 ('Disturbances: strikes in industry: communist instigated subversion') (Home Office F3 file 827723/325, formerly 823996/8, 'London Gas Strike. Prosecution of Certain Strikers') (Special Branch Report, 5 October 1950).

[96] See pp 97 and 169–170 above. The departmental policy was unlawful, as is discussed more fully in chs 11 and 12 below, especially at pp 213–16, 219, 237–38 and 241.

[97] TNA, HO 45/25546 ('Disturbances: strikes in industry: communist instigated subversion') (Home Office F3 file 827723/325, formerly 823996/8, 'London Gas Strike. Prosecution of Certain Strikers') (Special Branch Report, 5 October 1950).

[98] ibid.

even though they were bailed pending appeal. Only three prison sentences had been handed down in England and Wales during the war, despite there having been thousands of workers convicted for breach of Order 1305, and these had been quickly commuted to fines. The sentences in question had been passed – in relation to the Betteshanger dispute – on three full-time officials of the miners' union. Prior to the gas workers, there was no example of strikers having served a prison sentence for breach of Order 1305, not even in war-time. It seems that the magistrate had been encouraged to make an example of the men, and the whole purpose of the prosecution had been to serve as a warning to those taking or contemplating unofficial strike action, challenging claims that 'we are still under the rule of law', and that there was nothing 'political' about the prosecution.

VI. Conclusion

The gas workers' conviction was the first conviction under Order 1305 since the war. Having been authorised to prosecute in earlier disputes, Shawcross finally had his moment. In the end, the 1875 Act was a distraction, though its emergence as a possible basis for liability would have helped Shawcross' campaign to highlight the importance of contract law and the various potential implications of breach. But what had initially been an investigation by Special Branch aimed, on the orders of Frank Newsam, at securing the conviction for criminal conspiracy of a gang of ruthless Communists taking their directions from behind the Iron Curtain, had been scaled down to a token prosecution under Order 1305 against a group of gas workers who had a widely recognised industrial grievance. There were no Communist plots to uncover or plotters to bring to justice in the gas industry. The CSEU was even more guilty than the government: it was the Confederation's willingness to sign off on a poor deal that led to the prosecutions when it was clear that Isaacs and his colleagues were unwilling to go behind the official channels. Unimpressed, MI5's Guy Liddell wrote in his diary that:

> The D of P P said that the prosecution of the gas strike leaders had been somewhat muddled, since Jack Tanner had never been told. It appears also that Isaacs made his statement about a Communist plot without any prior consultation.[99]

With the strike still ongoing, approximately 1,000 gas workers attended a meeting at St Pancras Town Hall on the afternoon of the convictions. Admission was by union card and Special Branch again had to make do with an account of the meeting from an informer – 'a reliable source'. On the platform were representatives from the dockers and road haulage men, as well as the railway unions (said to be 'holding watching briefs'). Also on the platform were the 10 gas workers at liberty pending an appeal. On the front row were Haskell of the ETU and Berridge of the AEU and the Confederation. According to Special Branch, the union officers congratulated the men on their spirit while imploring them to return to work, telling them that to continue with the strike

[99] TNA, KV4/472 (Liddell Diary, 4 October 1950).

would be 'banging their heads against a brick wall'.[100] Confounding an earlier Special Branch assessment,[101] around 90 per cent of those present voted to go back to work, the Special Branch informant reporting that they had been motivated in part by a fear that they might lose their jobs following the deployment of the Navy in a few of the East End gas works.[102] This was good news for Noel-Baker and the chairman of the Gas Council, who had feared that the presence of the military would inflame the situation.[103]

[100] TNA, HO 45/25546 ('Disturbances: strikes in industry: communist instigated subversion') (Home Office F3 file 827723/325, formerly 823996/8 ('London Gas Strike. Prosecution of Certain Strikers') (Special Branch Report, 5 October 1950). There are two Special Branch reports in the file dated 5 October: one covers the trial, the other events afterwards.

[101] According to Special Branch: 'The general feeling among the men seemed to be that if a nominal fine is imposed, a resolution to return to work on Friday will be carried at the mass meeting to be held tomorrow.' If, on the other hand 'the men are sent to prison the strike may continue': ibid, Special Branch Report, 5 October 1950.

[102] On the day of the prosecution and the mass meeting, 175 sailors went to work in the Beckton Gas Works, and 43 in Bromley-by-Bow: ibid, Special Branch Report, 5 October 1950.

[103] See the Note to Shawcross by Noel-Baker, 26 September 1950: 'in the opinion of the Chairman of the Gas Boards concerned prosecution would embarrass these efforts [to end the strike] and I share that view. I am now advised, and must, I think accept the advice, that the intervention of troops would be worse than useless.' It is, however, notable that after the men had returned to work, the NTGB 'asked that troops remain available for the next day or two' in case there was another walk out: TNA, HO 45/25546 ('Disturbances: strikes in industry: communist instigated subversion') (Home Office F3 file 827723/325, formerly 823996/8, 'London Gas Strike. Prosecution of Certain Strikers'). As we have seen, Noel-Baker later changed his mind to support the prosecution.

10

Prosecution Over-reached

The Gas Workers' Appeal

I. Introduction

The gas workers' conviction represented a clear triumph for those Cabinet ministers who favoured a more robust use of criminal law to deal with illegal strikes, and unofficial strikes in particular. It also marked a clear passage from the earlier strategy of containment of industrial action by the use of troops and emergency powers rather than coercion. The importance of the criminal law was consolidated in the weeks to follow as the men prepared their appeal. Indeed, criminal law was no longer a weapon to be deployed against the Communists; on the contrary, its use paradoxically was ramped up as the Communist 'threat' was diminishing. Particularly significant in this respect were the wide-ranging Cabinet discussions which took place immediately after the trial. These revealed almost universal support for retaining the criminal law to deal with unofficial strikes, with a detailed examination of how Order 1305 might be replaced. Led mainly by Morrison and Chuter Ede rather than Isaacs, the discussions on 9 October in particular bring to mind the final sentence of George Orwell's *Animal Farm*: it was hard to believe that the participants were ministers in a Labour government.[1]

Apart from proposals to develop the criminal law, the period between the trial and the appeal saw the continuing presence of the criminal agencies of the state in the form of routine but intense surveillance of trade unionists, and in particular of workers engaged in disputes with their employer. The surveillance of the gas workers and their supporters – at a time when they were engaged in a lawful appeal and lawful protest against convictions – was staggering not only in terms of its breadth and depth, but also its propriety. Special Branch files provide a meticulous account of the campaign to support the gas workers' appeal and secure the revocation of Order 1305, as well as the hearing of the appeal and its aftermath. The files also record the steps proposed by the gas workers' leaders to make use of the Order 1305 procedures to avoid criminal liability in the future. They make clear that the workers were knowingly placed by the Minister of Labour in a position where they had no means of redress of their grievances other than by taking strike action which would inevitably bring them into conflict with the

[1] The point was not lost on MI5. Earlier in the year, Guy Liddell had reflected on 'a general tendency toward a strong-arm action', and speculated about 'what the Labour Party would have said to the Conservative Party if they had taken such action when they were in power', adding that 'it is somewhat paradoxical to find Labour using strong-arm methods against their own kind': TNA, KV4/471 (Liddell Diary, 11 June 1949).

criminal law. It is a sad story of betrayal, initially by a trade union and its officials, and then by a Labour government.

II. Cabinet's Response to the Convictions

By Monday, 9 October 1950, the gas workers were back at work except, according to Special Branch, the 10 convicted men, who were suspended on full pay pending the appeal.[2] The Cabinet was duly informed by Isaacs that the company had given the men the option of returning to work or being suspended on full pay.[3] Some ministers evidently thought this 'undesirable', given that the men were appealing only against their sentence, though it is not clear what the hardliners had in mind as being appropriate as an alternative to a return to work or suspension on full pay, the only options being suspension without pay or dismissal.[4] Isaacs also reported that, at the request of the North Thames Gas Board, the troops were being kept on standby for another few days. The Cabinet Conclusions for 9 October otherwise reveal a group of men fully vindicated by their coercive conduct, looking to press home the advantage on a number of fronts. Vindication was metamorphosing into vindictiveness.

Vindication would no doubt be reinforced by ministers' belief that public opinion supported the gas workers' convictions and the retention of Order 1305, an impression they must have gathered from press coverage of the prosecution. There was some regret about criticisms that the government had not moved quickly enough to bring in the troops and initiate prosecutions, but that was tempered by a belief that if they had moved too quickly, there was a danger they would not have taken the public with them. The only other regret it seems was that they had not been able to go further, the Lord Chancellor being recorded by Brook as saying that he wished they could have prosecuted the ringleaders for incitement. This was met by Shawcross' explanation that there was a 'lack of evidence of incitement', but that they had 'selected for prosecution the members of the Strike Committee'.[5] It was left to Bevin first to raise concerns about the continuing use of Order 1305 in light of the 'many undertakings given before it was made, in order to secure TUC agreement', noting second that 'many unions now favour its repeal – and Communists are cashing in on that feeling'.

Bevin also drew a response from Shawcross who claimed that 'while Order 1305 is there', he 'can't continually neglect to enforce it', but that he 'would like some modern

[2] TNA, HO 45/25546 ('Disturbances: strikes in industry: communist instigated subversion') (Home Office F3 file 827723/325A, formerly 823996/8, 'London Gas Strike. Prosecution of certain strikers') (Special Branch Report, 9 October 1950).

[3] TNA, CAB 128/18/23 (Cabinet Conclusions, 9 October 1950).

[4] They may have got the idea that the men should have been sacked from Chuter Ede. Sir Frank Newsam had telephoned in a report on the trial to the Home Secretary in which he stated that: 'Since the ten men who were prosecuted have been sentenced to imprisonment they will not be eligible for reinstatement unless the Gas Board and the Federation agree to some departure from normal practice': TNA, HO 45/25546 ('Disturbances: strikes in industry: communist instigated subversion') (Home Office F3 file 827723/325A, formerly 823996/8, 'London Gas Strike. Prosecution of certain strikers') ('Extract from Report Telephoned to S of S by Sir Frank Newsam 5.10.50').

[5] ibid.

legislation on the subject'.[6] The latter was in fact on the agenda, with the Cabinet Conclusions recording that: 'The Lord President [Morrison], with the Ministers departmentally responsible, was considering whether further powers should be taken to deal with Communist inspired strikes.'[7] The alternatives to be considered were either to extend the criminal liability for 'breach of contract in the public utility services' under the 1875 Act (and presumably effectively go further than the now repealed Trade Disputes and Trade Unions Act 1927, section 6(4)), or to require a secret ballot to be conducted before a strike in an essential service was started. On the question of unofficial strikes specifically, 'there would be advantage in taking fresh powers to deal with conspiracy or incitement to bring about [such] strikes, but it should be recognized that there were always great difficulties in securing evidence on which to base charges of conspiracy or incitement'.[8] It was also suggested that there could be a public inquiry 'into the whole subject before any fresh legislation was introduced'.[9]

These questions were revisited a week later. The main Cabinet agenda item on 16 October was 'Communist Incitement in Industrial Disputes',[10] the Lord President having been invited on 9 October 'to consider what further steps could be taken to counter Communist endeavours to cause industrial unrest and, in particular, whether the criminal law could with advantage be strengthened for this purpose'.[11] The Cabinet now had before it:

(i) a memorandum by the Lord President and the Home Secretary 'reporting their provisional conclusions on this question';[12] and
(ii) a memorandum by the Attorney General 'suggesting that the weapon of civil proceedings for damages for breach of contract should be used more extensively against persons taking part in unofficial strikes'.[13]

The Conclusions, and the Cabinet Secretary's Notebook,[14] record a fascinating discussion over the 'three possible courses of action':

- the extension of the Conspiracy and Protection of Property Act 1875, section 4 to a wider group of industries;

[6] TNA, CAB 195/8/33 (Cabinet Secretary's Notebook, 9 October 1950).
[7] TNA, CAB 128/18/23 (Cabinet Conclusions, 9 October 1950).
[8] ibid.
[9] ibid.
[10] The extensive account of this important and fascinating discussion in Sir Norman Brook's Notebook is headed 'Legislation Limiting Right to Strike': TNA, CAB 195/8/34 (Cabinet Secretary's Notebook, 16 October 1950). An extract from the Cabinet Conclusions relating to the meeting may be found in the Appendix on pp 296–97 below.
[11] TNA, CAB 128/18/24 (Cabinet Conclusions, 16 October 1950).
[12] TNA, CAB 129/42/29 ('Overseas Operations (Security of Forces Bill', Memorandum by the Lord President of the Council and the Home Secretary, 12 October 1950) (which included discussion of mandatory strike ballots).
[13] TNA, CAB 129/42/24 ('Legal Action in Connection with Unofficial Strikes', Memorandum by the Attorney General, 11 October 1950).
[14] TNA, CAB 128/18/34 (Cabinet Conclusions, 16 October 1950) and CAB 195/8 (Cabinet Secretary's Notebook, 16 October 1950).

- introducing an Act of Parliament making compulsory arbitration a 'permanent' feature of British industrial relations; and
- mandatory strike ballots (in this context particularly in essential services),

Morrison (Lord President) and Chuter Ede (Home Secretary) were effectively reheating in their joint memorandum balloting proposals which had been made by Tory backbenchers in the early 1920s.[15] In doing so, they were using the cover of the over-heated Communist threat as a pretext to reform labour law.

Extending the 1875 Act, section 4 to all essential services appears to have been the option favoured by Attlee.[16] However, colleagues pointed out that when the provision had first been implemented (and extended to electricity workers in 1919), workers in the utilities had generally enjoyed greater security of employment than most other workers, and consequently had been considered better able to sacrifice the freedom to strike.[17] In essence, it was thought that in the 1950s, workers in other equally essential but less secure jobs could not be expected to make such a sacrifice for the greater good of the community. Moreover, even where workers had comparative stability, 'under conditions of full employment, workers no longer prized security of tenure so highly as to be willing to accept in return for it, disabilities from which their fellows in other industries were free'. It was also pointed out by Shawcross – and duly acknowledged by ministers to be a significant drawback – that to take the course of expanding coverage of the 1875 Act 'would increase the number of criminal proceedings to be taken against persons taking part in in strikes'.

As for the proposal for compulsory arbitration to be introduced by primary legislation and thus become a 'permanent' element of British industrial relations, this was a step which found favour with Shawcross. The Attorney General told his colleagues that the prosecution of the gas workers had effectively forced his hand – he was now effectively obliged to prosecute in appropriate cases – and he would be more comfortable invoking provisions directly sanctioned by Parliament. Remarkably, during the course of the discussion on the retention of compulsory arbitration, Bevin, supposedly the architect of the 1940 Order, asked colleagues: 'If men comply with 1305, what can you do?' Shawcross was obliged to remind him that the Order is an 'absolute prohibition of any strike, official or unofficial – unless the Minister of Labour decides not to refer to arbitration'. More cogently, Bevin doubted whether workers would tolerate such measures in 'peacetime conditions', and claimed that compulsory arbitration was successful 'only in Communist countries where all strikes were prohibited'.

The veteran trade unionist told ministers that workers would never conform to compulsory arbitration, but that it was necessary to 'attract' them to arbitration, suggesting that the National Arbitration Tribunal be replaced by industry specific tribunals 'whose decisions would be accepted as final by both sides of industry'. Such an approach had, he assured his colleagues, worked in the boot manufacturing and steel industries, and, although he did not say it, accorded with the concept of Order 1305 as a form of collective agreement. Morrison countered that legislating to impose compulsory

[15] For a discussion of these earlier proposals, see KD Ewing, 'Strike Ballots' (1986) 5 *Journal of the Irish Society for Labour Law* 19.
[16] TNA, CAB 195/8/34 (Cabinet Secretary's Notebook, 16 October 1950).
[17] ibid.

arbitration would be 'controversial', but suggested that the 'Swedish model' might be considered. This was understood to mean the need for a central body that would enable the general economic situation to be taken into account when dealing with disputes. Generally, however, ministers, including Isaacs and Bevin, favoured a public enquiry into the matter, but Attlee warned that it was '[n]ot a good time for enquiry – Tories out to raise points on union structure'. Although it was pointed out (not entirely accurately) by Isaacs that both employers and unions were relatively happy for Order 1305 to continue in force,[18] ministers agreed that it was too soon:

> to give consideration to the long term development of the existing machinery for wage negotiation in industry. It was further agreed that, if developments followed the line of separate machinery for particular industries, care should be taken to ensure that the need for some central guidance on general economic conditions was not overlooked. In this connection it was suggested that further thought might be given to the role and functions of the trade unions in a planned economy under conditions of full employment and, in particular, to the functions of trade unions in nationalized industries.

The third of Morrison's and Chuter Ede's options, also favoured by Shawcross,[19] was to require strikes in essential sectors to be sanctioned by ballot, and for workers engaging in action which had not been approved by a majority in the union or unions involved to be a criminal offence. In the course of the Cabinet discussion, however, Isaacs made the pertinent point that it was unofficial rather than official action that was the problem and that a requirement for a ballot was not likely to discourage workers from walking out, and questioned whether all unions could be trusted to organise such a ballot.[20] Others pointed out that such strikes often lasted for no more than a day or so before the matter was settled, and in more protracted actions to permit unofficial strikers the opportunity to strengthen their case by use of a ballot would likely be counter-productive. Ultimately, '[i]t was the general view of the Cabinet that this proposal was not practicable'.[21] After all that had happened since the TUC Annual Congress in September, the whole September Revolution episode thus appeared to be ending rather quietly. Although wisely deciding that no approach be made to the TUC until the government had concrete plans in place, the Cabinet 'invited' the Prime Minister:

> to arrange for a Committee of Ministers, assisted by a group of official advisers, to formulate for consideration by the Cabinet specific proposals for (i) countering Communist endeavours to promote industrial unrest, particularly by means of unofficial strikes; and (ii) adjusting, in the light of current conditions, the existing machinery for the negotiation of wages settlements in industry.[22]

[18] He conceded that the unions 'want one or two minor changes' to the compulsory arbitration regime, but 'so do we': TNA, CAB 195/8/34 (Cabinet Secretary's Notebook, 16 October 1950).

[19] ibid.

[20] Isaacs said that he and his officials had contemplated discussing a requirement for strike ballots for official strikes with the TUC, but he preferred that there should be a public enquiry before taking that step: ibid.

[21] TNA, CAB 128/18/24 (Cabinet Conclusions, 16 October 1950). Isaacs reminded his colleagues that unofficial strikes were the problem; Attlee pointed out that most unofficial strikes were of very short duration (Isaacs confirming); and Bevin argued that a ballot would lend moral authority (TNA, CAB 195/8, Cabinet Secretary's Notebook, 16 October 1950).

[22] TNA, CAB 128/18/24 (Cabinet Conclusions, 16 October 1950).

Shawcross and Civil Proceedings for Damages Again

In addition to the matters in the text, at the Cabinet meeting on 16 October, Shawcross returned to an old theme to propose that 'more recourse might be had to civil proceedings for damages against persons who took part in unofficial strikes'.[23] This was a proposal for which some ministerial approval was forthcoming, 'largely on the basis of experience in the mining industry where it was believed that the fear of civil proceedings for breach of contract had in fact operated as a deterrent against unofficial strikes'.[24] Remarkably Bevan favoured such an initiative, provided it was 'preceded by publicity letting the men know', and he suggested the matter be raised with the TUC. There was, however, concern that 'civil proceedings were apt to be protracted, and that an unfortunate impression would be created if damages were awarded long after the strike had ended'.

Moreover, it was pointed out that in Scotland, strikers would be entitled to free legal aid in such proceedings, and it was also the case that many private employers provided essential services and – though this went unsaid – would not be likely to be prepared to sue their own workers. Doubts were also expressed about the Attorney General's proposal that 'the practice of instituting civil proceedings should be made general', but to apply in the first instance to the socialised industries. It was contended that if this policy were to be adopted, the criterion should be not whether an industry was socialised or not, but whether it provided an essential service, and it was arguable that some of the industries or services still under private ownership (such as food distribution) were more essential to the life of the community than some of those which had been brought under public ownership.

III. Joint Trade Union Defence Committee

While ministers were contemplating the future of Order 1305, trade union activists were outraged by the convictions and sentences. At the Cabinet meeting on 9 October, those present were made aware of a mass meeting in Hyde Park the previous day protesting against the convictions, and were told that 'the present Communist agitation' against the sentences passed on the 10 ringleaders 'might constitute contempt of court, since the matter was still *sub judice* pending the appeal'.[25] This raised the spectre of proceedings being brought against leading activists following speeches made at the Hyde Park event, Special Branch's Chief Superintendent Thompson reporting conveniently that all the speakers had been Communists. Remarkably, the point was taken seriously by an evidently nervous government, encouraged by the *Daily Telegraph*'s 'London Day by Day' column speculating about whether proceedings for contempt of court might be brought. This led an

[23] ibid.

[24] ibid. See *Ebbw Vale Steel, Iron & Co Ltd v Tew* (1935) 79 Sol Jo 593 for an illustration of this power being used; and *Fife Coal Co Ltd v MacBain* (1935) 52 Sh Ct Reps 84 for an indication of the problems that employers might encounter.

[25] TNA, CAB 128/18/23 (Cabinet Conclusions, 9 October 1950).

anxious and opportunistic Home Secretary to insist that the reports of the Hyde Park speeches should be submitted to the DPP.[26] The DPP replied on 16 October that there was no contempt, though it is clear that unknown to them, some of the speakers had come close to being charged.[27] While protest was expected, those who took part thus had to be careful: they were the subject of close surveillance pending the gas workers' appeal, and no doubt beyond.

Following the Hyde Park event, a meeting of what Special Branch called the London District Committee of the AEU was convened 'by Reginald BIRCH of the North London District Committee',[28] in Silvertown, East London to discuss the gas workers' prosecution and Order 1305. Reg Birch will be recognised by readers, having been encountered for the first time in Chapter Two: he was one of the first to be convicted under Order 1305, in his case for his involvement in the strike at Swift Scale in 1941. In those days he was an active member of the Communist Party, with which by 1950 he had become disillusioned because of the compromises he felt it had made. Originally scheduled for 27 September, the meeting was re-arranged for 12 October at very short notice, to the inconvenience of the police. According to a Special Branch report, '[i]n view of this it was not possible to make prior arrangements to cover the meeting', the police having to depend on a 'reliable informant' for details.[29] It is not expressly stated what were the 'prior arrangements' referred to. But it would be reasonable to speculate that it would have involved the use of recording equipment of a kind that had been used at other trade union meetings.

It is not known if AEU London District Committee meetings were under constant or regular surveillance, or if the interest in this case was generated by the subject matter, that is to say, the gas workers' prosecution and Order 1305, a discussion of which would not appear to be unlawful. Nevertheless, Special Branch were able to discover that this particular AEU London District Committee meeting had been addressed by Birch and James Wood of the London PWC, as well as by Wal Hannington, an AEU official who was the veteran of many progressive campaigns. Hannington was well known to Special Branch, having been the National Organiser of the National Unemployed Workers' Movement (NUWM) in the 1930s. It was in that capacity that he featured in *Elias v Pasmore*,[30] a leading case on police powers once familiar to students of constitutional law. A warrant having been issued for his arrest, the police waited until Hannington was at the offices of the NUWM before executing it. While on the premises, and without a search warrant, the police searched the property and seized documents which were subsequently used as incriminating evidence in the prosecution of Hannington and his colleague Sid Elias for offences relating to sedition.

[26] TNA, HO 45/25546 ('Disturbances: strikes in industry: communist instigated subversion') (Home Office F3 file 827723/325A, formerly 823996/8, 'London Gas Strike. Prosecution of certain strikers') (Special Branch Report, 9 October 1950).

[27] ibid ('Extract from Minute on 823,996/2' by 'T.M. [Theobald Matthews] D of PP').

[28] On Reginald Birch, see pp 23-24, above. Birch had been convicted under Order 1305 for his role in the Swift Scale strike in 1941.

[29] TNA, HO 45/25546 ('Disturbances: strikes in industry: communist instigated subversion') (Home Office F3 file 827723/327, 'Trade Union Defence Committee formed at a meeting of trade unionists held at Holborn Hall on 13-10-50') (Special Branch Report, 18 October 1950).

[30] *Elias v Pasmore* [1934] 2 KB 164.

In an important case which unsuccessfully challenged the legality of the police conduct, it was held by Horridge J that 'the interests of the State must excuse the seizure of documents, which seizure would otherwise be unlawful, if it appears in fact that documents were evidence of a crime committed by anyone'.[31] In other words, the police in the 1950s were taking similar liberties in relation to private property rights (and for the same reasons) as were their counterparts 20 years earlier with the blessing of the law. The experience had clearly not subdued Hannington, who was on his feet before the District Committee to tell the audience of only 28 that 'if it is the last thing we do, we must repeal this 1305 Act [sic]', and that 'we must not under any circumstances lose the right to strike'. The experienced activist recalled that when he was jailed in 1922 'for fighting for the rights of trade unionism', he was 'freed after only a few days in prison because of the workers' solidarity'.[32] With street marches having achieved the desired effect in influencing public opinion and consequently in changing the mind of government, Hannington suggested optimistically that if the same approach were adopted in relation to the prosecutions and the use of Order 1305, it would force the government to back down.

Following a resolution unanimously to support a campaign to raise awareness of Order 1305 and the recent convictions, all those present pledged to lobby MPs, distribute handbills, raise the matter at trade union meetings, and 'by every other means at his disposal'.[33] It is from this and presumably other trade union meetings that the Joint Trade Union Defence Committee (JTUDC) emerged to support the convicted gas workers and to campaign for the revocation of Order 1305. The Committee was endorsed by a wide cross-section of trade unionists, but membership was dominated by the ETU and the AEU, with members of the London Port Workers' Committee also playing an influential role. The inaugural meeting of the JTUDC took place at Holborn Hall, London on 13 October 1950, the day after the AEU District Committee meeting. Yet despite its purposes being clearly lawful, both of the major unions involved were regarded as being Communist-dominated, and it is probably for this as well as other reasons that the JTUDC was closely watched by Special Branch, which used various surveillance methods to monitor its activities and to keep the government informed. So, although the names and addresses and the union cards of those who attended the inaugural meeting were checked at the door, Special Branch had an informer among the 70 or so present, the informer's report being sent to MI5 – as well as to the Home Office.[34]

The Special Branch informer reported that the Chairman and Albert Knight were the only persons on the platform. Knight was a shop steward at De Havillands, 'an active Communist' who became the de facto leader of the campaign and secretary of the Committee. The names – sometimes only surnames – and workplaces of nine of the men who spoke from the floor were noted. A list of 14 men and one woman on whom Special Branch had already opened files was included in the report. Well-known

[31] ibid p 173. For a critique, see *Ghani v Jones* [1970] 1 QB 693.

[32] TNA, HO 45/25546 ('Disturbances: strikes in industry: communist instigated subversion') (Home Office F3 file 827723/327, 'Trade Union Defence Committee formed at a meeting of trade unionists held at Holborn Hall on 13-10-50') (Special Branch Report, 18 October 1950).

[33] ibid.

[34] ibid. Indeed, all Special Branch reports on the JTUDC and, it appears, all Special Branch reports relating to Order 1305 and industrial unrest generally were copied to MI5.

activists like Claude Berridge were identified, but 'unknowns' from vital industries appear to have been of particular interest. The presence of a Mr Bowhead from the Metropolitan Water Board, a Mr Thompson from an oil refinery, and a Mr Tattam from the Festival of Britain Site at Battersea were noted.[35] Otherwise, there is a record of what was a discussion of Order 1305 – its use to deter unofficial action and the failure of so many to grasp the extent to which the Order restricted industrial action as a whole. The men were urged to lobby their MPs, arrange meetings and collect funds. According to Berridge:

> [I]n my opinion the sentences passed on the ten gas workers were not imposed merely to punish these leaders but to set an example of what will happen in the event of a future strike … the government have taken this action because they realise that the cost of living will continue to rise owing to the great armament programme, and they are determined that wages shall not rise with the increase in the [cost] of living. War is coming and the workers have got to pay for it.[36]

Apart from the discussion of Order 1305, the business of what seems to have been a short but animated meeting also included the formal question of electing a standing committee to help advance the campaign for the revocation of Order 1305. Nineteen men were elected to a Committee some 20-strong – six were members of either the AEU or the ETU. Unusually, one woman, Elizabeth Rowe, was also elected. According to the police, Rowe was a member of the Communist Party. Berridge withdrew his nomination, apparently aware of the close interest taken in him by Special Branch: 'I already have a noose around my neck'. Indications of particular interest being taken in Berridge and occasional references to his covert encouragement of strike action are to be found in various Special Branch reports.[37] For example, at the end of the report on the trial of the gas workers at the Magistrates' Court, Special Branch say of Berridge that 'on instructions from the union he has instructed the men to go back to work, [but] unofficially he has done his best to prolong the strike'. Whether by private briefings given to Shawcross or reports sent to the Home Office which remain unreleased, it is likely that allegations of Berridge's alleged 'double dealing' would have been brought to the attention of ministers.

Almost certainly unknown to Berridge, he not only enjoyed the special attention of the police, but also the distinction of having been the subject of discussion at the Cabinet meeting on 9 October. There it is formally recorded in the Cabinet Conclusions that 'the trade unions concerned had not co-operated well with the Government' during the gas strike and that: 'There was much to be said for exposing in Parliament the way in which officials with Communist sympathies had sought to defeat the efforts of the Confederation to bring the strike to an end.'[38] The Cabinet were referring to the likes of

[35] Special Branch had learned that there was to be a meeting on the coming Sunday at the Festival of Britain site to discuss Order 1305. It turned out that they already had a file on Tattam.

[36] TNA, HO 45/25546 ('Disturbances: strikes in industry: communist instigated subversion') (Home Office F3 file 827723/327, 'Trade Union Defence Committee formed at a meeting of trade unionists held at Holborn Hall on 13-10-50') (Special Branch Report 16 October 1950).

[37] These are to be found in TNA, HO 45/25546 ('Disturbances: strikes in industry: communist instigated subversion'), the Home Office release to the National Archives which contains a number of files compiled by F3 Division.

[38] TNA, CAB 128/18/23 (Cabinet Conclusions, 9 October 1950).

Haskell and Berridge, the latter said to have 'sabotaged' attempts to arrange a meeting of the gas men which was thought likely to lead to a return to work. Embellishing the formal Cabinet Conclusions, the Cabinet Secretary's Notebook reveals Bevin and Shawcross to have been particularly angry. Berridge had given Percy Glading (Glading had been convicted of spying for the Soviet Union in 1938) a job at the AEU, which appeared to infuriate Shawcross: 'I want to see references in the House of Commons to union meetings, Berridge's activities and the existence of Glading'.[39] What is being talked about here is public denunciation under the cover of parliamentary privilege. As we will discuss later, Shawcross was himself publicly to denounce the pair in Parliament early in the New Year.[40]

IV. Surveillance Continues before the Appeal Hearing

The foregoing account tells us that the London District Committee of the AEU organised a meeting to support the gas workers and to campaign for the revocation of Order 1305, following the conviction and sentence of the former. This is overwhelming only for being so unremarkable. Why it is not only notable but also important is that our account draws almost exclusively from material in Special Branch reports. Such was the breadth and depth of the surveillance operation then in force. It is even more remarkable and even more important that this surveillance should not only have been set in place but should also continue during the period of the appeal when in modern parlance the proceedings were active. Remarkable because the state was in part spying on litigants in criminal proceedings, but also because by any account the JTUDC was a small 'organisation' of earnest commitment but little importance, as revealed by the relatively small – in proportion to the gravity of the matters with which it was concerned – attendance at the two meetings referred to above on 12 and 13 October. Paradoxically, perhaps that is something that can be said only as a result of impressive Special Branch surveillance.

The surveillance was nevertheless to continue until and beyond the appeal. Special Branch had an informant monitoring a meeting 'held inside Beckton Gas Works on Monday 16 October'. One of the chief speakers was Fred Lambert, a Boilermakers' Society shop steward at Beckton Gas Works, who it will be recalled from Chapter Nine was convicted under Order 1305 with the nine others. Lambert addressed about 70 of the men on the possibility of a strike in support of their claim to implement a new bonus scheme, this being the occasion when he had stated that his and Broadbent's selection for prosecution was a 'mystery'.[41] Learning from the lessons of his conviction, Lambert was under the impression (albeit soon to be disabused) that if union officials failed to press ahead with the claim on behalf of the workers, then the men themselves could take Order 1305 into their own hands by giving 21 days' notice of the dispute and then going on strike. In the words of Lambert when addressing the meeting: 'we will do it

[39] TNA, CAB 195/8/33 (Cabinet Secretary's Notebook, 9 October 1950). On Glading's conviction for espionage and his association with the Party after his release from prison, see KD Ewing, J Mahoney and A Moretta, *MI5 the Cold War and the Rule of Law* (Oxford University Press, Oxford, 2020) pp 57–58 and 97–98.

[40] HC Debs, 29 January 1951, col 685.

[41] See p 175 above.

in conformity with the wishes of Sir Hartley Shawcross. Everyone here and everyone concerned can forward the 21 days' strike notice to the Minister of Labour'.[42]

Special Branch also had an informer observing the activities of the JTUDC at the National Trade Union Club in Great Newport Street, Covent Garden, London, which was busy in the evenings and at weekends 'sending out circular letters to trade union branches, district committees, trades councils and shop stewards' committees, appealing for their support by protesting to Members of Parliament, raising funds etc'.[43] By the end of October, the police had obtained copies of a JTUDC leaflet written by Albert Knight, *Order 1305 Must Go*, focusing on the conviction of the 10 gas men and advertising a JTUDC 'Delegates' Conference' scheduled for the 11 November as well as a 'Great Demonstration of Protest' at Hyde Park on Sunday, 12 November.[44] Before these events took place, Special Branch had a presence at Holborn Hall again on 6 November to cover a meeting of the JTUDC at which they estimated that some 500 to 600 people were present. The only speakers from outside the gas industry were Albert Knight and Wal Hannington, and it was resolved that the gas men were to strike on Monday, 13 November in support of the 10 shop stewards and against Order 1305.[45] The appeal was set for Monday 21 November.

On 7 November, Special Branch reported on a local AEU meeting at Ilford when only 23 people had attended, despite the meeting having 'been widely circulated amongst trade unionists'. Remarkably, the report included the names and addresses of 18 out of the 23 present (identifying six as Communists). More remarkably still, Albert Knight, the main speaker, was able to confirm that the Ministry refused to accept notice of a trade dispute from unofficial committees or groups of workers. Knight reported that '[h]e had been told by Mr Isaacs that the shop stewards could not set this machinery in motion and that it could only be done through the trade union officials', thereby dashing plans Lambert had announced on 16 October. Nevertheless, Knight maintained that strike action was the only 'real weapon' available and that they must use it 'to strive for the acquittal of the 10 men, the abolition of 1305, and the dissolution of Special Branch'.[46] But while Knight was right that the strike (with the risk of conviction) was the only remedy if they were to secure an improvement to their wages, Special Branch was hearing that the proposed strike in support of the 10 shop stewards and against Order 1305 on 13 November was not something many of the gas workers supported, whatever the impression garnered at the mass meeting at Holborn Hall on 6 November to the contrary.

Thus, an informant at Beckton Gas Works reported that at a meeting on 8 November addressed by Broadbent and Lambert – two of the 10 convicted gas men – a vote on the

[42] TNA, HO 45/25546 ('Disturbances: strikes in industry: communist instigated subversion') (Home Office F3 file 827723/327, 'Trade Union Defence Committee formed at a meeting of trade unionists held at Holborn Hall on 13-10-50) (Special Branch Report, 20 October 1950). The report also covered a second meeting of 60 gas men from the East Ham Branch of the 'Boilermakers Society' at the Labour Hall, East Ham on 17 October.

[43] ibid. Special Branch Report, 24 October 1950. Albert Knight oversaw the volunteers and Claude Berridge was said to be a frequent visitor and advisor.

[44] ibid. Special Branch Report, 27 October 1950.

[45] ibid. Special Branch Report, 7 November 1950.

[46] A couple of members of the Labour League of Youth spoke up at the meeting in support of Order 1305 and of the government.

proposed strike saw 90 men vote against taking action, with only 27 in favour.[47] Such was the degree of disillusionment and distrust engendered by the failure of the strike and the publicity surrounding the prosecution that the men refused to allow their shop stewards a 'free mandate' at the Delegates' Conference scheduled for 11 November.[48] A second report received on the same day mentioned further setbacks for Broadbent and Lambert at Beckton. It appears that at '[v]arious departmental meetings' it had been decided to 'ignore the call for a one day's strike on 13.11.50', while information subsequently received tended to show that 'at a meeting of members of the Joint Trade Union Defence Committee the strike called for Monday next [13 January] has been cancelled'. Worse still, the demands of the men for an incentive bonus scheme, which had supplanted the original demand for an extra 3d per hour had been returned to the AEU London District Committee with a comment that it was a local and not a national issue, and would not be reported to the Ministry. The villain of the piece was a named CSEU full-time official.

Despite the lukewarm response from the convicted gas workers' colleagues, the proposed JTUDC Delegates' Conference referred to above nevertheless went ahead on 11 November, with Special Branch reporting that '[b]etween 300 and 400 delegates attended. They had been appointed by different trade union branches, trades councils and district committees, and claimed to represent 200,000 London workers'.[49] The main speakers were Albert Knight, DN Pritt KC and Wal Hannington.[50] During the course of the proceedings, nominations for a new committee were called for and submitted, the 'Standing Orders Committee' selecting the '20 most suitable'. Why a new committee was required was not made clear, either by the speakers or by Special Branch. The informant reported that at the end of the meeting, the names of the committee were read very quickly, but he managed to take down 16 of the surnames and the name of each man's union. These names were 'duly approved' by the conference. A full list was eventually obtained by Special Branch which was sent to MI5 and the Home Office, with eight of the 20 marked down as Communists. Oddly, a further three names were later added, two of whom were said to be Communist Party and the third a 'fellow traveller'.[51]

The three aims of the JTUDC were reported by the *Daily Worker* following the delegates' conference:

- the waging of a campaign for the acquittal of the 10 men;
- the ending of Order 1305 and any other resolution designed to restrict the workers' hard won right to withdraw their labour;

[47] TNA, HO 45/25546 ('Disturbances: strikes in industry: communist instigated subversion') (Home Office F3 file 827723/327, 'Trade Union Defence Committee formed at a meeting of trade unionists held at Holborn Hall on 13-10-50) (Special Branch Report, 10 November 1950). At a meeting of the gas shop stewards on 8 November at a pub in King's Cross, it was accepted that there was a lack of support.

[48] ibid.

[49] ibid, Special Branch Report, 12 November 1950. Unusually, the report listed the 'subject' as 'Informant's Notes', which was probably for the information of the DPP who was sent a copy of the report.

[50] ibid. DN Pritt was elected Labour MP for Hammersmith North in 1935. Following his expulsion from the Labour Party in 1940, he sat as an Independent Labour MP. He defended the seat in 1945, but lost it at the general election in 1950.

[51] ibid, Special Branch Reports, 21 and 30 November 1950.

- the disbanding of all police organisations set up to spy on trade unionists.[52]

According to the Special Branch report, the informant present at the delegates' conference heard one speaker, Bob Lovell, call:

> the attention of the delegates to the last of the three demands in the resolution – the disbanding of all police organisations set up to spy on trade unionists. He said that that sort of thing – spying on trade unionists – was to be expected under a Conservative Government, but not under a Labour one. It represented an indelible stain on the leaders of the Labour movement that they were allowing such a spy organization to come into being.[53]

Twelve speakers were allowed to speak for three minutes from the floor, including Claude Berridge of the AEU and Ted Dickens of the PWC. The Special Branch report noted that:

> All the speakers supported the resolutions and most of them spoke very bitterly about the formation of a department at New Scotland Yard concentrating on Trade Union activities.[54]

As for the proposed one-day strike for which support had ebbed, a statement was made to 'clear up misunderstandings' by Stanley Hale of the AEU. Hale claimed that on 6 November, the one day-strike had been called for by the ordinary gas process workers rather than the tradesmen who had walked out in September and whose stewards had been sentenced on 5 October.

Rather than strike on 13 November, it was now decided to wait until the appeal. Hale was a process worker and had at the earlier meeting argued against calling a strike on 13 November in order 'not to show their hand at this stage'. However, a resolution for a strike had undoubtedly been passed on 6 November, and it seems that Hale's intervention at the delegates' conference was a means of saving face. Nevertheless, the government will have taken comfort from the fact that support for the strikers in advance of the appeal seemed to be draining away. Not only was the planned strike called off, but the 'Great Demonstration of Protest' on 12 November proved literally to be a damp squib. According to Special Branch reports, some 400 protestors gathered around a podium set up in Hyde Park, the numbers dwindling to around 100 as rain set in:

> Four banners flanked the platform. They read a) Joint Trade Union Defence Committee. 1305 must go. Demand the right to strike. b) Festival of Britain. Battersea Park. Remove 1305. c) AEU banner. d) Ilford Branch of AEU banner.[55]

There were five speakers – four of whom were said to be Communists – including Claude Berridge and Wal Hannington. The report set out what was said, with verbatim accounts of each speech noted down in shorthand by a sergeant and three constables; these accounts were then sent on with the reports to the Home Office, MI5 and the DPP.

[52] *Daily Worker*, 13 November 1950.

[53] TNA, HO 45/25546 ('Disturbances: strikes in industry: communist instigated subversion') (Home Office F3 file 827723/327, 'Trade Union Defence Committee formed at a meeting of trade unionists held at Holborn Hall on 13-10-50) (Special Branch Report, 12 November 1950).

[54] ibid. Special Branch Report, 12 November 1950.

[55] ibid. Special Branch Report, 12 November 1950 (2nd Report).

V. The Gas Workers' Appeal

The government was clearly very concerned that the men's prison sentences might not be commuted. Reports in the *South London Press* some 11 days before the trial repeated comments made by the General Secretary of the Painters' Union about the likelihood of strike action if the gas men's prison sentences were upheld. This provoked Miss Harting of the Home Office's F3 to order Special Branch to track down a 'back copy' of the paper. Chief Superintendent Thompson sent her the two editions that had been published that day, and a copy of a Special Branch report on the matter. Both editions carried the same innocuous article – 'Gas Workers Will Walk out if 10 are Jailed',[56] which was then sent by the Home Office along with the Special Branch report to Shawcross and the DPP.[57] Anxiety levels were no doubt increased by a brief report of uncertain provenance submitted to F3 a few days later. The report drew on information supplied by Special Branch and MI5, claiming that although there was no official CPGB policy on the gas strike and the prosecutions, 'individual Party members are working actively to foment opposition to Order 1305', and described the convictions as a 'heaven sent opportunity of gaining sympathy among the rank and file of trades unionists'.[58] Moreover:

> [T]here is no evidence at present that the Communist Party line is likely to contravene the law, at any rate before the result of the appeals are known. It will probably be very difficult to obtain satisfactory evidence that the Communist Party are concerned in any attempts to intimidate the government … since the hostility of the workers as a whole is very clearly directed against Order 1305 and the prosecutions and they are quite likely to take action of their own initiative without particular prompting by the Communists.[59]

Special Branch reports of the hearing before the London Sessions Appeal Committee on 21 November were sent to MI5 as well as the Home Office.[60] Walter Monckton, who would be appointed Tory Minister of Labour in October 1951, represented the men, having waived his fee.[61] No doubt he would be sufficiently rewarded with political capital. The Press Association helpfully produced a verbatim account of the proceedings for the *Metalworker* journal, which does not need to be read very carefully to appreciate the cynical manipulation of the legal process on the part of the Labour government, and the Attorney General in particular.[62] Responding to the appeal, Christmas Humphries KC for the government made no apology for having secured the convictions: two million

[56] *South London Press*, 10 November 1950.

[57] Harting phoned Special Branch at 4 pm on 16 November. A Special Branch report written on 20 November (quoting the union officer in question as having stated that if the 10 men were sent to prison, 'no one will get any gas that day'), and the report plus the two different editions of the paper, were sent to Harting on 21 November, with a covering note by Thompson: TNA, HO 45/25546 ('Disturbances: strikes in industry: communist instigated subversion') (Home Office F3 file 827723/325A, formerly 823996/8, 'London gas strike Prosecution of certain strikers').

[58] ibid, 'A Note on the Communist Party and the Gas Strikers' Appeals, 14 November 1950.

[59] ibid.

[60] ibid, Special Branch Report, Gas strike prosecution, 21 November 1950.

[61] See N Fishman, '"A Vital Element in British Industrial Relations": A Reassessment of Order 1305, 1940–51' (1999) 8 *Historical Studies in Industrial Relations* 43, at pp 59–60.

[62] Press Association Special Reporting Service, 22 November 1950: Warwick Modern Records Centre, 'Gasworkers' Strike 1950', File MSS 233/3/3/11.

people were deprived of their gas and enormous inconvenience was caused, while there was a great loss of revenue mostly to small factories, and a definite danger to life. That apart, the prosecution was intended not just to punish the ringleaders, but also to serve as a warning to others that the criminal law still applied and that people who broke the law would be prosecuted: 'The purpose of the prosecution was to establish beyond doubt, and to make it as widely known as possible, that these persons were involved in an unofficial strike that was contrary to English law.'

Somewhat disingenuously, Humphreys added that 'the prosecution had no political implication whatsoever'. But although unrepentant about the prosecutions and convictions, it is clear that the government had second thoughts about the sentences, now that the purpose of the prosecution had succeeded. So much is revealed in the exchange between the Chairman of the Bench (Anthony Hawke) and Humphreys, who claimed that while Order 1305 had been continued after the war following an agreement with the employers and the trade union movement, it was 'just possible' that some of the men did not appreciate that it was 'binding on the trade union movement or was a criminal offence'. They might plausibly have thought that 'something under a statutory rule and order was removed from what they understood about an agreement', the prosecution thus now accepting that the men may not have known that Order 1305 still carried a legal obligation. This led to the following embarrassing exchange between Hawke and Humphreys, which makes it clear who was pulling the strings:

> Hawke: Are you inviting this committee to take the view in law that information you now have, and which was not before the learned Chief Magistrate [Sir Laurence Dunne] is that these men were not aware at the time they took the action that they were setting at defiance (sic) the existing law of the country?
>
> Humphreys: I merely said I modified what I said in the lower court, which was to the effect that these men must have known perfectly well they were committing a criminal offence. It may well be they did not appreciate it.
>
> Hawke: You have opened this appeal, no doubt with due discretion and on your instructions, as a matter which may be different entirely in gravity than that which you put before the Magistrate.
>
> Humphreys: I put before the learned Chief Magistrate that these persons must have known of the wording of this regulation to the extent that it sets out something that strikers in these conditions should not do. They were deliberately doing something which they knew that the parties – the employers and workmen – had agreed at least should not be done. I cannot say now that I am satisfied as I was then that they knew that what they were doing was a criminal offence as distinct as a breach of treaty or arrangement between employers and employees.[63]

Humphreys continued that such misunderstanding on the part of the appellants was 'no defence in trial', but was a matter which 'could be taken into consideration in mitigation of sentence'. After hearing Sir Walter Monckton, the bench retired for 12 minutes.

[63] ibid.

Greatly influenced by Humphreys' submissions, the magistrates spared the accused the 'disgrace' of imprisonment. The men were each fined £50, with no order as to costs: 'it has now been made clear to everybody that the action these appellants took is an offence against the criminal law and will result in severe penalties if it occurs again'.[64] The sum of £50 was nevertheless a very substantial one, equivalent to over £1,700 today. It was, moreover, considerably in excess of the largest fine recorded in war-time, and way beyond the usual ten shillings to £10 strikers might expect to pay.[65] Shortly after the appeal, however, Claude Berridge from the AEU announced that the men's fines would be paid from a fund that had been specially raised on their behalf, and that the fund already stood at £1,000, which included 20,000 francs from power and fuel workers of Paris.[66]

Although the appeal against the sentences had been successful, the *Daily Worker* headline on 22 November reflected the broad practical effect of the formal invocation of the penal provisions of Order 1305 for the first time since the war:

TEN GAS WORKERS ARE FINED £50 EACH
UNOFFICIAL STRIKERS WILL BE TREATED AS CRIMINALS

It was as if the government had legislated to prohibit strike action. As the paper put it in its lead article:

> In effect strikes have been declared illegal, and a striker is being turned into a criminal. One of the most cherished rights of the British working class, the result of a century or more of bitter struggle, the right to strike is being torn away from us by a Labour Government. This is being done not after a great discussion in Parliament or in the Labour movement. On the contrary it is being done quietly without discussion, by means of the wartime regulation 1305 … it exposes the Labour Government's repeal of the 1927 Trade Disputes Act for a gigantic piece of hypocrisy. The central issue in repealing this hated measure of Tory revenge was to restore peaceful picketing in strikes, to protect the right to strike. Now all this is being reduced to nothing by Order 1305 … The results of this prosecution will be to stiffen every employer and National Arbitration Board against the workers' legitimate demands. They know that if the workers resort to the final pressure of strike action, the ultimate resort making a reality of collective bargaining, the Government and the police will swoop down on the workers.[67]

[64] ibid.

[65] In England the fines handed down on conviction for breach of Order 1305 were typically much lower. For example, fines of between £2 and £35 were imposed upon the 83 diamond cutters and polishers following a strike from 14 April to 6 May 1943 for a wage increase of 50 per cent. Most of the fines were in the £10–£15 range and five defendants were dismissed on payment of costs from 4/- to £5. The £35 fine appears to have been the heftiest fine handed down during the war (see the fines recorded in TNA, LAB 10/173 ('Prosecutions of Strikers under Order 1305 (1) Undertaken (2) Contemplated').

[66] Press Association Special Reporting Service, 22 November 1950: Warwick Modern Records Centre, 'Gasworkers' Strike 1950', File MSS 233/3/3/11.

[67] *Daily Worker*, 22 November 1950.

Also on the day after the appeal, Lambeth Trades Council wrote to Isaacs informing him of a resolution passed at the previous meeting of the council:

> That this Council strongly protests at the action of the Labour Government in using the wartime National Arbitration Order to prosecute trade unionists for their part in labour disputes, even if unofficial, an action which under any other Government would not be tolerated by the Labour movement.[68]

This was the start of an avalanche of letters from trade unions, trades councils, and Labour Party branches to Isaacs, Chuter Ede, Aneurin Bevan, and Attlee. But now that the gas workers' enthusiasm for unofficial action had declined they were again at the mercy of the officials who had been condemned after the convictions of the 10 shop stewards. As we have seen, a CSEU full-time official had refused to report the dispute to the Ministry, thereby ensuring that any related strike would be unlawful.

But although the government felt vindicated by the convictions, this was nevertheless a poor case on which to deploy its legal strategy to the limit, the use of the criminal law having been justified initially as principally an anti-Communist weapon. Yet there was no Communist conspiracy, in this or indeed in any other case. Briefing the Cabinet on wage demands on 2 November, Isaacs told ministers that:

> Movements for wage increases is however official TU and orderly. TUs now able to take over from unofficial groups. Want to steer as much of this into tribunal [the National Arbitration Tribunal]. Workers are ready to accept their awards.[69]

Ministers even belatedly acknowledged that recent incidents at first suspected to have been sabotage had proved to have been accidents and the talk of Communist subversion which had characterised the Cabinet meetings of the summer and autumn disappeared from the Cabinet record, along with the last mention of the Overseas Operations (Security of Forces) Bill on 20 November 1950.[70] There may well have been Communist officials in the different unions, Communist activists in the JTUDC, and Communist Party members among the defendants. But the Special Branch records we have seen reveal that the influence of Communist officials in this and other disputes had been minimal.

[68] TNA, LAB 10/994 ('Resolutions urging the discontinuance of Order 1305') (Lambeth Trades Council to Isaacs, 22 November 1950). The Ministry received so many letters that they opened a file specifically for them.

[69] TNA, CAB 195/8/40 (Cabinet Secretary's Notebook, 2 November 1950).

[70] On 6 November, it was noted that suspected incidents of sabotage invariably turned out to be accidents, although there was a brief reprise of the comedic hysteria of the summer and autumn when reference to an incident at a REME depot at Aldershot saw a minister suggest that engineers tended to be drawn to Communism. Liddell's claim that Attlee chose to blame Communist saboteurs for political reasons is supported by Attlee's professed belief that: 'A clear sabotage case would rally public support' (TNA, CAB 195/8/41 Cabinet Secretary's Notebook, 6 November 1950). The Overseas Operations (Security of Forces) Bill was finally put to rest on 20 November, when the Chancellor stated that 'we should have to consult opposition before going on – as well as the TUC', before Attlee decided to 'postpone introduction of the Bill' (TNA, CAB 195/8/41 (Cabinet Secretary's Notebook, 6 November 1950). Later attempts to revive the Bill came to nothing.

VI. Conclusion

Although the convictions were upheld, the 10 gas workers allowed themselves a small celebration after the sentence of imprisonment was replaced by a fine for each of them. Special Branch must have deeply penetrated those immediately close to the defendants, with Home Office files reporting a dinner held for the men and their wives in December 1950 at which Berridge presented the men with £30 cheques, their wives with handbags, and the landlord of the pub they habitually used for meetings with a clock. At the end of the meal, Berridge introduced the party to Percy Glading and Wal Hannington.[71] The file also contains a copy of a commemorative photograph taken that evening. All of this was no doubt grist to Shawcross' mill, providing further evidence that the strike had been driven by the Communists and that he was right to prosecute. As we saw above, Shawcross had suggested at the Cabinet meeting on 9 October that he wanted to see 'references in the House of Commons to union meetings, Berridge's activities and the existence of Glading'.[72] The Attorney General duly obliged two months later in an important statement about Order 1305 prosecutions when he said in relation to the gas strike:

> I prosecuted in the case of the gas strike in North London recently because the public were being caused great inconvenience and hardship. Moreover, the information available to me showed that, whilst there was a pretence being made of urging strikers to return to work, the truth was that the Communists were anxious to see the strike continue. There was a Mr Berridge, who was the North London organiser for the Amalgamated Engineering Union, an avowed Communist, whose official duty it was to his union to secure a return to work, but who bent his unofficial efforts in the opposite direction. In his office, whether as a mere clerk, as nominally he is, or as an invigilator over Mr Berridge, as in accordance with Communist technique he may be, was a Mr Glading, a gentleman who was implicated in the Communist conspiracy in Meirut and who in this country in 1938 got six years' penal servitude for acting as a professional spy for Russia. In that case, the strike prosecution brought home to everybody that what was in point was not merely some matter of industrial regulation, but that the criminal law was being broken; and the prosecution had a salutary effect.[73]

Remarkably – though hardly unexpectedly since the general election nine months earlier had seen the defeat of the two Communist MPs elected in 1945 – no one asked about the source of the information for this parliamentary denunciation, or the legal basis by which it was obtained.[74]

What is notable about the foregoing passage is the principal reason given for mounting the prosecution: the strike caused 'great inconvenience and hardship'; not that it was politically motivated. Many strikes risk 'great inconvenience', which is a weak

[71] TNA, HO 45/25546 ('Disturbances: strikes in industry: communist instigated subversion') (Home Office F3 file 827723/325A, formerly 823996/8, 'London gas strike Prosecution of certain strikers').

[72] TNA, CAB 195/8/23 (Cabinet Secretary's Notebook, 9 October 1950).

[73] HC Debs, 5 December 1950, col 178.

[74] The Communist Party MPs were William Gallacher and Phil Piratin. The parliamentary denunciation of Berridge and Glading was a precedent for the public denunciation of Jack Gaster and a number of other individuals (not all them Communist Party members) by the Conservative government in 1954, following their travels to Korea during the Korean War. See KD Ewing, J Mahoney and A Moretta, 'Civil Liberties and the Korean War' (2018) 81 *MLR* 395.

justification for invoking criminal sanctions especially where the government is or was not prepared to provide alternative forms of dispute resolution. And even if it is the case that 'the Communists were anxious to see the strike continue', the Communists were not participants in the strike which they were anxious to continue. Nor was it the Communists who were put on trial and convicted. Indeed, rather helpfully if Reg Birch is to be believed, the Communist Party advised the men to plead guilty to the Order 1305 charge.[75] Leaving the complex politics of the Left to one side, this was a straightforward trade dispute processed by a group of workers who were poorly paid and badly let down by their unions, which – like the TGWU in the ports and at Smithfield – were too close to the government to enable them properly to represent their members. This was made clear at the meeting on 5 October at St Pancras Town Hall, where many of those present believed that they had achieved nothing. The strikers had, after all, sought a pay rise, not a confrontation with the government, and no matter how 'magnificent' the strike,[76] it had ended in failure. A Special Branch informant reported a contribution from the floor expressing a view that appears to have been shared by many others, and with which it is hard to disagree:

> if justice had been dealt out in a right and proper manner the men sentenced should have been the trade union officials and not the ten shop stewards. All trade union officials were doing was to draw 'fat salaries' and sit back, neglecting the men. The cost of living was rising and it should be the duty of trade union officials to press for increases in wages without having to be reminded by men taking strike action.[77]

[75] See W Podmore, *Reg Birch: Engineer, Trade Unionist, Communist* (Bellman Books, London, 2004), where the author refers to the 'the CPGB's shameful advice' (at p 29).

[76] The word used in a telegram said to have been sent by the Tilbury dock workers to the shop stewards read from the podium at the St Pancras meeting on the day the men were sentenced at the Magistrates' Court. 'Magnificent' was also the word one of the speakers used to describe the strike. According to Special Branch, the speaker's praise triggered '[s]houts of "What have we done? We have got nowhere"' from the assembled gas workers (from TNA, HO 45/25546 ('Disturbances: strikes in industry: communist instigated subversion') (Home Office F3 file 827723/325A, formerly 823996/8, 'London gas strike Prosecution of certain strikers') (Special Branch Report, 5 October 1950 – the third report on the strike and related events made that day).

[77] ibid.

PART V

Revocation of Order 1305: Victory for the Port Workers' Committee

11

Order 1305 and the Cabinet

Legal and Political Pressures

I. Introduction

The conviction of the gas workers was a warning to trade unionists everywhere that industrial action could bring with it criminal sanctions. Order 1305 was now more than simply a de facto offence to deal with the Communist Party. As such, it revealed the growing presence of the coercive power of the state and its agencies in industrial relations, all the more significant for the fact that state power was being deployed against those who had been neglected and overlooked. The prosecution and its aftermath were also important in exposing the critical role of the government's law officers in the management of industrial relations, and in particular the central role now occupied by Shawcross. As we have seen, the war-time practice of prosecutions under Order 1305 having been the responsibility of the Ministry of Labour appears to have broken down, with the lead being taken by Shawcross, who insisted that the law must be enforced. However, there does not appear to have been any formal handover of responsibility, which was not finally acknowledged publicly by Attlee until 7 November 1950, when he said in a parliamentary statement that 'it has become the practice for the question of prosecutions in such cases to be considered by the Director of Public Prosecutions. No particular date can be assigned to the commencement of this practice'.[1]

Although Shawcross claims not to have been consulted in advance of this statement being made,[2] his pre-eminence with respect to the exercise of the penal provisions and the interpretation of the Order was to be reinforced several weeks later, as we will discuss below. Coinciding with the formalisation of his responsibility for prosecuting under Order 1305, the Cabinet was being called upon to deal with an increasing number of problems which were arising as a result of the more coercive legal approach adopted to Order 1305. In December 1950 alone, five different disputes were brought to the attention of ministers for consideration, these concerned with two different but

[1] HC Debs, 7 November 1950, col 767.

[2] TNA, CAB 129/44/9 ('The Future of the Conditions of Employment and National Arbitration Order', Memorandum by the Attorney General, 11 January 1951): 'It was recently stated in Parliament by the Prime Minister that although the Minister of Labour had concurrent authority with me of initiating a prosecution, it had become the practice that the matter should be left to me. I was not consulted as to this transfer of responsibility but the transfer having been made, I accept it. I am sure that the object of the transfer was not to shift a disagreeable and difficult responsibility to the Attorney General but to ensure the due and detached enforcement of the law.'

connected issues: the first, in relation to strikes at the state-owned airline BOAC (British Overseas Airways Corporation) and at Duple Motor Bodies respectively, was whether those involved in strike action should be prosecuted; and the second was the equally difficult question whether the Minister of Labour had the power to accept reports of disputes from unofficial groups of workers, as a way of coercing trade union members to seek the resolution of their grievances through official trade union channels.[3] This in turn raised another question, which was whether having accepted a report, the Minister was then required to refer a dispute for resolution, or whether he had a power not to do so.

II. The BOAC Case

The first dispute relating to Order 1305 following the gas-workers' case was a closed shop dispute at Heathrow Airport which began on 22 November 1950. According to George Isaacs in a parliamentary statement on 5 December 1950,[4] two electricians employed by BOAC refused to join the Electrical Trades Union (ETU). When the other electricians employed by the corporation stopped work to hold a meeting (presumably to discuss the matter), they were suspended for the rest of the day. On the following day, 25 electricians were suspended for refusing to work overtime despite being contractually required to do so, at which point 125 other electricians stopped work, to be followed three days later by 25 more. Although the suspension of the initial 25 men who refused to work overtime was lifted on 28 November, there had been no resumption of work. And although the Ministry of Labour had met both sides, there was no sign of a resolution to the dispute despite 'severe dislocation of service', which was 'causing serious inconvenience to the public and heavy financial loss to BOAC'.[5] Notwithstanding losses which 'cannot yet be accurately gauged', BOAC had taken an uncompromising position: 'there must be a return to work before any discussions can take place'.[6]

On reporting on these details to the House, Isaacs was assailed from both sides about the strike, the message being the same regardless of the party. From his own side, Captain Albert Raymond Blackburn asked whether the Minister was 'aware that the General Secretary of the Electrical Trades Union, Mr Walter Stevens, is a declared and open member of the Communist Party', and that 'this strike has already caused a great blow to our prestige, and very great anxiety throughout the world'.[7] Blackburn was Labour MP for Birmingham King's Norton, and was later to lead a colourful life that saw him imprisoned for fraud and declared bankrupt. He was also to acquire notoriety amongst lawyers for his unsuccessful legal challenges to the Metropolitan Police Commissioner for failing to enforce the laws in relation to illegal gambling, and five

[3] As we saw in ch 9, a refusal to accept a report ensured that any strikes arising would inevitably be unlawful. A rejected report thus in effect amounted to a failure to report, both barring access to the NAT and preventing the operation of the built-in 'safety valve' which permitted those denied access to compulsory arbitration the opportunity to call a lawful strike.

[4] HC Debs, 5 December 1950, col 178.

[5] ibid col 179.

[6] ibid cols 178–79.

[7] ibid col 179.

years later in relation to obscene publications.[8] Between these cases he also failed in proceedings against the Attorney General in which he challenged the legality of the government's decision to join the EEC as it then was.[9] In 1950, however, Blackburn was concerned to bring the BOAC dispute to an end, and with this in mind asked Isaacs whether he would 'consider informing those who are responsible for this wanton breach of peace in industry that he will consider at least using the same powers as he used in the gas strike'.[10]

But Blackburn was no more persuasive in Parliament than he was to be in court. Refusing to be drawn on the claims of 'communist influence' or the 'political opinions of the general secretary', Isaacs explained that the Ministry had intervened by seeking to resolve the dispute by conciliation. Although it seems that the dispute had not been reported under the terms of Order 1305, the Ministry of Labour nevertheless persuaded the constitutional bodies within the industry to intervene. But they concluded unhelpfully that it was 'a matter for settlement between the firm and the union concerned'.[11] Faced with an impasse, Isaacs explained further that he could not refer the dispute to the NAT for arbitration under Order 1305 'because the Tribunal cannot and does not deal with questions relating to employment of non-unionists', which meant that 'we are left without an authority which can give binding decisions on the matter'.[12] When pressed further, Isaacs explained:

> Again, we get on to legal questions, and I may find myself saying something and apologising for it a couple of days afterwards. The point is that the strike would be illegal only if I had referred the dispute to the Tribunal, but I cannot refer to the Tribunal a matter with which the Tribunal has no power to deal. We have, therefore, a complicated question of legality or otherwise. Please do not ask me to try to answer it.[13]

No explanation was given for the position said to have been adopted by the Tribunal, though reference was made in *The Times* a few days later to a similar dispute several months earlier in which the Tribunal had 'ruled that the principle was not one which it could decide'.[14] In these circumstances the position adopted by Isaacs was perfectly understandable, even if the NAT's position was curious. That said, the NAT had already taken a narrow approach to its jurisdiction on a number of questions,[15] which suggests that Isaacs' account was not implausible. But in this case, there seemed to be little doubt that such disputes were covered, a trade dispute for the purposes of Order 1305 being defined to include disputes about the 'employment or non-employment' of 'any person'. That is exactly what closed shop disputes are about, and it is notable that there was jurisprudence to this effect in relation to the similar definition in the Trade Disputes

[8] *R v Metropolitan Police Commissioner, ex parte Blackburn* [1968] 2 QB 118; *R v Metropolitan Police Commissioner, ex parte Blackburn* [1973] 1 QB 241.

[9] *Blackburn v Attorney General* [1971] 1 WLR 1037.

[10] HC Debs, 5 December 1950, col 179.

[11] ibid col 180.

[12] ibid. Note that Isaacs did not appear to see the fact that the dispute had not been reported as an obstacle to referral.

[13] HC Debs, 5 December 1950, col 180.

[14] *The Times*, 7 December 1950. The principle here was the closed shop principle and the dismissal of non-unionists arising as a result.

[15] See *R v National Arbitration Tribunal, ex parte Crowther* [1947] 2 All ER 693, [1948] 1 KB 424.

Act 1906, conferring immunity from tortious liability for strike organisers acting in contemplation or furtherance of a trade dispute.[16] Nevertheless, having already decided that it did not have the power to order the reinstatement of a dismissed worker, it is unlikely that the NAT would have relished the power to require an employer to dismiss a worker who continued to refuse to join a trade union in order to settle a dispute where a closed shop operated.

Shawcross was much more sanguine. Addressing the Cabinet two days after Isaacs' parliamentary statement, he said unequivocally that although 'this strike was receiving a certain measure of recognition from the union concerned, it was clearly in contravention of Order 1305', though he did not address the Ministry's doubts.[17] Nevertheless, in accordance with constitutional propriety, Shawcross 'wished to know' from colleagues 'whether there were any considerations which the Cabinet would wish him to bear in mind in deciding whether to prosecute the principal members of the Strike Committee'.[18] While there was a chance the men might return to work on 11 December, Shawcross was nevertheless concerned that the strike might continue, and he needed to be ready to respond.[19] However, the Minister for Civil Aviation (Lord Pakenham) advised that BOAC was planning to take legal proceedings against the strikers if the matter was not resolved by 11 December (presumably for breach of contract), while other ministers noted that 'there would be some concern in trade union circles if a dispute arising out of a refusal of unionists to work alongside non-unionists led to criminal proceedings'.[20] Although ministers recognised Shawcross' familiar mantra that 'so long as Order 1305 remained in force, the Attorney General could not ignore flagrant breaches of its provisions',[21] the Attorney General was invited to take note of the foregoing points, and no prosecution was brought.

Shawcross circulated a memorandum the following day (8 December),[22] setting out the various considerations he had taken into account, referring in the process to his earlier memorandum of 28 June 1950.[23] First was the concern that the strike affected the public interest: 'important transport services were involved; heavy loss was caused and British prestige was affected'.[24] Indeed, the DPP had observed that it was 'perhaps the neatest example of an obviously illegal strike which we have had to consider', which meant that 'in the ordinary course [he] should have had no alternative but to prosecute'.[25] Second was Shawcross' belief that the strike had ended, though as it turned out, this was incorrect: the men did not return to work until 11 December. However,

[16] For a contemporary account of the jurisprudence, see NA Citrine, *Trade Union Law*, 2nd edn (Stevens & Sons, London, 1950), pp 478–79.

[17] TNA, CAB 128/18/43 (Cabinet Conclusions, 7 December 1950).

[18] ibid.

[19] ibid.

[20] ibid.

[21] ibid.

[22] TNA, CAB 129/43/55 ('Illegal Strikes and SR & O No 1305/40', Memorandum by the Attorney General, 8 December 1950).

[23] TNA, CAB 129/40/143 ('Illegal Strikes', Memorandum by the Attorney General, 28 June 1950). See p 134 above.

[24] TNA, CAB 129/43/55 ('Illegal Strikes and SR & O No 1305/40', Memorandum by the Attorney General, 8 December 1950).

[25] ibid.

the ending of the strike was not conclusive against prosecution, 'especially if strikers, by illegal action have gained their ends'. In weighing up these and other matters, Shawcross made clear that he discounted a third consideration, which was the extent of public or political support for the strike, said to be especially pertinent in this case. According to the Attorney General:

> The fact that, as in this case, the strike concerned the employment of non-unionists and would thus attract the sympathy of the Labour movement, as indeed it does my own, is I am afraid exactly one of those political considerations which I have as far as I can to exclude from consideration. It may be that opponents of the Labour movement regard such a strike as tyrannical and the Attorney General, in his legal capacity, cannot affect his legal and quasi-judicial action by his personal or political view of the merits on such a point.[26]

In the end, however, the critical consideration was the fact that had the dispute been reported (as it would have been had the Order 1305 regime been fully respected), it would not have been referred on to the NAT and would therefore (after 21 days) have become a lawful strike:

> I have, however, been greatly impressed by the Minister of Labour's statement that if the strike had been formally reported to him, he would not have referred it to arbitration and it would, therefore, after a lapse of time have become legal; it was no doubt on this ground that the Minister first stated that the strike was not illegal although he subsequently corrected this statement. I certainly think it would be wrong to prosecute for illegal striking those who, because of the administrative views of the Ministry of Labour, are denied the opportunity of arbitration. The only justification for making strikes illegal is that the better method of settlement provided by arbitration is available.[27]

When the BOAC case was revisited by the Cabinet on 11 December, Shawcross announced that the electricians had returned to work and confirmed to ministers his decision not to institute criminal proceedings against the strikers, principally because the dispute would not have been referred to arbitration even if it had been reported.[28] Shawcross was, however, 'anxious to explain, in reply to an arranged Parliamentary Question, that his decision was based mainly on the fact that the Minister of Labour would not have referred the dispute to arbitration',[29] a wish he had also expressed in his earlier memorandum. Evidently, the failure to prosecute had been criticised in the press and he felt the need to respond.[30]

There was a risk of course that such a statement would embarrass Isaacs, and lead to further questions directed at the Ministry of Labour. Perhaps as a result, Shawcross' insistence that he 'ought to be allowed' to make his reasons clear provoked a hostile response from Morrison, who was in the Cabinet chair on 11 December while Attlee was absent overseas. According to the Cabinet Secretary's notes, Morrison told Shawcross that if he wanted 'to make a reply in the H/C, submit draft to PM, who may want to consult M/Labour'.[31] The formal Conclusions are even more explicit: 'the Attorney General, before

[26] ibid.
[27] ibid.
[28] TNA, CAB 128/18/44 (Cabinet Conclusions, 11 December 1950).
[29] ibid.
[30] TNA, CAB 129/43/55 ('Illegal Strikes and SR & O No 1305/40', Memorandum by the Attorney General, 8 December 1950).
[31] TNA, CAB 195/8/52 (Cabinet Secretary's Notebook, 11 December 1950).

announcing his reasons for refraining from taking proceedings in respect of the recent strike of electricians employed by the British Overseas Airways Corporation, should consult with the Minister of Labour and the Prime Minister regarding the terms of the announcement which he was proposing to make'.[32] In other words, by being instructed by the Cabinet as to his parliamentary response, the Attorney General was being kept closely to heel. Ultimately, however, Shawcross deferred to Isaacs and Pakenham, who had 'strongly pressed' him not to tell the Commons why he had not prosecuted, subsequently complaining to Attlee that while he bears 'sole public responsibility for not enforcing the law', he was prevented from explaining why 'in the interest of other departments'.[33]

III. Duple Motors

The BOAC dispute was not the last time Shawcross was thwarted by his Cabinet colleagues, with the same happening almost contemporaneously in the dispute at Duple Motor Bodies Ltd, in Hendon, North London. This dispute had been brewing since May 1950, when a number of sheet metal workers were dismissed, ostensibly on the grounds of redundancy. The company had reinstated the men following a strike in June, but in October it subsequently initiated a larger redundancy programme threatening as many as 700 jobs. A strike of around 900–1,000 men involving multiple unions started on 19 October, though the bulk (80 per cent) of the strikers were members of the National Union of Vehicle Builders (NUVB). The strike had the support of the NUVB, which claimed that the company's action violated a national agreement and that there could be no resolution until workers already made redundant were reinstated. At a meeting between the unions and the employer on 2 December, an agreement was brokered by Ministry officials, but the proposed terms of settlement were rejected by the workers involved. At a further meeting of the parties on 7 December, the workers' representatives were said to be 'surprisingly aggressive', though the employer undertook to reconsider its plans.

On the same day as the latter meeting, the matter was brought to the attention of the Cabinet for the first time. The dispute having been reported to the Ministry of Labour and duly referred to the NAT, it was reported to ministers that the strike 'appeared to contravene Order 1305, although supported by the unions concerned', and that 'workers in a neighbouring factory owned by Park Royal Vehicles, Ltd, were raising contributions to enable strike pay to be distributed to the employees of Duple Motor Bodies, Ltd'. Isaacs was asked to prepare and circulate a memorandum on the dispute, which was done the next day (8 December), and from which the foregoing account largely draws.[34] The NAT arbitration was scheduled to take place under the

[32] TNA, CAB 128/18/44 (Cabinet Conclusions, 11 December 1950).

[33] TNA, LAB 10/1006 ('Conditions of Employment and National Arbitration Order SR&O, 1940 No 1305. Proposed Amendment of the Order') (letter from Shawcross to Attlee, 19 December 1950).

[34] TNA CAB 129/43/54 ('Duple Motor Bodies Limited, Hendon', Memorandum by the Minister of Labour and National Service, 8 December 1950). We also rely on Anon, *How Duple's Won* (C Short, London, 1951), written by members of the Strike Committee, for some factual detail.

chairmanship of Lord Terrington on 11 December. In these circumstances, it is surprising that the Cabinet should have been asked by the trigger-happy Shawcross on 11 December to consider whether he ought to prosecute under Order 1305, this questionable step perhaps explaining the evident irritation of some of his colleagues, who already had sight of the Attorney General's views of the dispute.

Thus, in his 8 December memorandum dealing with the BOAC dispute referred to above, Shawcross also wrote about the Duple Motor Bodies dispute. He did so in the following terms:

> (i) As I am informed, it started several weeks ago on the ground that the employers were dismissing certain workers for redundancy. In the result 800 men struck work because 400 were to be dismissed, a result most beneficial at present to the employers. The fatuity of this action or the fact that it was an official strike was not, however, a ground for not prosecuting. Nor, of course, is the fact that notwithstanding a reference to arbitration by the Minister, the strike still continues. I have up to now refrained from taking proceedings because the public interest did not appear greatly involved and no important production was being lost.
>
> (ii) The matter has assumed a different complexion, however, as a result of allegations in a Parliamentary Question put by private notice on Tuesday by Mr Lionel Heald, KC [subsequently appointed Attorney General by Churchill in 1951] to the effect that the Works Committee at Park Royal Vehicles Ltd were inducing employees of that firm to contribute towards a fixed levy for assisting the strikers at Duple's and were doing this by methods of intimidation and improper pressure. As far as the police have at present ascertained, these allegations appear well founded although not easy of proof.
>
> (iii) Assuming satisfactory evidence is obtained it would seem that those concerned at the Park Royal Works are guilty of aiding and abetting the illegal strike at Duple's and probably also of intimidation. I could hardly prosecute for these offences without also prosecuting the Union and other leaders at Duple's for counselling and procuring the illegal strike there.
>
> (iv) I should be glad to know if my colleagues are aware of any considerations affecting public policy to which I should have regard in deciding whether or not to prosecute.[35]

At the Cabinet meeting on 11 December 1950,[36] the Duple Motors' strike was discussed along with BOAC dispute, with Shawcross substantially repeating the points made in his 8 December memorandum, including the claim that the alleged illegal conduct of fundraisers at Park Royal Vehicles meant that prosecution of the strike leaders at Duple was unavoidable. Cabinet colleagues appeared bemused; it looks like Shawcross' epic display of his ignorance of the realities of unofficial activism during the Smithfield drivers' strike was being reprised before a wider audience.[37] In response to Shawcross' request about public policy considerations in deciding whether or not to prosecute, Morrison (in the chair in Attlee's absence) doubted whether prosecution was necessary, while Bevin weighed in to say that nothing unusual had been revealed, and that the Attorney General had discretion to overlook this sort of thing. For good measure, the Cabinet Conclusions record that 'difficult issues might arise if anything were done

[35] TNA, CAB 129/43/55 ('Illegal Strikes and SR & O No 1305/40', Memorandum by the Attorney General, 8 December 1950).

[36] TNA, CAB 128/18/44 (Cabinet Conclusions, 11 December 1950).

[37] See pp 112–115 above.

which could be construed as an attempt to restrict the rights of trade unions to raise funds for the support of a strike', a point made specifically by Bevin.[38]

Shawcross was duly informed that although the dispute had been referred to arbitration, there 'would be no public disadvantage if the Attorney General decided not to institute any proceedings in respect of this dispute',[39] Shawcross then being invited 'to take note of the views expressed in the Cabinet's discussion'.[40] Unsurprisingly, there was no prosecution of either the Park Royal or Duple workers. In correspondence to which Isaacs, Chuter Ede and Morrison were 'copied in', Shawcross later told Attlee that, as there were no threats of physical violence at Park Royal, the 'illegal and improper pressure' brought to bear was unlikely to constitute the offence of intimidation under the Conspiracy and Protection of Property Act 1875, section 7. While he thought 'the obvious offence' related to the fundraising 'is that of aiding and abetting an illegal strike contrary to Order 1305', such a prosecution would not be possible, given that he felt unable 'to fly in the face of the strongly expressed views of the Cabinet that a prosecution against the strikers themselves would not promote the public interest'. Recalling his earlier concerns at Smithfield in July 1950,[41] it seems that Shawcross was most exercised about the fundraising methods to support the strikers, as he had been earlier in the year.

Apart from advising the Prime Minister (and the three others who had been copied in) of his decision not to prosecute and the reasons for it, Shawcross took the opportunity in his correspondence with Attlee to address a matter that he had raised with Isaacs alone a few days earlier. Smarting from his humiliation in the BOAC case, Shawcross had written to Isaacs to say that he was 'not proposing in future to submit these cases to Cabinet since they involve discussion, the records of which might be extremely embarrassing', and that he intended 'to circulate a paper for the information of members' as to the course he would 'pursue in future in enforcing the Order', which he thought he was '*bound to do more drastically than hitherto*'.[42] Shawcross was notably more diplomatic in his correspondence with the Prime Minister than he had been with the Minister of Labour, saying that 'while very grateful for expressions of view by my colleagues', he thought that in future, rather than routinely to bring the question of whether to prosecute before the Cabinet, he ought to consult only where there are 'special reasons' to seek their opinions. He proposed that a more 'informal' approach be adopted in the future, with the Attorney General seeking only the advice of the Prime Minister and the Home Secretary, and any minister with a direct interest in the matter.[43]

Of these ministerial 'expressions of view', Shawcross stated that: 'My colleagues of course do their best to be helpful on these matters but whilst they are of course scrupulous to remind me that they share no responsibility for what I may decide, they indicate pretty clearly what they think that decision should be!' And as ever, Shawcross insisted

[38] TNA, CAB 128/18/44 (Cabinet Conclusions, 11 December 1950).
[39] ibid.
[40] ibid.
[41] See pp 112–115 above.
[42] TNA LAB 10/1006 ('Conditions of Employment and National Arbitration Order SR&O, 1940 No 1305. Proposed Amendment of the Order') (letter from Shawcross to Isaacs, 13 December 1950, emphasis added).
[43] ibid (letter from Shawcross to Attlee, 19 December 1950).

that while he did not like prosecuting under the penal provisions of Order 1305, until it was rescinded or reformed, he would nevertheless do so where he deemed it appropriate:

> I would like to emphasise once again the very strong view I hold that if Order 1305 is not repealed, I have no alternative as Attorney General but to see that it is enforced. So long as the Order is part of our law, my clear duty is to see that it is not allowed to become a dead letter and I accordingly in proper cases will have no alternative but to institute criminal proceedings. My own view is that the Order is not appropriate to present day circumstances and should be revoked or enforced.

Shawcross told Attlee that the Solicitor General, Sir Frank Soskice, took the same view and had long told him he had to enforce the law. Moreover, failing to enforce Order 1305 was now exciting adverse comment:

> I cannot in accordance with my duty allow it to be continually flouted with impunity and the matter is the subject of comment in legal and other circles.

Shawcross left it to Attlee as to whether he should circulate his letter as a Cabinet paper or merely send it as a formal Minute.[44] Attlee's reply was the real handover of full responsibility for prosecuting, subject to such consultation with colleagues as the Attorney General thought appropriate. The Prime Minister set it out by hand: 'done' was written in pencil at the top of the letter from Shawcross. This was followed by a formal Prime Ministerial Personal Minute to the Attorney General, Attlee agreeing with everything Shawcross had suggested, stating that only cases 'which involve matters affecting the safety and economic stability of the country' should be referred to the Cabinet by the Attorney General, as well as decreeing that the Cabinet should consider whether Order 1305 ought to be retained.[45] In the course of these exchanges, Shawcross had mentioned that Isaacs was preparing a memorandum on the prospect of reforming or rescinding Order 1305, ministers having requested that of Isaacs at the Cabinet meeting on 11 December. Taking his cue from the Attorney General, in a second Minute dated 21 December, Isaacs was invited by Attlee to give his views as soon as possible: 'I understand that you are preparing a paper on the future of Order 1305. I should like this brought to Cabinet early in the New Year.'[46]

Duple Motor Bodies Ltd and Order 1305

Although presented as a dispute about redundancy, this disguised the real nature of the Duple dispute, which appeared to be about the attempt by the coach-building firm to abandon the de facto recognition of eight unions. There were two strikes.

The first in June 1950 followed the dismissal of a number of sheet metal workers, including all of the sheet metal shop stewards, the Chairman of the Works Council and other activists. The dismissals were explained as redundancies. When the remaining sheet metal workers went on strike, the employer capitulated after

[44] ibid.
[45] TNA, PREM 8/1538 ('1951 Strikes and Industrial Disputes') (Prime Minister's Personal Minute, M150/50).
[46] ibid.

three weeks and either reinstated the men or withdrew the redundancy notices, the artificiality of the alleged redundancy situation subsequently being borne out when additional sheet metal workers were recruited, and overtime continued to be requested. The second and main strike took place over eight weeks during October–December and involved 900–1,000 men. The employer had announced that it proposed to cut production by five-sixths and that it would make that proportion of the workforce redundant, another attempt by management to rid the whole plant of trade union activists. The members of eight unions were involved and each union subsequently sanctioned the industrial action.

The employer evidently had high hopes that the NAT would favour them, presumably on the basis that the strike was unlawful and that following the *Crowther* decision relating to the NAT's powers,[47] it could not order reinstatement, and nor could it substitute its judgment for that of the management. However, after hearing from both sides (the unions were represented by the presidents of two of the unions involved, Duple's by a solicitor and a leading barrister), the members of the Tribunal had withdrawn to consider their decision. On their return, the chairman had stated 'that the Tribunal did not wish to hear the case any further at that stage, and that the most the Tribunal would be willing to do would be issue letters of advice to both parties', also indicating that 'they would be pleased if the two parties found themselves able to reach agreement without their intervention. He proposed to adjourn the hearing at that point and leave the two parties together'.[48]

Within hours, Duple's had conceded. This of course was viewed as a great triumph for the workers and their campaign, which had seen 250,000 leaflets distributed, MPs lobbied, marches held, and the Earl's Court Motor Show picketed. The men had also looked to the busmen, gas workers and dockers for financial help, organising collections at bus garages, power stations and building sites, including the Festival of Britain site. In a pamphlet produced afterwards by the strike committee drawing lessons from the dispute, it was pointed out that strike leaders had been permitted to attend NAT hearings, which was said to be a 'very encouraging sign in these times when TU officials and NEC's seem to be in some danger of losing contact with the ordinary member of the floor of the shop'.[49] It was also claimed that 'even in these modern times when strikes are no longer quite "the done thing" it is still possible to get official recognition', adding that 'it is still possible to get full time TU officials and NECs to stand in the face of the notorious Order No 1305 under which the gas workers were sentenced'.[50]

The pamphlet's authors would no doubt have been appalled if they had known that on 11 December – the day Lord Terrington delivered the fatal blow to Duple Motors – the Cabinet at Shawcross' initiative were deliberating on whether the strikers should be prosecuted.

[47] *R v National Arbitration Tribunal, ex parte Crowther* [1947] 2 All ER 693, [1948] 1 KB 424.
[48] Anon (n 34) p 22.
[49] ibid p 23.
[50] ibid p 24.

Durham County Council and Order 1305

A separate item on the Cabinet agenda on 7 December 1950 dealt with a dispute at Durham County Council, where the council had resolved that all employees must join a trade union.[51] The issue had been picked up by *The Guardian*, which had reported that employees had been told by letter that they were to indicate whether they were union members or not. Those who were not would be dismissed and re-engaged on new terms, which would include a requirement to be a trade union member.[52]

The Cabinet had considered the matter the week before (30 November), the Conclusions raising concerns about the political consequences of any such condition of employment. The concern related not only to the political capital it would provide the Conservatives, but also surprisingly to the political dissension it would create in Labour circles.[53] The Cabinet endorsed the steps taken by Bevan (Minister of Health) and Tomlinson (Minister of Education) to condemn the policy of the County Council, and agreed that the government must continue 'to offer uncompromising opposition to the enforcement of such a policy by a public authority'.[54] It was agreed that informal steps should be taken to encourage influential members of the Labour movement in Durham to take steps to persuade the County Council not to enforce the policy.[55]

Following the meeting on 30 November, Shawcross got into gear, circulating a quite extraordinary memorandum on 4 December,[56] examining what powers under public health and education legislation could be invoked against the County Council. While neither source of power seemed apposite, he nevertheless advised that 'by threatening to withhold financial assistance, and by other indirect methods [ministers] could exercise much influence'.[57] He also pointed out to the Minister of Education that he could intervene under the Education Act 1944, section 68 to issue directions to a local education authority he thought was behaving unreasonably. In this case there was no doubt that the Minister would be entitled to regard the letter to employees 'as an attempt to introduce an unreasonable condition of employment and as itself containing an unreasonable threat of dismissal'.[58]

Even more bizarrely, Shawcross was to write that on the presumed facts, it was 'clear' that if the County Council carried out its threat of dismissal, it would be conducting

[51] TNA, CAB 128/18/43 (Cabinet Conclusions, 7 December 1950).
[52] TNA, CAB 129/43/50 ('Action by Durham County Council in Regard to Membership of Trade Unions', Memorandum by the Attorney General, 4 December 1950). The Memorandum includes a copy of the letter to employees.
[53] TNA, CAB 128/18/39 (Cabinet Conclusions, 30 November 1950).
[54] ibid.
[55] ibid.
[56] TNA, CAB 129/43/50 ('Action by Durham County Council in Regard to Membership of Trade Unions', Memorandum by the Attorney General, 4 December 1950).
[57] ibid.
[58] ibid. This from a man who four days later wrote in relation to the BOAC dispute that 'the strike concerned the employment of non-unionists and would thus attract the sympathy of the Labour movement, as indeed it does my own' (TNA, CAB 129/43/55, 'Illegal Strikes and SR & O No 1305/40', Memorandum by the Attorney General, 8 December 1950).

a lock out in connection with a trade dispute in contravention of Order 1305. He added that 'in view of the issues of personal liberty involved', he could 'hardly neglect to take proceedings if this situation should unhappily arise'.[59] And for good measure, he claimed that the County Council may already have committed an offence under Order 1305, in that the letter to staff 'constitutes an act preparatory to a lock-out'.[60] Despite the threat, however, Shawcross concluded by expecting that an administrative or political solution would be found and that responsibility should not be 'thrown upon' him to invoke the criminal law'.[61] It had already been established by the House of Lords that Order 1305 applied to local authority staff.[62]

The matter was still unresolved on 7 December, but the Cabinet was told by Bevan that he was planning to meet the County Council with a view to bringing the 'present difficulties' to an end.[63] Isaacs then notified the Cabinet that he would not as a result notify the Council that they were in danger of contravening Order 1305. There is no record of further discussion of the matter by the Cabinet. But it seems that everyone had forgotten that the ban on the closed shop in local government had been removed by the repeal of the Trade Disputes and Trade Unions Act 1927 in 1946.[64] Indeed, in 1946 Shawcross had waxed lyrical about the benefits of closed-shop arrangements to employers, adding that the government saw 'no reason why democratically elected local authorities, or responsible statutory public authorities, should be discriminated against by the law in this matter'.[65]

IV. Kemsley Newspapers

The issues before the Cabinet on 11 December had related to the right to strike and the advisability or otherwise of prosecuting those taking industrial action, where the prosecution was addressed to action to enforce the closed shop, and the right of trade unions to levy their members to contribute to a strike fund.[66] That such action should give rise to the possibility of prosecution was rightly a matter of genuine concern. Nevertheless, the attempt politically to control the circumstances in which the law might be used gave rise to an important question of constitutional principle: should prosecution decisions be determined by ministers or by law officers? It is true that ministers were operating here to restrain rather than encourage prosecution. There were, however, clearly obvious dangers if the reverse were ever to be true. But just as ministers commissioned a review of Order 1305, a fresh problem made that review even more urgent. As explained above,

[59] TNA, CAB 129/43/50 ('Action by Durham County Council in Regard to Membership of Trade Unions', Memorandum by the Attorney General, 4 December 1950).
[60] ibid.
[61] ibid.
[62] *National Association of Local Government Officers v Bolton Corporation* [1943] AC 166.
[63] TNA, CAB 128/18/43 (Cabinet Conclusions, 7 December 1950).
[64] See p 62, above.
[65] HC Debs, 12 February 1946, col 214.
[66] TNA, CAB 128/18/44 (Cabinet Conclusions, 11 December 1950).

Isaacs operated a de facto policy of refusing to accept reports of unofficial disputes or refer unofficial disputes to arbitration. This was a policy that was to be challenged in the Kemsley Newspapers' case, which flipped attention from the prosecutorial discretion of Shawcross to the administrative discretion of Isaacs. The latter also had major implications for the right to strike.

The matter was raised in yet another memorandum, this time from Isaacs, circulated on 13 December, only two days after he was commissioned to conduct a review of Order 1305. In the latest memorandum, it was reported that the National Union of Journalists' chapels at Kemsley Newspapers (which published several titles, including the *Daily Graphic*) were concerned about heavy-handed management.[67] According to the Ministry of Labour, the dispute was 'rooted in a general sense of dissatisfaction on the part of the chapels with the way in which the management conducts its dealings with their members', the solicitor for the chapels supplying 'details of instances in the past where the firm are alleged to have acted harshly in dismissing workers or in other ways have not acted fairly towards the men'.[68] The Ministry took the view that 'vague and somewhat indefinite grievances about the general conduct of the firm are not matters which fall within the scope of Order 1305',[69] apparently on the ground that there was insufficient evidence of a 'trade dispute', a term which, it will be recalled, was defined in Article 7 to mean any dispute or difference 'between employers and workmen, or between workmen and workmen connected with the employment or non-employment, or the terms of the employment or with the conditions of labour of any person'.

Despite Isaacs' belief that he could reject reports from individual workers or unofficial trade union sources, the report of the dispute, made by the solicitor on behalf of the chapels (which were acting without the support of the union's executive), had evidently been accepted. While this seems curious, it is likely to reflect the chaotic state of the Ministry's procedures and the conflation of failing to accept a report and failing to refer a dispute (as well as perhaps that the report was made by a solicitor) than any change of policy at the Ministry.[70] However, having accepted the report, Isaacs was ultimately prepared to refer only one 'comparatively minor' matter to arbitration, the latter relating to 'the alleged wrongful dismissal of a particular worker'.[71]

[67] TNA, CAB 129/43/63 ('Conditions of Employment and Arbitration Order, Dispute between Kemsley Newspapers, Limited and Members of the *Daily Graphic* and Kemsley Newspapers (London) Chapels of the National Union of Journalists', Memorandum by the Minister of Labour, 13 December 1950). The Memorandum was not discussed by the Cabinet, although Shawcross responded to it in a letter to Isaacs: TNA, LAB 10/980 ('Kemsley Newspapers Ltd and Joint Negotiating Committee of the Daily Graphic Chapel and Kemsley Newspapers (London) Chapel of the National Union of Journalists. Notice of Trade Dispute under SR&O 1305', Letter from Shawcross to Isaacs, 2 January 1951).

[68] TNA, CAB 129/43/63 ('Conditions of Employment and Arbitration Order, Dispute between Kemsley Newspapers, Limited and Members of the *Daily Graphic* and Kemsley Newspapers (London) Chapels of the National Union of Journalists', Memorandum by the Minister of Labour, 13 December 1950). On the NAT's approach to dismissal disputes, see *R v National Arbitration Tribunal, ex parte Crowther* [1948] 1 KB 424.

[69] TNA, CAB 129/43/63 ('Conditions of Employment and Arbitration Order, Dispute between Kemsley Newspapers, Limited and Members of the *Daily Graphic* and Kemsley Newspapers (London) Chapels of the National Union of Journalists', Memorandum by the Minister of Labour, 13 December 1950).

[70] See TNA, CAB 129/44/8 ('The Future of the Conditions of Employment and National Arbitration Order', Memorandum by the Minister of Labour and National Service, 10 January 1951, para 6), discussed in ch 12 below.

[71] TNA, CAB 129/43/63 ('Conditions of Employment and Arbitration Order, Dispute between Kemsley Newspapers, Limited and Members of the *Daily Graphic* and Kemsley Newspapers (London) Chapels of the National Union of Journalists', Memorandum by the Minister of Labour, 13 December 1950).

That concession appears to have a been a step taken in response to the solicitor's demand that the Minister either refer the trade dispute on to arbitration or confirm that 'in the opinion of the Minister the provisions of the Order do not apply and that they are at liberty to advise the members of the chapels to take such action as they think fit'. No doubt provoking some alarm in the Ministry, Isaacs was also asked to confirm that in the event of the members of the chapels withdrawing their labour, no legal proceedings would be instituted against them,[72] though as a matter of practice that now would have been a decision for Shawcross.

It is unclear whether the chapels received a reply to the foregoing letter. If they did, they were obviously unimpressed, a subsequent letter from their solicitor, Barnett Janner, over two weeks later telling the Ministry that he had been instructed 'to inform the Minister that failure to deal with the dispute in the manner laid down by the Order by Wednesday next the 15th November will be regarded as a refusal for the purpose of an application to the King's Bench Division of the High Court of Justice for an order of mandamus'.[73] Isaacs presumably again refused to respond in the manner desired, and six days later the Lord Chief Justice granted the chapels' representatives leave to apply for mandamus to compel a reference to be made, an audacious claim for an administrative law remedy that was not easy to obtain. But if successful, the application could lead to a judicial order requiring a reference to arbitration of matters other than the wrongful dismissal claim. In bringing the matter to ministers' attention in his memorandum of 13 November, Isaacs pointed out that neither the report by the chapels to the Ministry of Labour nor the legal proceedings had the approval of the NUJ executive, presenting 'a plain case of a group of workers attempting to set in motion the machinery of Order 1305 against the wishes of their Union'.[74]

Isaacs had two concerns. The first and most obvious, though perhaps marginally the least important, was that the High Court would take the view that where a trade dispute had been reported under the Order, the Minister would be *required* 'to consider action under Article 2 of that Order for the purpose of effecting a settlement'.[75] In other words, he would have no discretion as to what disputes or which aspects of disputes needed to be considered. Second, however, he was also concerned that litigation would bring 'to the forefront an aspect of the Order which so far has not been of much practical importance',[76] namely the policy of the Ministry of refusing to accept reports of trade disputes from individuals or unofficial groups. Isaacs was noticeably careful to avoid explicitly stating that this had been the Ministry's policy, perhaps because it would so obviously raise questions of compatibility with Order 1305. The latter gave no express power to refuse to accept a report because of its source. Any such authority would have

[72] TNA, LAB 10/980 ('Kemsley Newspapers Ltd and Joint Negotiating Committee of the Daily Graphic Chapel and Kemsley Newspapers (London) Chapel of the National Union of Journalists. Notice of Trade Dispute under SR&O 1305') (Letter to the Secretary, Ministry of Labour and National Service from Barnett Janner, 26 October 1950).

[73] ibid.

[74] TNA, CAB 129/43/63 ('Conditions of Employment and Arbitration Order, Dispute between Kemsley Newspapers, Limited and Members of the *Daily Graphic* and Kemsley Newspapers (London) Chapels of the National Union of Journalists', Memorandum by the Minister of Labour, 13 December 1950).

[75] ibid.

[76] ibid.

to be implied by the rather unpromising provisions of Article 2(1), which says simply that the 'decision of the Minister as to whether a dispute has been so reported to him or not and as to the time at which a dispute has been so reported shall be conclusive for all purposes'.[77]

Rather than dwell on the legal position, Isaacs preferred instead to tell his ministerial colleagues that 'reports of disputes under the Order by unorganised workers are almost unknown'.[78] He also pointed out that 'the number of cases in which trade union members insisted on reporting a dispute against the wishes of their Executive has been so small as to be negligible,' and that 'the practice has been that when a report is received from a trade union official he or she was invariably asked whether the application is supported by the union's executive'.[79] In a telling passage, Isaacs continued by saying that:

> If, however, as the result of this case these 'rebellious' chapels succeed in setting the machinery of the Order in motion it may quite possibly lead to an extension of this sort of practice so that a disgruntled group of workers (for example, dockers) might report disputes against the advice of their own trade union. This would be a development which I have no doubt would be intensely resented by the trade unions who would naturally take the view that it was directly undermining their authority. It is true that the Order as it stands in theory permits this sort of thing, but, as I have stated above the practice has been very different.[80]

The politics are clear: a duty to accept reports from sources other than trade union executives would undermine the efforts that were being taken to deal with unofficial action, for which the gas-workers prosecution was an example; and as a practical consequence, it would empower groups of workers everywhere at the expense of their union executives.

If there was a duty to accept reports from unofficial groups of workers, the question would then arise as to whether the Ministry could refuse to refer them to arbitration, which was the issue in the Kemsley Newspapers' case. Here it seems that despite the legal action of the chapels, Isaacs had been advised that he had a discretion not to refer:

> I gather that the provision in Article 2(3) of the Order requiring me to take any steps which seem to me expedient might be interpreted as enabling me to take no steps in a case where I do not consider any steps are in fact expedient. I understand from the Law Officers that that at any rate is an arguable proposition and it would mean that where I take that view I would be under no obligation to refer the trade dispute to the National Arbitration Tribunal under Article 2(4) of the Order.

In exercising that discretion in cases 'dealing with an unofficial movement', there were 'of course' in his view 'good policy reasons for looking with a cold eye on any attempt by

[77] The main purpose of this provision would be to enable the parties to decide when the 21-day period had elapsed for the purpose of enabling industrial action to take place if the Minister had failed to take steps to deal with it. Once the reference date was settled, the 21 day limitation was firmly applied: *R v National Arbitration Tribunal, ex parte G A Cramp & Sons* (1947) 203 LT 160.

[78] TNA, CAB 129/43/63 ('Conditions of Employment and Arbitration Order, Dispute between Kemsley Newspapers, Limited and Members of the *Daily Graphic* and Kemsley Newspapers (London) Chapels of the National Union of Journalists', Memorandum by the Minister of Labour, 13 December 1950).

[79] ibid.

[80] ibid.

the workers concerned to invoke the machinery of the Order'. Indeed, it was 'probably' only in such a case that 'it would be practicable to refuse to take any action under the Order when a trade dispute has been reported'.[81] As we have seen, however, the problem with this is that if a dispute was not referred, it would enable strike action to be taken in unofficial disputes 'after 21 days from the report of the dispute'. This was the Article 4 'safety valve', which was meant to operate so that the strike prohibition was lifted when settlement of the dispute voluntarily or through compulsory arbitration was not possible. As Isaacs (or more likely his officials) put it:

> [T]he dilemma presented in these cases is between doing nothing and thereby facilitating a legal strike … or, on the other hand, referring an unofficial trade dispute for settlement under the Order and thereby accentuating the difficulties of the trade union in controlling their members. In view of the above considerations I am watching this case with particular interest.[82]

The problem would be solved if the Minister could refuse to accept reports on substantive grounds, so that the authors of unofficial action would be acting unlawfully while also not having an opportunity to have the matter resolved by arbitration. To his credit, this was a position that made Shawcross uneasy, writing to Isaacs to say:

> I have myself no doubt whatever that the Order applies to any 'trade dispute' whether or not the workers' side is supported by the appropriate trade union. As you appreciate, the Order prohibits strike action which has not been reported, but it would indeed be monstrous to prosecute workers for going on strike unofficially if, at the same time, although they had duly reported the dispute, they were denied recourse to the arbitral machinery laid down in the order.[83]

In these circumstances the best option would be to concede that the Ministry was bound to accept reports from both official and unofficial sources, but to accept that there was a discretion not to refer a dispute to arbitration. That at least would buy 21 days of peace, which might tend to de-escalate any tension. Possibly with this in mind, Shawcross sought to reassure Isaacs that he would be arguing in the Kemsley Newspapers' case that the Minister was 'not bound to refer every trade dispute reported to you to the National Arbitration Tribunal'.[84]

Order 1305, Article 2 and Ministerial Discretion

The power of the Minister – and the extent of his discretion – to refer a reported dispute to the NAT begins with Order 1305, Article 2(2). The latter used mandatory language, so that when a dispute was reported to the Minister, he 'shall' consider it, and if in his opinion there were suitable means for settling the dispute, he 'shall' refer it to these procedures accordingly.

[81] ibid.
[82] ibid.
[83] TNA, LAB 10/980 ('Printing Industry: Kemsley Newspapers Ltd and Joint Negotiating Committee of the *Daily Graphic* Chapel and Kemsley Newspapers (London) Chapel of the NUJ. Notice of Trade Dispute under SR&O 1305') (letter from Shawcross to Isaacs, 2 January 1951).
[84] ibid.

Where, however, the Minister was of the opinion that there were no suitable means for settling the dispute, Article 2(3) provided that he 'shall' take 'any steps that seem to him expedient to promote a settlement of the dispute', and 'may, if he thinks fit', refer the matter for settlement to the NAT. In the case of unofficial action, there may not have been suitable procedures in the industry in question, while at the same time it might not be desirable to refer the dispute to the NAT.

In these latter cases (unofficial action), the first question would have been whether the duty to take any steps the Minister deemed expedient included the right not to take any steps at all, where the Minister was of the opinion that no such steps were expedient for public policy or any other reason. If so, then the second question would be whether in such circumstances the Minister could exercise his discretion and refrain from referring the matter to the NAT on the ground that he did not think it fit to do so for the same reason.

Although it seems plausible to interpret Article 2 in this way, there would be two consequences in doing so: first, if challenged in judicial review proceedings, the Minister would have to explain these decisions, and perhaps also justify why they were taken; and second, where a dispute was not referred for settlement, it would be possible for the workers involved to take strike action 21 days after the dispute was reported.

V. Society of Town Clerks

The question whether or not any discretion existed in relation to the referring on of reported disputes was raised again in the last of the five disputes to trouble ministers in the weeks before Christmas in 1950. This was the dispute relating to the implementation of a pay settlement on behalf of town clerks, a relatively small group of senior local authority officers. As explained by Shawcross,[85] the Joint Negotiating Committee (JNC) for Town Clerks and District Council Clerks had been established in 1948 to make recommendations on pay. In 1949 the Committee recommended revised pay scales, by which the annual pay of individual town clerks would be based on the number of people living in the area for which they had responsibility: '£500–£800 in the case of areas with a population of under 5,000, to £3,000–£3,500 in the case of populations of 400,000 to 600,000, with complete discretion in the case of larger populations'.[86] Although the recommendations would lead to substantial pay increases in some cases, they were said nevertheless to be consistent with the government's pay restraint policy agreed with the TUC in 1948 as set out in the White Paper on *Personal Incomes, Costs and Prices*,[87] discussed in Chapter Five above.

[85] TNA, CAB 129/43/71 ('Legal Considerations Affecting Claims for Salary Increases by Town Clerks', Memorandum by the Attorney General, 18 December 1950).
[86] ibid.
[87] Cd 7321, 1948.

A number of local authorities refused to implement the recommendation, partly because 'the salary of town clerks should be related to their personal qualifications rather than to a flat rate based on population alone'.[88] As a result, the Society of Town Clerks reported disputes with 25 local authorities under Order 1305, which again caused Isaacs some embarrassment, explaining in yet another memorandum to ministers that there was 'a good deal of political opposition, particularly within the Labour Party, to the implementation of the recommendations of this Committee'.[89] There was also 'strong opposition amongst a number of local authorities who object to the recommendations on the merits and at the same time challenge the competence of the Committee in this matter'. Notably, Isaacs emphasised that the JNC 'does not possess the status or the authority of a Whitley Council'.[90] Legally, however, the question was whether a reference under Order 1305 to the NAT would be well made, Isaacs doubting whether 'a dispute concerning a single employee of a local authority can be a dispute within the meaning of [Order 1305]',[91] a question he put to the Attorney General for advice.

Although Shawcross thought it 'anomalous', nevertheless he 'reluctantly had to advise that under the language of the Order a town clerk is a 'workman' and a dispute between him and his authority is a trade dispute'.[92] And he did so despite the views of the Solicitor General, Frank Soskice, to the contrary. It is not clear on what basis Soskice gave his advice, or conversely why Shawcross should be so confident as to 'really have no doubt about the matter'.[93] One answer may lie in the decision in *National Association of Local Government Officers v Bolton Corporation*,[94] where the House of Lords rejected an argument that local authority employees were not 'workmen' for the purposes of Order 1305, explaining that:

> It is worth observing that, while the definition of 'trade dispute' [in Order 1305] is practically the same as in the Trade Disputes Act 1906, s 5(3), the definition of 'workmen' is entirely different and much wider than that in the Act of 1906. In that Act the workman had to be 'employed in trade or industry'. No such limitation appears in the definition of 'workman' for

[88] TNA, CAB 129/43/71 ('Legal Considerations Affecting Claims for Salary Increases by Town Clerks', Memorandum by the Attorney General, 18 December 1950).

[89] TNA, CAB 129/43/66 ('Salaries and Conditions of Employment for Town Clerks', Memorandum by Minister of Labour and National Service, 18 December 1950).

[90] ibid. The government regarded itself as effectively bound by the determinations of Whitley Councils.

[91] ibid.

[92] TNA, CAB 129/43/71 ('Legal Considerations Affecting Claims for Salary Increases by Town Clerks', Memorandum by the Attorney General, 18 December 1950).

[93] ibid. He was subsequently vindicated by the decision in *R v National Arbitration Tribunal, ex parte South Shields Corporation* [1952] 1 KB 46, which held that by virtue of the Interpretation Act 1889, a dispute involving one workman (which for these purposes would include a town clerk) would be covered by Order 1305. However, following the revocation of Order 1305 and its replacement by Order 1376 (on which see ch 14 below), existing disputes at the time of revocation and replacement were rolled over to be determined in accordance with Order 1376, provided the dispute fell within the restricted jurisdiction of the new Industrial Disputes Tribunal. However, it was held that unlike the NAT, the latter did not have jurisdiction under Order 1376 to deal with disputes involving single workers. It was held as a result in *ex parte South Shields Corporation* that the dispute in this case was not covered by the new law, and an order of prohibition was therefore granted at the request of the employer to prevent the IDT from hearing the case.

[94] *National Association of Local Government Officers v Bolton Corporation* [1943] AC 166. The case was not referred to in Shawcross' memorandum.

> present purposes, and the effect is to enlarge correspondingly the conception of 'trade dispute' itself.[95]

In addition, 'the position had already been somewhat compromised in this respect by the fact that the Departments concerned had previously regarded professional officers, such as, for instance, a medical officer of health and a director of education, as coming within the scope of compulsory arbitration orders'.[96]

This suggests that it was not open to Isaacs to refuse to accept the report, which appeared to fall squarely within the scope of Order 1305. According to Shawcross, however, 'the remaining question is whether, on such a dispute being reported to him, the Minister of Labour is obliged to refer it to arbitration', pointing out that it was 'at least arguable that the Minister has a discretion and that he is not bound to take any steps under the Order to promote a settlement if he does not think it expedient so to do'.[97] Here Shawcross appeared to provide a solution for Isaacs by asking whether 'political or administrative steps could have been taken or could still be taken now to point out the merely advisory character of the Joint Committee's recommendation, and the unsuitability of scale rates for professional officers whose qualifications and the extent of whose duties do not by any means universally correspond with the size of the populations which they serve'.[98] If, however, 'the matter has to be referred to arbitration under Order 1305', he continued, 'it will be difficult to avoid a general increase in all these salaries up to the recommended scales'.[99]

The Attorney General acknowledged that the existence of any such discretion on the Minister's part was one of the issues before the High Court in the Kemsley Newspapers' dispute, which had not yet been resolved. But although the Kemsley case was waiting to be heard, Shawcross was nevertheless confident enough to advise Isaacs that he 'probably [had] a discretion whether or not to refer these cases to the National Arbitration Tribunal' and that it was 'a matter of policy [for him] to decide what action to take'.[100] By now Isaacs appeared to find this advice unhelpful, and having decided that he was not minded to exercise any such discretion, proposed to refer the dispute to the NAT, despite the expectation of Shawcross about the likely outcome, and that as a matter of law, the recommendations of the NAT would have to be honoured.[101] Before doing so, however, in a Memorandum of 18 December, Isaacs sought the Cabinet's views, setting out what were in effect three reasons why he thought it was not open to him in this case to take advantage of the Attorney General's advice, suggesting that once a dispute was reported and accepted, the Ministry was simply a post box for references to the NAT.

[95] ibid p 175. This, however, did not address the issue subsequently raised in *ex parte South Shields Corporation* (n 93) about whether a dispute involving a single workman would be a trade dispute. There would be only one town clerk in most if not all local authorities, which were separate employers for these purposes.

[96] TNA, CAB 129/43/71 ('Legal Considerations Affecting Claims for Salary Increases by Town Clerks', Memorandum by the Attorney General', 18 December 1950).

[97] ibid.

[98] ibid.

[99] ibid.

[100] TNA, CAB 129/43/66 ('Salaries and Conditions of Employment for Town Clerks', Memorandum by Minister of Labour and National Service, 18 December 1950).

[101] TNA, CAB 129/43/71 ('Legal Considerations Affecting Claims for Salary Increases by Town Clerks', Memorandum by the Attorney General, 18 December 1950).

The first reason was that Isaacs' officials had already started to support efforts to resolve the dispute, and a failure on his part to refer it to the NAT following a failure of conciliation would involve a declaration on his part that he 'was not prepared to allow this dispute to be decided by the National Arbitration Tribunal whose impartiality and fairness should be beyond question'.[102] This was a decent argument based on the need to maintain the integrity of the NAT, and the need to avoid any refusal being misconstrued as a suggestion that the Ministry did not trust the body whose members it was responsible for appointing. A second concern driving Isaacs in the direction of a reference was that if he continued to postpone any decision to do so, the Society of Town Clerks would also apply to the High Court for an order of mandamus with a view to compelling him to make the reference. As Isaacs pointed out, it would be 'unfortunate if another application of this kind should follow so soon after the Kemsley Newspapers' case'. Third and decisively, 'it would be difficult to find any ground on which the application could be opposed'.[103] That would be a persuasive reason, which would have made the fear of legal action irresistible.

It appears nevertheless that the Minister of Labour was either persuaded or bullied to change his mind before the matter was considered by the Cabinet on 2 January, Isaacs now advising colleagues that:

> It would be unfortunate if a position was reached in which suggestions put forward by the Joint Negotiating Committee were imposed on local authorities by the National Arbitration Tribunal. While he would feel bound in the ordinary way to refer to the Tribunal a trade dispute between employers and a union, when efforts at negotiation had broken down, he felt justified in refusing to refer to the Tribunal the disputes between certain Town Clerks and their local authorities.[104]

The Cabinet Conclusions suggest that the pressure had come in the first instance from Shawcross, who was clearly concerned about the impact of any decision in the Town Clerks' cases for the forthcoming proceedings in the Kemsley Newspapers' case. Until that matter had been resolved by the High Court, Shawcross insisted that the Minister of Labour follow his earlier advice, and that he 'should not refer either that dispute or the cases of the Town Clerks to the Tribunal'. If, however, the High Court were to decide that Isaacs ought to have referred Kemsley Newspapers to the NAT, 'he thought that the Minister would be obliged to refer the cases of the Town Clerks as well'.[105]

The other pressure was political, and was led by a most unlikely source. Thus, the only view other than that of Isaacs and Shawcross to be recorded in the Cabinet

[102] TNA, CAB 129/43/66 ('Salaries and Conditions of Employment for Town Clerks', Memorandum by Minister of Labour and National Service, 18 December 1950).
[103] ibid. Shawcross had provided Isaacs with the means and the argument to justify refusing to make a reference: the Joint Negotiating Committee's recommendations were not binding, and he could have refused to intervene in view of 'the unsuitability of scale rates for professional officers whose qualifications and the extent of whose duties do not by any means universally correspond with the size of the populations they serve' (TNA, CAB 129/43/71 ('Legal Considerations Affecting Claims for Salary Increases by Town Clerks', Memorandum by the Attorney General, 18 December 1950)).
[104] TNA, CAB 128/19/1 (Cabinet Conclusions, 2 January 1951).
[105] ibid.

Conclusions on 2 January was that of Bevan (Minister for Health), who appeared to argue forcefully that:

> [T]he negotiations between the Town Clerks and local authorities, which had led to the recommendations put forward by the Joint Negotiating Committee, had not been of a satisfactory character; nor, in his view, had the findings of the Joint Negotiating Committee been of a nature which justified a reference to arbitration. The Government would have to consider whether the machinery set up under [Order 1305] was to be used to coerce local authorities. It was arguable that an elected local authority should not be compelled to accept arbitration machinery against its will.[106]

Perhaps predictably, the general view of the Cabinet was that neither the Kemsley Newspapers' case nor the Town Clerks' cases were to be referred to the NAT, and that the position should be reviewed 'in the light of the decision of the High Court on the application for an order of mandamus'. As we will see, however, the High Court avoided the hard questions, with the result that the issues about the scope of ministerial power identified in this chapter were never resolved before Order 1305 was revoked and replaced in September 1951.

VI. Conclusion

It seems remarkable that so much ministerial time should have been spent on what were typically relatively minor disputes. The five cases presented to the Cabinet nevertheless exposed serious problems with the way in which the government was now engaging with Order 1305. First, there were questions about whether and if so when the criminal powers should be deployed, with Shawcross now in a more prominent position and demanding that the criminal law be more widely used so long as Order 1305 remained in force. But he was frustrated by the Cabinet, which in the absence of any overt Communist engagement seemed to be reluctant to authorise prosecution, particularly where the strikes were concerned with core questions of trade union practice, which Shawcross did not appear to understand. Rather ominously, however, having been constrained by the Cabinet in his enforcement of the law, as we have seen, Shawcross was to win from Attlee the authority to prosecute without referring to the Cabinet other than in exceptional cases. From a constitutional point of view, that was a significant and principled move, though also a controversial and politically dangerous one in light of Shawcross' claim expressed in correspondence with Isaacs that he was 'bound to' prosecute 'more drastically than hitherto'.

But while Shawcross was becoming more belligerent, there was a profound lack of awareness on the part of the Ministry of Labour about its legal obligations. Isaacs had adopted an impossible position in which he refused to *accept* some categories of disputes, while also initially insisting on a power to refuse to *refer* disputes should he subsequently be required to accept them. The legal basis for the former approach in particular was highly

[106] ibid.

contestable as Isaacs appeared to accept and as Shawcross rightly pointed out. Although Isaacs' policies were understandable, enabling as they did the government to exclude from arbitration those disputes which could have politically embarrassing outcomes, they denied workers the opportunity to have their grievances addressed in circumstances where they were prohibited by law from taking industrial action. Although perhaps less important while the penal provisions were not being invoked against those who took unofficial strike action, this became a much more serious issue when Shawcross was given much greater freedom to prosecute. For as Shawcross himself recognised it would be 'monstrous to prosecute workers for going on strike unofficially if, at the same time, although they had duly reported the dispute, they were denied recourse to the arbitral machinery'.[107]

[107] See p 216 above.

12

The Cabinet Review of Order 1305

Irreconcilable Ministerial Tensions

I. Introduction

The disputes considered by Ministers in December 1950 and January 1951 reveal a number of problems with the operation of Order 1305. It was thus timely that on 11 December, Isaacs should have been asked to prepare a Memorandum on the future of the war-time powers, which was to be presented to the Cabinet in the New Year. The memorandum was duly circulated on 10 January 1951,[1] leading predictably to an immediate response on the following day from Shawcross, whose role had been enhanced by Attlee's agreement that Cabinet approval would not be necessary for all prosecution decisions. The disputatious Shawcross inevitably gave a different account of the problems arising under Order 1305, and in doing so helped to expose the differences within government about its operation.[2] We consider these notable memorandums in this chapter, along with the Cabinet's response, as well as the Cabinet's mediation of the differences between the two protagonists.

Behind the differences were contrasting philosophical approaches to the rule of law in industrial relations. Although operating in a legal framework, the Ministry of Labour focused on policy and saw the legislation as an irritant to be navigated. Shawcross on behalf of the Law Officers rejected this contextual approach, insisting that while he was uncomfortable with the legal constraints in Order 1305, the law nevertheless must be obeyed. This applied both in relation to the Ministry's arbitration powers, and in relation to the liabilities of workers who engaged in industrial action. The internal government tension could probably be accommodated while the law was being used principally as a political tool to deal with the Communist Party generally and problems within the TGWU in particular. But it was becoming more difficult to manage as it became harder to blame the Communist Party for worker discontent.

[1] TNA, CAB 129/44/8 ('The Future of the Conditions of Employment and National Arbitration Order', Memorandum by the Minister of Labour and National Service, 10 January 1951).

[2] TNA, CAB 129/44/9 ('The Future of the Conditions of Employment and National Arbitration Order', Memorandum by the Attorney General, 11 January 1951).

II. Isaacs' Memorandum

Isaacs' paper (the drafting of which was overseen by Chief Industrial Commissioner Sir Robert Gould) paid tribute to the effectiveness of compulsory arbitration in the post-war era. It was claimed that 'it would be difficult to overestimate the value and usefulness of the Order both during and since the end of the war as a complement to the normal negotiating machinery of industry'.[3] The existence of the National Arbitration Tribunal (NAT) in the background was said to have 'done much in a great number of cases to encourage the parties to come to agreement by negotiation'. While in other cases 'it may have had the effect of making one party or the other more intransigent', nevertheless 'it does give the assurance to both' that 'in the last resort a settlement of a trade dispute can be obtained compulsorily if need be'. The prohibition of strikes and lock outs together with compulsory arbitration 'have exercised considerable influence in restraining those who might otherwise have been tempted to take extreme measures'.[4] True, there had been stoppages of work throughout the lifetime of the Order. But 'no system of sanctions or of compulsory arbitration could entirely prevent them'.

Although 'without doubt' Order 1305 had been 'an important factor in our relative freedom from stoppages of work due to industrial disputes', now was the time to take stock. Isaacs had no reason to believe that either the British Employers' Federation (BEF) or the TUC no longer supported Order 1305 (although he had previously conceded that the unions would have liked to see some changes to the compulsory arbitration regime),[5] and he pointed to its extensive use: from the beginning of 1946 until June 1950, some 864 cases had been referred to the NAT, of which 804 had been reported by trade unions.[6] Paradoxically, it was 'those most vocal in their opposition' to the Order's continuance who had been 'most consistent in their use of it'.[7] However, restlessness on the part of trade unions over the strike prohibition was increasing, despite support for the continuation of Order 1305 at the TUC Annual Conference the previous September, which had been secured only by the General Council emphasising the right of unions to take intransigent employers to arbitration and 'slurring over' the strike restraints. Isaacs nevertheless acknowledged that the obvious resistance to Order 1305 had 'almost certainly been strengthened' by opposition to the restriction on what 'trade unionists and indeed some trade union executives' regarded as 'their immemorial right to strike'.

Indeed, Isaacs and his officials believed that the current level of concern meant that 'the Order in its present form will be impossible to administer', and that it was 'probably not unfair to say that an increasing body of trade union opinion is questioning the continued need for the Order'.[8] These concerns were compounded by two difficulties in the 'practical application' of the law. The first related to Isaacs' discretionary powers, and

[3] TNA, CAB 129/44/8 ('The Future of the Conditions of Employment and National Arbitration Order', Memorandum by the Minister of Labour and National Service, 10 January 1951), para 3.
[4] ibid.
[5] See p 184, above.
[6] For more details, see the box on p 228 below.
[7] TNA, CAB 129/44/8 ('The Future of the Conditions of Employment and National Arbitration Order', Memorandum by the Minister of Labour and National Service, 10 January 1951), para 4.
[8] ibid.

included (but were not confined to) the issues discussed in the previous chapter. These 'difficulties of interpretation' were explained in the following terms:

> (i) [T]he Minister may, for good cause, postpone the reference to the National Arbitration Tribunal beyond the twenty-one days provided for in the Order. The Order has been administered on the basis that in the case of postponement the prohibition on strikes and lock-outs continues in force. It now appears that if, within the twenty-one days, the Minister has not referred the dispute for settlement either to the machinery of the industry or to the National Arbitration Tribunal, the prohibition may lapse even though the Minister may have had good cause for the postponement of the reference. If that is a correct interpretation and if I wish to keep the prohibition alive, I have a maximum of twenty-one days in which to try for a settlement by conciliation or informal negotiation, and at the end of that time must refer the dispute to the National Arbitration Tribunal even though I have good reason to believe that a few more days discussion will result in a settlement by agreement. This was certainly not the intention.
>
> (ii) It has always been assumed that, in the case of failure to reach a settlement by other means, I *must* refer a dispute to the National Arbitration Tribunal. Some doubt has now arisen as to whether this provision is as mandatory as has been thought in the past. In general this is not a discretion which I should welcome.
>
> (iii) If reference to the Tribunal is mandatory, it appears that I must act even where the worker-party to the dispute is an individual workman or an unofficial committee of workers going behind the backs of their trade union executives. I need not point put to my colleagues how embarrassing this can be.[9]

Here we have Isaacs and his Ministry owning up to having misunderstood, misinterpreted, and misapplied Order 1305. The first of these three points had not been raised in any of the disputes covered in this book, and revealed an oversight in the drafting. Although the Minister could postpone making a reference to the NAT until after the 21 day period had elapsed where there were special circumstances to do so (art 2(4)), there was no corresponding qualification to the restriction on the right to strike or lock out in art 4, which could be exercised without qualification if the dispute had not been referred within 21 days of being reported. The second and third points were a reprise of concerns considered in Chapter Eleven, exposed by the Kemsley Newspapers' and Town Clerks' disputes respectively, which raised questions about who could report a dispute, as well as the responsibility of the Minister once a report had been accepted. That said, the concerns expressed by Isaacs on the second point seemed to be contradicted by his position at one stage in the Town Clerks' dispute in particular, which revealed the impracticability of operating without any discretion to refer. Other points – relating to the approach of the NAT to the scope of its jurisdiction raised by the BOAC and Duple Motors' disputes respectively – were not mentioned at this stage, though, as we will discuss below, they were picked up later.[10]

The other problem relating to the practical application of Order 1305 was 'the most difficult', and concerned 'the prosecution of workers for striking' – in other words, 'the enforcement' of Part II of the Order.[11] Here Isaacs acknowledged candidly that war-time

[9] ibid, para 6.

[10] These being the reluctance of the NAT to deal with the closed shop (as in the BOAC case), or de-recognition (which seems to have been at the bottom of the Duple Motors' dispute where the NAT was unable or unwilling to make a decision and returned the matter to the parties to resolve).

[11] TNA, CAB 129/44/8 ('The Future of the Conditions of Employment and National Arbitration Order', Memorandum by the Minister of Labour and National Service, 10 January 1951), para 7.

experience had shown that 'the penalties of the Defence Regulations did not deter workmen from striking if they felt strongly enough about the matter in dispute', while 'the sanctions were impossible to enforce where the numbers involved were large'. Since the war, moreover, there had been only one prosecution (London gas workers), and although prosecution had been 'considered' on a 'number of other occasions', it was not pursued 'because it was felt that it might prejudice the prospects of a negotiated settlement or because the number of workers involved was too large'. In an important passage, Isaacs continued:

> So long as the initiative in proposing prosecution in practice rested with me it was not too difficult to defend taking this kind of line, for after all my primary responsibility is to obtain a settlement of the dispute. But as was explained by the Prime Minister in his reply to a Parliamentary Question on 7th November, 1950, responsibility for initiating prosecution action has now been placed upon the Attorney-General. His view is that, so long as the Order remains in force, it is his clear duty to see that it is not allowed to become a dead letter; and that he can no longer refrain from prosecuting in such cases as appear to him to be appropriate. He is of the opinion that, unless the Order is to be enforced, it should be revoked.[12]

But although Shawcross' view was one which Isaacs had 'every sympathy',[13] it reflected a fundamental difference of attitude and approach: 'law enforcement' versus 'dispute resolution'.[14] In the former case, the law had to be applied and the parties were obliged to adapt their behaviour accordingly; in the latter case, the law had to adapt to the behaviour of the parties and to be applied accordingly. The question for Isaacs was how to absorb the new legal realities with industrial relations pressures. One option would be to retain Order 1305 as it then was, which with Shawcross now in charge would 'inevitably involve an increasing number of prosecutions'.[15] However, if in peace-time there were to be 'a succession of criminal prosecutions involving sentences of imprisonment', the TUC 'would almost certainly be forced to demand the revocation of the Order'. But if retention in its current form was not an option, nor was revocation. Apart from the continuing 'great value' of the restrictions on strikes and lock outs, Isaacs was unable to imagine 'a more inopportune time to take this step – a time when the international situation is full of danger, when our troops are fighting against heavy odds in Korea, and when production of armaments has again become a first priority'.[16]

[12] ibid. On the Prime Minister's explanation on 7 November 1950, see p 201, above; and on the Prime Minister's formal Minute on 19 December 1950 acknowledging the principal role of the Attorney General, see p 209, above.

[13] ibid.

[14] See also subsequently a similar tension under the Labour government in the 1970s: KD Ewing, '*Grunwick Processing Laboratories Ltd v ACAS*: The Social Contract, Trade Union Recognition, and the Rule of Law' in A Bogg, A Davies and J Prassl (eds), *Landmark Cases in Labour Law* (Hart Publishing, Oxford, 2022) ch 6.

[15] TNA, CAB 129/44/8 ('The Future of the Conditions of Employment and National Arbitration Order', Memorandum by the Minister of Labour and National Service, 10 January 1951), para 8.

[16] ibid. Isaacs also pointed out that if Order 1305 were to be revoked, the government would 'probably wish to re-enact in some other form Part III of the Order relating to the observance of recognised terms and conditions of employment' (ibid). As we saw in ch 4 above, provision had been made in the Wages Councils Act 1945 for the retention of a slightly amended version of Part III to be found in the Third Schedule of the Act ('Provisions of Part III of the Conditions of Employment and National Arbitration Order, 1940, as modified') to apply in the event of Order 1305 being revoked by the first Attlee administration, as had been expected.

So if neither retention (in its existing form) nor revocation was appropriate, this left the option of reform. This could be done in a number of ways, Isaacs writing in the first person as follows:

> (a) By deleting the provisions relating to the prohibition of strikes and lock outs. Although this would be welcomed by substantial numbers of trade unionists, I have reason to believe that some of the more responsible leaders regard these provisions as strengthening the hands of the Executives of the Unions and as helpful to them in their efforts to restrain their more hot-headed members.
> (b) By providing that the penalty for an offence against the strike and lock-out provisions should be a fine only and not imprisonment (I am advised that this would require an amendment of the appropriate Defence Regulation). This would remove much of the sting in the Order and would I think be greatly welcomed by the Unions and probably facilitate the endorsement of the Order at next September [TUC] Congress.
> (c) By providing that only established organisations habitually taking part in collective negotiations and acting through their Headquarters, and not individuals or unofficial committees, may report disputes under the Order.
> (d) By excluding from the scope of the Order, disputes relating to recognition or non-unionism, neither of which are readily susceptible of settlement by compulsory arbitration. So far as recognition disputes are concerned, such exclusion would merely make clear what is already generally understood to be the law.[17]

In presenting these four options or potential combinations of options, Isaacs suggested that there might be a fifth, 'such as limiting the period of strike prohibition to the first twenty-one days after the dispute has been reported',[18] which would allow strikes to take place thereafter regardless of whether the dispute had been referred to arbitration or elsewhere.

However, Isaacs and his officials acknowledged that 'the whole question requires the most careful consideration', referencing again 'the present critical international situation'.[19] Consequently, before making any specific recommendations, Isaacs proposed to seek the advice of both sides of industry 'whose interests are so vitally engaged in every aspect of this matter'.[20] To this end, an early meeting of the Joint Consultative Committee of the National Joint Advisory Council was to take place, 'with a view to placing before them the problems that have arisen in connection with Order 1305'. Isaacs would then report back to his colleagues. But although he had given a full account of the problems facing the Ministry of Labour, Isaacs nevertheless appeared completely to misunderstand the critical weakness, which his suggested solutions would only reinforce. The fact that individual workers or unofficial groups of workers had difficulties that could not be resolved through official channels suggested that there might

However, Order 1305, including the original Part III, remained in force until August 1951, when it was supplanted by the provisions relating to 'issues concerning recognised terms and conditions of employment' in Order 1376, the relevant provisions of the 1945 Act (Part III, s 19) having expired on 31 December 1950 as the 1945 Act required.

[17] TNA, CAB 129/44/8 ('The Future of the Conditions of Employment and National Arbitration Order', Memorandum by the Minister of Labour and National Service, 10 January 1951), para 8.

[18] ibid para 9.

[19] ibid.

[20] ibid.

be problems with these official channels. This was a matter that demanded a response. It should not have been left to the Attorney General to point out that to deny the workers involved both access to arbitration and the right to strike was wholly untenable.

Table 12.1 Cases referred to the National Arbitration Tribunal

Year	Number referred	Reported by or on behalf of employers	Reported jointly on behalf of employers	Reported by or on behalf of workers
1946	142	6	5	131
1947	164	9	3	152
1948	174	12	1	161
1949	247	14	5	228
To 30 June 1950	137	4	1	132
Total	864	45	15	804

Source: TNA, LAB 10/1006 (Conditions of Employment and National Arbitration Order SR&O, 1940 No 1305. Proposed Amendment of the Order) (Ministry of Labour, 'Cases Referred to the National Arbitration Tribunal)).[21]

III. Shawcross' Response

Order 1305 thus created two major but inter-related problems that had to be addressed, both of which were at the heart of the difference between Isaacs and Shawcross. The first was the operation of the system of compulsory arbitration, with the Ministry demanding control at the point of entry to the system. And the second was the enforcement of the prohibition of strikes and lock outs (though mainly the former), whether or not the dispute was capable of resolution by arbitration. Indicating that Order 1305 was a significant contemporary pre-occupation, Shawcross responded to Isaacs with a Memorandum of his own.[22] Dated 11 January (the day after Isaacs' Memorandum), Shawcross addressed three questions:

- the administration of Order 1305 and the Ministry of Labour's understanding of what it required;
- his own role in enforcing the law in the event of any strike or lock out taking place in breach of its provisions; and
- his own ideas for the retention and reform of Order 1305, along with his own ideas for the role of the law in industrial relations generally.

[21] The headings in the table do not imply that disputes were accepted from individual workers or unofficial groups. The term 'workers' in this context is a synonym for trade unions.

[22] TNA, CAB 129/44/9 ('The Future of the Conditions of Employment and National Arbitration Order', Memorandum by the Attorney General, 11 January 1951).

In dealing with the first of these questions, Shawcross responded to the various matters identified by Isaacs, including Isaacs' point about postponing a reference to the NAT beyond the normal period of 21 days because there is 'good reason to believe that a few more days' discussion will result in a settlement by agreement'.[23] As we have seen, Isaacs had written that:

> It now appears that if, within the twenty-one days, the Minister has not referred the dispute for settlement either to the machinery of the industry or to the National Arbitration Tribunal, the prohibition may lapse even though the Minister may have had good cause for the postponement of the reference. If that is a correct interpretation and if I wish to keep the prohibition alive, I have a maximum of twenty-one days in which to try for a settlement by conciliation or informal negotiation, and at the end of that time must refer the dispute to the National Arbitration Tribunal even though I have good reason to believe that a few more days discussion will result in a settlement by agreement. This was certainly not the intention.[24]

Shawcross made clear that 'the prohibition against strike or lockout action lapses at the end of the 21 day period if no reference has been made by then'.[25] He also made the obvious point that if a dispute was so close to a settlement, 'the mere fact that a reference has not been made within the 21 days and that, therefore, the prohibition against strike or lockout action has lapsed', would not necessarily lead to a strike or lock out taking place.[26]

Perhaps more importantly, Shawcross expressed surprise that Isaacs had eschewed the thought of a discretion to refer disputes to the NAT, given that he appeared effectively to have acknowledged the existence of and need for such a power in the BOAC,[27] Kemsley Newspapers', and Town Clerks' disputes.[28] Rather exasperated, the Attorney General stated that he 'had always understood that the Minister desired to retain a discretion' not to refer, and had '*on this understanding*, advised him [in relation to the Town Clerks' and Kemsley/*Daily Graphic* cases] that it is possible to argue that the Order gives him the right so to do'.[29] Shawcross advised that if Isaacs wished to avoid a ruling in the Kemsley Newspapers' case that he had a discretion not to refer, then the action for a mandamus 'should not be resisted'.[30] The reluctance of Isaacs and his officials to accept reports from unofficial sources or refer unofficial disputes to the Tribunal also drew a stinging response from Shawcross. Essentially he reiterated the argument made first when the Cabinet was considering the BOAC strike, and subsequently to Isaacs in

[23] TNA, CAB 129/44/8 ('The Future of the Conditions of Employment and National Arbitration Order', Memorandum by the Minister of Labour and National Service, 10 January 1951), para 6.
[24] ibid.
[25] TNA, CAB 129/44/9 ('The Future of the Conditions of Employment and National Arbitration Order', Memorandum by the Attorney General, 11 January 1951), para 2.
[26] ibid.
[27] In fact, in the BOAC case, the dispute was not reported, though Isaacs said he would not have referred it had it been reported. In the Kemsley case, the matters in dispute were reported, but only one of those matters was deemed to be a trade dispute and referred on. The Town Clerks were waiting for the Kemsley case to be heard, though the discretion point was dropped in the Ministry's defence and was not dealt with by the court. See below, pp 238–239.
[28] TNA, CAB 129/44/9 ('The Future of the Conditions of Employment and National Arbitration Order', Memorandum by the Attorney General, 11 January 1951), para 2.
[29] ibid, emphasis in original.
[30] ibid.

relation to the Kemsley Newspapers' dispute, that the Order applied 'to all trade disputes whether supported by a trade union or not', adding that '[i]t would be quite intolerable to prohibit unofficial strike action unless those who desired to strike had, as an alternative right, recourse to the National Arbitration Tribunal'.[31]

This brought Shawcross to his second question, which was his own role in the enforcement of the law, a role which he said was exercised 'concurrently with the Minister of Labour', and one which he insisted the Attorney General should retain: 'the occasional device of giving a Minister or someone else an exclusive power to prosecute is undesirable'.[32] Although he had 'on many occasions refrained from prosecuting' in deference to the opinion of his colleagues that prosecution would prejudice an expected settlement by negotiation, and sometimes for technical reasons,[33] Shawcross clearly remained of the view that so long as the law was on the books, he had a duty to enforce it. This was not to say that he was in favour of the criminal law being deployed in industrial relations, arguing that if it was to be used, then he 'would prefer to see a completely revised system of national arbitration capable of regular enforcement'. But even with changes of this kind, he continued, 'the criminal law as a method of preventing strikes will remain at best an uncertain, uneven, and risky weapon'.[34] Alternatively, 'but no doubt less efficaciously', he would have preferred to see 'a law delaying strike action either by the necessity of giving notice terminating the contract of employment', or 'by a secret postal ballot'.

Shawcross thus conceded that the use 'of the criminal law may all too easily bring about the opposite to the desired result; there may be a widespread extension of the strike, those prosecuted tend to be represented as martyrs and antagonism is caused against the law and the police'.[35] But while the criminal law remained in force and although he had a discretion on whether to prosecute, Shawcross railed against demands that he be deflected by political considerations in exercising that discretion. In an interesting passage which reveals a desire to push back against the pressure to which he appears to have been under in order not to prosecute, Shawcross said clearly with recent disputes in mind:

> [T]he implications of the present Order are not always understood, and it is sometimes considered that, in deciding whether or not to prosecute, the Law Officers should have regard to considerations to which (however attractive they may be politically) the Law Officers must in truth always close their eyes. Thus the fact that a prosecution in relation to a strike arising out of a refusal of Trade Unionists to work alongside non-Unionists might cause concern in Trade Union circles is one which, as the Lord Chancellor pointed out, I am constitutionally bound to ignore.[36] So also the suggestion that before prosecuting for alleged intimidation I would doubtless satisfy myself that the action had not been with the knowledge and approval of the Trade Union since action which is otherwise a breach of the criminal law is not the less so because approved by a Trade Union.[37] Equally misconceived is the argument recorded in

[31] TNA, CAB 129/44/9 ('The Future of the Conditions of Employment and National Arbitration Order', Memorandum by the Attorney General, 11 January 1951), para 2.
[32] ibid para 2(iv).
[33] ibid.
[34] ibid para 3.
[35] ibid.
[36] This is reference to a discussion at TNA, CAB 128/18/43 (Cabinet Conclusions, 7 December 1950).
[37] This is reference to a discussion at TNA, CAB 128/18/44 (Cabinet Conclusions, 11 December 1950).

> the same Minute that there would be 'misunderstanding if criminal proceedings were taken in respect of a dispute which had already been referred to arbitration' since the very object of the Order is to prohibit strike action whilst matters are the subject of arbitration and the only sanction for the system of compulsory arbitration which the Order establishes is that of criminal prosecution.[38]

These comments simply reflect the extent to which Shawcross felt that his independence had been compromised by yielding to political pressure on grounds to which he ought to have closed his ears.

Shawcross' third question followed naturally from his 'embarrassment' in having to enforce the criminal law against trade unionists,[39] the Attorney General accepting that it would be implausible to revoke Order 1305. Even though he would 'gladly see it removed', Shawcross accepted that Order 1305 had to be retained for the extraordinary reason that it was necessary to deal with the Communist Party, despite the fact that it applied only to 'trade' disputes:

> I realise that the revocation of the Order would not only put an end to a system of arbitration which has been generally most useful, but might also be politically unwise at the present time. The danger of strike action being used for political or subversive ends has, I suppose, much increased since we repealed the Trades Disputes Act 1927 five years ago. It is, however, in practice most difficult to obtain evidence that a strike is a seditious conspiracy, and if the present Order were repealed there would, apart from the limited sanction under the Conspiracy and Protection of Property Act 1875, be no provision in the criminal law effective to prohibit strikes in aid of political objectives. Whether requested or not by one side or the other of industry, I think it would be difficult now to revoke the Order completely.[40]

In terms of possible reforms, Shawcross canvassed the option of a fine rather than imprisonment for breach of the Order, with 'a daily penalty of £1, so long as the strike continued, recoverable at the suit of the individual employer against each striker, or by each locked out worker against his employer, as the case may be'. But although this odd proposal would take enforcement outside the realm of the criminal law, it was likely to be opposed by employers 'who much prefer the opprobrium for enforcement action to lie on the shoulders of the Government or the Attorney-General'.[41]

Otherwise, Shawcross strongly opposed Isaacs' suggestion to restrict standing to report disputes to 'established organisations habitually taking part in collective negotiations and acting through their Headquarters': 'If the prohibition on strike action were left as it is, this would impose an intolerable limitation on the right of individuals to strike.' On the other hand, if the prohibition on strike action 'was to be removed' (meaning presumably for those who would be excluded from the right or duty to report disputes), 'this would encourage unofficial strikes which are exactly the ones against which the Order should be directed'.[42] As for Isaacs' belief that strikes relating to recognition and the closed shop were outside the embrace of Order 1305, Shawcross appeared

[38] 'The Future of the Conditions of Employment and National Arbitration Order', Memorandum by the Attorney General, 11 January 1951), para 4.
[39] ibid para 5.
[40] ibid.
[41] ibid para 6.
[42] ibid.

to contradict him (at least in relation to recognition disputes): 'In general, as the law now stands such disputes are clearly within the Order.'[43] However, Shawcross had no comment to make on whether these or closed shop disputes should be excluded, though he acknowledged the Ministry of Labour's view that 'the National Arbitration Tribunal does not consider that it can usefully decide them'.[44] But as it happens, Isaacs' understanding of the law was to be revealed by the Kemsley Newspapers' case as having been correct.[45]

In the penultimate paragraph of his Memorandum, Shawcross dwelt on his often expressed distaste for invoking the criminal law against strikers and his preference for discouraging strikes through civil actions brought by employers. If the matter had not been complicated 'by the present facts of the international situation which may make any action difficult', he would have suggested that 'permanent legislation should be undertaken establishing a system of national arbitration on a peace-time basis, rather than as a hangover of war-time regulations'.[46] Under the Shawcross plans, the revised legislation would have 'prohibited strike or lockout action *until* the arbitration machinery had run its course (not absolutely as at present)'.[47] The penalty would be a civil one, 'recoverable summarily at the suit of the employers or workmen, with a right in the employers or workmen and perhaps also in the Attorney-General to go to the Court and secure an injunction against strike or lockout action in advance of the arbitrator's award'. In the case of action by the Attorney-General, legal proceedings would be possible 'only if it was in the interest of the community generally that such an injunction be granted'. According to Shawcross, such a power already existed, 'but is attended by such difficulties and doubts that it has fallen into desuetude'.[48]

IV. The Cabinet's Response

The Isaacs and Shawcross memorandums reveal that there was no squeamishness about using the law to deal with collective bargaining disputes or strikes. Indeed, the debate between the pair was not about whether there should be a role for the law, but what that role should be. Although the differences between them were important, they were in some respects nevertheless quite narrow. Both started from the position that there should be a strong role for the state in dispute resolution, and both were reluctant, at least for the time being, to remove rather than revise the restraints on strikes. The main divisions dealt with how the existing arrangements could be made to work more effectively. Specifically, these related mainly to the right of individual workers and unofficial groups of trade unionists to have access to arbitration, and whether the Minister had

[43] ibid.
[44] ibid.
[45] *R v Minister of Labour and National Service, ex parte Manning* (1951) Sol J 238. See p 240 below.
[46] TNA, CAB 129/44/9 ('The Future of the Conditions of Employment and National Arbitration Order', Memorandum by the Attorney General, 11 January 1951), para 7.
[47] This suggests intentionally or otherwise a complete ban on the right to strike, if all disputes were to go to arbitration and if arbitration awards were binding.
[48] TNA, CAB 129/44/9 ('The Future of the Conditions of Employment and National Arbitration Order', Memorandum by the Attorney General, 11 January 1951), para 7.

a discretion to refuse to refer unresolved disputes to arbitration. These questions were closely intertwined and posed a real dilemma for the Ministry of Labour, which was determined not to empower individuals or unofficial groups by allowing them access to arbitration, but was just as determined to restrain unofficial strikes particularly in light of recent experience.

What is notable, however, is the acceptance that restrictions on strikes should continue to operate via the criminal law, with only Shawcross presenting (what were hastily composed) proposals for the use of civil remedies, which would be tied – it seems – to a new statutory regime for compulsory arbitration. The continuing focus on the criminal law perhaps reflected Shawcross' earlier suggestion that employers understandably preferred the State to do their dirty work,[49] though it will not have been overlooked that the employers in the BOAC dispute appear to have been willing to sue strikers for damages,[50] as Shawcross had advocated in his many memorandums. Absent from the discussion, however, was any reference to the other common law powers of employers, which may reflect a sense that the tort dragon had been slain by the Trade Disputes Act 1906, the *Crofter* case in 1942, and the Trade Disputes and Trade Unions Act 1946.[51] To this end, it is striking that the industrial action during the period of the Attlee government produced only one reported piece of tort-based litigation at the suit of an employer, this being the injunction sought by the ship owners to prevent the occupation of the *Beaverbrae* in the Canadian seafarers' dispute of 1949.[52]

The memorandums of the two protagonists were considered by the Cabinet on 15 January 1951.[53] Introducing the agenda item on industrial disputes to his colleagues, the Cabinet Conclusions reveal that Isaacs focused exclusively on the arbitration provisions of Order 1305 and was doing his best to avoid confessing that he and his officials had misinterpreted the provisions of the Order:

> [T]he administration of this Order had run smoothly until recently, when a number of difficulties had been raised about its interpretation. First, it now appeared that if the Minister, for good cause, postponed a reference to the National Arbitration Tribunal beyond the twenty-one days prescribed in the Order, the prohibition on a strike or lock-out lapsed; secondly, it was not clear whether it was mandatory on the Minister to refer to the Tribunal all cases in which there was a failure to reach a settlement by other means: and thirdly, if reference to the Tribunal was mandatory, it was not clear whether the Minister must act even where the workers who were party to the dispute were an unofficial body acting against the wishes of their trade union executive.[54]

As anticipated by his Memorandum of 10 January, Isaacs added that he had arranged for a meeting of the NJAC's Joint Consultative Committee to be held on 24th January, 'with a view to placing before them the problems which had arisen in the interpretation of the Order and ascertaining their views on the form which it should take in the future'.[55]

[49] ibid para 6.
[50] See p 204 above.
[51] *Crofter Hand Woven Harris Tweed Co Ltd v Veitch* 1942 SC (HL) 1: 'The right of workmen to strike is an essential element in the principle of collective bargaining' (Lord Wright).
[52] *Canadian Pacific Railway v Gaud* [1949] 2 KB 239. The dispute was one to which Order 1305 did not apply, as Shawcross pointed out in his 11 January memorandum. On the dispute, see pp 73–74 above.
[53] TNA, CAB 128/19/3 (Cabinet Conclusions, 15 January 1951).
[54] ibid.
[55] ibid.

According to the Conclusions, Isaacs repeated his concern that 'unless agreement was reached between the two sides of industry on the form in which the Order should continue in force, a motion for its revocation might be carried at the next meeting of the Trades Union Congress'.[56] There was no enthusiasm amongst other ministers for revocation or for the position to change drastically. According to the Cabinet Secretary's Notebook,[57] the Chancellor of the Exchequer, Hugh Gaitskill, argued that Order 1305 should not be revoked at present; the Minister of Health, Aneurin Bevan, was in favour of postponing consideration because of the international situation; and the Colonial Secretary, Jim Griffith, thought it desirable to keep going with Order 1305 in some form.[58] Griffith was particularly concerned by the Kemsley Newspapers' case and the possibility that 'unofficial communist leaders are enabled to get [disputes] to arbitration'.[59] He was also concerned that if the groups of unofficial workers were permitted to use Order 1305, the TUC would withdraw its support, and the government would be obliged to revoke it in line with undertakings previously given in 1945 when Order 1305 was retained.

Cabinet Discussion on the Future of Order 1305

The political sensitivity around Order 1305, as revealed in the full account of the discussion on 15 January recorded in the Cabinet Secretary's Notebook, is of interest:

AttG [Not heard]

HG Shd, not revoke at present. Amendment I favour only (b).[60]

AB P'pone consideration until we know implicns of n armament.

JG Desirable to keep Order going in some form. Easy for Comm leadership to get men out. If Kemsley decision enables them to use it – TUC will decide next time that Order shd go. And M/L still pledged to end it, if one side asks for its revocation. ie if held that M/L has no discretion and unoffl comm leaders are enable to get to arbitn (?).

GAI Wd like to canvass views on JCC – especially if we prefer to delay final decision.

PM Throw it open: or put proposals?

GAI Throw it open for general discussion.

AttG On 3 (c) in M/L memo.[61] Is it meant that prohibn of unoffl strikes to continue. Diff to forbid them to go to arbitn and at same time to prohibit them to strike.

GAI Diff: for don't want Order swamped by multitude of small applicns. Want TU views on that question.

Agreed: get general views of JC

[Exit LO's].

[56] ibid.

[57] TNA, CAB 195/8/57 (Cabinet Secretary's Notebook, 15 January 1951).

[58] ibid.

[59] ibid.

[60] This was option (b) presented in Isaacs' memorandum of 10 January: 'providing that the penalty for an offence against the strike and lock out provisions should be a fine only'.

[61] This was the reference to 'excluding from the scope of the Order, disputes relating to recognition or non-unionism'.

Note: the personnel in question in descending order were Shawcross, Gaitskell, Bevan, Griffith, Isaacs, Attlee, Isaacs, Shawcross, and Isaacs. LO's were the Law Officers, Shawcross and Wheatley (Lord Advocate) present for this item only.

Source: TNA, CAB 195/8/57 (Cabinet Secretary's Notebook, 15 January 1951).

These and other points are captured in the formal Cabinet Conclusions, which reinforce the concern to proceed cautiously and to reform rather than revoke. The latter reveal – perhaps more so than the informal record – the Cabinet to be preoccupied with finding a solution that would not require the Minister to refer unofficial disputes to arbitration procedures, without confronting the problem of how the problem of unofficial action might otherwise be addressed. They also suggest as a result that Shawcross was winning the argument on the need for the Minister of Labour to retain discretionary powers of referral as one way of ensuring that unofficial disputes were kept away from the NAT:

> The dispute between Kemsley Newspapers and certain chapels of the National Union of Journalists raised the question whether the Minister of Labour was entitled to refuse to refer to the National Arbitration Tribunal grievances of an indefinite character, which were being pressed against the advice of the National Executive Committee of the National Union of Journalists. If the Minister of Labour was not prepared to argue, in the legal action now before the Courts, that the Order gave him a discretion whether or not to refer a dispute to the Tribunal, the only point at issue would be whether the dispute amounted to a trade dispute within the meaning of the Order. If the case went against the Minister and the Order was not amended, the law might play into the hands of the Communists who could foment unofficial disputes and demand that the Minister should refer them to the Tribunal. If such a state of affairs developed, the Trades Union Congress would almost certainly ask for the revocation of the Order; and it had been understood from the beginning that, if either side made such a demand, the Order would not be continued in force. There would be difficulties in amending the Order to provide that only disputes recognised by a trade union could be reported under it, but these difficulties would have to be examined if the Kemsley case went against the Minister.[62]

It was also thought that 'if the Order were to be amended by general agreement, it would be desirable to make it clear that the dispute between certain boroughs and their Town Clerks did not fall within its scope'.[63]

Underlining the message that they were not ready for radical changes to Order 1305 or the regime it created, Ministers decided that further consideration should be postponed until Isaacs had the chance to speak to the Joint Consultative Council on 24 January 'about the difficulties which had arisen in the administration of [Order 1305]'.[64] It was also agreed that, in the light of that discussion and of the imminent decision in the Kemsley Newspapers' case, 'the Cabinet should consider at a later date whether, and if so in what respects, the Order might be amended'.[65] In the course of the meeting, however, Shawcross once again made the point that it was difficult to justify prohibiting

[62] TNA, CAB 128/19/3 (Cabinet Conclusions, 15 January 1951).
[63] ibid.
[64] ibid.
[65] ibid.

unofficial strikes while also denying workers the right to have grievances dealt with by arbitration.[66] Further underlining ministerial caution and the absence of any principled objection on the part of others to existing arrangements, the Conclusions nevertheless record that 'it would be undesirable to delete the provisions of the Order relating to the prohibition of strikes and lock-outs; but it might be useful to provide that breach of the Order should be punishable only by a fine, and not by imprisonment, and to exclude from its scope disputes relating to recognition or non-unionism'.[67]

The Attorney General's role in exposing the hypocrisy of workers risking prosecution by taking strike action in the course of disputes that the Ministry of Labour would not permit to be reported or referred to arbitration is as surprising as it is commendable. Surprising because perhaps more than any other person in the Attlee government, Shawcross identified unofficial action with Communist instigation, and had spent several years looking for evidence with which to pursue the activists in question, as we have seen above. However, it would be a mistake to be too effusive in our praise of the Attorney General, who despite his simultaneously thoughtful and spikey memorandum of 11 January was reported as having said that now was not the time to make any such 'major alteration', being disposed to conclude that, for the present, the Order should continue to be in force 'more or less in its existing form'.[68] Perhaps the key passage in his Memorandum was the observation that if Order 1305 were revoked, there would be no adequate provision in the criminal law 'effective to prohibit strikes in aid of political objectives', following the repeal of the Trade Disputes and Trade Unions Act 1927.[69] That said, Order 1305 should have had no application to such strikes.

V. Isaacs Resigns

On the same day as the Cabinet meeting on 15 January, Isaacs wrote to Shawcross as part of the preparations for the Kemsley Newspapers' case.[70] Isaacs now appeared to accept that there were legal concerns under Order 1305, the impact of which he was keen to minimise. The main purpose of the letter was to consider the 'discretion to refer' point which was likely to arise in the litigation, and whether the case should be defended on the ground that he acted lawfully in refusing to refer the full matter to the NAT. In his letter to Shawcross, Isaacs stated that he had first encountered the argument that the Order afforded him 'discretion to refer' in the advice the Attorney General had given him in the Town Clerks' case (though the record shows that the matter had been considered earlier, during the Kemsley Newspapers' exchanges).[71] Making clear that the advice was unwelcome, Isaacs repeated his understanding that he had an obligation to refer disputes *not settled by other means* to the NAT, adding

[66] ibid.

[67] ibid.

[68] ibid.

[69] TNA, CAB 129/44/9 ('The Future of the Conditions of Employment and National Arbitration Order', Memorandum by the Attorney General, 11 January 1951), para 5.

[70] TNA, LAB 10/1006 ('Conditions of Employment and National Arbitration Order SR&O, 1940 No 1305. Proposed Amendment of the Order') (letter from Isaacs to Shawcross, 15 January 1951).

[71] See p 215 above.

that only when he judged that there was no trade dispute within the meaning of the Order would he decline to refer the matter on.[72] This perhaps reflected further misunderstanding. If there was not a trade dispute, there would arguably be no power to accept the reported case in the first place. It would be a dispute of a kind to which Order 1305 did not apply.

Isaacs referred to the fact that in the Kemsley Newspapers' case, he had taken the view that only one of the matters reported by the chapels could be said to be a trade dispute within the terms of the Order and that considering himself bound to refer that dispute, he had done so. Whatever his motives for making that referral,[73] this would incidentally appear to indicate that he had now accepted that he could not arbitrarily refuse to accept reports from unofficial sources. Indeed, it appears from a paper prepared for Isaacs on 12 January by five senior Ministry officials – which was to provide the basis of a letter to Shawcross – that Isaacs' long-held refusal to accept reports of disputes from unofficial sources was known to be unlawful. In the paper from officials, Isaacs was reminded that 'departmental advice to the Minister has always been that the Order applied to all trade disputes covered by the definition and the Minister could not and should not refrain from taking action simply because of the source of the report'.[74] The officials continued by saying that: 'Administratively we have always tried to secure that the Trade Union take charge and we have been successful up to now, but we would not resist the Attorney's view that it would be intolerable to prohibit strike action if access to the Tribunal was …'[75]

The final words of the sentence have been lost, but while the phrase 'Administratively we have always tried to secure that the Trade Union take charge' reads very like a qualified admission that officials had made it very difficult for individuals or unofficial groups to report trade disputes, it is safe to say that the Ministry long understood that if an unofficial group were denied access to binding arbitration, then they should not be denied the right to strike. However, the Ministry officials did not entirely take Shawcross' side. On the contrary, his grasp of the Order 1305 prosecution procedure was also challenged, with officials making the very pertinent point that while responsibility for initiating prosecution might rest with Shawcross, normally before cases were considered by the Attorney General and the DPP, they had first to be referred to them by the Ministry of Labour:

> Whilst the Attorney General may not have refrained from taking proceedings because of the numbers involved, the fact is that cases hitherto have not been referred to him out of consideration of the fact that we did not think the proceedings would be useful. [However, we] would not challenge his view that any cases brought to his notice would have to be decided strictly according to the legal position.[76]

[72] TNA, LAB 10/1006 ('Conditions of Employment and National Arbitration Order SR&O, 1940 No 1305. Proposed Amendment of the Order') (letter from Isaacs to Shawcross, 15 January 1951).

[73] See ch 11 above.

[74] TNA, LAB 10/1006 ('Conditions of Employment and National Arbitration Order SR&O, 1940 No 1305. Proposed Amendment of the Order') (paper by Sir Guildhaume Myrrdin-Evans, 12 January 1951). The contents were agreed with four other senior Ministry officials. Sir Guildhaume Myrrdin-Evans was by now Deputy Secretary in the Ministry of Labour.

[75] ibid.

[76] ibid.

This is the reality to which Shawcross himself may have been alluding when he referred (in his 11 January memorandum) to always having had 'a responsibility (concurrently with the Minister of Labour) for enforcing the Order'.[77] Nevertheless, as Chapters Seven to Ten make clear, Shawcross did not wait for cases to be referred by the Ministry of Labour, and was perfectly content to take the initiative, particularly in cases where Order 1305 was being used as an offence against the state.

So although it was beginning to appear that Isaacs could not refuse to accept reports from unofficial sources (as was the situation in the Kemsley Newspapers' case, where the reporting of the dispute was opposed by the NUJ),[78] the main point of Isaacs' letter was to emphasise to Shawcross that he had no desire to have any discretion over whether to refer on for dispute resolution a trade dispute that had been lawfully reported and accepted. He told the Attorney General that while the application for mandamus should be resisted, it should not be on the ground that the Minster of Labour has a discretion to decline to refer reported trade disputes not settled by other means to the NAT. He explained that:

> [P]icking and choosing between what I would do for different types of people reporting disputes to me would cause criticism and controversy, and would, I think, tend to bring the administration of the Order, and ultimately the Order itself into disrepute.[79]

As we have seen, the Attorney General seemed slightly bemused by Isaacs' position on the discretion point, given that he 'had always understood that the Minister desired to retain a discretion and I have, *on this understanding*, advised him that it is possible to argue that the Order gives him the right so to do *although I think this doubtful*'.[80] In view of the position that had been taken by Shawcross hitherto, the last words in added italics are equally extraordinary.

Isaacs was not around when the Kemsley Newspapers' case was argued in court a few months later. The Cabinet meeting on 18 January 1951 was to be his last. 'Feeling the need for some relaxation' after five years in the job, he claimed subsequently that he had asked to be relieved of his duties, and was appointed to the less exacting role of Minister for Pensions, which did not carry with it a seat in the Cabinet.[81] It is not clear to what extent Order 1305 and the dispute with Shawcross contributed to his fatigue. Nor is it clear whether he fell on his sword as a direct result of the mismanagement of Order 1305

[77] TNA, CAB 129/44/9 ('The Future of the Conditions of Employment and National Arbitration Order', Memorandum by the Attorney General, 11 January 1951), para 2(iv).

[78] See TNA, CAB 129/43/63 ('Conditions of Employment and National Arbitration Order; Dispute between Kemsley Newspapers Limited and Members of the 'Daily Graphic' and Kemsley Newspapers (London) Chapels of the National Union of Journalists: Memorandum by the Minister of Labour and National Service', 13 December 1950), para 5.

[79] TNA, LAB 10/1006 ('Conditions of Employment and National Arbitration Order SR&O, 1940 No 1305. Proposed Amendment of the Order') (letter from Isaacs to Shawcross, 15 January 1951).

[80] TNA, CAB 129/44/9 ('The Future of the Conditions of Employment and National Arbitration Order', Memorandum by the Attorney General, 11 January 1951), para 2, emphasis in original.

[81] As he explained in his resignation letter: GG Eastwood, *George Isaacs: Printer, Trade-Union Leader, Cabinet Minister* (Odhams Press, London, 1952), p 198. We do not know if this was the real reason. But Isaacs – who had been the longest-serving Minister of Labour in the history of the office – appears to have been highly regarded by Attlee (and widely by others), who wrote an affectionate preface to his biography (ibid).

and his understandable desire to eschew legalism and elevate policy beyond the law. Whatever the explanation, Aneurin Bevan 'father of the NHS' and arguably the safest pair of hands in the Cabinet, became Minister of Labour. Perhaps reflecting the importance of Order 1305 at the time, Shawcross wrote to the new Minister on 19 January (only a day after Isaacs resigned) reminding him of the Kemsley Newspapers' case, explaining to Bevan that an order of mandamus was being sought.[82] He also explained that the two key points were whether or not a trade dispute had existed or was apprehended at the *Daily Graphic*, and whether or not the Minister was required to refer unresolved disputes to the NAT or whether he had a discretion not to do so.

According to Shawcross, the first point was of little importance ('could be left to a junior'), unlike the second, which was of considerable importance. He recalled that in the Town Clerks' cases, Isaacs had been advised that:

> It was arguable that under the terms of the Order the Minister did possess a discretion. I must say, however, that the more I think of the matter, the less attractive this argument becomes and I certainly do not wish to raise it … in the present case if, in fact, you prefer to have no discretion in the matter. Perhaps you would be good enough to let me know what your view is.[83]

Bevan told Shawcross in reply that 'the question of 'discretion' bristles with difficulties', and he agreed with his predecessor that the Minister's case 'should rest on the question of whether there is or is not a trade dispute',[84] despite what appeared to be the weight of ministerial opinion at the Cabinet meeting on 15 January.[85] Presumably Bevan was now representing the departmental line, having argued only a few weeks earlier when Minister of Health that the Town Clerks' cases raised issues which suggested that they ought not to be referred to the NAT. In doing so, Bevan had suggested not only the need for a discretion of the kind now being questioned by Shawcross, but also the grounds on which it might be exercised to refuse a reference in the Town Clerks' cases.[86]

Although there was much fumbling and stumbling about the discretion point, it is perhaps understandable that the Ministry's lawyers would be anxious about a power rather than a duty to refer unresolved disputes to the NAT. It would expose every failure to refer to the possibility of what is now called judicial review There is also the possibility that it would expose to challenge – particularly by employers – decisions to refer to arbitration.[87] That said, administrative law was not in the same state of development as it is today, and the Court of Appeal had obliged the government in the seminal *Wednesbury Corporation* decision in 1947 (albeit wholly unrelated to industrial relations and labour law) by making it clear that in the post-war era, the courts would not be

[82] TNA, LAB 10/1006 ('Conditions of Employment and National Arbitration Order SR&O, 1940 No 1305. Proposed Amendment of the Order') (letter from Shawcross to Bevan, 19 January 1951).

[83] ibid.

[84] TNA, LAB 10/980 ('Kemsley Newspapers Ltd and Joint Negotiating Committee of the Daily Graphic Chapel and Kemsley Newspapers (London) Chapel of the National Union of Journalists. Notice of Trade Dispute under SR&O 1305') (letter from Bevan to Shawcross, 30 January 1951).

[85] See p 235 above.

[86] See p 221 above.

[87] See *R v National Arbitration Tribunal, ex parte Midgley Harmer Ltd* [1947] 1 All ER 196; and *R v National Arbitration Tribunal, ex parte Crowther* [1948] 1 KB 424.

too aggressive in questioning the vastly expanding governmental powers across a wide range of social and economic activity.[88] Nevertheless, Ministry lawyers would have been mindful of the dangers of judicial intervention, and it is clear from Isaacs' response to the Society of Town Clerks that this was something he was keen to avoid. But they need not have worried. Kemsley Newspapers proved to be a massive anti-climax, the High Court holding that there was no trade dispute.[89]

By the time the case reached the High Court, the nature of the dispute had become clearer, relating to an alleged breach of a recognition and procedure agreement between the company and the NUJ chapel 'to facilitate discussions between the management and the editorial staffs employed at Kemsley House on matters in which either or both of the editorial chapels were concerned'.[90] More specifically, the dispute related to an allegation that management had gone behind the procedure in one case and dealt directly with an individual employee rather than with the chapel, a similar problem some 40 years or so later subsequently giving rise to another seminal dispute.[91] According to the chapel in the Kemsley Newspapers' dispute, this was a trade dispute, which had been reported to the Minister, who had refused to take any steps to deal with it. In seeking mandamus to compel the Minister to consider the reference, it is not clear how the applicants anticipated the dispute being resolved by the NAT, which presumably is where they wanted it to go. But in agreeing with the Minister that this was not a trade dispute, the Lord Chief Justice (Lord Goddard) said that it was 'merely a dispute relating to the procedure which had been designed to prevent trade disputes from arising'.[92] As a result, it was not necessary to address the critical question of minister's powers, which as pointed out in Chapter Eleven was a problem never resolved until Order 1305 was revoked and replaced later in 1951.

[88] *Associated Provincial Picture Houses Ltd v Wednesbury Corporation* [1948] 1 KB 223. See J Griffith, *Judicial Politics since 1920* (Blackwell, Oxford, 1993), pp 48–64 on the role of post-war judges, and Lord Greene MR in particular.

[89] *R v Minister of Labour and National Service, ex parte Manning* (n 45). Geoffrey Bing KC and Mark Smith appeared for the applicants, the future Lord Diplock for Kemsley Newspapers, and Shawcross for the Ministry of Labour. For a discussion of some of the wider issues raised by the case, see C Schmitthoff, 'The Growing Ambit of the Common Law' (1951) 29 *Canadian Bar Review* 469. For the full transcript, see TNA, LAB 10/980 ('Kemsley Newspapers Ltd and Joint Negotiating Committee of the Daily Graphic Chapel and Kemsley Newspapers (London) Chapel of the National Union of Journalists. Notice of Trade Dispute under SR&O 1305') (R v Minister of Labour and National Service, ex parte James Lionel Manning and Gerald John Byrne (from the shorthand notes of WB Gurney, Sons & Funnell, 55 Victoria Street, Westminster, SW1)).

[90] *R v Minister of Labour and National Service, ex parte Manning* (n 45). The issue is not without contemporary significance and reinforces the view that trade union recognition legislation remains necessary even under a system of sectoral collective bargaining and the extension of recognised terms and conditions of employment as in Order 1305, Part III and subsequent measures which included the Employment Protection Act 1975, s 98, Sch 11. The 1975 Act notably also contained a trade union recognition procedure, albeit one that was inadequate. See Ewing (n 14). Admittedly, the judicial review process was much more intrusive in the 1970s than in the 1940s.

[91] See *Wilson and Palmer v United Kingdom* [2002] ECHR 552, (2022) 35 EHRR 20 in a very different legal climate from that in which *R v Minister of Labour and National Service, ex parte Manning* (n 45) was decided.

[92] ibid. Contrast the Privy Council decision in *Beetham v Trinidad Cement Ltd* [1960] AC 132 about a recognition dispute on a similar definition of trade dispute, albeit under different legislation some eight years later. The modern definition of a trade dispute applies to 'machinery for negotiation or consultation, and other procedures, relating to any of the foregoing matters, including the recognition by employers or employers' associations of the right of a trade union to represent workers in any such negotiation or consultation or in the carrying out of such procedures'. See Trade Union and Labour Relations (Consolidation) Act 1992, ss 218, 244.

VI. Conclusion

Despite various issues having been raised at the Cabinet meeting on 15 January, everything remained at large pending the outcome of the Kemsley Newspapers' case, ministers preferring that Order 1305 should be retained for the time being in one form or another, with or without amendments. In the end, Kemsley Newspapers was inconclusive on one of the major issues, with the result that the government would operate as if the Minister was required to refer disputes to arbitration, subject to cases which were truly exceptional, such as those arising in the Town Clerks' cases.[93] And until it was challenged in the courts or elsewhere, the Ministry also remained free in practice to continue to restrict the operation of Order 1305 to official disputes, and to continue as a result to refuse to accept unofficial disputes, thereby ensuring that participation in such action would be an offence, even though the practice of refusing to accept such disputes had been recognised by officials for some time to be unlawful. However, the problems left unresolved would be problems for someone else to sort out. Aneurin Bevan resigned from the government on 23 April in protest about prescription charges, replaced by the inexperienced Alf Robens, upon whom fell the responsibility for the future of Order 1305. Harold Wilson also resigned from the government, to be replaced by Sir Hartley Shawcross as President of the Board of Trade.

If collective paralysis because of Kemsley Newspapers was one notable feature of the ministerial debates about Order 1305 between 10 and 15 January 1951, another was the inadequate analysis of the gas workers' case. Although it was referred to by Isaacs,[94] there is no attempt to assess its implications or the lessons to be learned from the prosecution, other than to propose a fine rather than imprisonment for breach of the strike and lock-out provisions. Given the Ministry of Labour's desire to retain the law in one form or another, this was disappointing, as was the lack of effort to address the underlying problems that made the future of Order 1305 in its original form now unsustainable. Why was it that workers felt the need to take unofficial action? What was wrong with the industrial relations system that worker concerns could not be addressed by collective bargaining procedures and compulsory arbitration? How could these problems be resolved? It was not until the 1960s that these questions would seriously be addressed by a royal commission chaired by Lord Donovan.[95] Yet despite the wishes of ministers to the contrary, by now it was probably too late to save Order 1305, its fate about to be sealed by its clumsy use by Shawcross before his elevation to the Board of Trade and a seat in the Cabinet. The occasion was the ongoing saga between the Labour government and the nation's dock workers.

[93] Paradoxically, the Town Clerks' case was eventually referred by the Minister to the NAT following the report to the Minister by the Society of Town Clerks of a dispute between the Town Clerk of South Shields and the South Shields Corporation. See *R v National Arbitration Tribunal, ex parte South Shields Corporation* [1952] 1 KB 46.

[94] TNA, CAB 129/44/8 ('The Future of the Conditions of Employment and National Service Arbitration Order', Memorandum by the Minister of Labour and National Service, 10 January 1951), para 4.

[95] See Royal Commission on Trade Unions and Employers' Associations, 1965–68, Report, Cmnd 3623, 1968.

13

Prosecuting the Port Workers' Committee

The Trial Collapses

I. Introduction

Shawcross now had his tail up and seemed to assume responsibility for determining whether all strikes – 'Communist-inspired' or not – were to end up in prosecution. A man of many memorandums as well as contradictions, Shawcross' memorandum of 11 January 1951 appears to have been designed in part to prepare his colleagues for a robust application of the criminal law, which until he had recently brought it to bear on the gas workers, had not been used in the five years he had been Attorney General. Whether ministers were entirely convinced about the sympathy he professed to feel for their likely embarrassment at the renewal of such prosecutions, or his claim that he would be happy to see the Order withdrawn, is unknown.[1] Nevertheless, the highly talented but controversial law officer prevailed over George Isaacs and officials at the Ministry of Labour, and in the course of doing so had won over the Cabinet. A fortnight after the Cabinet meeting on 15 January 1951, Shawcross was given an opportunity to win over the House of Commons in an Adjournment Debate in which he provided a seminal statement about the role of the Attorney General, with specific reference to the prosecution of strikers.

As we saw in Chapter Eight, Sir Frank Newsam had created a new framework for cooperation between F3 Division at the Home Office, Special Branch and MI5, with a view to closing down the Port Workers' Committees in order to stop disorder in the ports. This was done it seems in the belief that the hidden hand of the Communist Party was behind the troubles on the waterfront. Indeed, it is only on that basis that the involvement of the Security Service could be justified. As we discussed earlier, however, the discontent in the docks had deep industrial roots grounded in what were perceived to be poor working conditions and inadequate rewards for very heavy and physically demanding work. The failure to address these concerns adequately led to fresh unofficial strike action in 1951. Although much more muted than in 1949, the action nevertheless provided the government with the opportunity to pursue its vendetta against key activists who were assumed to be in the vanguard of the unrest. However, the prosecution of

[1] TNA, CAB 129 /44/9 ('The Future of the Conditions of Employment and National Arbitration Order 1940', Memorandum by the Attorney General, 11 January 1951).

the PWC leadership was to lead to a major humiliation for Shawcross on the eve of his re-shuffling to the Board of Trade almost immediately thereafter, it seems for reasons unconnected with the dockers' case.

II. Shawcross Prepares for Prosecution

It will be recalled that the TGWU National Docks Delegate Conference in 1945 adopted a programme for the improvement of working conditions in the ports as the official policy of the union.[2] The aims of what was subsequently referred to as the Dockers' Charter included a wage of twenty-five shillings a day, two weeks' paid holiday, payment for statutory holidays, a reduction in the working week to 40 hours and a pension for retired workers. By the summer of 1950, dock workers were still being paid nineteen shillings a day, about which Shawcross accepted there was 'a great deal of discontent'.[3] On 22 January 1951, the workers' side of National Joint Industrial Council for the Port Transport Industry (NJIC) – which was the 'recognised constitutional machinery for settling wage claims' – decided to recommend a deal which included an increase of two shillings a day.[4] Critically, however, there was a much greater increase for workers engaged on piece rates, which accounted for about 90 per cent of the workforce.[5] A conference of union delegates from the docks voted on 1 February to accept the recommendation and an agreement was duly concluded between the employers' side and the trade union side on the NJIC.

Following the introduction of Newsam's surveillance programme in September 1950, Special Branch was presumably picking up disquiet about the settlement among rank-and-file trade unionists on Merseyside, where the workforce was 'not piece work minded',[6] so that the agreement was much less attractive as a result. With this in mind, it is surely no coincidence that two days before the conference of union delegates – the outcome of which is likely to have been expected to be a foregone conclusion – Shawcross was invited to make a statement to Parliament, ostensibly about the role of the Attorney General, but more probably to warn against unofficial action in the ports in the aftermath of the pay deal having being sealed. The occasion was an Adjournment Debate initiated by Lynn Ungoed-Thomas, Labour MP for Leicester North East,[7] who sought to obtain from the Attorney General 'as comprehensive a statement as possible with regard to his responsibility for prosecutions', adding that, with recent industrial action clearly

[2] See p 119 above.

[3] *The Times*, 10 April 1951 (Sir Hartley Shawcross, opening the prosecution of seven dockers).

[4] ibid.

[5] *The Times*, 16 February 1951.

[6] ibid.

[7] Between 1945 and 1950, Ungoed-Thomas had been MP for Llanduff and Barry before the constituency was redistributed. He advised Shawcross in the Town Clerks' dispute discussed in ch 11 (Shawcross rejected his advice about the matter being a 'trade dispute'). See TNA, CAB 129/43/321 ('Legal Considerations Affecting Claims for Salary Increases by Town Clerks', Memorandum by the Attorney General, 18 December 1950). Having been returned at the 1950 election, Ungoed-Thomas was to become Solicitor General in April 1951. He later became a High Court judge, sitting notably in *Lawlor v Union of Post Office Workers* [1965] Ch 712. On Ungoed-Thomas, see H Shawcross, *Life Sentence* (Constable, London, 1995), pp 189–90.

in view, it is 'a matter that has created a great deal of confusion in the public mind and particularly with regard to quasi-political matters, such as illegal strikes'.[8]

The statement on 29 January was made at a time of criticism of the government – most notably in the *Daily Telegraph*, to whose tune it is surprising Shawcross felt the need to dance – for not invoking Order 1305 often enough and for not enforcing the law. He gave a bravura performance in response, definitively setting out the responsibilities of the Attorney General in prosecutions, to explain what is still current practice.[9] Even Reginald Manningham-Buller (a future Tory Attorney General and subsequently Lord Chancellor as Viscount Dilhorne) acknowledged that the statement made by Shawcross would 'put the position and, indeed, the duties of the Attorney-General beyond doubt and beyond dispute'.[10] MPs liked what they heard about the Attorney General occupying a quasi-judicial office and performing a quasi-judicial role, and that while he consulted colleagues, he did not take instructions from anyone. Although recognising the difficulties of using the criminal law against strikers in peace-time, Shawcross made it clear that he would not hesitate to prosecute in 'appropriate cases' and 'at the appropriate time', adding that 'the public cannot be held to ransom nor the law as it is at present be brought into complete disrepute'.[11]

Maintaining that he could not 'pretend to lay down in advance' any rules on which he should act in these matters, Shawcross was 'always loth to proceed against the rank and file in an industrial dispute where the real inciters and leaders have succeeded in covering up their activities'.[12] Nevertheless, it had not been possible to prosecute in the 1949 dock strike – it was not a trade dispute – nor in several others where he was about to intervene before the strike collapsed. In the gas strike, in contrast, Shawcross prosecuted 'because the public were being caused great inconvenience and hardship'. Moreover, the information available to him showed that 'whilst there was a pretence being made of urging strikers to return to work, the truth was that the Communists were anxious to see the strike continue'.[13] But although he would not – and indeed could not – prosecute in all cases, Shawcross made it clear that he had an 'unfettered discretion', that he would 'look at each case on its merits', and that he would prosecute when 'with a knowledge of all the circumstances, it seems in the public interest so to do'.[14]

If this was a warning, it was to fall on stony ground in Birkenhead, where dockers were unhappy with the settlement approved by union delegates on 1 February, voting at a dock gate meeting on the following day in favour of strike action, which they sought thereafter to extend to other ports on Merseyside and later London. They were voting to reject what Jack Dash described as a "spit-in-the-eye' wage increase',

[8] HC Debs, 29 January 1951, col 679.

[9] See *R (Corner House Research) v Director of the Serious Fraud Office* [2008] UKHL 60.

[10] HC Debs, 29 January 1951, col 690.

[11] ibid col 684. Here he was referring to a speech he had made on 6 October 1950 to which *The Times* and *The Daily Telegraph* had responded, the latter in most disobliging terms. For an account of the newspaper reports, see HC Debs 29 January 1951, col 679 (Lynn Ungoed-Thomas).

[12] ibid col 685.

[13] ibid.

[14] ibid cols 685–86. It was in the course of this speech that the Attorney General used the cover of parliamentary privilege to denounce Claude Berridge and Percy Glading, a practice which was adopted by ministers in the course of the next 15 years or so. See p 197 above.

negotiated by a team led by Arthur Deakin,[15] demanding the full implementation of the Dockers' Charter. By Monday 5 February, the matter had become sufficiently grave for a ministerial statement to be made to Parliament. However, Aneurin Bevan, the new Minister of Labour, reported that 'apart from Merseyside and Salford all ports are working normally', adding that 'on Merseyside, out of a total register of 18,000 about 8,100 are on strike'. By 'the efforts of the union' the strike had been contained, the union having 'prevented an extension of the stoppage to the other ports'.[16] But although contained, the Cabinet Emergencies Committee was told two days later that nearly all the dockers in Birkenhead and Salford, along with half of the Liverpool complement, were on strike.[17]

Not only that: 450 strikers at the Royal Docks in London were holding rallies and trying to persuade the rest of the 27,000 London dockers to join them.[18] This was clearly the opportunity Shawcross was waiting for, using the Cabinet Emergencies Committee meeting on 7 February as the occasion to consult his colleagues about whether to prosecute. In his Commons speech, the Attorney General had made clear that in deciding whether to prosecute, it was not enough that there was sufficient evidence of an offence; it was necessary also to consider whether prosecution was in the public interest. In acquainting himself of all relevant considerations, Shawcross explained that the Attorney General:

> may, although I do not think he is obliged to, consult with any of his colleagues in the Government; and indeed, as Lord Simon once said, he would in some cases be a fool if he did not. On the other hand, the assistance of his colleagues is confined to informing him of particular considerations which might affect his own decision, and does not consist, and must not consist, in telling him what that decision ought to be. The responsibility for the eventual decision rests with the Attorney-General, and he is not to be put, and is not put, under pressure by his colleagues.[19]

It should be noted that Shawcross is not saying that it would be good practice formally to consult the Cabinet, which he had done hitherto, only constantly to be rebuffed. Rather, he is saying, consistently with an earlier letter to Attlee dated 19 December 1950 and Attlee's response thereto,[20] that he might in certain circumstances consult his colleagues in the government. That was something altogether different: the Attorney General could choose who to consult, when to consult, and how to consult.

[15] J Dash, *Good Morning Brothers!* (Lawrence & Wishart, London, 1969), p 80. An altogether different account of the agreement was provided by Sir Colin Anderson of the National Association of Port Employers in *The Times*, 16 February 1951.

[16] HC Debs, 5 February 1951, col 1345.

[17] TNA, CAB 134/179 (Cabinet Emergencies Committee, 7 February 1951).

[18] ibid. In discussion, it was suggested that the strike was in effect being financed by PAYE tax rebates, a matter that Bevan said had been taken up with the Chancellor. This was an issue addressed by the Heath and Thatcher governments. See M Partington, 'Unemployment, Industrial Conflict and Social Security' (1980) 9 *ILJ* 243.

[19] HC Debs, 29 January 1951, cols 683–84.

[20] TNA, PREM 8/1538 ('1951 Strikes and Industrial Disputes') (Shawcross to Attlee, 19 December 1950, and Prime Minister's Personal Minute, M150/50, 21 December 1950). See ch 11 above.

The question of prosecution having been raised before the Cabinet Emergencies Committee, the record goes on to state that sufficient evidence was available to enable criminal proceedings to be brought – against some of the London dockers and those from Merseyside who were assisting them – on a charge of 'conspiring to incite others to strike'.[21] This is an altogether curious formulation, which revealed the purpose of the prosecution: it was the London dockers who were being asked to support the Merseyside dockers rather than the other way round, but it was the former who were the real targets of the prosecution. Although the Attorney General thought that 'it would be difficult to refrain from operating the ordinary processes of the law', he felt that he ought 'to seek the advice of the Committee on the question of public policy that might be involved by the institution of proceedings which was, of course, solely within his own discretion'.[22] The record continues:

> The general view of the committee was that it was difficult to assess the results which might follow the institution of proceedings. It was however, appreciated that it would be difficult to justify proceedings against gas workers and not dockers. There was, moreover, some indication that on this occasion the ringleaders had little support and to take action against them might weaken rather than strengthen their position with the rank and file. This was the first strike which had occurred since an attempt had been made by the PWC to co-ordinate the organisation of strike action at all major ports. The Attorney General said that he would await results of the meetings being held by the dockers later in the day before making a decision.[23]

The report does not tell us if the 'general view' was a unanimous view of the Committee or if there was hesitation on the part of any of its members. Nina Fishman has written that although he had been a member of the Cabinet Emergencies Committee, the new Minister of Labour opposed the prosecution, but that he was swayed by both the Home Secretary (Chuter Ede) and the Secretary of State for Scotland (Hector McNeill), who were strongly in favour.[24] According to Fishman, the latter pair argued that 'this was the moment to attack', as 'the inciters were on their knees and should be knocked out' – 'on their knees' presumably because they were failing to take the overwhelming majority of dockers with them. Thus although support on Merseyside and at Salford was strong, it was not solid, *The Times* reporting that 9,589 out of 16,090 Merseyside dockers were on strike, though all but 128 out of 2,505 were on strike at Salford.[25] It was also reported, however, that the strikes had 'failed to make an impression' on the 27,000 London dockers, despite the PWC's persistent attempts to bring them out. Their efforts to do so had to be abandoned, *The Times*' Labour correspondent noting that the PWC was in 'danger of becoming a laughing stock'.[26]

[21] TNA, CAB 134/179 (Cabinet Emergencies Committee, 7 February 1951).
[22] ibid.
[23] ibid.
[24] N Fishman, 'A Vital Element in British Industrial Relations: A Reassessment of Order 1305, 1940–51' (1999) 8 *Historical Studies in Industrial Relations* 43, at p 68. On this account, Bevan wrote subsequently to Shawcross two days later to express his opposition to the prosecution. For his part, Shawcross recollects an exchange with Bevan 'in the corridors' when the latter told him to 'go for them now', and cites Bessie Braddock as having claimed that Bevan subsequently lied about not supporting the prosecution: Shawcross (n 7) p 73.
[25] *The Times*, 8 February 1951.
[26] ibid.

III. Dock Workers Arrested

By coincidence, Thursday 8 February was Ministry of Labour questions in the House of Commons. As would be expected, Bevan was asked to comment on a wide range of issues including the industrial unrest, with Reginald Bevins, recently elected Tory MP for Liverpool Toxteth, inviting him to make a statement about 'the strike of dockers on Merseyside organised by the port workers' committee'.[27] Responding in the afternoon of 8 February, Bevan appeared to suggest that the problem was receding and that the strike was burning itself out. Thus, 'the position on Merseyside and at Manchester shows some improvement this morning and it is clear that the very extensive efforts to involve other ports have completely failed'.[28] As he spoke, however, plans were already afoot to arrest some of the organisers of the industrial unrest, Special Branch presumably having been tipped off that several Merseyside men had travelled or were travelling to London to meet representatives of the PWC. With the men under surveillance, it seems implausible that Bevan and Ministry officials would have been unaware that arrests were imminent when the parliamentary statement was made.

Arrest warrants issued by the Bow Street magistrate were executed on the evening of 8 February at a meeting between two Liverpool dockers and a group of about 12 members of the London PWC at the White Horse pub in Stepney. Six men were arrested, two from Liverpool and four from London, the latter including Harry Constable and Ted Dickens, both of whom we encountered in Chapter Seven and both of whom the government was clearly determined to convict. The arrests followed what appears to have been a delicate operation by Special Branch involving multiple methods of surveillance, including the use of interception and/or recording devices. Commander Burt of Special Branch is said to have told Guy Liddell on a visit to MI5:

> about his various exploits in connection with the arrest of members of the Dockworkers' Committee. He said that he had run considerable risks in obtaining information and asked whether we thought our various technical devices could assist him from time to time, since he realised that our equipment was probably far superior to his own.[29]

The impression is that Special Branch had sailed 'close to the wind'. We would expect nothing less.

The six were taken to Bow Street Police Station. A seventh arrest was made on Merseyside, 'Liverpool CID' confirming to *The Times* early on the following morning that 'a member of the Merseyside Port Workers' Committee had been detained and

[27] HC Debs, 8 February 1951, col 1913.

[28] ibid.

[29] TNA, KV4/473 (Liddell Diary, 15 February 1951). Liddell also recorded that he 'showed him the piece of tele-check on [redaction] which suggested that somebody had been leaking from Special Branch about the arrests'. In relation to locating the source of the 'leaks', Burt told Liddell that CID could not gain access to Special Branch files without his permission, or the permission of Thompson, his second in command, but also that there were 200 men in the Metropolitan Police Special Branch and 'he could not be certain of the loyalty of every one'. Burt concluded that he would have to look into the possibility of implementing the 'Y Box' system employed in the Security Service Registry. Certain files with particularly sensitive information were categorised as 'yellow files'. Access to these files was tightly restricted. Liddell recorded that Burt 'intended to look into this matter, with particular reference to his recent operations in connection with the Dockworkers' Committee'.

was being taken to London'.[30] All seven now in custody, they were brought before the Bow Street magistrate, Mr Bertram Reece, on 9 February, where they were charged with having between 8 October and 6 February conspired with others unknown to incite dock workers to take part in strikes in connection with trade disputes, contrary to Order 1305, Article 4.[31] If nothing else, the arrests did something which the Birkenhead dockers had failed to do, which was to arouse a significant body of London dockers, leading to strike action in support of those who had been arrested. It was reported that on the following day (10 February), more than 6,700 London dockers joined the 11,500 strikers in the north-west, with an estimated 300 of the former making their way to Bow Street Magistrates' Court. Some 50 of their number were allowed inside, the rest waiting in the rain 'for nearly two hours until the proceedings ended',[32] the defendants being greeted by an approving crowd following their release on bail.

However, the strike action by the London dockers was not undertaken for the same reasons as the strike that led to the prosecutions. Rather, their action was a protest against the arrests and the prosecutions: for some no doubt a challenge to the 'rule of law'. It is clear nevertheless that passions ran high. According to a press report of a London dockers' meeting held on the eve of the subsequent committal proceedings:

> Nearly all the speakers at the meeting protested bitterly about the use of the arbitration order which, they insisted, was a wartime emergency measure and should be abolished at once. While members of the port workers' committee, to which some of the seven men belong, were prominent in this agitation, there was evidence of genuine feeling among the rank-and-file dock workers at the meeting. However mistaken their view may be, it is providing inflammable material for those who want to bring London docks to a standstill and for the so-called joint trade union defence committee.[33]

The aforementioned committal proceedings began in the week after the meeting on which *The Times* correspondent had reported. They were conducted by the Chief Magistrate, Sir Laurence Dunne, who we encountered in Chapters Nine and Ten in the action against the gas workers, the proceedings beginning on 20 and 21 February before concluding following an adjournment on 14, 15 and 16 March.[34]

Although the strike in Liverpool was by now petering out,[35] the action continued in solidarity with those who had been charged. *The Times* reported on 21 February that thousands of dockers in London, Manchester, and on Clydeside had the previous day taken part in a 'one-day token protest strike'. Moreover, hundreds of dockers attended the proceedings at Bow Street on 20 February, the police being required to close the court doors after announcing that the public gallery was full, leaving 350 or so dockers milling around

[30] *The Times*, 9 February 1951.

[31] *The Times*, 10 February 1951. The seven in question were Robert Crosbie, Joseph Harrison, and William Johnston (all from Merseyside), and Harry Constable, Joe Cowley, Ted Dickens, and Albert Timothy (all from London).

[32] *The Times*, 11 February 1951. Among those outside was Vic Marney, arrested for an offence under the Public Order Act 1936, s 5 (using threatening, abusive or insulting words or behaviour calculated to cause a breach of the peace). On pleading guilty, he was fined ten shillings (ibid). Marney had previously been disciplined by the TGWU for his part in the 1949 strike, and his presence is referred to in several earlier chapters.

[33] *The Times*, 13 February 1951.

[34] *The Times*, 21 and 22 February, 15, 16 and 17 March 1951.

[35] *The Times*, 21 February 1951.

outside. While JF Bass was addressing the Chief Magistrate on behalf of the DPP, the National Dock Labour Board announced that 10,860 men were on strike in London and that 13,940 were at work.[36] Yet despite the challenge to the majesty of the law, there was no question of a prosecution being brought under Order 1305 against those who had participated in this wildcat action. Apart from anything else, a strike to protest against arrests and prosecutions was not a trade dispute within the meaning of Order 1305, though it would have been possible to bring charges similar to those set out in Counts two and three of the main proceedings discussed below. But no such steps were taken.[37]

So far as the committal proceedings are concerned, the case against the accused seemed straightforward, though it was necessary to distinguish between the conduct of the Liverpool men and their London co-accused. The first few days of the proceedings were preoccupied with the Merseyside defendants, who had been dissatisfied with their working conditions and had as a result 'put their heads together to foment this discontent, not only against employers but also against the men's elected representatives'.[38] The Liverpool accused had encouraged their fellow workers to strike against the advice of their own union officials, and had set about spreading their strike with a view to putting pressure on the union leadership responsible for negotiating terms and conditions of employment. Although they were 'comparatively unsuccessful' in London, this did not deter them from inciting dockers elsewhere, or continuing the pressure on the London dockers with the threat of returning to London 'with thousands of strikers marching to shame the London dockers into coming out on strike'.[39]

When the proceedings resumed on 14 March, police officers present at dockers' meetings in Liverpool gave an account of what they alleged had been said,[40] while the following day was 'occupied with the evidence of police officers who took notes of speeches in London dock areas'.[41] On day five, the Chief Magistrate heard from the defence, the Liverpool men represented by Sydney Silverman, the Labour MP for Nelson and Colne.[42] According to Silverman, a solicitor on the Left of the Labour Party who had served on Liverpool City Council in the 1930s, the evidence had shown that the defendants he was representing had no case to answer, the prosecution having failed to prove that the accused had intended either to take part in an unlawful strike, or to use unlawful means to bring about the strike. No trade dispute was involved as that term was defined in Order 1305, Article 7, the only dispute disclosed being between TGWU members and officials of the union, adding that the latter were 'neither employers of the members nor fellow workmen with them'. If there was no trade dispute, then, as submitted by Silverman, there was no strike to which Order 1305, Article 4 applied.

Alluding to the unspoken allegations of a Communist presence behind the prosecution, Silverman claimed that 'there was no justification for the hint that there was some hidden hand – some kind of nefarious conspiracy on the part of a number of

[36] ibid.
[37] It would have been foolish to have done so, even though the dockers' protest action was repeated throughout the different phases of the trial. See *The Times*, 17 March 1951.
[38] *The Times*, 21 February 1951.
[39] ibid.
[40] *The Times*, 15 March 1951.
[41] *The Times*, 16 March 1951.
[42] ibid.

people – not genuinely to deal with grievances and remove them but to exploit them in some other interests'.[43] The four London men were, however, represented by Jack Gaster, a well-known solicitor and member of the Communist Party. He submitted on their behalf that even if there was a strike, 'there was no evidence that the London defendants were associated with it'.[44] Nevertheless, the Chief Magistrate concluded predictably that there was enough evidence to send the men for trial on the charge of conspiring to incite dockworkers to strike in breach of Order 1305, though, as he pointed out, this did not mean that the indictment would be drawn in these terms. That was a matter for the prosecution, which might choose to 'include any number of charges'.[45] Perhaps rather ominously, however, the last day of the committal proceedings was also to see strike action by London dockers, some of whom again attended the court proceedings. According to *The Times*, 9,440 men were on strike, with 16,980 working. Out of 148 ships in London docks, 83 were either idle or undermanned.[46]

Surveillance Continues

As we saw in Chapter Eight, Home Office files make it clear that the dockers had been the subject of intense surveillance since October,[47] this coinciding with Newsam's initiative of 16 September 1950 and the conviction of the 10 gas workers. The files contain details of the surveillance operation, including the charges, as well as Special Branch monitoring of the trial, and correspondence from Shawcross about the conduct of the proceedings. The extensive surveillance operation also included the surveillance of bodies such as the Joint Trade Union Defence Committee (JTUDC), which we encountered in Chapter Ten in rather hapless circumstances. The fact that it was clearly an organisation of little clout was no reason to spare the expenditure of police resources in monitoring its activities for purposes that could only have related to the fantasies of the intelligence community.

Special Branch had been aware of the stirrings of the JTUDC since an emergency meeting at the Trade Union Club in WC2 on 18 February shortly after the dockers' arrests. The police obtained a very detailed account of who attended and what was said, even though those present were limited to ten in number. Plans were made for an anti-Order 1305 rally in Trafalgar Square which took place on 4 March while the committal proceedings were adjourned.[48] A JTUDC 'recall conference' was convened on 10 March 1951, the draft resolution noting that the TUC

[43] ibid.
[44] ibid.
[45] *The Times*, 17 March 1951.
[46] ibid.
[47] TNA, HO 45/25546 ('Disturbances: strikes in industry: communist instigated subversion') (Home Office F3 file 827723/343, 'Prosecution of the seven dockers accused of inciting illegal strikes') ('Special Branch Report, Dock Strike – Prosecution', 20 April 1951). Interestingly, the file has 'MI5' written on the cover and under 'RELATED PAPERS' it lists 827723/332 'London Port Workers', and 863200/628 'Communist interference in Industry'.
[48] TNA, HO 45/25546 ('Disturbances: strikes in industry: communist instigated subversion') (Home Office F3 file 827723/327, 'Trade Union Defence Committee formed at a meeting of trade unionists held at Holborn Hall on 13-10-50').

General Council had requested the withdrawal of the penal clauses of the Order, but also that 'pressure exists for the retention of the anti-strike legislation'.[49] The Committee proceeded to threaten 'solidarity action throughout the country' should the prosecutions not be withdrawn.

Having already obtained and passed on to the Home Office a copy of the resolution, Special Branch reported that the 'recall conference' was opened by Albert Knight, who expressed his belief that:

> Order 1305 and police spies were putting trade unionism back 100 years … the national press was asserting that the present industrial unrest was due to 'infiltrators' into trade unions, but the fact was that the likes of Sir Hartley Shawcross were the infiltrators. He was the man, who with consummate professional skill had defended the owners of the Creswell Colliery against widows and children.[50] The trials of the gas workers and dockers were 'try outs' of Order 1305, and it was now quite clear that it was to be used against workers but not employers. Denouncing police spies and MI5 he said that shop stewards and convenors were now being singled out for attack.

Before closing his speech, the Special Branch report continues, 'Knight asked for 20 volunteers to submit their names to form a new and active JTUDC in order to combat the work of police spies and MI5 who were poisoning the mind of the public against the workers'.[51] A fresh committee was approved and the police listed the 20 men. Special Branch had already opened files on seven of them.

Charlie Broadbent, one of the 10 convicted gas men, told the conference that he considered himself 'qualified' to speak about MI5 who had 'sorted him out' during the gas strike. He said 'there had always been spies among the workers'. As we have seen, Broadbent had been selected for prosecution in the gas workers' strike following information obtained about his union work both at Beckton Gas Works and at public meetings. Wal Hannington wound up the debate:

> Commenting on police spies and MI5, he said that he knew plenty about them but nothing to their credit. In 1936 he said, there were 135,000 political spies in America who were paid 80 million dollars by the employers. Holding up a cutting from the previous Saturday's [3 March] *Evening Standard*, he said that it was reported that Scotland Yard was conducting extensive political enquiries in various factories in London. The position now was that any worker (not necessarily a communist) who spoke up for his rights, was subsequently spied upon and made subject of a file at Scotland Yard.

Quite what purpose was served in collecting, storing or processing this information relating to a public meeting is frankly hard to fathom. There are no secrets here and it is the type of information that in the modern world would be communicated to the world at large by social media.

[49] ibid, 'COPY JOINT TRADE UNION DEFENCE COMMITTEE. RECALL CONFERENCE 10-3-51 DRAFT RESOLUTION'.

[50] A total of 80 miners were killed in the Creswell Colliery, north Derbyshire disaster of 26 September 1950.

[51] TNA, HO 45/25546 ('Disturbances: strikes in industry: communist instigated subversion') (Home Office F3 file 827723/327, 'Trade Union Defence Committee formed at a meeting of trade unionists held at Holborn Hall on 13-10-50') ('Special Branch Report, Recall Conference of JTUDC', 12 March 1951).

MI5, the Communist Party and Dock Strikes

The Home Office files relating to the prosecution of the dock workers give some insight into the operation of the network forged under the direction of Frank Newsam in September 1950, as the fruits of MI5 and Special Branch investigations were being shared with the Home Office. These are useful for telling us more about the anxieties of the intelligence community than the threat posed by the Communist Party.

One of the items on file records PA Osmond of MI5's specialist trade union section B1D writing to Oakley at the Home Office on 6 April, telling him that the Communist Party hoped to arrange a strike of port workers on the first day of the dockers' trial, which had been set for 9 April. F3 were also told that the Party believed that should the seven men be convicted and prison sentences handed down, the dockers and allied trades would walk out of their own accord. Osmond's breezy confidence in this intelligence – undoubtedly garnered from speculative conversations picked up by 'special facilities' located at the Communist Party's King Street offices, and from the gossip peddled by infiltrators and other informers – gave the impression that a master plan had been hatched by the CPGB, the details of which had been obtained by MI5.

Anyone who has read sufficient of the King Street 'special facilities' transcripts, or the often ludicrous reports from other sources, will be aware that the Service would have picked up little more than office gossip, and the predictions of Party members with only a sketchy grasp of the events at hand. Besides, the various unofficial committees like the PWC, the JTUDC, and the Road Haulage and Allied Trades Committee were not, whatever the political loyalties of the committee members, under the control of the CPGB, and the influence that these committees exercised over the workers was, at best, tenuous. It was highly unlikely that the CPGB would have hoped to be able to engineer a walk out on the first day of the trial. The Party was not delusional. As for the likelihood of a walk out by the dockers in the event of the seven men being convicted and sent down, that was stating the obvious. The men would be very likely to go on strike.

Nevertheless, maintaining the fiction that King Street could persuade the dockers to strike and that the CPGB conspired to arrive at secret collective decisions, Osmond chose to tell Oakley that:

> It seems that the Communist Party will be best pleased if the dockers are given sentences of one month because it feels that a protest strike could be continued for the whole of that period. It feels also that the workers on the Festival of Britain site would be certain to follow the dockers, and since the sentences would be announced shortly before the Festival is due to be open, particularly effective dislocation from the communist view would be caused.

Osmond hedged his bets by adding that there were some indications that the attempt at a full protest strike would not necessarily take place on the announcement of the verdict, but at a date to be fixed in advance by the Communist Party.

IV. The Dock Workers' Trial

The trial opened at the Old Bailey on 9 April before the Lord Chief Justice, Lord Goddard. Goddard is remembered as an enthusiast for capital punishment and for having campaigned for the restoration of flogging as a penalty. He has been described as 'a domineering bully with viciously punitive views on all aspects of criminal justice policy'.[52] Shawcross – who is said to have 'recommended' Goddard for the appointment in 1946 (at the age of 68)[53] – was assisted in the prosecution by Christmas Humphreys (whose father sat with Goddard in several high-profile post-war criminal trials) and JF Bass from the DPP's office. Rose Heilbron KC, David McNeil and David Turner-Samuels appeared for the Liverpool dockers, while Roy Wilson KC and Ralph Milner appeared for their London counterparts. Both Turner-Samuels and Milner were or were to become the subject of MI5 surveillance as members of the Communist Party Lawyers' Group, as was Jack Gaster, who appeared for the London dockers in the committal proceedings, their presence no doubt increasing speculation about the Communist hand behind the port strikes.[54]

As anticipated by the Chief Magistrate, two further charges had been added to the indictment, the government having been alerted in the committal proceedings to the defence against a charge under Order 1305 alone. It was now alleged that between 5 October 1950 and 8 February 1951, the defendants were engaged in:

- conspiracy to incite to strike in connection with trade disputes contrary to Order 1305, Article 4;
- conspiracy otherwise than in contemplation or furtherance of a trade dispute to induce workers employed under the Dock Workers (Regulation of Employment) Order 1947 to breach their contract of employment;
- conspiracy otherwise than in relation to a trade dispute to interfere with the conduct of the employers' business by inducing workers employed under the 1947 Order 'to the great damage of the said employers'.[55]

Note that the charge was conspiracy, not participation in an illegal strike (as in the gas workers' case). This was an extraordinary step. As we have seen, the gas workers were tried in summary proceedings before a magistrate. No such discourtesy for the PWC and the Liverpool men swept up in the same net. For them, it was the full force of the law: prosecution for conspiracy on indictment before a jury at the Old Bailey with the prospect of sentences on being found guilty which would greatly exceed those set out in Order 1305.

[52] M Berlins, 'A Chief Justice Got away with Murder', *The Independent*, 22 October 2011.

[53] J Morton, 'Obituary: Lord Shawcross', *The Independent*, 11 July 2003. For a fuller account of the circumstances of Goddard's appointment to a position which by convention could potentially have been claimed by Shawcross himself, had he not been a 'stripling of forty three' at the time, see P Devlin, *Easing the Passing: The Trial of Dr John Bodkin Adams* (Faber & Faber, London, 1985), pp 92–93.

[54] See KD Ewing, J Mahoney, and A Moretta, *MI5, the Cold War and the Rule of Law* (Oxford University Press, Oxford, 2020), p 180.

[55] *The Times*, 10 April 1951.

It is unclear whether the first charge was brought under the Defence Regulations or at common law.[56] Either way, there was the possibility of a harsh sentence. If the former, the penalty could have been up to two years' imprisonment (or a £500 fine).[57] If the latter, until the Criminal Law Act 1977, 'the penalty for conspiracy is at large, which means that a court may impose a very long sentence of imprisonment for an agreement to commit an offence which has not actually been committed, even though the offence itself attracts only a small penalty'.[58] Charges two and three were clearly brought at common law and, as such, were alternatives to the charge brought under Order 1305. These charges meant that if the jury considered that there had not been a trade dispute, then the men could still be convicted. Convictions could thus be secured *either* on the first charge, *or* on one or both of the other two charges. The latter were essentially the common law offence of conspiracy deployed in *R v Bunn*,[59] where it was held that an agreement by workers to break their contracts of service without just cause would be an illegal conspiracy at common law. As discussed in Chapter Four, the latter was preserved by the Conspiracy and Protection of Property Act 1875 for action which was not undertaken in contemplation or furtherance of a trade dispute.

The prospects for the seven men thus appeared bleak, and further confrontation with the dock workers seemed inevitable. Indeed, the first day of the trial was met with another protest strike, *The Times* reporting that 8,220 London men had not turned up for work, with the result that 100 ships were either idle or undermanned. The number of men of all grades working normally was said to be 17,550.[60] It was also reported that a group of 30 or so PWC members meeting at Tower Hill 'in steady rain in the afternoon' had recommended a return to work on the next day. But they did so:

> on the ground that the dock workers should prepare themselves for a much greater demonstration when the result of the trial is known. The strikers were warned that this last round would come in seven or eight days and that then not merely 10,000 but 20,000 or more dock workers should join in.[61]

The protest strikes were addressed by the Attorney General inside when opening the case for the prosecution, referring to the 'large numbers of otherwise loyal and honest citizens' who were 'striking against what they mistakenly believed to be the object of [the] prosecution and in the vain hope of altering its course'.[62] The jury was to disregard

[56] Conspiracy 'with any person to commit' an offence under the Regulations or any Order made thereunder was an offence, and was 'punishable in like manner as the said offence' (Defence Regulation 90(1) (as amended)).

[57] Defence Regulation 92(1)(b)).

[58] HC Debs, 3 May 1977, col 238 (Home Secretary, Merlyn Rees).

[59] *R v Bunn* (1872) 12 Cox CC 316.

[60] For a colourful account of the first day of the trial, see J Dash, *Good Morning Brothers!* (Lawrence & Wishart, London, 1969), p 86. Dash was a well-known London dockland trade union activist and Communist Party member.

[61] *The Times*, 10 April 1951. It was also pointed out that at this meeting, notes were taken by plain-clothes police who, with uniformed officers and press representatives, nearly outnumbered the strikers present' (ibid).

[62] This paragraph draws on the report in *The Times*, 10 April 1951.

any such protests: 'The greater the clamour, the greater the demonstrations that there might be about the case, the more important it was to emphasise that the jury were concerned with nothing more than the enforcement of the rule of law.'

But the rule of law was not the only principle on which the Attorney General relied. Thus, the defendants were condemned for not being 'content to rely upon constitutional methods and machinery in order to secure what they believed to be their just demands'.[63] The constitutional methods to which Shawcross was referring in his opening speech were not the methods familiar to constitutional lawyers. Rather, he was referring to the methods familiar to the industrial relations practitioner, though given the role of trade unions and collective bargaining in the post-war era, the two might plausibly be regarded as synonymous. As subsequently pointed out by Lord Goddard,[64] the appropriate response of the accused was to campaign within the official structures of the union for the rejection of the settlement and the negotiation of a new one. Having lost the vote in favour of the agreement, it was not legitimate to seek to undermine it by illegal action. But just as important as the need to obey the law and follow desired industrial relations procedures were the consequences of failing to do so. Although he acknowledged the failure to extend the strike to London, Shawcross was nevertheless concerned that the alleged illegal action was taken in the knowledge that the docks were 'the life-line' of the country, and that a national dock strike would 'strangle the nation'.[65]

The second day of the trial was devoted to the evidence of eight police officers from the Birkenhead Borough Police and the Liverpool City Police respectively, each of whom 'gave extracts of speeches alleged to have been made by the defendants' at various dockers' meetings on 24 September, 8 October and 2 February.[66] By the end of the second day, it appears that the prosecution's focus was with Count one, with Rose Heilbron KC on behalf of the three Merseyside defendants responding to the prosecution's case at the beginning of day three by arguing unsuccessfully that the second and third Counts should be dropped on the ground that there was no evidence against her clients. Anticipating that this point would be taken, Goddard dismissed it, saying that if the men were found not guilty on Count one, he would consider Counts two and three, at which point any matters Heilbron desired to raise could then be considered. He also rejected her submission that the prosecution had failed to prove that the strike was illegal on the first Count, on the ground that it was 'not the result of a trade dispute between employers and the dockers, but the result of a domestic dispute between the union and the men'.[67]

The case for the prosecution was followed by three days (the third, fourth and fifth days) of evidence for the defence,[68] the jury hearing from the Liverpool defendants on the first two of those days. Their case was built on disappointment with the NJIC award, one of their number explaining that the focus of their action was not the employers,

[63] ibid.

[64] *The Times*, 18 April 1951. See below, p 257.

[65] *The Times*, 10 April 1951.

[66] *The Times*, 11 April 1951.

[67] *The Times*, 12 April 1951. On the contrary, 'there was a great deal of evidence that the strike was over whether the men were to get the Dockers' Charter' adding that the jury might conclude that 'if the employers had been willing to pay the twenty-five shillings a day asked for the men would have gone back the next day' (ibid).

[68] *The Times*, 12–14 April 1951.

but the 'main enemy', namely union officials who 'refused to come to grips with the shipowners'. The whole purpose of the strike was to press the union to open negotiations with the employers for the Dockers' Charter, and it was with this in mind that they had gone to London to seek the support of the London PWC.[69] Heard on day five, Albert Timothy explained that the role of the London PWC was to 'ginger up' the union, and that its quarrel was not with the employers, but with Arthur Deakin, the union's General Secretary. He was followed by Ted Dickens, who said that the Liverpool strike was ill-advised, adding that 'once it had started, as good trade unionists, it was necessary to get the utmost support for it from the London dockers'. Likewise, Joe Cowley admitted that he was a member of the London PWC and that as soon as the Liverpool men arrived in London asking for support, he gave them his 'full co-operation'.[70]

In his closing speech on day six, Shawcross reminded the jury that there were three issues to consider:

- were the men acting in concert and agreement about something they set out to do in connection with the Dockers' Charter;
- was their action and agreement designed to bring the dockers out on strike; and
- was the strike to be one in connection with a trade dispute, or one which involved a breach of contract or injury to the employers?[71]

Insisting in reply that 'the right to withhold labour was a tradition fought for over hundreds of years', Rose Heilbron added that 'it was the only weapon the workers had'.[72] On the question whether the defendants had come into conflict with the law, it was 'ridiculous' to suggest that this was a dispute between the men and their employers: 'If the union had said they would re-open negotiations with the employers the strike would not have lasted another ten minutes', Heilbron insisting that 'the only quarrel the dockers had was with their union officials'.[73]

V. The Prosecution Collapses

In his summing up on the following day, the Lord Chief Justice began by saying that 'this was really quite an ordinary prosecution for an alleged breach or crime against public order',[74] a remarkable comment to have made, not least because this was only the first time since 1941 that the Old Bailey had hosted an Order 1305 trial, and only the second time since the war that there had been a prosecution.[75] But it did emphasise the extent

[69] *The Times*, 13 April 1951.
[70] *The Times*, 14 April 1951.
[71] *The Times*, 17 April 1951.
[72] ibid.
[73] ibid. These submissions were echoed by Roy Wilson KC for the London dockers: 'this was a dispute between the trade union and the workers, and if the jury accepted that, it was not a trade dispute within the meaning of Order 1305'.
[74] *The Times*, 18 April 1951.
[75] The first followed the Swift Scale strike of April–May 1941 led by Reg Birch. The trial saw the defendants found guilty but merely bound over. See W Podmore, *Reg Birch: Engineer, Communist, Trade Unionist* (Bellman Books, London, 2004), pp 12–13 and 223–26. See also pp 22–25 above.

to which Order 1305 had metamorphosed from a war-time instrument of industrial discipline to a post-war offence against the state. Thereafter, however, Goddard gave a fairly balanced account of the issues, identifying the trade dispute question as 'really the great question the jury would have to decide', making it clear that a 'dispute between a trade union or trade union officials and the men would not amount to a trade dispute within the meaning of Order 1305'.[76] The decision for the jury was 'whether the object of the strike was the Dockers' Charter which was concerned with wages and conditions of employment', or 'whether it was because the union officials had not put forward the men's views, and the men desired further negotiations to take place'.[77]

Although he was not prepared to direct the jury that a strike against the union's performance would be a trade dispute within the meaning of Order 1305, the Lord Chief Justice nevertheless made it clear that he disapproved of strike action taken in response to the alleged failings of union officials. If the officials were 'out of touch with the men', the 'proper way' to respond he suggested was 'not to urge a strike throughout the ports of the country but to remove the officials from office'.[78] This was all very well. But one of the grievances of the PWC raised at the trial was that there was no means available to the dockers to enable them to remove lazy, corrupt, incompetent or unresponsive officials, which was why the PWCs were formed in the first place.[79] Of course, it may be that the officials were not 'out of touch', but were behaving satisfactorily for a majority of the members. If that was the case, thought Goddard, it would be a 'serious matter' if 'the country could be held up to ransom by a strike because the officials of a union failed to please one section of their members who might be in a minority'.[80]

The Lord Chief Justice was clearly very troubled by the consequences of the strike action. If the strike had spread to all the ports, then 'a very serious state of affairs would have arisen'.[81] There would have been a 'stranglehold on the nation which would have entailed hardship on the whole community and would have imperiled the economic recovery of the country'.[82] Before concluding, Goddard made it very clear that he was unhappy not only with the potential consequences of the defendants' action, but with the conduct of those outside the court who had taken action to support them at various points in the trial:

> Strikes intended to overawe courts or juries were illegal, and if anybody doubted it they had better have that doubt removed from their minds. People who struck with the object of influencing or intimidating courts or juries were guilty of an offence.[83]

It is not clear what offences the Lord Chief Justice had in mind. The conduct was clearly not a breach of Order 1305 for the reasons explained above, though he may have been contemplating the common law offence of perverting the course of justice. The latter

[76] *The Times*, 18 April 1951.
[77] ibid.
[78] ibid.
[79] This is a point that had been made forcefully by the Merseyside defendants in particular. See generally J Goldstein, *The Government of British Trade Union: A Study of Apathy and the Democratic Process in the Transport and General Workers Union* (George Allen & Unwin, London, 1952).
[80] *The Times*, 18 April 1951.
[81] ibid.
[82] ibid.
[83] ibid.

applies widely to include 'interference with jurors with a view to influencing their verdict'.[84] It may also have been a contempt of court, but contempt of court is not a crime. So far as we are aware, there was no such prosecution.

The jury spent two and a half hours on day seven considering Count one. Despite being told that it was merely 'a matter of common sense', the jurors returned to the judge for further guidance on the definition of a trade dispute. The foreman was handed a copy of Order 1305, and Goddard drew an unhelpful parallel with what he imagined to be an event from everyday life in an attempt to assist jurors reach the verdict:

> Supposing you, in your own businesses, said to your clerks or servants, as was said here: 'We will pay you 21/- a day' – that is the employers' offer which has been accepted – and if then your man, without necessarily coming to you, walked out and let it be known that they would not work until they got 25/-, then you have to ask yourselves whether that is or is not a dispute. Perhaps you will return to your room and see if you can agree.[85]

About half an hour later, the foreman returned to say they were still unable to agree on the question of whether there had been a trade dispute. Consequently, they could not arrive at a verdict on the first charge. Goddard then asked Shawcross whether he wanted him to go on to instruct the jury to 'consider Count two or do you wish me to discharge the jury altogether?'[86]

Shawcross suggested that the jury go on to consider Count two. This is despite the fact that by this stage, he was concerned that the accused would be jailed if found guilty. We know this because he had written to Chuter Ede, Morrison and Bevan at the weekend following day five to say that he anticipated that the dockers would be sent to prison following what appeared to be some unconvincing evidence on the part of two of the defendants:

> If the men are convicted I think it improbable that they will not receive fairly stiff sentences. All the men gave evidence and I have rarely seen men so thoroughly discredit themselves … In the circumstances, *I am afraid it would be impossible for me to make any intervention at all about their sentences beyond the one which I told you privately I had already made.*[87]

The jury was nevertheless duly discharged from considering Counts one and three, and was instructed to concentrate only on Count two. About 20 minutes later, the jurors returned, the foreman announcing that they had found the defendants guilty on Count two. The Attorney General now had to consider whether there should be a retrial on Count one and an arrest of judgment on Count two.[88]

Having been invited by Goddard to reflect on the verdict overnight, on the eighth and final day of the trial, Shawcross told the judge that, in the interests of justice, he felt

[84] Crown Prosecution Service, Public Justice Offences, as revised 18 September 2024.

[85] TNA, HO 45/25546 ('Disturbances: strikes in industry: communist instigated subversion') (Home Office F3 file 827723/343, 'Prosecution of the seven dockers accused of inciting illegal strikes') ('Special Branch Report Dock Strike – Prosecution', 20 April 1951).

[86] *The Times*, 18 April 1951.

[87] TNA, HO 45/25546 ('Disturbances: strikes in industry: communist instigated subversion') (Home Office F3 file 827723/343, 'Prosecution of the seven dockers accused of inciting illegal strikes') (Shawcross to Chuter Ede, 14 April 1951), emphasis added. The impression given is that he was seeking to stave off the threat of widespread strikes. Shawcross told Chuter Ede that he was 'writing in similar terms' to Morrison and Bevan.

[88] *The Times*, 18 April 1951.

compelled to say that he was abandoning the case,[89] by means of a prerogative power that enabled the prosecution to discontinue the proceedings. The reasons given for the Attorney General's change of heart were said to be purely technical, namely the illogicality of the jury's verdicts:

> It seemed impossible to reconcile the jury's verdict on Count 2 with their disagreement on Count 1. Although it may not have been the intention of the jury, the Attorney General said he had come to the conclusion that the illogical findings of the jury compelled him, in fairness to the defendants, to discontinue these proceedings, and subject to the Lord Chief Justice's better judgment, he proposed to do that by not moving for judgment under Count 2, and by entering a *nolle prosequi* to the whole indictment. Important as this case was, it was even more important that the proceedings against the defendants should not be in any way or oppressive.
>
> Under Count 1 it was necessary for the jury to decide whether or not there was a trade dispute in existence, and as to that they could not agree. Under Count 2 it was equally necessary for them to decide whether there was a trade dispute. The Attorney General said he thought the jury would have followed the same course they had taken in the first count, and disagreed on the second count. He would then have been left with the unfettered discretion to ask for a new trial on the whole indictment. But it seemed to him impossible for the jury logically to disagree on the existence of a trade dispute under Count 1 and then to agree about it, almost in the next breath, under Count 2.
>
> There must have been at least some members of the jury who thought under Count 1 that there was a trade dispute, and they could not logically have changed their minds when they came to consider the second count. It may have been that the jury thought the defendants should be convicted of something, but they were not quite sure of what. In these circumstances … he did not think it possible to sustain a verdict, and he proposed to enter a *nolle prosequi* to the whole indictment.[90]

No doubt a crushing blow, Shawcross blamed Goddard for 'an unusual lack of clarity in the summing up'.[91] Nevertheless, it is impossible to exclude the possibility that he was influenced by wider political considerations when reflecting on the verdict overnight. There were already 9,000 London dockers on strike, with several hundred demonstrating outside on day seven of the trial,[92] the jury's confusion providing a convenient opportunity to de-escalate what would almost certainly have been further industrial troubles if the dockers had been found guilty. It is not known what interventions Shawcross had made on the weekend after day five about the likely sentences, or to whom he had spoken so candidly to convince him that jail was the likely outcome for the dockers. The details were clearly so sensitive that they could not be relayed to colleagues in print even confidentially, which will no doubt inform speculation about the identity of the person

[89] *The Times*, 19 April 1951.

[90] ibid. The *nolle prosequi* means simply that the Crown is abandoning the case. According to Lord Devlin, writing about another famous case (the trial of Dr John Bodkin Adams) where it was employed a few years later, a *nolle prosequi* 'is used mostly for the protection of the guilty on the rare occasions when it is in the public interest that justice should not be done': Devlin (n 53) p 180. Devlin provides a good account of the *nolle prosequi* procedure (pp 179–81). Now rarely used, its use in the Bodkin Adams case was especially controversial: see HC Debs, 1 May 1957, col 292. See further AW Bradley, KD Ewing, and CJS Knight, *Constitutional and Administrative Law*, 18th edn (Pearson, Harlow, 2022), p 291.

[91] Shawcross (n 7) p 73.

[92] *The Times*, 19 April 1951.

concerned.[93] But with the likelihood of long prison sentences, it is impossible to exclude the possibility that further private conversations took place with different people on the evening of the verdicts, and that Shawcross was subjected to pressure from ministerial colleagues when he was giving 'a good deal of thought to the situation' before making his decision.[94]

Shawcross nevertheless remained defiant despite this great personal setback. He wished it to understood not only that strikes in connection with trade disputes were still unlawful by virtue of Order 1305, but also that strikes which were not in connection with trade disputes could still give rise to criminal liability at common law. This was because by virtue of the Conspiracy and Protection of Property Act 1875, the protection from criminal conspiracy at common law applied only to acts done in contemplation or furtherance of a trade dispute, as that latter term was defined by the Trade Disputes Act 1906. Just to be clear, Shawcross emphasised that 'if there were no trade dispute a strike calculated to cause a breach of contract, or interfere with the course of justice, or interfere or affect the policy of the State, or interfere with the interests of the State might constitute a grave political offence'. And in response to comments made by the Lord Chief Justice in his summing up, Shawcross added that he would not be deterred from taking action 'in the case of a strike calculated to intimidate juries where it was appropriate', advising that the DPP would 'institute proceedings in order to ensure that such matters could be brought before the court'.[95] It was nonetheless poignant that on the day after the funeral of its author, Order 1305 should itself have suffered a fatal blow in such ignominious circumstances.[96]

VI. Conclusion

The dockers walked out of the Old Bailey on 18 April to be met, according to the Special Branch account, by 'an enthusiastic reception by the crowd which then numbered about 500–600 persons'.[97] About fifty moved on to Transport House (TGWU headquarters): this number gradually increased and shouts of 'Three cheers for the seven dockers', 'We want the Charter' and 'Down with Deakin' were raised. About eighty men entered Transport House, 'chanted slogans and left'.[98] In the words of Jack Dash, despite the failure of the union to 'lift a finger to free the seven', they were 'saved from imprisonment', and the British labour movement was released from 'the shackles of Order 1305', with 'the right of free men to withdraw their labour restored after eleven

[93] Fuelling speculation is the information provided by Shawcross in his autobiography that Goddard 'often' spent the weekend at 'Peckhams', Shawcross' 'country house': Shawcross (n 7) p 222.

[94] *The Times*, 19 April 1951.

[95] ibid.

[96] *The Times*, 18 April 1951, announcing that Mrs Attlee would represent the Prime Minister at Bevin's funeral service at Golders Green Crematorium. A motion proposing that the latter's remains be interred in Westminster Abbey 'in view of his services to the British people in the cause of defeating those who sought to enslave the world' had already been tabled in the Commons by Raymond Blackburn, the controversial Labour MP we encountered in ch 11 above: ibid.

[97] TNA, HO 45/25546 ('Disturbances: strikes in industry: communist instigated subversion') (Home Office F3 file 827723/343, 'Prosecution of the seven dockers accused of inciting illegal strikes') ('Special Branch Report Dock Strike – Prosecution', 18 April 1951). See also Dash (n 60) pp 86–87.

[98] Special Branch Report 18 April 1951 (ibid).

years'.[99] The next day's *Daily Worker* celebrated 'A Glorious Victory', demanding that 'All trade unionists must see that Order 1305 goes immediately', adding that 'Pollitt says: Shawcross must go'.[100] The *Daily Worker* also reported that on the evening of the trial's collapse, the seven men had returned to the pub where they had been arrested. Here 'parodies of popular songs guying Sir Hartley Shawcross were sung', it being observed that the 'only people who did not take part in the victory celebrations were two plain-clothes police officers who stood sipping their beer and resenting the wisecracks made about them by the dockers'.[101]

Wounded pride and battered reputations aside, the main effect of the trial paradoxically was to bring down the very law which the government had sought to enforce. Never used again, Order 1305 was quickly revoked. Although the dockers' case suggested that juries could not be relied upon, Order 1305 could still have been enforced without a jury, as in the gas workers' case. But the London dockers had signalled that workers were not prepared in peace-time to be restrained by it, the government consequently being 'forced to abandon' long-cherished ambitions to jail the PWC leadership,[102] who emerged as victors in what had been a skirmish on the margins of the Cold War. But although the prosecution was undertaken principally to bring down the leadership of the London PWC, the latter had by now 'lost much of its raison d'etre',[103] reinforcing the sense that Newsam, Chuter Ede and Shawcross had exaggerated the influence of the Communist Party in the ports, a case that had been made frequently by MI5's Guy Liddell.[104] As Bevan pointed out without referencing the dockers' case, it 'can be an awfully lazy habit' always 'to look for Communists under the bed'.[105] It is no surprise then that with London dockers in particular 'quite happy' with the NJIC settlement in January, the ports were, in the words of Colin J Davis, about to experience 'a remarkable calm after the tumultuous years of 1948–51'.[106]

[99] Dash (n 60) p 87.
[100] *Daily Worker*, 19 April 1951.
[101] ibid.
[102] CJ Davis, *Waterfront Revolts: New York and London Dockworkers, 1946–61* (University of Illinois Press, Urbana, 2003), pp 202–03, 206.
[103] ibid p 206.
[104] See pp 106, 160.
[105] HC Debs, 15 February 1951, col 730. See Fishman (n 24) p 69.
[106] Davis (n 102) pp 202–03, 206. Working conditions at least in the London docks are said to have improved as a result of the 1951 settlement, with *The Times* Labour correspondent writing about labour shortages and 'the men taking home heavy pay packets': *The Times*, 8 February 1951.

14

Revocation and Legacy of Order 1305

I. Introduction

The dockers' case was remarkable for highlighting just what is involved when the criminal law is used against trade unionists.[1] A number of words or phrases stand out in the narrative in Chapter Thirteen, emphasising the scale of the state infrastructure that needs to be deployed to prosecute workers. Suspected criminals must be kept under surveillance, however primitive the surveillance machinery; the strike as a crime needs to be investigated; evidence needs to be gathered; a prosecution needs to be mounted; a jury needs to be sworn; a trial needs to take place; and guilt needs to be determined before sentences need to be imposed. Labour lawyers thus encounter what ought to be an alien world inhabited by Special Branch, MI5, F3 Division at the Home Office, the Criminal Investigation Department (CID), police detectives, criminal charges, bail, committal proceedings, the Old Bailey, police evidence, imprisonment, and so on. In the dockers' case admittedly, there had been no sentences handed down and thus no imprisonment, though that would have been the logical outcome if the trial had not been mismanaged by the prosecution. The failed prosecution brought all that to a sudden end. The trial put Order 1305 beyond use and its revocation inevitable.

As we have seen in Chapter Twelve, on 23 April 1951 Aneurin Bevan and Harold Wilson resigned from the Cabinet. This left vacancies at the Ministry of Labour and the Board of Trade respectively, with Alfred Robens promoted to the former and Hartley Shawcross appointed to the latter, to be replaced by Frank Soskice as Attorney General.[2] Together, Robens and Soskice moved to de-escalate industrial relations tension. It is true that disputes continued to be reported to and discussed by the Cabinet, as in the case of a Manchester dock strike,[3] and a strike by road haulage workers a few days later.[4] But with the exception of the negotiations over miners' pay and conditions, the discussions were brief and they revealed no appetite for the drama of the preceding six years.[5] There appears also to have been a more relaxed approach to the Communist

[1] On the role of the criminal law in labour relations, see A Bogg, KD Ewing and A Moretta, 'The Persistence of Criminal Law and Police in Collective Labour Relations' in A Bogg, J Collins, M Freedland, and J Herring (eds), *Criminality at Work* (Oxford University Press, Oxford, 2020), ch 19.

[2] Robens replaced Bevan (who had replaced Isaacs on 17 January 1951). Bevan resigned on 23 April 1951 after only a few months in protest about the introduction of NHS prescription charges.

[3] TNA, CAB 128/19/36 (Cabinet Conclusions, 22 May 1951) (Manchester Dock Strike).

[4] TNA, CAB 128/19/37 (Cabinet Conclusions, 28 May 1951) (Road Haulage Dispute).

[5] TNA, CAB 128/19/2 (Cabinet Conclusions, 8 January 1951). For the Cabinet Emergencies Committee it was, however, business as usual, with, for example, the Cabinet Emergencies Committee on 20 May

Party, whose fortunes were on the wane, as revealed at the General Election in 1950 when the Party lost its two MPs. This is not to say of course that the Communist Party was no longer an obsession of MI5 or the government,[6] but merely to acknowledge that there were no concerns about Communist Party industrial saboteurs being brought to Cabinet, and no more claims in Cabinet Conclusions about Communist Party sedition.

II. Decommissioning of Order 1305

The effect of the failed dockers' prosecution was to hasten the demise of Order 1305, which was immediately decommissioned by the DPP. This was revealed by a miners' strike in South Wales in 1951 which seemed to meet the core criteria for prosecution: it was unofficial and it was said to be Communist-influenced if not instigated. The strike had been called at the Wern Tarw mine in Pencoed, Glamorgan on 7 June 1950 in protest at the closure of two seams, and the transfer of 87 miners to another colliery. It was suspected that this was the start of a running down of the colliery prior to closure. With two other pits having already come out in support of the Wern Tarw men, on 12 June the Lodge Committee at the mine urged more fellow miners to join them in the strike. The action was, however, opposed by the NUM South Wales Area, the Executive Committee of which advised the men to return to work, only to be defied by the strikers who printed and published 3,000 'flyers' justifying their action. Three days after publication of the flyers, the Chief Constable of Glamorgan, Joseph Jones, sent a report to WH Cornish of F3 at the Home Office, and to MI5, by which time the strike affected eight collieries.

The Chief Constable's report included the following information:

> The Lodge Committee of the Wern Tarw Colliery consists of twelve members, five of whom are known communists. Of these five the following three have been most active in attempting to spread the strike to other local collieries:
>
> Frank HAYWARD, 12, Mill Street, Tonyrefail (Secretary)
>
> Penry JONES, 2, Lewis Street, Llwyncelyn, Porth (Chairman)
>
> David DAVIES, 'Woodlands' Derwen Cottages, Coity (Compensation Secretary)
>
> David Davies has an Austin saloon motor car Reg. No WN 8051 which he has been using extensively to convey members of the Wern Tarw Lodge and other union officials to other local collieries in an effort to bring the workmen out in sympathy with the strikers at Wern Tarw.[7]

considering the precautions which might be taken should the then current rail dispute result in a strike (TNA, CAB 134/177, Cabinet Emergencies Committee, 20 May 1951), and on the following day expressing concern at the potential reaction of the US government if it should learn that the UK was struggling to bring much-needed raw materials ashore (TNA, CAB 134/177, Cabinet Emergencies Committee, 21 May 1951). Nevertheless, there was perceptibly less appetite for overt intervention.

[6] The Cabinet Emergencies Committee had heard that the Manchester strike had 'begun over small grievances which had been seized upon by the Communist leaders of the unofficial PWC': TNA, CAB 134/177, Cabinet Emergencies Committee, 20 May 1951.

[7] TNA, HO 45/25546 ('Disturbances: strikes in industry: communist instigated subversion') (Home Office F3 file 827723/346, 'The Chief Constable of Glamorgan. Unofficial Colliery Strikes') ('Report from Chief Constable of Glamorgan', 15 June 1951).

The report also included the names and addresses of other trade unionists, the carefully logged details making it clear that the Glamorgan police had been investigating and recording the activities of local Communists and trade unionists for a long time.[8] Indeed, generations of first-year law students have known about such practices in South Wales since the early 1930s, the High Court in a leading case from South Wales having established the right of Special Branch officers to be present at political meetings (despite being asked to leave) where there was an apprehension of sedition or a breach of the peace.[9]

From information provided by employers at the various pits, Jones also passed on details of the collieries affected, the numbers of men out on strike, as well as the estimated daily 'loss' of coal: 3,805 miners out, with approximately 4,390 tons of coal lost every day. But although the Chief Constable claimed that the action appeared to fit the bill for proceedings under Order 1305, there was hesitation about proceeding. Jones was mindful of the failed dockers' prosecutions, and was also aware of plans now under way to scrap Order 1305:

> A significant feature of these disputes is the agitation of communists who are doing all they can to spread the strikes over as large a field as possible, and it is learned from a reliable source that it is the intention of these persons to bring out all the South Wales coalfields if they can do so.
>
> I have considered whether the actions of these agitators constitute a breach of the law, and whether there is evidence of a conspiracy to incite miners to take part in strikes in connection with trade disputes contrary to the provisions of Article Four of the Conditions of Employment Act and National Arbitration Order, 1940 – Order 1305. In view, however, of the decisions reached at the trial of the seven dockers at the Old Bailey in April last, and the fact that the withdrawal of Order 1305 is at present under consideration, I am reluctant to instruct my officers to commence inquiries into the matter without further advice. This is a matter which you may wish to give consideration to yourself, and I am enclosing an extra copy of this report so you may, if you wish, pass it on to the appropriate authority for a considered opinion.[10]

When Jones referred to a reluctance to instruct his officers 'to commence inquiries into the matter without further advice', he was asking whether he should start working with a view to making arrests and bringing criminal charges. A Minute note by Helen Harting of the Home Office's department F3 observed that 'a new Order, replacing [Order] 1305 is to be put before the Minister of Labour by a sub-committee set up to advise him under the chairmanship of Mr Williamson, General Secretary of the GMWU in the

[8] While the Chief Constable of Glamorgan did not attend either of the Home Office meetings on 19 and 26 September (on which see ch 8), he was subsequently informed of the new arrangements by Special Branch.

[9] *Thomas v Sawkins* [1935] 2 KB 249.

[10] TNA, HO 45/25546 ('Disturbances: strikes in industry: communist instigated subversion') (Home Office F3 file 827723/346, 'The Chief Constable of Glamorgan. Unofficial Colliery Strikes') ('Report from the Chief Constable of Glamorgan', 15 June 1951). For good measure, Jones added that 'a lot of people are unaware of the part taken by communists in these disputes, and it may be that if the National Coal Board were to give a little publicity to this aspect of the stoppages it would open the eyes of those involved and improve the situation considerably'.

near future',[11] and suggested that in the circumstances 'an investigation at this moment might be considered pointless'.[12] In another note on the same day, a senior F3 official (AS Oakley) observed that following 'the recent failure of the prosecution of the seven dockers it might be thought an inopportune moment to take steps to enforce the present Order', adding that 'there have been many precedents' for ignoring failures to comply with it. Notably, however, the matter was 'one of policy and the Ministry of Labour might be consulted'.[13] Oakley had of course correctly assessed the political situation, though he also consulted MI5, to be told that it was not for them to advise the Chief Constable 'on whether to pursue enquiries with a view to prosecuting under Order 1305'.[14]

The surveillance remained ongoing pending a decision about prosecution. When MI5 advised the Home Office that it was not for them to advise Jones about a prosecution, they were careful nevertheless to capitalise on the intelligence opportunities which the dispute provided, replying also that 'the investigations into subversive activities, however, are of the greatest value to us,' and that MI5 was 'anxious that the investigation into the South Wales coal strike, from this point of view, should be continued'. An MI5 officer had already written to Jones 'thanking him for the results of his investigations so far', and looking forward to the receipt of 'further material of this nature'.[15] The Glamorgan constabulary not only obliged, but did so enthusiastically. A second report from Jones on 21 June informed both MI5's B1D and the Home Office's F3 that 'Frank HAYWARD and other members of the Wern Tarw Lodge Committee continue their activities in spreading the strike', and that 26 pits were now affected. With almost 10,000 miners having walked out,[16] Jones gave more details of various events relating to the strike, while more names, addresses and car registration numbers of known and suspected Communists were supplied.

A Home Office F3 official (Cornish) sent Jones' reports of 15 and 21 June respectively to the DPP (Sir Thomas Mathew), who told Jones on 27 June that he 'did not advise commencing police inquiries into illegal aspects of these unofficial strikes at this stage,' and that he would be notified 'if and when inquiries should be undertaken with a view to prosecution',[17] it being confirmed on the following day by Harting (of F3) that 'the Home Office appears to have no further interest in the matter'.[18] Jones' third report

[11] Williamson had been in favour of the prosecution of the gas workers. A Home Office official told the Home Secretary that the Minister of Fuel and Power wanted Chuter Ede to know that Williamson had 'told him that he approved the prosecutions … one of the ten was a member of his own union. He had asked for legal assistance from the union and had been refused' (TNA, HO 45/25546 ('Disturbances: strikes in industry: communist instigated subversion') (Home Office F3 file 827723/325A, 'London gas strike Prosecution of certain strikers', 4 October 1950).

[12] TNA, HO 45/25546 ('Disturbances: strikes in industry: communist instigated subversion') (Home Office F3 file 827723/346, 'The Chief Constable of Glamorgan. Unofficial Colliery Strikes').

[13] ibid, Minute note by Mr Oakley, 21 June 1951.

[14] ibid, from REC Broadbent 21 June 1951. B1D had a 'Special File' 452/5 for the information received.

[15] ibid. In his report of 15 June, Jones also said that he had 'already sent a brief preliminary report to the Security Department on these unofficial strikes, having regard to the dominant communist influence present, and am also forwarding a copy of this report to the Department'. The Security Department was of course MI5.

[16] There was another breakdown of numbers of strikers and tonnage 'lost' at each of the 26 pits.

[17] TNA, HO 45/25546 ('Disturbances: strikes in industry: communist instigated subversion') (Home Office F3 file 827723/346, 'The Chief Constable of Glamorgan. Unofficial Colliery Strikes') ('Report from the Chief Constable of Glamorgan', 27 June 1951).

[18] ibid, Minute sheet entry by Helen Harting, 28 June 1951.

(sent on 27 June) not only included information about the decision not to prosecute (which surely would have been known by its recipients),[19] but also additional information about the strike. The latter information was sent despite the fact that there was not to be a trial, and therefore no justification for continued intelligence gathering or sharing. The information shared included material about the strike already in the public domain gleaned from the pages of the *Western Mail* (a cutting from which was supplied by Jones),[20] as well as a Circular drafted by Hayward for distribution to the South Wales Lodges.[21] For their part, MI5 were no doubt interested to receive a cutting from the *South Wales Echo* that Alfred Davies – the President of the union – had 'severed connections with the Communist Party'.[22]

In the days before the internet, London-based agencies such as the Home Office F3 and MI5 relied on such sources for information even of this basic kind. But the information supplied on 27 June also included material that could only have become available by intrusive covert surveillance, and is notable for giving even more insights into the scale of the surveillance operation:

> On 21st June it is known that a telephone message was received by Frank HAYWARD at about 10.50 pm from a man (unidentified) named Thomas, asking Hayward to come down from the Glyncorrwg Colliery at 6 am the following morning to address the colliers on the day shift. He told Thomas that he had another engagement but was asked by Thomas to put it off as the Glyncorrwg pit was more important. HAYWARD promised to attend and did address the collieries in that district, where workmen were gathered for the morning shift. Normal working was not affected.

Apart from phone tapping, as the foregoing would suggest, it appears also that activists were the subject of other surveillance methods, in the form of either the use of informers or police/Special Branch observation. Thus, Chief Constable Jones reported that:

> [O]n 22 June leaflets were distributed to workmen at the Cwm Colliery, Tyrant; and in the streets at Tonyrefail, by Arthur COOPER, 32, Pengarreg Rd, Tonyrefail. On the same day David DAVIES and John Emylyn EVANS, of the Wern Tarw Lodge, distributed leaflets to workmen at the Wyndam Colliery, Ogmore Vale at 6.5 am. They left in Davies's car. They later visited the Western Colliery, Nantymoel, but left when spoken to by the police.

The delegates at a Coalfield Conference held at Cardiff on 29 June voted to support a resolution to return to work by 56,100 votes to 39,600.[23] Normal working was resumed on 2 July. On the following day, this news was passed to Cornish (who seemed to be the link between the Home Office and the DPP) in a handwritten note by a colleague (KE Hughes, who appears to have been the main Home Office link with Special

[19] This information is likely to have been known to the Home Office before then, perhaps as early as 25 June.

[20] *Western Mail*, 26 June 1951.

[21] A copy of the circular, dated 19 June 1951 is in TNA, HO 45/25546 ('Disturbances: strikes in industry: communist instigated subversion') (Home Office F3 file 827723/346, 'The Chief Constable of Glamorgan. Unofficial Colliery Strikes').

[22] *South Wales Echo*, 26 June 1951 (cutting supplied by Jones in his 27 June Report).

[23] *Western Mail*, 30 June 1951. Alf Davies – the Communist President of the union – declared the vote to have been a vote of confidence for the NUM leadership. But he added that: 'We have received repeated complaints that the police were at collieries when their presence was entirely uncalled for. Their presence aggravated the strike. But for the fact that the police were there a number of the men who stayed out would have returned to work.'

Branch).[24] It quoted an unnamed source as describing the vote as 'an overwhelming majority', though there was nothing secret about the conference resolution, which was widely reported. With the strike over, Cornish wrote to the DPP referring to the Chief Constable Jones' report of 27 June:

> May I take it that you do not particularly wish to have this further report. The Chief Constable has also said that there have been no reports of disorder and that those who seem to be active in promoting the strike have been most careful not to cause trouble and to comply with police requirements. As you no doubt know, the strike is now over.[25]

The DPP agreed that 'in the circumstances' he 'need not worry' Cornish to send 'the further report in this matter'.[26] Of course, it is unlikely that there was ever any question of bringing any prosecutions, especially after the dockers' case. Nevertheless, we are again indebted to the Home Office for having sent this material to the National Archives confirming what many people suspected about the surveillance of trade union activists. Even so, it is possible that some of the documents relating to still more intrusive monitoring have been removed from the file.

III. Robens and Soskice Memorandums

Shortly after the DPP decided that he would not be launching a prosecution of the Welsh miners, formal steps were taken at a political level finally to lay Order 1305 to rest. To this end, Memorandums were presented to ministers by Robens and Soskice, dated 20 and 24 July 1951 respectively.[27] Robens had reported that the Ministry of Labour had consulted the TUC, which was no longer willing to accept penal sanctions for strikes, but that it would welcome a new instrument preserving some of the existing provisions of Order 1305.[28] This is what was to be done, Robens explaining that Order 1305 had to go because its penal provisions had 'outlived their usefulness and have become a serious embarrassment in present circumstances'.[29] The main differences between Order 1305 and the new one he was to present to Cabinet were as follows:

(a) The prohibition of strikes and lock outs would be entirely removed.
(b) The scope of the Order would be confined to disputes concerning wages and conditions of employment and would exclude disputes arising from such matters as the employment of non-unionists and claims for re-instatement. Experience

[24] TNA, HO 45/25546 ('Disturbances: strikes in industry: communist instigated subversion') (Home Office F3 file 827723/346, 'The Chief Constable of Glamorgan. Unofficial Colliery Strikes') (Hughes to Cornish, 3 July 1951).
[25] ibid, Draft letter to DPP, 3 July 1951.
[26] ibid, Sir Theobald Mathew to Cornish, 4 July 1951.
[27] TNA, CAB 128/20/5 (Cabinet Conclusions, 26 July 1951).
[28] TNA, CAB 129/46/71 ('The Future of the Conditions of Employment and National Arbitration Order', Memorandum by the Minister of Labour and National Service, 20 July 1951).
[29] ibid para 5.

had shown that such matters were not 'susceptible of settlement' by compulsory arbitration.

(c) 'Compulsory arbitration' – in the sense of one party to a dispute being able to take the other party to arbitration against their will – would be retained and a tribunal like National Arbitration Tribunal would continue to function, though under a different name.[30]

As we will discuss below, however, the proposals for compulsory arbitration were very different from the understanding of compulsory arbitration in Order 1305. In the meantime, the new Minister of Labour explained that this third feature of his proposed new Order would exclude applications by 'trade union branches acting without the authority of their union, groups of unorganised workers and also professional associations'.[31] This was of course a direct response to the problem that had exposed Isaacs, and gave effect to what had been the policy of the Ministry of Labour until its unlawfulness had been revealed by Shawcross. The explicit exclusion of professional associations from standing to make a report addressed a problem that had arisen more recently following an attempt to use the procedure by the Society of Town Clerks,[32] doubts being expressed about its status as a genuine trade union on the ground that 'its principal objects were not the regulation of the relations between workmen and masters or any of the other statutory objects referred to in [the Trade Union Act 1913, section 1(2)]'.[33]

Moreover, in trades or industries where there were voluntary procedures, as a further restriction, it would be possible for complaints to be taken to the new tribunal – the Industrial Disputes Tribunal (IDT) – only by employers or trade unions who were party to these procedures, 'so that in practice unrecognised or break-away unions would be excluded'.[34] Where there were no such procedures, it would be possible for a complaint to be made only by an employer, or by an employers' organisation, or by a trade union 'having a substantial proportion of employers or workers in the trade or part of the trade concerned'.[35] Finally, in what was a major regression, the benign provisions of Part III of Order 1305 – requiring collective agreements to have *erga omnes* effect – would also be rescinded, to be replaced and diluted as follows:

> [A]n organisation of employers or a trade union which habitually takes part in the settlement of terms and conditions of employment in the industry or section of industry concerned would be able to report an issue as to whether a particular employer should observe recognised terms and conditions, and the Tribunal might require the employer to observe such terms and conditions (or such as it might determine to be not less favourable).[36]

[30] ibid para 3.
[31] ibid.
[32] See TNA, CAB 128/19/1 (Cabinet Conclusions, 2 January 1951). See pp 217–221 above.
[33] TNA, CAB 129/46/71 ('The Future of the Conditions of Employment and National Arbitration Order', Memorandum by the Minister of Labour and National Service, 20 July 1951, para 3).
[34] ibid.
[35] ibid.
[36] ibid.

Soskice went over the same ground as Robens in his parallel Memorandum a few days later,[37] albeit in more detail, beginning with the jurisdiction of the new tribunal, which would deal with 'disputes' and 'issues':

> Employers or trade unions may report to the Minister 'disputes'; or 'issues'. A 'dispute' is a 'dispute in a trade or industry or section of a trade or industry or in an undertaking, connected with terms of employment or conditions of labour' [but not trade union membership as a condition of employment]. An 'issue' is an issue as to whether an employer should observe terms and conditions recognised in the district, that is, in effect, established by voluntary negotiation or arbitration.[38]

Like Robens before him, Soskice further explained that 'when there is machinery for voluntary settlement of the terms and conditions of employment', only recognised or representative organisations would be permitted to make a claim, to ensure that 'dissident non-affiliated unions would in general be excluded'.[39]

The new scheme was designed to foster the voluntary settlements of disputes, so that when a 'dispute' or 'issue' was reported to him, the Minister would be empowered to take steps to promote a settlement. In the case of a 'dispute' (as distinct from an 'issue'), however, he would be required to refer the dispute to any suitable negotiation or arbitration machinery to which the parties had access and had not yet exhausted. A 'dispute' not otherwise settled was to be referred to the Industrial Disputes Tribunal within 14 days, though again learning from the operation of Order 1305, the Minister would have a general discretion to defer a reference, with a specific power to defer while industrial action was taking place. The only 'sanction' under the new procedure was that any terms and conditions specified in a Tribunal award (whether a 'dispute' or an 'issue') would become implied terms of the contracts of employment between the employers and the workers to whom the award related. It would no longer be an offence to take part in a strike or lock out before referring a dispute under the procedure, nor would it be an offence to take part in a strike or lock out in relation to a dispute that had been so referred.

Like Robens four days earlier, Soskice also highlighted the dilution of the *erga omnes* principle in relation to collective agreements.[40] But it is clear that in agreement with the Minister of Labour, his major concern was the need to remove the criminal sanctions relating to strikes and lock outs. To this end, Robens gave the following 'strong reasons' for doing so:

> (i) in general it is doubtful whether the criminal law can ever be an effective weapon to restrain strikes;
> (ii) it would be impossible to continue any criminal provisions in an Order – if it were desirable to have them, they should be enacted by Statute;
> (iii) if there is any criminal provision whether in an Order or a Statute, it is impossible to allow it to be continually disregarded; but prosecutions are difficult to institute and

[37] TNA, CAB 129/46/74 ('The Future of the Conditions of Employment and National Arbitration Order', Memorandum by the Attorney General, 24 July 1951).

[38] ibid para 2.

[39] ibid. Soskice conceded that 'there might be breakaway unions which complied with the requirement that they should represent substantial numbers of workers'.

[40] ibid para 4. See Box on pp 275–276 below.

> may often involve risk of greatly aggravating the dispute and even possibly provoking a wholesale disobedience to the law. As my colleagues will know, the penal provisions of Order 1305 have been a source of constant difficulty, particularly to the Law Officers.[41]

Soskice was to add that 'if it were desired to retain some criminal sanction, this would have … to be done by Statute after full debate in Parliament, and then … would be possible only in a very restricted form'.[42]

There was no evidence of Order 1305 being required any longer to deal with Communist-inspired industrial action. Soskice nevertheless thought it worth reminding colleagues (should the point be raised in Parliament) that there was adequate legal machinery to deal with political strikes, as his predecessor had pointed out five years earlier in the debates about the Trade Disputes and Trade Unions Bill.[43] In a Schedule to his Memorandum, Soskice helpfully reminded his readers that it was:

> [A] criminal offence to conspire to do or to incite others to do an unlawful act or to do a lawful act by unlawful means. Therefore to bring about a strike not in connection with a trade dispute is prima facie an indictable offence, but in practice the remedy can only be used in exceptional cases.[44]

Basically, Soskice – a Labour Attorney General – was relying on the common law of conspiracy which had been used against the gas workers in *R v Bunn*,[45] and which had been expressly preserved by the Conspiracy and Protection of Property Act 1875 for use in cases where the industrial action was not 'in contemplation or furtherance of a trade dispute'.[46]

So far as existing remedies were concerned, for the sake of completeness, Soskice addressed the potential civil remedies, having toyed with the idea of making it actionable (without saying by whom) to incite others to strike without resorting to negotiation or arbitration. The idea was rejected, however, quite properly on the ground that it too would require primary legislation.[47] Although not referred to by Soskice, any such initiative would mean re-opening the settlement secured by the Trade Disputes Act 1906, which appeared now to be remarkably robust. The Trade Disputes and Trade Unions Act 1946 had fully restored the legal protections introduced in 1906 following their limitation in 1927, while separately (as we have pointed out in several occasions) the tortious liability to which that settlement was a response had been questioned in the *Crofter* case.[48] The latter effectively took the tort of conspiracy to injure out of active service in industrial relations by recognising the legitimacy

[41] ibid para 5.
[42] ibid para 6.
[43] ibid. As we have seen, however, Shawcross had complained repeatedly about the problems in finding usable evidence to bring a prosecution for criminal conspiracy.
[44] ibid, Schedule para 1.
[45] *R v Bunn* (1872) 12 Cox CC 316.
[46] Conspiracy and Protection of Property Act 1875, s 3. See ch 4 above. Soskice also drew attention to the criminal liability contained in the 1875 Act, ss 4 and 5, there obviously being no intention to repeal either provision. Equally, there is no known example of either being brought into active service following the botched gas workers' prosecution in 1950, as pointed out by the Donovan Commission. See Royal Commission on Trade Unions and Employers' Associations, 1965–68, Report, Cmnd 3626, 1968, paras 834, 842.
[47] TNA, CAB 129/46/74 ('The Future of the Conditions of Employment and National Arbitration Order', Memorandum by the Attorney General, 24 July 1951, para 6).
[48] *Crofter Hand Woven Harris Tweed Co Ltd v Veitch*, 1942 SC(HL) 1.

of the 'right to strike'. It would almost certainly have led to conflict with the TUC if the government had proposed to qualify the scope of the restored and expanded 1906 settlement, either by narrowing the definition of a protected trade dispute, or by creating a new head of liability for breach of a new statutory duty.[49]

IV. Revocation and Replacement of Order 1305

The Robens and Soskice Memorandums were considered by the Cabinet on 26 July 1951.[50] Rather than deal with their substance, the main question considered by ministers was the timing of a Commons debate about what was to become Order 1376.[51] It was decided to arrange a date to ensure a full attendance of Labour backbenchers in case of any trouble, so it was not until 2 August that the matter was considered by Parliament in advance of the new Order coming into force on 14 August.[52] Robens' parliamentary announcement – in which he emphasised the role of the new Order as being supplementary to existing voluntary procedures – was welcomed on both sides of the House. In what reads remarkably today, RA Butler for the Conservatives rose to say that it was the Opposition's desire to give the new Order 'a fair wind,' and that they 'certainly accept[ed] the Minister's view that the voluntary bargaining system should be maintained in this country and supported on all occasions'.[53] Perhaps even more notable, however, was the Conservative Party's appreciation of the removal of restrictions on strikes:

> I should also like to welcome the fact that the Minister has stated that the Order contains no provision prohibiting lock-outs or strikes. That is in accordance with what we have already expressed and in accordance with the policy which we had already adopted as ours.[54]

Writing shortly afterwards, Kahn Freund referred to the revocation of Order 1305 as 'an important event in the development of British labour law'.[55] As he pointed out, reflecting contemporary opinion, 'the attempt to use the machinery of the criminal law for the furtherance of industrial peace has ended in failure'.[56] But as indicated above, there was more to Order 1376 than the removal of the ban on strikes. These included the retention of an arbitration procedure for the resolution of disputes, albeit in a manner heavily modified from its original form in Order 1305. But as trailed

[49] Also on the question of civil liability, Soskice pointed out in a Schedule to his paper that: 'If a worker breaks his contract of employment, eg, if in the case of a weekly contract he stops work before the week is out, his employer may sue him for damages for breach of contract. The damage is generally small in money, and may be nominal. In practice, it has been found that employers, particularly the nationalised undertakings, hesitate to take these proceedings although they have been successfully taken on occasions. The remedy, however, is a remedy open to the individual employers and is not equivalent to some remedy in the hands of the State as a whole': TNA, CAB 129/46/74 ('The Future of the Conditions of Employment and National Arbitration Order', Memorandum by the Attorney General, 24 July 1951, Schedule, para 3).

[50] TNA, CAB 128/20/5 (Cabinet Conclusions, 26 July 1951).

[51] Industrial Disputes Order, SI 1951 No 1376.

[52] HC Debs, 2 August 1951, col 1624.

[53] ibid col 1626.

[54] ibid.

[55] O Kahn Freund, 'Industrial Disputes Order' (1951) 14 *MLR* 467.

[56] ibid p 468.

by Robens on 20 July, the definition of a trade dispute was narrowed so that certain disputes could not be reported and referred to arbitration. It was now expressly provided that the definition did not 'include a dispute as to the employment or non-employment of any person or as to whether any person should or should not be a member of any trade union'. This gave effect to the desire to exclude closed shop disputes from the scope of the arbitration procedures. As we saw in Chapter Eleven in relation to the BOAC dispute, however, Order 1305 had been effectively dis-applied in such cases by Ministry of Labour and NAT practice, which Shawcross as Attorney General had endorsed by refusing to prosecute.

This limit on the IDT's jurisdiction meant that the dispute then brewing in the newspaper industry about the right to be a trade union member could not be referred to arbitration, even if there had been a desire on the part of the unions to do so. This was the bitter dispute at DC Thomson Ltd, the Dundee-based publisher of several well-known titles, including *The Beano* and *The Dandy*. Since at least the General Strike in 1926, the company had operated a 'union free' policy, by which it was a condition of employment that all staff should sign what was referred to as the 'document' whereby they undertook not to join a trade union, those refusing to sign the 'document' being dismissed.[57] Although the TUC Annual Congress approved a motion in 1951 seeking the TUC General Council's support to challenge the company's practice,[58] trade unionists continued to be dismissed at the company's site in Manchester. Following the dismissal of James McKay on 21 March 1952 after 31 years' service, the National Society of Operative Printers and Assistants (NATSOPA) took industrial action to secure his re-instatement and in the following month, a number of trade unionists at the company's Glasgow works joined the action until the non-union condition was withdrawn. Although beyond the scope of Order 1376, the resolution of this dispute nevertheless required government intervention at the highest level, to which we return below.[59]

More controversial than the foregoing, however, was the requirement anticipated by both Robens and Soskice that disputes could be reported to the Minister only by employers or employers' associations, or by trade unions. Cue the intervention by Tory backbencher Sir Herbert Williams, who was prompted to ask what was to be done 'when people went on strike against the advice of their own union, given that the Industrial Disputes Tribunal would have no jurisdiction to deal with such disputes?'.[60] Robens was notably unconvincing in response, claiming that the new Order did not take away any of the Minister's other powers nor his capacity to exert 'a moral influence'.[61] Yet only a year earlier the problem of unofficial action was so acute that Isaacs responded to Eden by saying that he was prepared if necessary to legislate to deal with it. In what was an extraordinary volte-face on behalf of a government which had been preoccupied if

[57] The Webbs refer to requirements to sign the 'hated' document as an instrument of union-exclusion going back to the 1830s, noting its presence at various points in their famous history and optimistically asserting that by the late 1850s, 'the old expedient' had 'fallen somewhat into discredit': S Webb and B Webb, *The History of Trade Unionism, 1666-1920* (Longmans, Green & Co, London, 1920), p 255.

[58] TUC Annual Report 1951, pp 332–33.

[59] See pp 277–278 below.

[60] HC Debs, 2 August 1951, col 1628.

[61] ibid.

not obsessed by industrial action unsupported by union hierarchies, Robens continued in his reply to Sir Herbert by claiming that:

> There will be many cases where people will not observe what has been laid down and in these cases we must do as we have always done, bring the two sides together and preach a little sweet reasonableness. I am certain – and things are moving in this direction – that there is a greater sense of responsibility on the part of both workers and employers in relation to industrial disputes. It is the basis of our democracy to encourage self-discipline among individuals.[62]

But although the foregoing were significant changes, Order 1376 reset the law in an even more fundamental way, confounding earlier ministerial claims by creating what was in effect no more than 'an elaborate apparatus of permissive arbitration'.[63] Because of the lifting of the restraints on the right to strike, arbitration was no longer compulsory as it had been under Order 1305. On the contrary, the effect of Order 1376 was to make arbitration optional on the part of the union, even where it satisfied the reference criteria of (i) habitually taking part in the settlement of terms and conditions of employment, or failing which (ii) being representative of a substantial proportion of the workers in the industry concerned, or a section thereof. Thus, a union was free to report a dispute to the Minister if it was so inclined, but it was free not to do so and to take industrial action instead. According to the Donovan Royal Commission, which in 1968 provided a retrospective assessment of Order 1376's operation, some trade unions preferred to 'rely on their industrial strength' rather than arbitration.[64] But even if a dispute was reported to the Minister – either by the employer or by a union – the reference could effectively be vetoed or aborted by industrial action. Thus, as pointed out by Soskice on 24 July, it was not possible for the Minister to refer a dispute to the Tribunal while industrial action continued, 'if in his opinion it would be undesirable to do so'.[65]

A union could thus in effect choose to arbitrate or strike, or strike and then arbitrate. If it chose to arbitrate, the union remained free to strike if it did not like the arbitration award. Although Article 10 provided that 'it shall be an implied term of the contract between the employer and workers to whom the award applies that the terms and conditions of employment to be observed under the contract shall be in accordance with the award', Article 10 also provided that these terms would apply unless:

> varied by agreement between the parties or by a subsequent award of the Tribunal or until different terms and conditions of employment in respect of the workers concerned are settled through the machinery or negotiation or arbitration for the settlement of terms and conditions of employment in the trade or industry or section of trade or industry or undertaking in which those workers are employed.

There was nothing to stop a union from taking industrial action to secure better terms than those provided in the award. It is not clear to what extent this was a problem in practice, though it is a sign of the extent to which Order 1376 had changed labour

[62] ibid.
[63] DN Pritt and R Freeman, *The Law versus the Trade Unions* (Lawrence & Wishart, London, 1958), p 105.
[64] Royal Commission on Trade Unions and Employers' Associations (n 46) para 238.
[65] SI 1951, No 1376, art 8(3), which continues: 'where the Minister has referred a dispute to the Tribunal and thereafter notifies the Tribunal that one of the parties to the dispute is taking any such action as aforesaid, all proceedings thereon shall be stayed until the Minister cancels such notification'.

law dramatically. Arbitration was no longer compulsory, and did not necessarily give rise to meaningfully binding outcomes; it was now entirely voluntary, and all coercive restraints were removed.

The unilateral arbitration provisions under Order 1376 were thus in effect a one-way bet for the unions. According to Donovan, they tended to be relied on by organisations operating in 'poorly organized industries and trades', noting that 'the great majority of references seem to have concerned comparatively weak groups of workers'.[66] But although IDT awards were 'by and large in line with settlements being reached by other means',[67] employers nevertheless grew to dislike the procedures, Donovan claiming that:

> A feeling developed among employers that the Industrial Disputes Tribunal procedure worked in a one-sided way and that while its awards could be effectively enforced by employees, it was difficult for employers to benefit from awards in their favour. The knowledge that arbitration was available which in practice worked in this way tended in the employers' view, to undermine negotiation.[68]

It had always been understood that unilateral arbitration should 'continue only so long as it had the support of both sides of industry'.[69] With employers' support thus having been lost, an opportunity to remove Order 1376 was provided in 1957 when the then Conservative government decided to abolish the Defence Regulation under which Order 1376 was made, the government making it clear that it was doing so because the instrument had 'proved not to be acceptable to the British Employers' Confederation'.[70]

It is notable nevertheless that the revocation of Order 1376 was opposed at the time by the Labour Party, then in Opposition. Indeed, it was Alfred Robens himself as Shadow Minister of Labour who moved the prayer to annul the Regulation introduced to revoke Order 1376.[71] According to Robens, Order 1376 had played a major part in 'preventing a tremendous number of disputes',[72] adding in a long speech defending the instrument he had authored that it was particularly important for unions like NALGO which at the time had renounced the right to strike, 'a very substantial principle' to which it had adhered, 'no doubt in the interests of the public generally'.[73] Without binding arbitration, there was no way by which NALGO would be able to process disputes. But although the annulment motion predictably failed, the government unwilling to compromise on 'disputes', it was, nevertheless, prepared to concede on the retention of the provisions relating to the unilateral arbitration of 'issues' – that is to say, the provisions of Order 1376 relating to the extension of collective agreements made by parties who represented a substantial proportion of the employers and workers in a particular industry. As a result of a 'very far-reaching' amendment to the Terms and Conditions of Employment Bill then

[66] Royal Commission on Trade Unions and Employers' Associations (n 46) para 238.

[67] ibid.

[68] ibid para 239.

[69] ibid.

[70] HC Debs, 19 November 1958, col 1173 (Iain Macleod, Minister of Labour and National Service). The procedure came to an end in 1959, by which time the IDT had made over 1,270 awards.

[71] HC Debs, 19 November 1958, col 1155. The Order in question was the Industrial Disputes (Amendment and Revocation) Order, 1958 (SI 1958 No 1796).

[72] HC Debs, 19 November 1958, col 1163.

[73] ibid col 1164.

before Parliament,[74] unions were thus empowered by primary legislation to refer a 'claim' to the Industrial Court that a renegade employer was not acting consistently with the terms of such an agreement.[75] The Industrial Court could then make an award requiring the employer in question to comply, the terms of the agreement being implied into the contracts of employment of the workers concerned.

Regulatory Effect of Collective Agreements

As anticipated by Robens in his Memorandum on 20 July 1951, Order 1376 made provision for the reporting of 'issues' as well as 'disputes'. 'Issues' related to claims against employers who were failing to apply the terms and conditions of employment prescribed by relevant collective agreements. As indicated in the text, there was a difference between the provisions of Order 1305 and its replacement. Under Order 1305, there was a legal duty that 'all employers in that trade or industry in that district shall observe the recognised terms and conditions or such terms and conditions of employment as are not less favourable than the recognised terms and conditions'.[76]

Recognised terms and conditions were defined widely to include, for example, 'any decision of a joint industrial council, conciliation board or other similar body constituted by organisations of employers and trade unions which are representative respectively of substantial proportions of the employers and workers engaged or employed in the trade or industry in the district in which the employer is engaged'.[77] The role of the NAT in such cases was to enforce that duty, by determining the appropriate recognised terms and conditions, deciding whether the employer was not complying, and if so inserting them as an implied term of contracts of employment if necessary.

Order 1376 retained the *erga omnes* principle, albeit in a limited way. There was no longer an express statutory duty on all employers to comply with recognised terms and conditions as set out in relevant collective agreements. The duty was now at best implicit: an issue concerning a failure to comply with recognised terms and conditions could be reported to the Minister and thereafter referred to the IDT, but the latter now had a discretion whether to require these terms and conditions to be extended. By virtue of Order 1376, Article 9(3), it was provided that:

> Where an issue has been referred by the Minister to the Tribunal and the Tribunal is of opinion that there are recognised terms and conditions applicable to the case and that the employer concerned is not observing those terms and conditions or terms and conditions of employment which, in the opinion of the Tribunal, are not less favourable than those terms and conditions, it may by its award require the employer to observe the

[74] HL Debs, 27 April 1959, col 991 (Lord Silkin).

[75] The Industrial Court had been established by the Industrial Courts Act 1919. It took over the IDT's jurisdiction, the latter abolished following the revocation of Order 1376. See Terms and Conditions of Employment Act 1959, s 8.

[76] SR&O 1940 No 1305, art 5(1).

[77] ibid art 5(2)(b).

recognised terms and conditions or such terms and conditions of employment as may be determined by it to be not less favourable than the recognised terms and conditions.

Following the revocation of Order 1376, these latter provisions were re-introduced in an adapted form by the Terms and Conditions of Employment Act 1959, section 8. The *erga omnes* principle was now in primary legislation for the first time albeit in diluted form, in the manner described in the text.[78] The 1959 Act was amended by the Industrial Relations Act 1971, before being repealed and replaced by the Employment Protection Act 1975, section 98 and Schedule 11, revising and expanding the operation of unilateral arbitration for the extension of collective agreements and other terms and conditions of employment. The latter procedure was abolished in 1980 by the first Thatcher administration.[79]

Northern Ireland

As discussed in Chapter Three, Order 1305 did not apply in Northern Ireland, where an equivalent measure – Order 1508 – applied. Order 1508 was not revoked until the Conditions of Employment and National Arbitration (Amendment and Revocation) (NI) Order 1958 (Order No 169), made under Regulation 58AA of the Defence (General) Regulations 1939. Regulation 58AA had continued to have effect by virtue of the Supplies and Services (Transitional Powers) Act 1945 as extended by the Supplies and Services (Extended Purposes) Act 1947 and the Supplies and Services (Defence Purposes) Act 1951, and continued in force again by the Supplies and Services (Continuance) Order 1957.[80] The penal provisions of Order 1508 were not invoked after 1945.

V. A Gradual Reorientation

While the threat of criminal liability for organising and participating in strike action (though not for picketing and other strike related activities) had been lifted in August 1951,[81] the spectre of the common law continued to lurk, albeit held back in relation to the criminal law by the Conspiracy and Protection Act 1875, and in relation to tortious liability by the Trade Disputes Act 1906. The question now was when the judiciary, notoriously hostile even to the concept of organised labour for as long

[78] See also Royal Commission on Trade Unions and Employers' Associations (n 46) para 240.
[79] For full details, see B Bercusson, *Fair Wages Resolutions* (Mansell, London, 1978).
[80] See PRONI, CAB 9C/11/8 ('Contracts of Employment and Redundancy Payments Bill Compulsory Arbitration').
[81] There are many examples of the criminal law being used subsequently for picketing and other strike-related activities, with the cases of the Shrewsbury pickets in the 1970s and the miners in the 1980s being particularly notable.

as there could be said to have been an English legal system, would start to restrict the freedom to take industrial action workers now enjoyed. As we saw in Chapter Four and as alluded to above, the House of Lords had exercised restraint during the war to reset the foundations of tortious liability (at least in relation to conspiracy).[82] But although that restraint was to change following the revocation of war-time powers, it was not immediate, as revealed by the Court of Appeal decision in *DC Thomson & Co Ltd v Deakin*.[83] The latter reflected the prevailing sentiment reflected in Order 1376 that legal restraints on the right to strike were finally to be removed and the freedom of trade unionists restored.

In retrospect, however, the case is significant not only for the fact that the employer thought to use the civil law, but also that it was indulged at first instance on three occasions. As we have seen, the firm – which had long refused to employ trade unionists – had dismissed a Manchester-based employee because of his trade union membership. This led to industrial action by 79 colleagues of the dismissed worker, 74 of whom were also dismissed, leading in turn to the company being declared 'black' by the men's union. Secondary action against the firm followed, much of it orchestrated ironically by the TGWU, as a result of which DC Thomson took its legal action. An *ex parte* interlocutory injunction was granted against Arthur Deakin on 9 May 1952 to stop interference with the supply of paper from Bowaters Sales Ltd, to which the General Secretary of the Paper Workers' Union was added on 13 May, before the injunction was discharged on 26 May. A second *ex parte* interlocutory injunction was granted on 16 May 1952 against officials of NATSOPA and the Paper Makers' Union respectively to stop interference with the contracts between DC Thomson and WH Smith, the newspaper distributor, the injunction later being discharged on 27 May.[84]

DC Thomson & Co Ltd appealed against the discharge of the first injunction. But in upholding the decision of the High Court, the Court of Appeal declined to recognise that a prima facie 'actionable interference with contractual rights' had been established. Nevertheless, the Court of Appeal did accept that intentionally procuring the breach of a commercial contract between an employer and a third party could give rise to tortious liability, planting a seed that was to flower a decade later to disrupt the protection from tort liability secured in 1906. That said, the secondary action against DC Thomson had limited effect, though it was only the intervention of the Prime Minister that brought the dispute to an end,[85] Churchill regarding a ban placed by an employer on his employees as 'intolerable'. Having been 'against the action of the Durham County Council', he was

[82] *Crofter Hand Woven Harris Tweed Co Ltd v Veitch* (n 48).

[83] *DC Thomson & Co Ltd v Deakin* [1952] Ch 646.

[84] An interim interdict was also granted by Lord Blades in the Court of Session on 22 May 1952 against a number of ASLEF and NUR officials in Dundee 'restraining them from interfering with the company's legitimate right to trade'. It was alleged that they had incited their members to refuse to run trains carrying goods belonging to Thomson's and to have threatened to strike. Unlike the interim injunctions which were discharged, it is unclear when the interim interdict was recalled: it was still in force on 28 August.

[85] Cabinet papers on deposit in the National Archives confirm the TUC's account of Churchill's role: A Moretta, 'Benchmarking Workplace Rights' (PhD dissertation, University of Liverpool 2019), pp 142–43 (available at: https://livrepository.liverpool.ac.uk/3060675). For the full story, see the report of the Court of Inquiry set up under the terms of the Industrial Courts Act 1919: *Report of a Court of Inquiry into a Dispute between DC Thomson and Company Limited and Certain Workpeople, Members of the National Society of Operative Printers and Assistants*, Cmd 8607, 1952.

'equally opposed to the position adopted by DC Thomson which was "the closed shop the other way round"'.[86] The company agreed to 'cease insistence on anyone signing an agreement not to belong to a trade union' – 'in deference to the express request of the Minister arising from the Government's position in relation to ILO Convention 98' (which the previous government had ratified in 1950). But it refused to re-employ the strikers.[87]

A few years after the *DC Thomson* case, the Court of Appeal appeared to reveal a second possible challenge to the right to strike in the post-Order 1305 era. This was the attempt by the National Coal Board (the industry had been nationalised in 1947) to sue one of its own employees for breach of contract following industrial action. In *National Coal Board v Galley*,[88] a group of pit deputies at Oxcroft Colliery in Derbyshire refused to work contractually agreed Saturday overtime. The obligation to do so was set out in a collective agreement concluded by their union (on this occasion NACODS), the terms of which had been implied into their contracts of employment. Attempting to do what Shawcross had wanted the gas employers to do in 1950 (and to which Soskice had drawn attention in his Memorandum on 24 July 1951),[89] in 1956 the National Coal Board brought proceedings against the defendant to recover damages for losses incurred as a result of the industrial action. It was claimed that because of the overtime ban by the defendant and his colleagues, these losses amounted to £535 for the day that was the subject of the claim, and £3,395 in total over a period of two months. The deputies each earned £16 and ten shillings weekly.

According to the Court of Appeal, the action was 'not strictly a test case', but 'the first of 85 actions brought by the plaintiffs against other defendants raising similar issues'.[90] A successful outcome for the NCB would thus send a chilling message to all its employees about the risks associated with taking industrial action. Not only that: it is a message which would have implications going well beyond the mining industry, the consequences potentially affecting all trade unionists. It was necessary to go back as far as the Lancashire Cotton Corporation case in 1942 to find a similar example of such retribution.[91] There, eight Lancashire weavers were each required to pay £8 (presumably the loss sustained by the company as a result of the withdrawal of each individual's labour during a two-day strike). The employer, however, appears to have decided against demanding the same from the other (approximately) 92 weavers, very likely having become aware of the catastrophic impact such a step would have on industrial relations

[86] On the Durham County Council case, which was a long-running saga, see pp 211–212 above.

[87] This account is based in part on a TUC minute of a meeting between the Prime Minister and a TUC delegation on 8 September 1952. The TUC minute is held at the Warwick Modern Records Centre, University of Warwick and was accessed on 20 September 2021.

[88] *National Coal Board v Galley* [1958] 1 WLR 16. The case was heard by the Court of Appeal over a few days in October and November 1957. See also *Ebbw Vale Iron and Coal Co v Tew* (1935) Sol Jo 593; and *Fife Coal Co Ltd v MacBain* (1935) 52 Sh Ct Reps 84. On *Galley* and *Tew*, see KD Ewing, *The Right to Strike* (Oxford University Press, Oxford, 1991), pp 18–20. *Tew* appears to have given the coal industry the reputation for suing its employees referred to by ministers and officials in previous chapters. See p 74 above. The employer in *MacBain* was unsuccessful on the facts.

[89] See, for example, pp 173–174, and 186. On Soskice, see p 271 above, note 49.

[90] *National Coal Board v Galley* (n 88) p 17 (Pearce LJ).

[91] See TNA, LAB 10/173 ('Prosecutions of Strikers under Order 1305 (1) undertaken (2) Contemplated').

and on the firm's reputation. In *Galley*, nevertheless, the NCB won at first instance, and ominously the defendant was ordered to pay £100 with costs.

The victory was, however, short-lived, the Court of Appeal appearing to go to great lengths to allow (in part) Mr Galley's appeal and reduce the award by a very considerable margin, tacitly making it clear that the threat of a claim for breach of contract could not be allowed to restrict the freedom to strike to the extent suggested at first instance. First, the writ was issued within days of the first day which was not worked, the court holding that subsequent days of action would have been seen as separate causes of action requiring separate claims.[92] Second, after reasoning which might charitably be described as impenetrable, the Lords Justices of Appeal required Mr Galley to pay only for the cost of obtaining a replacement on the Saturday which was the subject of the claim – £3, eighteen shillings and two pence. It seems that this would be payable, although 'no productive work' had been done that day due to the absence of other deputies and shot-firers. As highlighted by the headnote author, it was held that 'although the defendant was undoubtedly acting in concert with others in failing to report for duty on the day in question, it was not shown that his breach of contract contributed to the loss of output of coal sustained on that day'.[93] Shawcross' blueprint for dealing with strikers thus proved to be difficult to implement in practice, despite the vigour and persistence with which it had been advanced.

It would nevertheless be a significant blow to workers on strike if they were not only to lose their wages for taking such action, but required also to pay the wages of their replacement. However, it was not the use of contract law that was to lead to a reorientation of the post-Order 1305 ceasefire, but the development of tort law, the DC Thomson case proving to be no more than a false start. The occasion was another closed shop dispute at Heathrow airport,[94] this time between BOAC and the Association of Engineering and Shipbuilding Draughtsmen (AESD). There the company 'accepted that if any shop achieved 100 per cent union membership then they would not disrupt that state of affairs by introducing a non-union recruit'.[95] When Douglas Rookes – a previously active and enthusiastic member – resigned from the union in November 1955, 'the men ran strongly against him',[96] and a few weeks later, the three defendant officials of the union threatened the company that unless Rookes was removed from the Design Office, all AESD members would withdraw their labour. Any such action would have been unconstitutional in the sense that a National Joint Industrial Council Agreement for Civil Air Transport concluded in 1949 provided for the resolution of disputes by arbitration.[97]

[92] *National Coal Board v Galley* (n 88) p 27.

[93] ibid, at p 17.

[94] For a previous closed shop dispute involving BOAC at Heathrow airport, see pp 202–206 above.

[95] R Bagshaw, 'Rookes' Tale' in J Adams-Prassl, A Bogg and ACL Davies, *Landmark Cases in Labour Law* (Hart Publishing, Oxford, 2022), p 99.

[96] KW Wedderburn, *Cases and Materials on Labour Law* (Cambridge University Press, Cambridge, 1967), p 503.

[97] Bagshaw (n 95) p 100. However, he was not dismissed at the request of the union or its members, who insisted only that he be removed from the office: P Smith, 'The Law behind the Law: *Rookes v Barnard*, the Common Law and the Right to Strike' (2017) 38 *Historical Studies in Industrial Relations* 38 – a superb account.

As pointed out by Roderick Bagshaw, there was no strike: Rookes was suspended and then dismissed.[98] After a lengthy delay, the case was heard in the High Court in 1961. Rookes was awarded £7,500 following a jury trial, a decision overturned by the Court of Appeal, before being restored by the House of Lords.[99] The Lords held that the officials were liable for 'tortious intimidation', and that the Trade Disputes Act 1906, sections 1 and 3, while worded to protect against liability for tortious inducements to breach contracts of employment, did not extend immunity to trade union members and officials who threatened to induce a breach unless harm was caused to the plaintiff. According to the *New Statesman* (retrieved by Bagshaw), 'the Lords first of all extended an obscure and unfamiliar civil wrong, and then decided that the 1906 Act gives no protection against it'.[100] And according to the AESD's General Secretary George Doughty: 'The intention of the 1875 Act was breached by the House of Lords' judgment in the *Taff Vale* case. The intention of the 1906 Act was breached by *Rookes v Barnard*.'[101] Although the legal merits of the decision have been hotly contested,[102] it was nevertheless the harbinger of a new era of judicial attacks on trade union freedom.

VI. Conclusion

So, although the courts initially showed some reluctance to engage with industrial action following the revocation of Order 1305, the civil law gradually began again to fill the gap left by the retreat of the criminal law. *Rookes v Barnard* was the first of a pair of House of Lords decisions which indicated that *Crofter*, *DC Thomson* and *Galley* were to give way to a more robust judicial approach. The other decision was *JT Stratford & Son Ltd v Lindley*,[103] which was another 'blacking' case, in which the plaintiff company claimed to have suffered the same deliberate and direct 'actionable interference' with a commercial contract that had been contemplated by the court in *DC Thomson*. It was held that by inducing their members to break their contracts of employment, the respondents had unlawfully procured a breach of commercial contracts between the target of the action (who was an associate of an employer with whom the defendants had a recognition dispute) and its customers.[104] By a remarkable irony, Lord Reid was a dominant presence in the House of Lords in both *Rookes v Barnard* and *Stratford v Lindley*. As Lord Advocate, James Reid had been responsible for the enforcement of Order 1305 in Scotland during the war, and as Conservative MP for Glasgow Hillhead

[98] ibid.
[99] *Rookes v Barnard* [1964] AC 1129.
[100] ibid p 101 (referring to passage in *New Statesman*, 24 January 1964).
[101] TUC Report 1964, p 523, quoted in C Wrigley, 'Trade Unions and the 1964 General Election' (2007) 21 *Contemporary British History* 325.
[102] Bagshaw (n 95).
[103] *JT Stratford & Son Ltd v Lindley* [1965] AC 269. See also *Torquay Hotel Co Ltd v Cousins* [1969] 2 Ch 106.
[104] It was also held that the action was unlawful on the additional ground that 'the respondents threatened to induce the men of their union to break their contracts and thereby threatened to use unlawful means to interfere with the appellant's business' (at p 325).

had been the young Hartley Shawcross' tormentor in strongly opposing the repeal of the 1927 Act after the war.[105]

Legislation was passed in 1965 to neutralise the effect of *Rookes v Barnard*, but not the instability caused by other legal decisions at the time. The British model of labour law was now under pressure, with judicial developments adding to a sense that 'the basic principles of our system of industrial relations are in question'.[106] A Royal Commission was appointed to consider whether these principles should be 'restored, revised or replaced'.[107] But by the time the Royal Commission reported, the post-war consensus had evaporated. The year 1970 saw the election of a combative Conservative government and the ambitious attempt by Edward Heath's Cabinet to supplant the post-war settlement with a comprehensive set of statutory controls. A highly structured legal framework overseen by a National Industrial Relations Court was the basis of the new regime, the failure of which has been told elsewhere.[108] The replacement of the 1971 Act by a union-friendly government in 1974 and 1975 led to the brief revival of a third period of judicial activism since 1900,[109] before Thatcherism obliterated any remaining notions of economic democracy through collective bargaining and trade union representation in government. Although the government was responsible for the new restrictions on the right to strike, responsibility for their enforcement was outsourced to employers, and to the civil rather than the criminal law.

[105] It was ironic too that Hartley Shawcross played a part in advising Rookes' legal team: see Smith (n 97).

[106] Royal Commission on Trade Unions and Employers' Associations (n 46) para 45.

[107] ibid.

[108] See M Moran, *The Politics of Industrial Relations* (Macmillan, London, 1977); B Weekes, M Mellish, L Dickens, and J Lloyd, *Industrial Relations and the Limits of the Law: The Industrial Effects of the Industrial Relations Act 1971* (Basil Blackwell, Oxford, 1975).

[109] See *Grunwick Processing Laboratories Ltd v ACAS* [1978] AC 655; *NWL Ltd v Woods* [1979] ICR 867; *Express Newspapers Ltd v McShane* [1980] ICR 42; and *Duport Steels v Sirs* [1980] ICR 161.

PART VI

Conclusion

15

Conclusion

I. The Context

We have seen in the pages above that the period from 1945 to 1951 was characterised by relatively low levels of industrial action. It was, however, also a period in which a number of high-profile disputes took place, and in which some of these disputes were politically challenging for the government, particularly those in the ports, which had implications for the availability of food, already in short supply. The unrest on the docks was no doubt paradoxical in light of the changes that had been made at the beginning of the war and retained thereafter to improve working conditions and enhance job security. Dock work had been notorious for its casual nature, George Isaacs recalling the days 'when there were thousands of men lining up at the dock gates and it was really a question of the survival of the fittest'. Recalling too an occasion when he saw how men were 'literally fighting for a job'.[1] These observations were made when introducing what became the Dock Workers (Regulation of Employment) Act 1946 to establish a permanent registration scheme for dock workers and dock employers.

As a result, only registered employers could employ people on dock work, which was normally restricted to registered dock workers. Terms and conditions of employment – which included guaranteed payments for times when work was not available – were set by the National Joint Industrial Council (NJIC) for the Port Transport Industry, which drew its membership from the National Association of Port Employers as well as various trade unions. In addition to dealing with terms and conditions of employment, the NJIC nominated eight of its number to the National Dock Labour Board, which was responsible for the general policy and administration of the national dock labour scheme. These arrangements, based on the principle of 'dual control' in the management of the industry,[2] were clearly not enough to prevent disputes, to which we have seen the government responded by adopting a number of strategies, beginning with the use of troops under defence powers, escalating to the use of the Emergency Powers Act 1920, and escalating further to the use of criminal sanctions under Order 1305. All were big steps for a Labour government to take.

[1] HC Debs, 12 November 1945, col 1753.
[2] Ministry of Labour, *Industrial Relations Handbook* (HMSO, 1961 edn), p 58.

II. A Dysfunctional Activity

The experience of Order 1305 generally provided some important insights into the role of the state under the post-war Labour government. In particular, it highlighted the diminished influence of the traditional constitution in law making in what was a new economic democracy with a greater role for trade unions and the TUC in the process of government. Order 1305 was made under powers contained in the Emergency Powers (Defence) Acts 1939–40, in which Parliament delegated to ministers the power to make Defence Regulations to require the compulsory arbitration of trade disputes and to impose restrictions on the right to strike, a right said by Pritt to be derived from the common law.[3] These powers were continued in force by the Supplies and Services (Transitional Powers) Act 1945, with the result that while the power to introduce and continue Order 1305 in operation had statutory authority, the sub-delegated content of Order 1305 and the restrictions contained therein at no point had parliamentary approval. Crucially, however, they were introduced in 1940 with the agreement of the TUC and the British Employers' Confederation, both organisations consenting to the retention of the restrictions five years later, on the condition that they could be revoked at any time.

With the renewal of the agreement in 1945 forged within the framework of the tripartite National Joint Advisory Council, trade unions thus played a part in the formal *process* of determining the rules by which they were governed, along with the *substance* of the rules which were to apply, in what was an alternative form of law making. In doing so, they were engaged in what were new forms of constitutional legitimacy for legal regulation, and were able to insist that the law be changed when it ceased to be appropriate. The constitutional innovation that led to the renewal of Order 1305 was by no means isolated, as the development of the wage restraint bargain between the government and the TUC in 1948 was also to reveal, leading to the White Paper on *Personal Incomes, Costs and Prices* having regulatory effect.[4] This form of regulation was just as binding on those to whom it was addressed as it would have been if contained in an Act of Parliament. It too was based on consent, and it too had to be withdrawn after it no longer retained the support of the TUC. All of which is to highlight what appears not to be obvious: British labour law was developed principally in the shadow of the administrative state, alongside the bright lights of primary legislation.

In the emerging social democracy, the administrative power of the state was being used not only to contain trade unions, but also to empower them as regulatory bodies engaged in making the rules by which workers were employed. Despite the focus of this book on the right to strike, the other important feature of Order 1305 was the application of the *erga omnes* principle to industry-wide collective agreements, which were given direct legal effect, binding everyone in the sector in question. In the new social democracy, terms and conditions of employment were regulated not unilaterally by employers through the contract of service, or politically by the state through legislation,

[3] HC Debs, 28 April 1944, col 1103.

[4] *Personal Incomes, Costs and Prices*, Cmd 7321, 1948. For an attempt to apply this precedent as part of the Social Contract in 1974, see KD Ewing, 'The Politics of the British Constitution' [2000] *PL* 405.

but principally by collective agreements which were for all practical purposes 'legislative' instruments. Under such arrangements, however, it was essential for trade unions to operate democratically, and for officials to behave in a responsive and responsible way on behalf of their members to whom they ought to have been accountable. Yet this was to become an Achilles' heel of the system as it developed after the war, as highlighted by evidence on day three of the dockers' trial where one of the defendants was reported as complaining of a 'great deal of dissatisfaction in the union because we cannot elect our own officials'.[5]

So while unofficial action may have been dysfunctional in an idealised social democracy of the kind which the post-war government was developing, in such circumstances it was perfectly rational as an important safety valve. The point is well made in a quite brilliant insight by Joseph Goldstein, who refers to a letter from a docker to the *News Chronicle* which gives an account of rank-and-file suspicions of full-time officials, who they saw as having been co-opted by the new Labour government into different state functions. In these circumstances, wrote Goldstein:

> The strike in the period of transition from a capitalist economy to a socialist economy is becoming as much a means of informing the Trade Union leader of his membership's grievances, as it is a weapon against the employer. When socialist demands are being made of workers living in what is essentially a profit-motivated society in transition, the average workers must be kept more closely in touch than ever before with what leaders are thinking and doing. The strike as a means of communication between leader and rank and file is both expensive and dangerous, and one the community can ill afford.[6]

By failing to acknowledge this point, trade unions were in danger of becoming engines of oppression rather than liberation and participation, and of losing sight of the importance not only of securing better working conditions, but also the processes by which these conditions were achieved. It was concerns of this kind that led Bevan provocatively to have asked in the debates about Regulation 1AA in 1944 whether Parliament ought not 'to consider all the rules of the unions', with a view to ensuring that officials are elected and accountable to the rank and file.[7]

But in the new social democratic constitution, innovation was to emerge not only in relation to law making, but also in relation to law enforcement (in its widest sense), bringing to the forefront classical notions of the rule of law. Here we find a contrast between the pragmatic approach of the Ministry of Labour and the increasingly strident position of the Law Officers led by Sir Hartley Shawcross. The departmental or administrative approach was fairly relaxed about matters of legality, renewing the operation of Order 1305 despite the advice of the Ministry of Labour's Chief Industrial Commissioner (CIC) that 'we are not at present in a position to apply the sanctions of the Order when an illegal strike occurs'. Because 'the Order has ceased to have public support and its early revocation is expected',[8] such inaction

[5] *Daily Worker*, 12 April 1951. One of the accused is reported as saying on the same day that the Birkenhead dockers had no confidence in their officials: *The Times*, 12 April 1951.

[6] J Goldstein, *The Government of British Trade Union: A Study of Apathy and the Democratic Process in the Transport and General Workers Union* (George Allen & Unwin, London, 1952), p 64.

[7] HC Debs, 28 April 1944, col 1073.

[8] TNA, LAB 10/ 581 ('Minute Note by R M Gould, Ministry of Labour', 15 December 1945).

would be difficult to justify after a decision had been taken deliberately to retain the law. The CIC's views were – perhaps unwittingly – echoed by Shawcross only two days after the renewal of Order 1305 took effect. Speaking in the Commons during the Committee stage of the Trade Disputes and Trade Unions Bill, he defended the repeal of the 1927 Act (which had restricted the right to strike following the General Strike) on the ground that 'no Government has ever been able effectively to stop or to prevent a strike'.[9]

Presumably with Order 1305 and Betteshanger particularly in mind, Shawcross acknowledged that there had been hundreds and possibly thousands of prosecutions during the war, with workers fined and sentenced to terms of imprisonment. But as he pointed out, 'the fines were incapable of enforcement, or collection, and the prisons were incapable of receiving people who have been sentenced to go there'.[10] The Ministry's response was to be seen subsequently in a departmental paper in 1947, which suggested that it had no intention to enforce the law,[11] a position reflected without any hint of embarrassment in a parliamentary statement by Isaacs in 1950 when he said that:

> The number of stoppages of work arising from industrial disputes reported as beginning in the 12 months ended August, 1950, was 1,334; the great majority of these were stoppages of brief duration, involving only small numbers of men. The question whether these stoppages were in contravention of the Conditions of Employment and National Arbitration Order, could only be authoritatively determined in the courts, and I have not thought it appropriate to institute proceedings in the courts in respect of any of these stoppages.[12]

But the departmental approach to enforcement was to be seen also in the practice of not referring unofficial disputes to arbitration. Although the policy was clearly unlawful, to refer such disputes would undermine the centralised structures that were developing and the authority of full-time trade union officials. It would also risk undermining the government's pay policy, as explained in Chapter Five. Formal legality had to give way to economic reality and should not be allowed to encourage processes or practices that risked subverting the structures built so carefully.

This pragmatic approach was initially supported and indeed encouraged by Shawcross. But he changed his mind and was subsequently to take the view that the law must be enforced and that departmental policy must yield to the formal requirements of the law. Having contradicted himself once, Shawcross was to contradict himself a second time, insisting in the Adjournment Debate on 29 January 1951 that the law need not be enforced all the time, and that prosecution was both a matter of law and discretion, which was to be exercised in the public interest.[13] As we saw in Chapter Thirteen, Shawcross used the Adjournment Debate in part to reply to

[9] HC Debs, 26 February 1946, col 1807.

[10] ibid.

[11] TNA, CAB 129/19/190 ('Development of National Arbitration Machinery, Memorandum by the Minister of Labour and National Service, 3 July 1947), para 5.

[12] HC Debs, 16 September 1950, col 1691. At this point Isaacs appeared to believe that he still had some notional responsibility for initiating prosecutions. In practice, this power had been exercised by Shawcross as we have seen throughout, before being formally transferred to the latter, as acknowledged by Attlee in a parliamentary statement on 7 November 1950: HC Debs, 7 November 1950, col 767.

[13] HC Debs, 29 January 1951, cols 679–90.

comments made by *The Times* and the *Daily Telegraph* in response to a speech he had made several months earlier.[14] The latter had disobligingly questioned the Attorney General's view that the law must be enforced 'in appropriate cases at the appropriate time'. In questioning this qualification, the *Daily Telegraph* asked whether it is not in fact 'a basic principle of the rule of law that the operation of the law is automatic (except when the law is specifically permissive and not mandatory) where the offence is known or suspected?'. For traditionalists, there was thus the prospect, of the law being arbitrarily enforced, and similar cases being treated differently.

Indeed, with a cutting nod to what is in effect Dicey's first principle, the *Daily Telegraph* questioned whether 'the arbitrary implementation of the law' is 'just as offensive to the elementary notion of justice as an arbitrary law'.[15] Responding on 29 January, Shawcross claimed that he must 'in a quasi-judicial way consider the effect of prosecution upon the administration of law and of government in the abstract rather than in any party sense'.[16] The meaning of a 'quasi-judicial way' was not made clear, though it did impress most if not all of those who heard it. While he would 'consult with any of his colleagues in the Government', 'the assistance of his colleagues is confined to informing him of particular considerations which might affect his own decision, and does not consist, and must not consist, in telling him what that decision ought to be'.[17] Responsibility for the eventual decision rests with the Attorney General, who 'is not to be put, and is not put, under pressure by his colleagues in the matter'.[18] This was a pitch for unconstrained power, in the exercise of which Shawcross would not be accountable to anyone. Behind the façade of a quasi-judicial role, the pragmatic industrial relations approach of the Ministry of Labour was to be displaced by the more legalistic approach of the law officers.[19]

III. A Weapon of Cold War Politics

In asserting his authority to decide when the law was to be applied, Shawcross also said that no Attorney General could possibly allow himself to be 'influenced by political considerations' in deciding whether or not to prosecute.[20] While some of the rest of his comments referred to above were disingenuous, this was plainly untrue in the case of Order 1305, which was clearly used for political purposes against the Communist Party and its activists.[21] As pointed out in Chapter Four, it was used principally as

[14] See above, pp 243–244.

[15] See AV Dicey, *Introduction to the Study of the Law of the Constitution*, 9th edn (Macmillan, London, 1939). The 10th and most recent edition was published in 1959. Dicey is still referred to as 'our greatest constitutional lawyer': *Jackson v Attorney General* [2005[UKHL 56, at para 95 (Lord Steyn).

[16] HC Debs, 29 January 1951, col 683.

[17] ibid.

[18] ibid col 684.

[19] The same tensions were to arise under the Labour government in the 1970s, albeit in different circumstances. In the 1970s liberal constitutional values were to triumph much more clearly and much more effectively. See Ewing (n 4); and KD Ewing, '*Grunwick Processing Laboratories v ACAS*: The Social Contract, Trade Union Recognition and the Rule of Law' in J Adams Prassl, A Bogg, and ACL Davies (eds), *Landmark Cases in Labour Law* (Hart Publishing, Oxford, 2022), ch 6.

[20] HC Debs, 29 January 1951, col 686.

[21] Indeed, Shawcross claimed in his 29 January speech that a factor in the gas workers' prosecution was the presence of Communists 'anxious to see the strike continue' (col 685).

an offence against the state directed at those who were members or supporters of the Communist Party or those whose conduct was believed to have been influenced by it. In this way, the use of Order 1305 revealed a tension about the role of trade unions, which were simultaneously instruments of government in the new social democracy but also vehicles for subversion, all the more dangerous for the fear that the subversion was to aid a foreign power at a time of heightened security concerns. So despite Shawcross' claims in the Adjournment Debate on 29 January, Order 1305 was used principally to deal with political enemies. Admittedly, its use was not confined to such cases: it was used against the dockers in 1951 for purely vindictive purposes where there was no practical need to do so.

Order 1305 had thus become unintentionally, and inadvertently, but necessarily, a weapon in Cold War politics, a role for which, as explained in Chapter Four, it was ill-suited. But although Shawcross was to realise that it would have been better to have kept the 1927 Act if this was the purpose for which the law was to be used, that too would not have been effective to deal with the big disputes on the waterfront, whether the two strikes in 1949 and 1950 in relation to solidarity with the Canadian seafarers and then with their own colleagues disciplined by the union, or any of the other industrial action by dock workers. New legislation to target the exaggerated Cold War mischief considered by the government was hastily dropped after being vetoed by the TUC, ministers unwilling to proceed without its consent. So despite being the principal (but not the only) tool available, Order 1305 was limited in the sense that it made illegal only strikes related to trade disputes. It did not apply to political strikes, unless there was some deeply submerged political motivation. The gas workers' prosecution was perhaps an example of such a case, at least in Shawcross' mind. Given the hyperbole and political drama in the ports in particular, that single conviction seems a rather modest haul, though it does emphasise the limitations of Order 1305 as an instrument for dealing with the industrial activities of the Communist Party.

In any event, as suggested by MI5's Guy Liddell, it is likely that claims about Communist Party subversion were greatly exaggerated. Otherwise it would have been possible to have used the other powers that Shawcross had been most anxious to deploy had the evidence been available, notably the law relating to sedition, extraordinary as that may seem. Which is not to deny a Communist Party presence in the trade unions or in the Port Workers' Committee or elsewhere. The major problems faced by the government, however, were the unresolved grievances of dockers and the lack of sufficient progress with the Dockers' Charter. It was the latter which fuelled the disputes, and it was salutary that once the grievances of the vast majority of the dockers had been addressed in January 1951, the problems of unofficial action dissipated noticeably. It was salutary too that the failed prosecution of the dockers in 1951 tended to show that the jury thought the dispute to be a dispute between the union and its members. As such, it was a consequence of the weakness of the post-war model and its insufficient efforts to resist what Robert Michels famously referred to as the 'iron law of oligarchy' which tended to capture labour movement organisations.[22] In

[22] R Michels, *Political Parties: A Sociological Study of the Oligarchical Tendencies of Modern Democracy* (Hearst's International Library, New York, 1915).

other words, it was a direct challenge to Deakin's management, uninformed by Cold War politics.

Although this was to be the last time that the criminal law was to be used against trade union activists for organising industrial action, this is not to say that with the revocation of Order 1305, the criminal law was removed from the statute book. Frank Soskice reminded Cabinet colleagues in 1951 of the residual liabilities as a result of the Conspiracy and Protection of Property Act 1875, section 3, and the continuing operation of sections 4 and 5 of the same Act, still applying to render participation in a strike a criminal offence. Although much of the 1875 Act has gone, the section 5 offence has been carried over to the Trade Union and Labour Relations (Consolidation) Act 1992, though it has attracted curiously little attention. It is nevertheless a criminal offence wilfully and maliciously to break a contract of service 'knowing or having reasonable cause to believe that the probable consequences' of doing so will be to endanger human life, cause serious bodily injury, or expose valuable property to destruction or serious injury. The 'very wide' scope of the latter provision was highlighted by the Royal Commission on Trade Unions and Employers' Associations in 1968, which recommended nevertheless that section 5 should be retained, taking the view that repeal 'might be construed as an express licence to do that which the criminal law now forbids'.[23]

More importantly, however, the continuing casual conflation of trade unionism with subversion is witness to the continuing and at times intense engagement of state agencies such as MI5 and the Metropolitan Police Special Branch with the monitoring and surveillance of trade unionists. The nature of these practices is laid bare in Chapters Six to Ten, with Home Office files not only making clear the existence of state surveillance, but also exposing its scope and methods. Even if Cold War politics provided any justification, that surveillance was clearly being undertaken for reasons unrelated to the Communist Party. More worrying is the possibility that trade unions were being supplied with information by the police to facilitate the expulsion of members following the 1949 dock strike. Forget about trade unions and state abstention. Trade unions were deeply penetrated by the state, with which some trade union leaders actively collaborated, despite Bevin's powerful defence of the trade union meeting as a privileged place of assembly for the conduct of business, to be attended only by those entitled to be present, free from the prying eyes of the state and its agents, with nothing said to be used as evidence in a police court.[24]

The casual conflation of trade unionism with subversion was of course to continue under both Labour and Conservative governments in the context of industrial action in the 1950s and beyond in order to justify the continuing surveillance of trade union activity. With the passage of time, the surveillance is less likely to have been undertaken

[23] Royal Commission on Trade Unions and Employers' Associations, 1965–68, Report, Cmnd 3623, 1968, para 846. However, it has never been used, and the focus of the law since 1951 has changed from an ineffective strategy of punishment by prosecution to a much more effective one of restraint by injunction. See *BBC v Hearn* [1977] ICR 685 and *Express Newspapers Ltd v Keys* [1980] IRLR 247 in the context of 'political' strikes. That said, strike-related activities continue to attract the attention of the criminal law and the police, while breach of an injunction can have punitive consequences for contempt of court.

[24] HC Debs, 28 April 1944, cols 1129–30.

for the investigation of crime or the defence of the realm (as during the early Cold War). On the contrary, it was more likely to have been undertaken to obtain information and to crush those who would challenge the authority of the government (most notably during the Thatcher era). In this way, surveillance techniques were used not to preserve, but to undermine democracy. Whatever the justification, the continuation and development of practices identified in the 1940s and 1950s are illuminated thereafter by two well-known examples. The first is the seafarers' strike in 1966, which famously led to the Prime Minister's condemnation of 'a tightly knit group of politically motivated men'. But it also led to a lengthy parliamentary statement by the Prime Minister which revealed an unhealthy level of knowledge about the operation of the National Union of Seamen, its officials, and the role of the Communist Party.[25] At various points in the course of a lengthy speech (delivered in the presence of an MI5 officer),[26] Wilson (himself a veteran of the dock strikes of the 1940s) told the Commons that:

> [T]here are no Communists on the executive council of this union and that the number of Communists among the membership of the union is extremely small.[27]
>
> [T]he Communist Party, unlike the major political parties, has at its disposal an efficient and disciplined industrial apparatus controlled from Communist Party headquarters.[28]
>
> For some years, the Communist Party has had as one of its objectives the building up of a position of strength not only in the Seamen's Union, but in other unions concerned with docks and transport.[29]
>
> The bid that the Communists are making is directed to next year's conference [of the union] at which the rules can be changed and at which steps can be taken also to change the full-time officers. In this union, for the reasons I have given, the full-time officers have an unusual degree of power to influence … the union's activities.[30]
>
> The Communist Party's industrial organiser is Mr Bert Ramelson, who, in January, succeeded Mr Peter Kerrigan. He has three full-time officials on his staff and in the London area, where the docks provide his hunting ground, his principal lieutenant is Mr Dennis Goodwin. Round this full-time nucleus has been gathered a small group of active trade unionists in the NUS and other trade unions.[31]
>
> The objectives of the Communist Party in this dispute were, first, to influence the day-to-day policy of the executive council; secondly, to extend the area of the [strike]; and, thirdly, to use the strike not only to improve the conditions of seamen – in which I believe them to be genuine – but also to secure what is at present the main political and industrial objective of the Communist Party – the destruction of the Government's prices and incomes policy.[32]

[25] HC Debs, 28 June 1966, col 1719.
[26] C Andrew, *The Defence of the Realm: The Authorized History of MI5* (Penguin, Harmondsworth, 2008), p 528. Wilson apparently greatly appreciated MI5's contribution to the handling of the strike, and particularly appreciated the product of phone taps and listening devices. Evidently Wilson was 'sometimes briefed daily, or even twice daily' by MI5 during the strike, after the then Cabinet Secretary Burke Trend had 'decided to inform the Prime Minister of the intelligence the Service was obtaining' about Communist involvement.
[27] HC Debs, 28 June 1966, col 1612.
[28] ibid col 1613.
[29] ibid col 1614.
[30] ibid col 1615.
[31] ibid.
[32] ibid col 1616.

> Time and again in this dispute the Communist Party's objectives have rapidly become the policy of the [union's] executive. This is particularly true in relation to the determination of the party to spread the strike.[33]
>
> The policy of extending the [strike] was, however, conducted by Mr Ramelson, Mr Goodwin and a number of other influential Communists whose influence extended to unions beyond the NUS. The most prominent of these was Mr Harry Watson, the President of the Lightermen's Union, and such well-known figures as Mr Jack Dash and Mr Danny Lyons, who are both members of the unofficial liaison committee in the London docks, together, of course, with Mr Gordon Norris and Mr Jack Coward representing the seamen.[34]

Critically, however, as Wilson 'want[ed] to make clear', 'none' of this was 'in any way illegal'; nor was there any 'suggestion of any interference in this strike from overseas'.[35] It was all 'indigenous'.[36]

Before turning to our second illustration – the miners' strike of 1984–85 – what the seamen's strike tells us is that state surveillance and monitoring of trade unions had become normalised, and that trade unions had become deeply penetrated by the state.[37] It was not a precondition of surveillance that it was motivated by a concern about the Communist Party acting as an agent of a foreign state, or that there was suspicion of illegality that was the subject of investigation. The Prime Minister's recognition that everything had been 'rooted in our own doctrines of freedom of association and action' begs many questions. Why was MI5 involved in the first place? Why the surveillance on the detailed scale that would be required to make these and other statements? Why were trade unionists publicly denounced in Parliament under the cover of parliamentary privilege?[38] What were the surveillance methods used to collect this information about the union, its procedures, officers and members? Some of the information would clearly have been in the public domain. But some of it would have been acquired by the bugs at Communist Party HQ, which are now well enough known, while some of it was likely to have been acquired from informers and the active surveillance of others.

But not only had surveillance become normalised, it was to be significantly expanded in terms of scope and resources, with Seumas Milne referring to the 'huge increase in activity against the left and the trade-union movement in the 1970s and early 1980s',[39] a claim that tends to be confirmed by MI5 whistleblowers. One of the MI5 areas targeted for growth was F Branch, responsible for monitoring 'domestic subversion'.[40] So far as the miners' strike is concerned, it is necessary to refer here to only a few points to

[33] ibid col 1619.

[34] ibid cols 1619–20. In a later passage he referred again to Jack Dash 'who, as his numerous speeches in the docks indicated, took a more moderate line because he was torn between his loyalty to the party and his loyalty to his union, which was resisting all pressures to take the Communist line': col 1621.

[35] ibid col 1614.

[36] Ibid.

[37] Despite ILO Convention 87, which requires 'the public authorities [to] refrain from any interference which would restrict this right or impede the lawful exercise thereof': ILO Convention 87, art 3(2).

[38] The speech was substantially reproduced, including the names of the individuals, in Wilson's autobiographical account: H Wilson, *The Labour Government 1964–70* (Penguin, Harmondsworth, 1974), pp 308–11.

[39] S Milne, *The Enemy Within* (Verso, London, 1994), p 276.

[40] ibid pp 276–77.

emerge from Milne's rich account. In a neat summary following the publication of Stella Rimington's memoirs, Rimington being an ex-Director of MI5, Milne wrote that:

> As assistant MI5 director in charge of F2 branch, targeting trade unions, Rimington supervised the most ambitious counter-subversion operation ever mounted in Britain. Under her guidance, MI5 infiltrated Arthur Scargill's inner circle, oversaw the country's largest-ever bugging and telephone-tapping effort in cooperation with GCHQ, coordinated the legal onslaught against the NUM and helped organise the strike-breaking effort.[41]

MI5's authorised historian has written that 'the Service was less fearful of subversion than the Prime Minister', reporting in April 1984 that 'subversive organisations were not making a significant impact on events', but that Thatcher and some of her ministers 'seem to have been unpersuaded'.[42]

IV. Tragic Consequences

Rather poignantly, Bevin died on the Saturday following the fifth day of the dockers' trial in 1951, the architect almost surviving the collapse. But with its revocation long overdue, Order 1305 had been broken by two ill-judged prosecutions. The first against the gas workers was an abuse of process, using industrial legislation as a tool against a supposed political enemy. The second against the dock workers was an act of folly, the law being used for no apparent reason than that it was there. The Attorney General was embarrassed by his hubris, though Isaacs was spared any humiliation by his resignation shortly before the fateful dockers' prosecution was launched. But the gas workers case and the Cabinet obsession about Communists in the trade unions are reminders of the historic (and continuing) alignment of trade unionism with subversion,[43] and of the historic (and continuing) presence of the state in the surveillance and control of trade union activity. That surveillance does not take place for benign reasons; nor is it evidence of collective laissez-faire. In this as in other ways, the state is and has been a constant presence in industrial relations, from the monitoring of and sharing information about activists, to channelling activity through state-supported structures, to interfering with the autonomous operation of these structures.

[41] S Milne, 'The Truth about MI5's Role in the Miners' Strike Will Not Come out in Rimington's Memoirs', *The Guardian*, 3 October 1990. Milne's important work makes it clear that the surveillance activity was not confined to the NUM. Note too the report that the Secretary of State for Employment in the Thatcher government boasted that 'the level of briefing he received from the police was so detailed that he knew where trade unionists went on holiday': Unite the Union, 'Norman Tebbit's Admission about Government Involvement in Spying on Trade Unionists Must Be Fully Investigated', 17 March 2021, www.unitetheunion.org/news-events/news/2021/march/norman-tebbit-s-admission-about-government-involvement-in-spying-on-trade-unionists-must-be-fully-investigated.

[42] C Andrew, 'The Threat of Subversion' (nd), www.mi5.gov.uk/the-threat-of-subversion. Studies of this surveillance continue to yield yet more disturbing material, including claims that 'MI5 leaked confidential details of NUM bank accounts and the movements of union officials to Price Waterhouse, seemingly based on covert surveillance and phone tapping': M Hollingsworth, 'For Years, I Suspected MI5 Interfered in the Miners' Strike. The Truth was Even More Shocking Than I Thought', *The Guardian*, 7 March 2024.

[43] On which see further A Bogg, KD Ewing, and A Moretta, 'The Persistence of Criminal Law and Police in Collective Labour Relations' in A Bogg, J Collins, M Freedland, and J Herring (eds), *Criminality at Work* (Oxford University Press, Oxford, 2020, ch 19).

As Kahn Freund warned at the time, Order 1376 was no answer to the problem of unofficial action which had been a principal cause of Order 1305's demise.[44] Order 1376 avoided rather than addressed the problem, expressly denying unofficial groups the opportunity to have their grievances peacefully resolved, though it no longer exposed them to the risk of criminal sanctions when they took industrial action. The matter was not addressed until the Donovan Royal Commission did so in 1965, leading to a diagnosis based on the informality of workplace industrial relations and the remoteness of national bargaining structures,[45] a diagnosis compounded by Jack Jones' autobiographical account of lazy full-time trade union officials.[46] Unfortunately, Donovan's diagnosis led to a prescription for change which, although widely applauded by scholars at the time, proved in the long run to be counter-productive. It contributed to a major reset of the role of the state in industrial relations, designed to engineer a re-structuring of collective bargaining, with a decentralisation of activity from the sector to the enterprise. The attempts to deal with unofficial action were ultimately successful, but at the price of destroying the institutional framework in which it was seen by conventional wisdom to be dysfunctional. In retrospect it was a tragedy.

[44] O Kahn Freund, 'Industrial Disputes Order' (1951) 14 *MLR* 467.
[45] Royal Commission on Trade Unions and Employers' Associations (n 23).
[46] J Jones, *Union Man: An Autobiography*, 2nd edn (Warren & Penn, London, 2008), p 165.

Appendix
Extract from Cabinet Discussion of 'Industrial Disputes. Communist Incitement'

Cabinet Conclusions, 16 October 1950[1]

The Cabinet first discussed the question of introducing fresh legislation on this subject and considered the three alternative possibilities described in paragraph 3 of [the paper circulated by the Lord President and the Home Secretary]. The first of these was that the provisions of the Conspiracy and Protection of Property Act, 1875, should be extended to cover all essential employments. It was pointed out in discussion that, in defining 'essential employments' for this purpose, it would be difficult to decide where to draw the line. Moreover, the Act of 1875 had been based on the fact that the workers whom it covered had enjoyed greater security of tenure than those in other industries: this would not apply in some of the other industries which would now be regarded as essential to the life of the community, and in any event, under conditions of full employment, workers no longer prized security of tenure so highly as to be willing to accept in return for it disabilities from which their fellows in other industries were free. Finally, this course had the disadvantage that it would increase the number of criminal proceedings to be taken against persons taking part in strikes.

The second possibility was to enact in permanent form provisions on the lines of the Conditions of Employment and National Arbitration Order. *The Attorney General* said that, so long as this Order was continued in operation, it would become increasingly difficult for him to evade his responsibility for enforcing it – particularly now that he had invoked it in the recent proceedings against ten men who had taken part in the London gas strike. If it was to be kept in operation and enforced, he would prefer that it should have the direct authority of Parliament. On the other hand, *The Foreign Secretary* said that he was doubtful whether a requirement of compulsory arbitration for industrial disputes could be maintained much longer under peace-time conditions. In trade union circles in the past the view had always been taken that, under normal conditions, the workers would not accept compulsory arbitration; and this system operated effectively only in Communist countries where all strikes were prohibited. He believed, therefore, that some new approach would have to be made to this problem; and he had been wondering whether this might not take the form of establishing, in place of

[1] TNA, CAB 128/18/24 (Cabinet Conclusions, 16 October 1950).

a single national tribunal, separate arbitration tribunals for the main industries whose decisions would be accepted as final by both sides of the industry. This method had worked satisfactorily in the boot trade and in the steel industry, and it might be capable of extension to other industries. The Cabinet were informed that, for the moment, both sides of industry seemed to be willing that the Conditions of Employment and National Arbitration Order should be continued in force, though it was thought that the trade unions would wish to see some minor amendments made in it. Despite this, there was general agreement in the Cabinet that it was not too soon for Ministers to give consideration to the long-term development of the existing machinery for wage negotiation in industry. It was further agreed that, if that development followed the line of separate machinery for particular industries, care should be taken to ensure that the need for some central guidance on general economic conditions was not overlooked. In this connection it was suggested that further thought might be given to the role and functions of the trade unions in a planned economy under conditions of full employment and, in particular, to the functions of trade unions in nationalised industries.

The third possibility discussed … was that it should be made an offence for any person to take part in a strike in an essential service until the members of the trade union or unions concerned had all voted in favour of strike action by a secret ballot. In discussion it was pointed out that many unofficial strikes were sudden and spontaneous demonstrations against some minor grievance, and that such disputes were often [resolved] within a day or so. On such occasions it would usually be impossible to restrain the men from withholding their labour until steps had been taken to hold a secret ballot; and it would be neither desirable nor practicable to prosecute them after the event for having gone on strike before a ballot had been held. There would also be practical difficulties in determining who should hold the ballot – in an unofficial strike, it would be unreasonable to expect the union to do so – and in defining the classes of worker in the industry among whom the ballot should be held. There was also the disadvantage that, if the ballot went in favour of the strike, the moral position of the strikers would be greatly strengthened. It was the general view of the Cabinet that this proposal was not practicable.

BIBLIOGRAPHY

Official Publications

Committee on Industry and Trade, Final Report, Cmd 3282, 1929
Lord Denning's Report, Cmnd 2152, 1963
Ministry of Labour, Annual Report 1933
Ministry of Labour, Annual Report 1937
Ministry of Labour, Annual Report 1939–1946
Ministry of Labour, *Industrial Relations Handbook* (HMSO, 1961 edn)
Ministry of Reconstruction, Committee on Relations between Employers and Employed, Interim Report, Cmd 8606, 1917
Personal Incomes, Costs and Prices, Cmd 7321, 1948
Report of a Court of Inquiry into a dispute between DC Thomson and Company Limited and Certain Workpeople, Members of the National Society of Operative Printers and Assistants Cmd 8607, 1952
Review of the British Dock Strikes, Cmd 7851, 1949
Royal Commission on Trade Unions and Employers' Associations, 1965-68, Report, Cmnd 3263, 1968

Books and Articles

Allen, VL, *Trade Unions and the Government* (Longmans, London, 1960)
Andrew, C, *The Defence of the Realm: The Authorised History of MI5* (Penguin, London, 2010)
Bagshaw, R, 'Rookes' Tale' in J Adams-Prassl, A Bogg and ACL Davies, *Landmark Cases in Labour Law* (Hart Publishing, Oxford, 2022)
Beer, SH, *Modern British Politics* (Faber & Faber, London, 1965)
Bennett, G, *The Zinoviev Letter: The Conspiracy That Never Dies* (Oxford University Press, Oxford, 2018)
Bercusson, B, *Fair Wages Resolutions* (Mansell, London, 1978)
Black, B, 'A Triumph of Voluntarism? Industrial Relations and Strikes in Northern Ireland in World War Two' (2005) 70 *Labour History* 5
Bogg, A, Ewing KD, and Moretta, A, 'The Persistence of Criminal Law and Police in Collective Labour Relations' in A Bogg, J Collins, M Freedland and J Herring (eds), *Criminality at Work* (Oxford University Press, Oxford, 2020)
Bradley, AW, Ewing KD, and Knight, CJS, *Constitutional and Administrative Law*, 18th edn (Pearson, Harlow, 2022)
Brodie, D, *A History of British Labour Law, 1877–1945* (Hart Publishing, Oxford, 2003)
Brodie, D, 'The Scottish Case – *Crofter Hand Woven Harris Tweed v Veitch*' in KD Ewing (ed), *The Right to Strike: From the Trade Disputes Act 1906 to a Trade Union Freedom Bill 2006* (Institute of Employment Rights, Liverpool, 2006), Chapter 6
Brown, DH, 'The Craftsmanship of Bias: Sedition and the Winnipeg General Strike 1919' (1984) 14 *Manitoba Law Journal* 1
Bunyan, T, *The History and Practice of the Political Police in Britain* (Quartet Books, London, 1977)
Carswell, R, and MacDermott, JC, *Dictionary of Irish Biography* (Royal Irish Academy, online at www.dib.ie)
Citrine, NA, *Trade Union Law*, 2nd edn (Stevens & Sons, London, 1950)
Clegg, HA, *A History of British Trade Unions since 1889, Vol III, 1934–1951* (Clarendon Press, Oxford, 1994)

Cooper, Lord, *The Scottish Legal Tradition*, 3rd edn by MC Meston (Saltire Society, Edinburgh 1969)
Cullen, PV, *Stranger in Blood; The Case Files on Dr John Bodkin Adams* (Elliot & Thompson, London, 2006)
Dash, J, *Good Morning Brothers!* (Lawrence & Wishart, London, 1969)
Davis, CJ, *Waterfront Revolts, New York and London Dockworkers 1946–61* (University of Illinois Press, Urbana, 2003)
Davies, P and Freedland, M, *Labour Legislation and Public Policy: A Contemporary History* (Clarendon Press, Oxford, 1993)
Devlin, P, *Easing the Passing: The Trial of Dr John Bodkin Adams* (Faber & Faber, London, 1985)
Dicey, AV, *Introduction to the Study of the Law of the Constitution*, 9th edn (Macmillan, London, 1939)
Dicey, AV, *Introduction to the Study of the Law of the Constitution*, 10th edn with an Introduction by ECS Wade (Macmillan, London, 1959)
Doyle, B, 'A Substitute for Collective Bargaining? The Central Arbitration Committee's Approach to Section 16 of the Employment Protection Act 1975' (1980) 9 *ILJ* 154
Dukes, R, *The Labour Constitution: The Enduring Idea of Labour Law* (Oxford University Press, Oxford, 2014)
Eastwood, GG, *George Isaacs: Printer, Trade-Union Leader, Cabinet Minister* (Odhams Press, London, 1952)
Ewing, KD, '*Grunwick Processing Laboratories Ltd v ACAS*: The Social Contract, Trade Union Recognition, and the Rule of Law' in A Bogg, A Davies and J Prassl (eds), *Landmark Cases in Labour Law* (Hart Publishing, Oxford, 2022)
Ewing, KD, '"A Just Share of the Fruits of Progress": The Role of Collective Bargaining' in K Arabadjieva, N Countouris, B Luna Fabris and W Zwysen (eds), *Transformative Ideas: Ensuring a Just Share of Progress for All* (European University Institute, Brussels, 2023)
Ewing, KD, 'Strike Ballots' (1986) 5 *Journal of the Irish Society for Labour Law* 19
Ewing, KD, 'The Politics of the British Constitution' [2000] *Public Law* 405
Ewing, KD, *The Right to Strike* (Oxford University Press, Oxford, 1991)
Ewing, KD, 'The South Shields Case: Subverting the Trade Disputes Act 1906?' in KD Ewing (ed), *The Right to Strike: From the Trade Disputes Act 1906 to a Trade Union Freedom Bill 2006* (Institute of Employment Rights, Liverpool, 2006)
Ewing, KD, 'The State and Industrial Relations: Collective Laissez Faire' Revisited' (1998) 5 *Historical Studies in Industrial Relations* 1
Ewing, KD, and Gearty, CA, *The Struggle for Civil Liberties, Political Freedom and the Rule of Law in Britain, 1914–1945* (Oxford University Press, Oxford, 2000),
Ewing, KD, Mahoney, J and Moretta, A, 'Civil Liberties and the Korean War' (2018) 81 *MLR* 395
Ewing, KD, Mahoney, J and Moretta, A, *MI5, the Cold War and the Rule of Law* (Oxford University Press, Oxford, 2020)
Field, GG, *Blood, Sweat and Toil: Remaking the British Working Class, 1939–1945* (Oxford University Press, Oxford, 2011)
Fishman, N, 'A Vital Element in British Industrial Relations: A Reassessment of Order 1305, 1940–51' (1999) 8 *Historical Studies in Industrial Relations* 43
Fishman, N, *The British Communist Party and the Trade Unions 1933–45* (Scolar Press, Aldershot, 1995)
Gallacher, W, *The Case for Communism* (Penguin, Harmondsworth, 1949)
Goldstein, J, *The Government of British Trade Union: A Study of Apathy and the Democratic Process in the Transport and General Workers Union* (George Allen & Unwin, London, 1952)
Goodhart, AL, 'The Legality of the General Strike in England' (1927) 36 *Yale Law Journal* 464
Griffith, J, *Judicial Politics since 1920* (Blackwell, Oxford, 1993)
Ince, Sir Godfrey, *The Ministry of Labour and National Service* (George Allen & Unwin, London, 1958)
Johnston, TJ, *The History of the Working Classes in Scotland* (Forward Publishing Co Ltd, Glasgow, 1922)
Jones, J, *Union Man: An Autobiography*, 2nd edn (Warren & Penn, London, 2008)
Jones, M, 'CAC and Schedule 11: The Experience of Two Years' (1980) 9 *ILJ* 28
Kahn Freund, O, 'Collective Agreements under War Legislation' (1943) 6 *MLR* 112
Kahn Freund, O, 'Industrial Disputes Order' (1951) 14 *MLR* 467
L, JG, 'Collective Agreements and Collective Labour Disputes' (1930) 55 *Scottish Law Review* 45
Lyddon D and Smith, P, 'The 1906 Act: The First Fifty Years: Industrial Relations, Picketing and the Employers' Challenge, in KD Ewing (ed), *The Right to Strike: From the Trade Disputes Act 1906 to a Trade Union Bill 2006* (Institute of Employment Rights, Liverpool, 2007)
MacDermott, Lord, *Protection from Power under English Law* (Stevens, London, 1957)

MacFarlane, LJ, *The Right to Strike* (Penguin, Harmondsworth, 1981)
McIlroy J, and Campbell, A, 'Beyond Betteshanger: Order 1305 in the Scottish Coalfields during the Second World War, Part 1: Politics, Prosecutions and Protest' (2003) 15 *Historical Studies in Industrial Relations* 27
McIlroy, J and Campbell, A, 'Beyond Betteshanger: Order 1305 in the Scottish Coalfields during the Second World War, Part 2: The Cardowan Story' (2003) 16 *Historical Studies in Industrial Relations* 39
Mahoney, J, 'Civil Liberties in Britain during the Cold War' (1989) 33 *American Journal of Legal History* 53
Mak, A, 'Spheres of Justice in the 1942 Betteshanger Miners' Strike: An Essay in Historical Ethnography' (2015) 36 *Historical Studies in Industrial Relations* 29
Michels, R, *Political Parties: A Sociological Study of the Oligarchical tendencies of Modern Democracy* (Hearst's International Library, New York, 1915)
Milne, S, *The Enemy Within* (Verso, London, 1994)
Moffatt, A, *My Life with the Miners* (Lawrence & Wishart, London, 1965)
Moran, M, *The Politics of Industrial Relations* (Macmillan, London, 1977)
Morgan, KO, '1906: Blissful Dawn' (2006) 51 *Journal of Liberal History* 32
Morris, GS, 'The Emergency Powers Act 1920' [1979] *Public Law* 317
Morris, M (ed), *The General Strike* (Penguin, Harmondsworth, 1976)
Newsam, Sir F, *The Home Office* (Allen & Unwin, London, 1954)
Novitz, T, *International and European Protection of the Right to Strike: A Comparative Study of Standards Set by the International Labour Organization, the Council of Europe and the European Union* (Oxford, Oxford University Press, 2004)
Ollerenshaw, P, 'War, Industrial Mobilisation and Society in Northern Ireland, 1939–1945' (2007) 16 *Contemporary European History* 169
Orwell, G, *Animal Farm* (Penguin, Harmondsworth, 1948)
Page Arnot, R, *A History of the Scottish Miners* (George Allen & Unwin, London, 1955)
Page Arnot, R, *The Miners in Crisis and War: A History of the Miners' Federation of Great Britain from 1930 Onwards* (George Allen & Unwin, London, 1961)
Partington, M, 'Unemployment, Industrial Conflict and Social Security' (1980) 9 *ILJ* 243
Pelling, H, *A History of British Trade Unionism*, 3rd edn (Penguin Books, Harmondsworth, 1976)
Pelling, H, *The British Communist Party* (A&C Black, London, 1975)
Phillips, J, 'Labour and the Cold War: The Politics of Anti-communism, 1945–55' (1999) 64 *Labour History Review* 48
Phillips, J, *The Great Alliance: Economic Recovery and the Problems of Power 1945–1951* (Pluto Press, London, 1996)
Podmore, W, *Reg Birch: Engineer, Communist, Trade Unionist* (Bellman Books, London, 2004)
Pritt, DN, *Law, Class and Society: Book One, Employers, Workers and Trade Unions* (Lawrence & Wishart, London, 1970)
Pritt DN and Freeman, R, *The Law versus the Trade Unions* (Lawrence and Wishart, London, 1958)
Schmitthoff, C, 'The Growing Ambit of the Common Law' (1951) 29 *Canadian Bar Review* 469
Shawcross, H, *Life Sentence* (Constable, London, 1995)
Simon, Sir J, *Three Speeches on the General Strike* (Macmillan, London, 1926)
Simpson, AWB, *In the Highest Degree Odious: Detention without Trial in War-Time Britain* (Oxford University Press, Oxford, 1992)
Smith, P, 'The Law behind the Law: *Rookes v Barnard*, the Common Law and the Right to Strike' (2017) 38 *Historical Studies in Industrial Relations* 38
Stammers, N, *Civil Liberties in Britain during the Second World War* (Croom Helm, London, 1983)
Tyndall, A, 'Patriotism and Principles: Order 1305 and the Betteshanger Strike of 1942' (2001) 12 *Historical Studies in Industrial Relations* 109
Wade, ECS, 'Seditious Libel and the Press' (1948) 64 *LQR* 203
Wade, ECS and Phillips, G G, *Constitutional Law*, 5th edn by ECS Wade (Longmans, Green & Co, London, 1955)
Webb, S and Webb, B, *The History of Trade Unionism, 1666–1920* (Longmans Green, London)
Wedderburn, KW, *Cases and Materials on Labour Law* (Cambridge University Press, Cambridge, 1967)
Weekes, B, Mellish, M, Dickens, L and Lloyd, J, *Industrial Relations and the Limits of the Law: The Industrial Effects of the Industrial Relations Act 1971* (Basil Blackwell, Oxford, 1975)
Williams, DGT, *Not in the Public Interest: The Problem of Security in Democracy* (Hutchinson, London, 1965)

Wilson, H, *The Labour Government 1964–70* (Penguin, Harmondsworth, 1974)
Wrigley, C, 'Trade Unions and the 1964 General Election' (2007) 21 *Contemporary British History* 325

Other Publications

Anarchist Federation, *War Commentary*, Vol 4, No 23, October 1943
Anon, *How Duple's Won* (C Short, 1951)
Andrew, C, 'The Threat of Subversion' (nd), www.mi5.gov.uk/the-threat-of-subversion
Berlins, M, 'A Chief Justice Got away with Murder', *The Independent,* 22 October 2011
Crown Prosecution Service, Public Justice Offences, as revised 18 September 2024, online at www.cps.gov.uk/prosecution-guidance/public-justice-offences
Dalyell, Lord, 'Obituary: Lord Mellish', *The Independent*, 11 May 1998
Deakin, A, 'A Challenge to Democracy! And Our Answer', *Transport and General Workers' Union Record,* January 1950
Deakin, A, 'British Trade Unions and the Communist Conspiracy' (1952) 139 *National & English Review* 337
Deakin, A, 'Trade Unionism v Communism: The Gloves are off!', *Transport and General Workers' Union Record,* July 1949
Farquhar, J, 'Lessons of the Smithfield Strike', *Socialist Review*, 1 September 1958, p 2
Hollingsworth, M, 'For Years, I Suspected MI5 Interfered in the Miners' Strike. The Truth was Even More Shocking Than I Thought', *The Guardian*, 7 March 2024
Labour Party, *Let Us Face the Future* (1945)
Milne, S, 'The Truth about MI5's Role in the Miners' Strike Will Not Come out in Rimington's Memoirs', *The Guardian*, 3 October 1990
Moretta, A, 'Benchmarking Workplace Rights' (PhD dissertation, University of Liverpool 2019) (https://livrepository.liverpool.ac.uk/3060675)
Morton, J, 'Obituary: Lord Shawcross', *The Independent*, 11 July 2003
Socialist Equality Party, *The Historical and International Foundations of the Socialist Equality Party, Part 3*, 12 March 2011: www.wsws.org
Trades Union Congress, Annual Report 1950
Trades Union Congress, Annual Report 1951
Trades Union Congress, Annual Report 1964
Trades Union Congress, Annual Report 1976
Trades Union Congress, *The Tactics of Disruption; Communist Methods Exposed* (TUC, 1949)
Trades Union Congress, *The TUC and Communism* (TUC, 1955)
Unite the Union, 'Norman Tebbit's Admission about Government Involvement in Spying on Trade Unionists Must Be Fully Investigated', 17 March 2021
Upham, M, *The History of British Trotskyism to 1949, Part Two (1938–1944)*, 6 April 2004, www.marxists.org

INDEX